D0164482

Women in Literature

Reading through the Lens of Gender

Edited by Jerilyn Fisher
and Ellen S. Silber

Foreword by David Sadker

GREENWOOD PRESS
Westport, Connecticut • London

Library of Congress Cataloging-in-Publication Data

Women in literature : reading through the lens of gender / edited by Jerilyn Fisher and Ellen
S. Silber ; foreword by David Sadker.
     p. cm.
   Includes bibliographical references and index.
   ISBN 0–313–31346–6 (alk. paper)
   1. Women in literature.   2. Literature, Modern—History and Criticism.   I. Fisher,
Jerilyn. II. Silber, Ellen S.
   PN56.5.W64W65   2003
   809'.93352042—dc21   2002035212

British Library Cataloguing in Publication Data is available.

Library of Congress Catalog Card Number: 2002035212
ISBN: 0–313–31346–6

First published in 2003

Greenwood Press, 88 Post Road West, Westport, CT 06881
An imprint of Greenwood Publishing Group, Inc.
www.greenwood.com

Printed in the United States of America

The paper used in this book complies with the
Permanent Paper Standard issued by the National
Information Standards Organization (Z39.48–1984).

10 9 8 7 6 5 4 3 2 1

This book is dedicated

To Jules, Arielle, Devan—who make all good work possible

To the beloved memory of Herman and Lilly, who come to mind
whenever there's cause for celebration . . .

J. F.

To Al and Kenny, my wonderful family

To Mother and Pearl, and the knowledge we might have shared

E.S.S.

Contents

CONTENTS ix

CONTENTS   xiii

CONTENTS   xv

Foreword

When my late wife, Myra, and I first began our research documenting sexism in schools, we were astonished to discover that even skilled and gifted teachers made boys the center of their instructional efforts. Teachers asked boys more questions than they asked girls; and awarded boys more praise, meted out more criticism, and directed more instructional help to them as well. Even when the teacher did not call on boys, boys would simply shout out their answers and comments, and the teacher would accept those callouts. Either way, boys were capturing the instructional spotlight.

Then we became educational cartographers, mapping student seating patterns. We discovered yet another gender divide, only this time a geographic one. About half the classrooms that we observed were characterized by gender-segregated seating. Boys enjoyed property rights to certain areas of the class, while girls staked out other seats. And not surprisingly, teachers would gravitate, as if drawn by a magnet, to the "boy neighborhoods." Once again, males became the location of instruction. We reported our findings in a series of scholarly articles and books, and then in *Failing at Fairness*.

One of the sad ironies of our research is that teachers are unaware of these gender discrepancies; most are clueless. Masked by the rapid pace of classroom life, these patterns do not strike teachers' notice easily. In fact, teachers become quite upset when they discover that their effectiveness in the classroom is compromised by gender bias.

Guess what? This same lesson needs to be learned about the curriculum. Subtle—and not-so-subtle—sexism short-circuits even our most cherished books, and teachers and their students need to be taught to see the sexism. *Women in Literature: Reading through the Lens of Gender* fits us with the glasses we need to see the gender insights found on the pages of these books. Let's go to a classroom for an example.

There you are, about to teach Chaucer's *Canterbury Tales* (yet again!), and you look at your students and think, "How will I bridge these centuries?" While Chaucer's women tell tales that are nearly a millennium old, Michael Cornelius explains how they continue to speak to the realities and dualities facing today's women. The freethinking Wife of Bath boasts of her sexual talents as a way to achieve what she wants, and has the temerity to know, voice, and try to satisfy her desires. The Clerk's Tale of Griselda, on the other hand, portrays a wife so meek and loyal, so traditional and subservient, that years of indignity and even cruelty cannot shake her devotion to her abusive husband. Those who listen to these tales, the fellow travelers, find the independence of the Wife of Bath quite threatening, while the obedience shining through in Griselda's story wins their admiration. The adulterous and obedient wives in the *Canterbury Tales* speak to the continuing conflict between women who want to escape their submissive role and those who accommodate an abusive relationship.

For literature teachers, protected only by their worn copy of *Canterbury Tales, Silas Marner*, or *The Good Earth*, finding, analyzing, and teaching about these sexist literary lessons is an enormous challenge. Connecting these ideas with a generation raised on MTV, Britney Spears, and Ashanti is yet another challenge. Can the Wife of Bath be *that* relevant?

Watch out, Ashanti, here comes *Women in Literature*. What Jerilyn Fisher and Ellen Silber have done in editing this marvelous collection of essays on the classics (and then some) is both incredibly simple and remarkably useful (like in, "Why didn't I think of that?"). The authors identified the canon, the most commonly taught books in high school (and often colleges as well). Then they contacted colleagues who knew these books, taught them, and could examine them through a lens that today's students too rarely use, the lens of gender. The result is a rich collection of succinct essays about these frequently taught books, a collection filled with stimulating points of view and immediately useful ideas for lessons and learning.

The gender connections and themes that Fisher and Silber describe could not be more on target for this generation of students. I am constantly amazed (and disappointed) at the historical and social amnesia displayed by so many students unable to grasp the persistent gender barriers that still channel and inhibit their own growth. It has become conventional wisdom among many if not most high school and college students that good jobs, equal pay, and rapid promotions are now all but guaranteed for anyone who works hard. We have arrived at VGB Day, Victory over Gender Bias.

Many students today think women can have it all. They can go to work and find a terrific job, with pay and promotions equal to men, not to mention the Audi, BMW, or Volvo parked in their two-, oops, three-car garage. True, a woman might decide to take a little time off for children, but then if she chooses, it's back into that high-powered position that the company kept open waiting for her return. Today's "modern" husband happily shares in childcare, and will even be an equal partner in housekeeping. Gender stereotypes are little more than a vestige of a bygone era. Even the term "feminism" is viewed as an antiquated word, no more relevant than bohemian or hippie.

Then there is a group of students who see labels like "feminist" as dangerous, a new "F" word to be avoided at all costs. These are the "traditional" students, women and men who see tomorrow as a romantic reflection of a more simple and pleasant yesterday. These women will choose to stay at home, tending to children and creating a safe family harbor. Their traditional husbands will venture into the world of work to earn wages and "provide" for their families. Rejecting the concept of flexible gender roles and expanding options, these traditionalists seek more familiar and comfortable roles.

That's not to say young feminists, male and female, are extinct, but they probably feel endangered. Thus the majority of my students seem to fall into three categories: those who reject feminist goals entirely, those who believe that gender bias is a remnant of the past, and a smaller group of students willing to voice their feminist beliefs. The irony is that in a few short years, life will teach all these students some pretty tough gender lessons. Many of them will someday discover that they have become angry adults confronting a society where sex discrimination is very much alive. Given today's far-right political agenda, including curtailing Title IX protections in school, abolishing the Women's Bureau at the Department of Labor, and reversing *Row v. Wade*, the future may be not only far from utopian, it may be disturbingly similar to the sexist past. Given that danger, this book is now even more important.

And it is not only the majority of students who are out of the loop in terms of feminist ideas, gender challenges in society, and related themes in literature; many instructors could use a refresher course as well. That is one reason why I consider this book to be of so much potential value. In addition to helping a new generation of students come to terms with gender bias, it can help a generation of teachers unravel themes, garner new perspectives, and see some of their literary favorites through newly "gendered" eyes. I have always thought that one secret to good teaching is the ability to discover fresh dimensions in celebrated material; in a sense, to see the familiar as new again. Jerilyn Fisher and Ellen Silber have done just that.

This volume offers a tour of gender insights hidden away in many of our great books. *Invisible Man* provides a powerful insight into the racism confronting African Americans, but as Yolanda Pierce explains, it also reflects the simplistic duality of Ralph Ellison's portrayal of women. Women are defined by their relationships to men, with race only the most obvious layer of bias. Ellison's women seem unable to escape the confining roles of "madonnas or whores." While Sybil plays out the white woman's rape fantasy and is an overtly sexual figure, Mary, the black woman, is desexualized and presented as the "mammy," whose only purpose is to meet the needs of others. In fact, when there are no such needs, Mary disappears for hundreds of pages. Based on the shallow coverage of African-American women, the book might better be entitled *Invisible Woman*.

Between the covers of *Women in Literature* you will find ways of seeing and analyses that may surprise and inform your perceptions of some great books. You may also come across newer works not found in the historic canon, since the editors of this volume have wisely included several contemporary, multicultural authors and some older but less well-known stories such as Cisneros' *The House on Mango Street*, Tan's *The Joy Luck Club*, Staples' *Shabanu: Daughter of the Wind*, Williams' *Dessa Rose*, Emecheta's *The Bride Price*, Gilman's *Herland*, and de Pizan's *The Book of the City of Ladies*.

The essays in this book expose the sexist limitations of even our most renowned writers, providing a sense of connection for today's feminists, literary confirmation that their concerns are genuine. This book will also raise unsettling questions for those students who believe that gender equity is no longer an issue, or that traditional gender roles provide a safe haven. Jerilyn Fisher and Ellen Silber have constructed an informative, book-by-book analysis of the uphill struggle of women in fiction (and often in reality as well). *Women in Literature* offers fresh understandings and energizing ideas for the study of literature. And that is a wonderful gift for teachers and students.

David Sadker
American University, Washington, DC

Preface

WHAT READERS WILL FIND IN THIS VOLUME

Women in Literature: Reading through the Lens of Gender contains ninety-six essays examining literary representations of femininity and masculinity. In collecting these essays, we wish to explore how writers spanning time and place have conceived gendered aspects of the self, as characters navigate the complex psychic and social worlds they inhabit. Our goal is to provide examples of how fictional texts, both canonical and new, can be approached freshly by putting at the center of analysis girls' and women's different perceptions, their distinct predicaments, and their varied experiences.

The whole notion of a canon conveys a supposed universal standard of excellence embodied in a list of certain texts; that designation is passed down from generation to generation, conveying prestige and assuring literary stature. In the majority, these "great books" represent mainly what men of educational privilege have most valued as writers and readers. As a result, the canon marginalizes at least half the human experience. Yet, teach these texts we do, often with ambivalence—fondness and admiration edged with discomfort about bias and stereotypical representations. Responding to this dilemma, the essays gathered here offer feminist analyses of images and themes, revealing the customary yet profound significance of gender in our lives.

While most of the essays in this volume explore the best-known and most often taught novels and plays, others introduce less well-known titles that offer positive female role models and new insights into culturally diverse women's situations. Librarians and teachers will be interested in seeing how these new titles can lend balance to the traditional curriculum. Each essay includes within it suggestions for teaching that can heighten students' awareness of themes related to gender and offers a selective list of resources for further study.

To facilitate use of this volume by teachers, students, and librarians, we have provided an appendix of salient themes that can be found in *Women in Literature*. Librarians and teachers alike will find this compendium helpful in organizing a syllabus or curriculum, or in making decisions about library purchases or text selections for courses or units that will foster discussion of a particular gender issue.

The book is arranged alphabetically by title, beginning with Mark Twain's *The Adventures of Huckleberry Finn*. To find out if a particular text is included in this volume, readers can check either the Contents, which, reflecting the book, lists titles alphabetically, or the Index of Literary Works by Author, which appears at the end of the book.

WHAT THIS BOOK AIMS TO ACCOMPLISH

During the latter half of the twentieth century, the resurgent Women's Movement, increased public visibility for women, and the expansion of women's studies as an academic discipline worked together to change almost everyone's ideas as well as the general discourse about gender roles. Yet to what extent have such changes in the social and intellectual climate influenced critical interpretations of literature? Although a growing percentage of teachers have become committed to making courses gender-balanced with regard to both curriculum and pedagogy, many continue to teach traditional content in traditional ways. Without faculty development activities in women's studies, most high school and college teachers lack direct exposure to feminist perspectives that might influence what they teach or might provide impetus to consider new fiction specially suited to the gender-sensitive classroom.

The publication of *Women in Literature* presumes that, still today, teachers of literature and humanities need accessible resources should they wish to teach titles in the core curriculum from a woman-centered point of view. Thus, we have included here a majority of essays that treat commonly taught literary texts; and we have also sought essays about lesser-known novels and plays that teachers describe as "tried and true" in their capacity to offer complex, inspiring portraits of girls and women. Generally, the books we've chosen to represent are those that can engage students in discussion of gender and sex differences, patriarchal society, women as subjects—not objects—of study, feminism as an inclusive social movement, and feminist literary theory.

For the most part, teachers tend to select texts and develop critical insights based on what they themselves have learned. Typically, for teachers of English and the humanities, this means drawing from a list of works which, over time, have become part of the established canon and which teachers are, for the most part, expected to teach, and which their students are expected to know. Thus, it is understandable that most instructors make text selections from among traditional titles. Additionally, without specific models of feminist literary study, teachers generally glean their interpretations of literary texts from critical sources that reflect conventional readings. Yet, these interpretations alone, however valid and interesting as literary criticism, are unlikely to help students resist the imposition of narrow sex roles, or question stereotypical views of race, class, and sexual orientation. Nor will they help teachers to recognize the damaging effects of exclusion when textual representations repeatedly ignore or devalue "everything female in literature: female authors and readers, works written by and for women, portrayals of female experiences, styles and genres thought to be feminine" (Messer-Davidow 72). By calling attention to gender, sex, race, and class as major dimensions of literary works, *Women in Literature* provides teachers and students with practical, stimulating analyses that rethink traditional scholarship.

One common situation that is *not* conducive to new readings occurs when teachers of introductory-level literature courses are handed a list of books or an anthology from which they must teach. Specifically, in the case of the many hardworking adjunct instructors or substitutes, these teachers are frequently assigned survey courses at the last minute, often leaving little time to prepare and think in new ways about old texts. Understandably, these teachers may hesitate to venture into critiques that differ from what they know best. Thus, circumstances sometimes render literature classrooms a place where students learn primarily from established interpretations, particularly of books in the core curriculum.

As Donnalee Rubin notes, we can't assume that all women read like feminist critics (and, she adds, neither can we assume that no men do) (21). The objective of this volume, then, is to support those who would like to "read like feminist critics" by providing an alternative approach to a variety of texts, an entry point for use in actual classroom sessions. Written largely by feminist scholar-practitioners with instructional experience in high school and/or college, the essays gathered here will help teachers by laying the groundwork for critical discussion, pointing out, in particular, some of the identity issues and thorny questions that frequently stem, organically, from the soil of gendered reading.

As for the many teachers who now claim considerable expertise in feminist studies, we expect that they would each recall having, at times, felt uneasy in classroom discussions of specific subjects (i.e., sexual orientation, the human body, and white or middle-class privilege). They know that confronting these topics can stir personal controversy for impressionable students. For those new to the field who might hesitate, for example, to teach lesbian content or call attention to literary images of menstruation or incest, some of the essays can serve as guides for introducing material that is both politically and personally sensitive. Since our authors are practitioners whose classroom approaches to controversial subjects have met with success, it is our hope that teachers reading *Women in Literature* will feel encouraged to reinterpret familiar texts in these ways, and to consider assigning works outside the canon. We hope, too, that students will feel more confident trying out feminist interpretations, inspired by the readings and approaches offered within these pages.

The essays in this book situate each work in its literary time and place. Contributors attend to social forces surrounding the work's production, and sometimes, in the case of various women writers, the controversy surrounding its reception. We recognize, with feminist critic Amy Ling, that all of literature represents "the written voice of a specific group of people at a specific time," and we agree with her in this: that if we, the readers, open our minds to the writings of those who have been raised quite differently from ourselves; if we take interest in a wide range of multicultural, sexually distinctive voices as they "sing their individual and communal songs," we more fully enjoy the "richness and depth in this chorus that is America"—and all the world, Ling might add today (157, 159). Our aim is to help students understand this aspect of literary history—that what an author writes, the critical notice the work receives, and who reads it are all influenced profoundly by sexual, racial, political, and historical realities. Recognizing this, students may come to appreciate that inclusive feminist criticism, in its effort to rediscover and reclaim neglected women writers, can not only free from oblivion the writers themselves, but it can also liberate readers who unexpectedly come to see both themselves and others in a "lost" writer's work.

Yet, if the reading of fiction can serve as an open door for students to enter into important discussions of gender roles, oppression, and power relations, we find it unsettling to learn that in teacher-education textbooks which train our future teachers, reading methods is singled out as the discipline which experts devote the "least space to" (Zittleman and Sadker 173). Through their review of these instructional materials, Zittleman and Sadker observe that while verbal commitment to promoting gender equity may be expressed, "specific resources and strategies to achieve that goal are often absent" (168).

With this in mind, we have directed *Women in Literature* to teachers and students who seek resources and strategies for dismantling stereotypical images that justify women's subordination and other forms of social inequality. Moreover, by providing discussion of refreshing works by women of color and white women, works that balance the traditional curriculum, we mean to facilitate both students' and teachers' learning from those who, historically, have been eclipsed by the dominant culture.

Even teachers who are seasoned feminist critics will be pleased to have the rich multitude of activities and assignments offered within these pages. For example, one dilemma that all high school and college feminist teachers confront in today's multicultural classrooms concerns the choice of books to assign: how to decide if a newly discovered woman writer, one not represented among the so-called classics, is good enough—that is, sufficiently worthy of classroom time—to take the place of an author whose work is widely accepted as important. With specific ideas for generating discussion and a list of literary, gender-related resources about each work, the essays in this book may help with such decisions.

HOW WE CHOSE THE TEXTS

Our objectives in selecting the texts were twofold: to research and compile a list of the most popular novels and plays in high school and college English and Humanities classrooms, and to augment that list with a number of less commonly taught, teacher-recommended works which feature positive female role models. We sought cultural diversity in our final list, which resulted in our choosing texts with fictional situations of both a temporal and geographical range. We began our task by reviewing published lists of literary works frequently taught, discovering these in the following seven sources:

1. "Outstanding Books for the College Bound: Fiction," www.ala.org/ yalsa/booklists/obcb/fiction.html.

2. P.A.C.T. Program—Reading List for High School Students—Appendix for Language Arts Standard 13: Level IV, www.jps.net/bmoom/ pact/currclm/hslit.htm, used by permission from *Mcrel*, the Midwest Continent Regional Educational Laboratory, June 1997.

3. "Variety and Individualism in the English Class: Teacher-Recommended Lists of Reading for Grades 7–12" by Sandra Stotsky and Philip Anderson, sponsored by the NEATE, a listing of Suggested Pre-College Reading, compiled by consulting English professors in the New England colleges concerning which works of literature they believe students would benefit from reading before college study.

4. Applebee Report from the Center for the Learning and Teaching of Literature, 1989: Titles Required in 30 Percent or More of the Public Schools, Grades 7–12.

5. Outstanding Books for the College-Bound: Choices for a Generation (Young Adult Library Services Association, Marjorie Lewis, Editor).

6. High school and college syllabi, available online, using "high school English classes" or "college English classes" as the key for a search.

7. National Council of Teachers of English, Women in Literature and Life Assembly (WILLA).

In addition to consulting these sources, we issued a call in *Equity* (published by the Institute for the Education of Women and Girls at Marymount College of Fordham University, Tarrytown, New York) addressed to teachers from places around the country who are interested in women's studies. In this call, we solicited contributors and also asked for recommended books that these feminist teachers most often taught or thought should be *more* often taught in high school and introductory college literature classes. Their recommendations have been invaluable in our decision making about what to include in this volume.

Last, we drew from personal experience, reviewing titles we ourselves have taught that have generated lively, constructive discussion of sex roles in our own classrooms: *The Book of the City of Ladies*; *Breath, Eyes, Memory*; *The Bride Price*; *Dessa Rose*; *Florence*; *Herland*; *The Left Hand of Darkness*; *Memoirs of an Ex-Prom Queen*; *Rubyfruit Jungle*; *So Long a Letter*; *Shabanu*; *Trifles*. As a whole, these books, some more familiar by now than others, offer readers a chance to study literary images of female and male dynamics from a fresh, though sometimes startling or painful perspective.

Any set of choices has limits. We regret not having essays about James Baldwin's *Go Tell It on the Mountain*, Louise Erdrich's *Love Medicine*, George Orwell's *Animal Farm*, Chaim Potok's *The Chosen*, Ntzoke Shange's *Betsy Brown*, and Virginia Woolf's *To the Lighthouse*. In some cases we could not match a popular text with a qualified contributor; in others, space became the obstacle to inclusion. Still, notwithstanding these regrettable omissions (as well as other "favorites" our readers will surely wish were here), we believe we have collected a broad, plentiful spectrum of essays, which use tools of feminist criticism to illuminate the texts.

HOW WE RECRUITED CONTRIBUTORS

Once our list of texts was gathered, we searched for writers through calls for contributors in journals and by networking with our publisher and among our contacts in the fields of women's studies and feminist criticism. We also used the Internet to locate specialists whose work centers on particular authors we sought to represent. We feel fortunate that so many scholars of serious reputation quickly became interested in participating in this project, seeing it as a much-needed resource, a worthy educational "cause."

Lynn Malloy, our editor at Greenwood, was exceedingly helpful in directing us to writers who had previously published articles or books about authors to be included in this volume. We also used the online listing of calls for papers published by the University of Pennsylvania and used the venue of women's studies and English discipline conferences to solicit interest in *Women in Literature*. We took advantage of our own professional networks to identify faculty with expertise in particular books or authors. Finally, our own contributors have been quite generous in their willingness to contact colleagues prepared to write on gender analysis, with expertise on a specific literary text.

While we had begun our search for essay writers thinking that a few key scholars could take, for example, the nineteenth century in American literature, we were soon struck by the attractiveness of having contributors represent not only geographical range but also a range of teaching approaches. As a result, essays have been written by contributors who live and work in Hawaii, Alaska, England, India, Germany, the Midwest, the West Coast, the South, and all down the eastern seaboard, reminding us that women's studies is being "done" in classrooms and by scholars across the globe from a similar critical lens but informed by the individual's professional context and experiences.

ACKNOWLEDGMENTS

Many people have helped us in the writing of this book. We are first and foremost deeply indebted to our contributors for their generosity, creativity, and patience.

We are most grateful to our editor at Greenwood, Lynn Malloy. She acquainted us with many of the scholars who wrote for this volume and gave us background materials, plus wise advice and counsel when we needed it. Her commitment to this volume as a classroom resource has been a guiding force since our work began. Thanks also to Anne Thompson, who helped us in the later stages of readying the manuscript for publication.

A special thank you to Jules Trammel for his expert technical support and to Jo Ellen Morrison at the Marymount College of Fordham University, Tarrytown library for providing critical sources.

We wish to thank Lucy Morrison for introducing us, at a particularly important juncture, to several of her colleagues, who contributed to the book.

Early on we appreciated the help of Jack Lynch, Rutgers University, in showing us online sources of Web sites for high school English class curricula and places to post a call for contributors.

As ever, we appreciate each other's talents, especially as we engage together in this life's work we share: doing what we can to improve gender equity and encouraging dreams and possibilities for girls and women, boys and men. Not a day has gone by when we haven't been thankful for the precious friendship between us that has been strengthened by both the challenges and the joys of collaboration.

WORKS CITED

Ling, Amy. "I'm Here: An Asian American Woman's Response." *New Literary History* 19.1 (1987): 151–60.

Rubin, Donnalee. *Gender Influences: Reading Student Texts*. Carbondale and Edwardsville: Southern Illinois UP, 1993.

Introduction

Engaged in the world of a good writer's imagination, we read ourselves as we project ourselves into the situation of the text, reflecting on our received values and entertaining new ideas about living. As Judith Fetterley suggests, literature is itself political (xi, xii); likewise, Patricinio Schweickart reminds us that the point

> is not merely to interpret literature in various ways; the point is to *change the world* . . . reading and writing [are] an important arena of political struggle, a crucial component of the project of interpreting the world in order to change it. (39)

Feminist criticism is a moral as well as a political enterprise: "it takes a stand" (Donovan ix). Thus, it has the capacity to alter the way that readers understand themselves and conceptualize their surroundings. Reading through a feminist lens that examines gender, students may find their assumptions about women and men disrupted as they learn about power, privilege, authority, point of view, and "otherness." Indeed, they may find themselves reconsidering almost everything humans do with or say to one another. Perhaps it is for this reason that Lillian Robinson speaks of feminist literary study as " 'criticism with a Cause,' " that is, criticism that seeks to correct the devaluation of women, "to alleviate the oppressive effects of literature on women . . . transforming the institutions of literature, criticism, and education" (Messer-Davidow 69).

Barbara Smith, in her 1977 landmark essay "Toward a Black Feminist Criticism," emphasizes the connection between the women's movement and feminist inquiry:

It took the surfacing of the second wave of the North American feminist movement to expose the fact that these works [books by white women] contain a stunningly accurate record of the impact of patriarchal values and practice upon the lives of [these] women and more significantly that literature by white women provides essential insights into female experience. (159)

By extension, in sowing seeds for a specifically Black feminist criticism, Smith charges that such an endeavor must occur in the context of Black feminist political theory, since the politics of sex, race, and class are "crucially interlocking factors in the works of Black women writers" (158–59).

"Doing" feminist literary criticism, then, involves asking at least these several questions: Does reading literature by diverse women foster reevaluations of resistance, oppression, and the so-called "feminine" themes such as the domestic sphere or the nuances of relationship? How are gender, race, and class imprinted in works by particular authors whose lives span time and place? Has the traditional scale of literary judgment kept some women writers from assuming greater authority, more enduring voices, and positions of power? Reading literature written by men—especially male-authored works in the canon—from the perspective of female experience, what can we learn about gender relations, about the "masculine mystique," about long-valued interpretations of these texts themselves, and about a culture's dominant social and aesthetic values? Do female characters face moral or relational dilemmas different from those confronting male characters? How does an author's gender influence the creation of a novel's narrative voice? And finally, what effect does an author's gender have on the imagined male or female reader? A book reviewer? A textbook selection committee? Generally speaking, contributors approach the texts they analyze in *Women in Literature* with more than one of these questions in mind, demonstrating how many ways there are to "do" feminist criticism.

"Entering an old text from a new critical direction," as poet Adrienne Rich is well-known for saying (35), can renew for us those works we have been teaching for years. How, for example, have male portraits of women been read in the past, and how as feminist critics can we revise those readings to more fully understand women in literature? One widely known fictional character is Mrs. Morel, Paul's mother in D. H. Lawrence's *Sons and Lovers*. While traditional critics have labeled Mrs. Morel as overprotective and sexually fixated on her sons, Maria Margaroni re-visions this aspect of the mother–son relationship, analyzing it *politically* as the "product of Mrs. Morel's frustrations within a culture that denies her any direct access to power" (272). Mrs. Morel seeks consolation in her sons, Margaroni says, because only they can do what she wants to do and cannot attempt, let alone accomplish.

Female characters drawn by established women writers have not necessarily fared better with traditional critics. In Emily Brontë's *Wuthering Heights*, Catherine Earnshaw, famous for her wild and carefree childhood, lived in close association with her foster brother, Heathcliff. Living temporarily with the wealthy, established Linton family, she decides to marry their son, Edgar. Soon afterward, a jealous Heathcliff leaves, but after he returns, Catherine becomes ill, both mentally and physically, and dies at a young age. A traditional interpretation has her dying because she cannot reunite with her true love, Heathcliff, but Barbara Thaden, in "Procrustean Bed: Gender Roles in Emily Brontë's *Wuthering Heights*," suggests that the underlying cause of Catherine's death lies in the repression of so much of her core self, "her rage against [the] restrictive bonds" necessary to fulfill "the role of conventional wife and mother" (307) amidst the landed gentry of mid-nineteenth-century England.

Feminist criticism not only sheds new light on women characters; it also revises our understanding of how masculinity and lesbian and gay relationships are portrayed in literature. (Although there are teachers and scholars today who prefer the term "gender criticism" as a critical label because it seems to more directly include discussion of sexuality and sexual orientation, we use the term "feminist criticism," embracing its origins in feminism as a social movement.) Feminist criticism, as it is practiced today, critiques inequalities and oppressions in the context of various and diverse interpersonal, sexual, and social relations. Feminist critics move easily from analysis of the female into examination of images of oppression in its various forms, connecting gender bias to other forms of domination. While feminist critics may emphasize the study of women in literary works, because women and men coexist in innumerable and intimate ways, a fresh view of one gender necessitates heightened awareness of the other. As Eve Kosofsky Sedgwick notes, "feminist studies . . . specif[y] the angle of an inquiry rather than the sex of either its subject or its object" ("Gender Criticism" par. 2).

It is our hope that the essays in *Women in Literature* will lead young adult students to question socially constructed notions of "women" and "men" that influence the lives of real women and real men who find love in both heterosexual and homosexual relations. Additionally, we hope that students using this book will feel increasingly comfortable using the term "feminist criticism," understanding its potency as a critical lens for studying literary and cultural representations of gender.

CRITIQUING NORMS

As part of any feminist literary project, when we study literature by both women and men, we must avoid "replicat[ing] the dangerous cultural fiction that men are not gendered" (Baym 61). When boys and young men in a coeducational classroom are assigned a text that treats strictly the lives of girls and women, they can sometimes read unsympathetically, seeing the characters' concerns as female and therefore trivial, disregarding the work as a major reading experience. More typically, when girls are assigned texts exclusively featuring boys and men, the characters and their dilemmas assume universal significance and are not identified as gendered. Not subjecting conventional portraits of masculinity to gender analysis may lead, unintentionally, to a mistaken premise to which we are all prone: that men's lives are normative and the term "gender" does not apply to them.

Books by men about male subjects, ones in which women are totally absent or obviously peripheral, have elicited surprising interpretations by feminist critics. Kim Martin Long, for example, discusses the absence of female characters in Melville's *Moby-Dick*. She shows male dominion as it characterizes this classic, but by looking for "female presences," Long finds that symbols of women's existence, such as the powerful sea and the storm, which Melville personifies as feminine, "actually win out over the male-dominated aggression that pervades the story" (201). Long's analysis will help feminist teachers approach this novel without simply indicting Melville "for gender bias only by examining the few images of 'real' female characters in *Moby-Dick*" (201).

Black Boy by Richard Wright, an autobiographical novel focused on male experience, tells the story of this African-American writer's life from his childhood in the South through his days in Chicago. Wright pictures the women in his life as not understanding his need for independence and limiting his intellectual horizons. He characterizes them as having nothing more going for them than "a false church, a whiskey bottle, and . . . a peasant mentality" (70–71). But Kenneth Florey urges us not to accept Wright's negative images of women at face value. He suggests that we encourage students to "see through" them and recognize instead, by closely reading the facts that Wright records, the nurturing, protective influence these women actually provided.

Our contributors have a special role to play as well in their interpretation of books by writers who cast girls and women at the literary center, narrating their stories of empowerment from within the gender-biased societies they inhabit. For example, a feminist work such as Alice Walker's *The Color Purple* focuses readers' attention on how women help each other to grow. Celie's transformation from abashed, abused, and silent to "living proud and in full possession of her voice" comes from the protagonist's relationships with women, forged through song, letter writing, and work. Ernece Kelly's essay tracks these other women in Walker's novel who, "in following their unique paths toward personal fulfillment, guide Celie to explore and honor her own" (75). Reaching out to the subjugated Celie, sexy Shug Avery, bold Sofia, and courageous Mary Alice empowers Walker's protagonist by modeling for her different ways that different women overcome men's relentless efforts to limit and disable those they deem "beneath" them. Walker knows that without supportive female friendship and love, a woman like Celie would remain isolated and self-critical, unable to challenge the pitiful men who attempt to debase her.

While Walker's female characters all become outspoken in their resistance to oppression, Shabanu, the title character in Suzanne Fisher Staples' novel, must learn to internalize her struggle against patriarchal tyranny. Zarina Hock shows how this young girl, growing up in a Pakistani desert culture, "comes to terms with oppressive practices of a male-dominated society" and learns to "see her self-worth when she is 'betrayed and sold' " (260, 261). Hock points out that Shabanu's favorite aunt, Sharma, a woman who dared leave her abusive husband and who lives independently, becomes "an instrument of agency" for her niece. Sharma teaches the 12-year-old girl, who is about to be wed to a man she has run away from home to avoid marrying, that "a woman's dreams of freedom must remain hidden" (261). This advice allows Shabanu to create inside herself an "inner space—a space untouched by male tyranny" (261). Through Hock's culturally sensitive analysis of Shabanu's story we see that female characters find the resolve to rebel against oppression quite differently, and importantly, we see that there is no "one right way" to resist male dominion. Hock's discussion asks readers to interrogate their own cultural bias as they read stories of girls coming of age in distant places.

Providing balance in the number of selections that feature protagonists of each gender, we aim to disrupt "one particularly unfortunate assumption" that teachers sometimes hold, one about which Zittleman and Sadker express concern in their study: that "boys will refuse to read stories about girls, an insight that does not encourage equity and respect" (174). This attitude—that privileges boys' preferences and their socialized hostility toward anything "girly"—still makes its way up the scholastic ladder, not infrequently distorting both high school and college curricula.

But gender is only a single factor that shapes an individual's inner life and choices. Clearly, other identity markers such as race, ethnicity, class, sexual orientation, and religion cannot, in everyday life, be easily separated, even for the purposes of classroom discussion. Fortunately, across high school and college campuses today, celebrating multiculturalism is an honorable, well-respected pursuit. Yet, in our academic experience, educational activities aimed at recognizing cultural diversity tend to show more interest in racial, ethnic, and class variables than gender or sexual preference; rarely do such programs highlight sufficiently the complex, intrinsically connected ways that bias exists in an ordinary woman's or man's life, as well as in social policy. Many have found that both curricular and extracurricular programs promoting inclusiveness often signal that gender discrimination, by its omission from the center of discussion, is a less significant form of bias than race or class. As one teacher says from her experiences in school:

> We start with gender and within minutes, we are pursuing arguments about race. We start with gender again, and immediately head in the direction of teenage violence. We mean to start with gender next. But gender is the piece which is mentioned less often by name in the staff room, in professional development workshops, in the newspapers, or in the classroom. (Ginsberg et al. 164)

It is not uncommon today to hear high school and college students expressing the view that, unlike racial and class discrimination, women's problems have, by this time, been alleviated through gains in employment equity and access to higher education. This view, however, ignores the reality of most women's lives: being female head of household, taking sole responsibility for childcare, or succumbing to unfair expectations for gendered divisions of labor in the home; worrying daily about body image and trying to keep up with unrealistic fashion and beauty dictates—all of which put severe limits on what girls and women can do and how they feel about themselves and their potential. While commonalities among people who grow up female can be greater than their differences, teachers may find it easier (that is, more "politically correct") to talk about inequities experienced by a single racial group than to discuss the fact that diverse women have been and are discriminated against in similar ways; for example, in terms of money and power. Unfortunately, there are multiple anecdotal examples of occasions when well-intentioned teachers convey the idea to students that problems associated with gender bias—assumed to be women's problems and not men's—are less urgent than other forms of bias, and therefore less worthy of classroom time.

Another related and equally fallacious assumption that we hope to interrupt is that books largely about white culture are not about race. The assumption that because whiteness prevails as a racial norm, it is neutral and need not be mentioned is analogous to the idea that because what is male is normative, gender need not be raised in books about men. As Nellie McKay writes,

> while many white middle-class feminists are now sensitive to the special problems in the combination of race, class and gender, they can (and some still do) concentrate their resources on strategies that deal with female oppressive patriarchal structures, which may or may not include

ideas of race, class, and gender [together] as necessary components of their feminist ideologies.

This, McKay continues, means, "feminists of color, must, at all times, address white male and female (including feminist) racial oppression and black male patriarchal dominance as well" (163). Regrettably, only several essays in *Women in Literature* directly take into account the effect of characters' whiteness on the story's racial dynamics or how the author's whiteness may have influenced her/his literary creation (*Dessa Rose, Florence, Herland, Jane Eyre, Shabanu, Uncle Tom's Cabin*). In each of these novels, race concerns are portrayed as an aspect of the plot or characterization and the white characters' awareness of their racial privilege becomes woven into the story. Through compiling this book we recognize keenly that the effect of whiteness on literary production is an area to which white feminist scholars need to give more critical attention, through discussion of race in texts whose story lines and white protagonists seem oblivious to their own white privilege.

As the essays in *Women in Literature* show, the approaches feminist teachers take to the study of literary texts are varied. But any approach that centralizes questions of women's status and equity can warm up the "chilly climate" for female students by validating social and intellectual concerns most girls face. Additionally, by providing essays that treat patriarchy and female resistance to it, we hope to help students begin envisioning possibilities for rereading and posing feminist critical questions about prevailing norms, questions that they might not otherwise have asked.

Feminist critics, even in the early days, now more than three decades ago, quickly perceived, as Lillian Robinson points out, the limitations of simply "expos[ing] sexism in one work of literature after another" (qtd. in Kolodny 547). Since that time, feminist criticism has broadened its scope to challenge the accuracy and adequacy of established literary history, with male writers and critics at the center of influence; the traditional canon taught in secondary, undergraduate, and graduate classrooms nationwide; the "loss" of brilliant writings by women, works that gained recognition only posthumously, such as Chopin's *The Awakening* or Hurston's *Their Eyes Were Watching God*; or women of genius, such as Harriet Beecher Stowe and Lorraine Hansberry, who did not find in their circumstances hospitable conditions for writing more than one or two great works. Barbara Smith underscores the important political role that criticism plays "in making a body of literature recognizable and real . . . for books to be real and remembered they have to be talked about" (159). In *Women in Literature*, our most expansive goal is to promote feminist discussion of the traditional canon and to bring into the classroom less-recognized novels and plays that will be remembered for their power to engage students in examining literary images of gender. Ideally, the essays published here should spark debate and prompt new awareness; indeed, we think that readers will find our contributors' interpretations not only useful but also memorable, well worth talking about in classrooms across the country.

With so many needs, purposes, and promises to fulfill, what, we might ask, does most feminist criticism have in common? Perhaps it is the effort to examine any aspect of a text, by a man or by a woman, for signs of female presence or absence that we might not otherwise see because masculine values and experience have long been considered normative in our culture. Written from behind a lens of feminist inquiry, the essays gathered here aim to expose the bias of standard literary critiques that may restrict rather than expand our students' imaginations and curtail insights about women's and men's lives. We anticipate that *Women in Literature* will contribute to inclusive discussions that will honor different female voices, visions, and meditations alongside those created by men.

WORKS CITED

Baym, Nina. "The Feminist Teacher of Literature: Feminist or Teacher?" *Gender in the Classroom: Power and Pedagogy.* Ed. Susan L. Gabriel and Isaiah Smithson. Urbana and Chicago: U of Illinois P, 1990, 60–77.

Donovan, Josephine. "Introduction to the Second Edition: Radical Feminist Criticism." *Feminist Literary Criticism: Explorations in Theory.* Ed. Josephine Donovan. Lexington: UP of Kentucky, 1989, ix–xxi.

Fetterley, Judith. *The Resisting Reader: A Feminist Approach to American Fiction.* Bloomington: Indiana UP, 1978.

Ginsberg, Alice E., Joan Poliner Shapiro, and Shirley P. Brown. "Opening GATE (Gender Awareness Through Education): A Doorway to Gender Equity." *Women's Studies Quarterly* 28.3–4 (Fall/Winter 2000): 164–76.

Kolodny, Annette. "Dancing through the Minefields: Some Observations on the Theory, Practice, and Politics of a Feminist Literary Criticism." *Women's Voices: Visions and Perspectives.* Ed. Pat C. Hoy II, Esther H. Schor, and Robert DiYanni. New York: McGraw-Hill, 1990, 546–64.

McKay, Nellie. "Response to 'The Philosophical Bases of Feminist Literary Criticisms.' " *New Literary History* 19.1 (1987): 161–67.

Messer-Davidow, Ellen. "The Philosophical Bases of Feminist Literary Criticisms." *New Literary History* 19.1 (1987): 63–103.

Rich, Adrienne. "When We Dead Awaken: Writing as Re-Vision." *On Lies, Secrets, and Silence.* New York: W. W. Norton & Company, 1979, 33–49.

Robinson, Lillian S. "Dwelling in Decencies: Radical Criticism and the Feminist Perspective." *College English* 32.8 (1971): 879.

Schweickart, Patrocinio. "Reading Ourselves: Toward a Feminist Theory of Reading." *Gender and Reading: Essays on Readers, Texts, and Contexts*. Ed. Elizabeth A. Flynn and Patrocinio P. Schweickart. Baltimore, MD: The Johns Hopkins UP, 1986.

Sedgwick, Eve Kosofsky. "Gender Criticism: What Isn't Gender." www.duke.edu/~sedgwic/WRITING/gender/htm, n.d.

Smith, Barbara. "Toward a Black Feminist Criticism." *But Some of Us Are Brave: Black Women's Studies*. Ed. Gloria T. Hull, Patricia Bell Scott, and Barbara Smith. New York: Feminist Press, 1982, 157–75.

Wright, Richard. *Black Boy* [1991 version]. New York: Harper, 1993.

Zittleman, Karen and David Sadker. "Gender Bias in Teacher Education Texts: New (and Old) Lessons." *Journal of Teacher Education* 53.2 (2002): 168–80.

Women's Roles and Influence in Mark Twain's *The Adventures of Huckleberry Finn* (1885)

Melissa McFarland Pennell

Often described as an archetypal novel of male friendship and a boy's journey toward understanding, Mark Twain's *Huckleberry Finn* features numerous female characters. Through his female characters and the various roles they play, Twain reveals gender codes and expectations of his day and the ways that women are sometimes limited by these social forces. The range of female characters contributes to the complexity of the novel and to the texture of the antebellum world that Twain conveys. Like many of the men in the novel, the women are also affected by the racist mentality of slavery.

The biggest contrast between men and women in the novel involves mobility. Huck and Jim travel through much of the narrative, as do the Duke and Dauphin. Some male characters, such as Peter Wilks, make significant journeys, while others are free to come and go in the local areas in which they live. Female characters, in contrast, are typically bound by place. They are usually encountered in their homes, underscoring women's ties to the domestic sphere. One of the few female characters who leaves her assigned space is Sophia Grangerford, whose elopement sets off another battle in the Grangerford–Shepherdson feud, costing her younger brother Buck his life. Through her actions, Twain suggests the perils that attend a woman's decision to defy patriarchal authority and pursue her own course.

The female characters who appear in *Huckleberry Finn* can be divided into three basic groups: mothers and mother-substitutes; older, single women without children; and girls or young women. Each group introduces distinctive gender issues and allows Twain to present the world of Huck Finn as it would have appeared to an adolescent boy.

Within the domestic sphere, mothers and mother-substitutes execute a degree of authority, especially through their ability to maintain order within the household. Often Huck, especially in the company of his friend Tom Sawyer, attempts to fool these women and disrupt the household. Teachers can ask students how this form of defiance by boys raised by women serves as a means for the boys to test boundaries and gender roles. But in another way these mother figures demonstrate authority; they also reveal—through their perceptive comments—experiential wisdom they have gained. When Huck tries to pass himself off as a girl to Mrs. Judith Loftus, she quickly sees through his disguise and tells him what he does wrong. She cautions: "Don't go about women in that old calico. You do a girl tolerable poor, but you might fool men, maybe" (684). Aunt Polly and Aunt Sally, like Mrs. Loftus, display tolerance for the antics of boys and a genuine affection for them. Late in the novel, Tom's Aunt Sally, who has endured the mischief within the plot to free Jim, says to Huck, "Oh, go on and call me Aunt Sally, I'm used to it, now, and 'tain't no need to change" (909), as she draws him into the family circle. Huck, however, realizes that these bonds of affection will require accommodation to women's rules that he endeavors to resist.

In contrast to the acceptance he meets from mothers, Huck has difficulty with Ol' Miss Watson. Brittle and harsh, she has little patience for what she perceives as others' failings. Twain uses her character to reflect what he considers the deep-seated hypocrisy of early nineteenth-century culture, especially the conflict between professing religious beliefs and owning slaves. Her notions of class status and propriety create an unbridgeable gulf between her and Huck, while Twain uses Miss Watson's spinster status to underscore her lack of sympathy. Huck fares better with the Widow Douglas. Although she has no children of her own, she has taken in Huck, hoping to provide him greater stability and guide him toward more acceptable, middle-class social conventions. Huck chafes against the code of behavior she imposes, but unlike Ol' Miss Watson, who has been neither wife nor mother, Huck perceives that the Widow Douglas does care for him and that her efforts are well-intentioned.

On his journey, Huck encounters a number of young women or hears about them from others. Some reflect attributes that Twain critiques, while others embody values that he endorses. Emmeline Grangerford's funereal drawings and poems identify her with popular sentimentality and false sympathy. Teachers can explore how Twain uses Emmeline as a target of humor, questioning whether her characterization represents the author's belief that women assume artificial behaviors to perpetuate illusions of a pseudo-aristocratic society. Can Emmeline's thin veneer of cultivation obscure the underlying culture of violence that destroys her family? Her false sentiment stands in contrast to the genuine sorrow expressed by Boggs' daughter and the compassion expressed by Mary Jane Wilks. Twain suggests, however, that compassion for others makes young women vulnerable to con men who see them as easy targets;

that young women, like the Wilks sisters, are easily victimized in a society that accepts appearances as reality. Such ideas about female vulnerability fostered the nineteenth-century belief that middle-class women need male protection from life's harsh realities. This point of historical interest may lead teachers to ask whether it is women's perceived vulnerability that elicits male chivalry, reinforcing genteel beliefs and practices (such as door-opening) that disempower women and skew power relations between the sexes. Do women need men's chivalry as a buffer against tough circumstances beyond their capacity to negotiate? What strengths do Mary Jane Wilks and her sisters reveal? Can—and should—women also practice chivalry in their treatment of men?

Huckleberry Finn is often read as a *bildungsroman* that traces a boy's development. Certainly, Huck and Jim's joint quest for freedom has been considered the core of the novel. To help students appreciate Twain's approaches to gender issues, teachers can encourage a close look at Huck's interactions with female characters. From each exchange, Huck gains an important lesson or piece of knowledge that shapes his character or helps him on his journey. Students can identify these lessons and determine which are most significant. Huck also evaluates concepts of masculinity by comparing his experiences to those of girls and women. His recognition that in his culture, the world of women, of home, and family, means limitations and confinement leads to his desire to "light out for the Territory ahead of the rest" to avoid Aunt Sally's plan to "adopt . . . and sivilize" him (912).

WORK CITED

Twain, Mark. *The Adventures of Huckleberry Finn* [1885]. *Mississippi Writings.* New York: Library of America, 1982, 617–912.

FOR FURTHER READING

Stahl, John D. "Mark Twain and Female Power: Public and Private." *Studies in American Fiction* 16.1 (1988): 51–63.

Stein, Regina and Robert Lidston. "The Mother Figure in Twain's Mississippi Novels." *Mark Twain Journal* 21.3 (1983): 57–58.

The War against the Feminine: Erich Maria Remarque's *All Quiet on the Western Front* (1929)

Mary Warner

In the epigraph the author suggests that "[the book] will try simply to tell of a generation of men who, even though they may have escaped shells, were destroyed by the war." Remarque alludes here specifically to the destruction that permeates the spirit of this generation of men who fought in World War I. Certainly, the human spirit must be described as including the capacity for compassion, sensitivity, and other life-affirming feelings. In casting sensitive poet Paul Bäumer as narrator, Remarque exposes the successful war against the feminine that was and is part of any military campaign.

Paul and his classmates, enlisting at eighteen, had been labeled by their teacher as the "Iron Youth"; however, they find in the first terrifying, disillusioning moments at the Front that they are neither "iron" (unfeeling and invulnerable) nor are they any longer youth. Combat and glorification of the "Fatherland" impel Paul and his young peers not only to fight for their lives and their country but also to battle an interior war against their "feminine" sides in order to triumph in physical battle.

The opening chapter highlights several ways the feminine spirit is crushed. Speaking of Kantorek, schoolmaster and proponent of the male-oriented world, Paul says: "He was about the same size as Corporal Himmelstoss, the 'terror of Klosterberg.' It is queer that the unhappiness of the world is so often brought on by small men" (10). Paul's observation raises interesting questions for the classroom about the pressure boys and men experience to appear strong, and the ways that they sometimes "compensate" for having short stature or slight build in a culture still saturated with tall, muscular, agile prototypes for male success. Kantorek, indeed, suggests such "compensation" in his being no less than a martinet, indoctrinating Paul and his schoolmates about the honor of enlisting; the schoolmaster's "long lectures" continue until all the boys enlist, including Joseph Behm, a "plump, homely fellow" (11). Paul's description of Behm associates him with the stereotypically feminine: He is less athletic and therefore less "soldier-like" than the other boys; he enlists to avoid ostracization by his peers, and tragically, though perhaps inevitably, he is the first to fall in battle. And there can be no tears shed by any of the "spirit scarred" remnant.

Remarque devotes extensive text to those dying and to the guilt of the living young soldiers. When Kemmerich dies, Paul faces the greatest pathos, having come from Kemmerich's hometown, and he is haunted by the image of Kemmerich's mother, "a good plump matron," crying as she implored Paul to

> look after Franz. . . . Indeed he did have the face like a child, and such frail bones that after four weeks' pack-carrying he already had flat feet. But how can a man look after everyone in the field. (15)

The male "ironness" must dominate; there is no "looking after" others, even one's comrades. Paul cannot allow his friend's softness to pierce the soldier's shield of stoicism for more than a few seconds. Just outside the dead man's hospital room, he reluctantly gives away Franz Kemmerich's boots, seeming to give away with them much of his anger and grief at losing his childhood playmate.

Paul experiences his helplessness here and indeed, there is no haven from heartless, dehumanizing conditions at the front. But his earlier description of Kemmerich's mother (which mirrors that of other mothers in the text) portrays the maternal as physically ample—capable, in absentia, of providing images of comfort. Symbolically, Paul's lengthy descriptions of shelling further illuminate the consolation that mothers and, by extension, Mother Earth provides:

> To no man does the earth mean so much as to the soldier. When he presses himself down upon her long and powerfully, when he buries his face and his limbs deep into her for fear of death by shell-fire, then she is his only friend, his brother, his mother; he stifles his terror and his cries in her silence and her security; she shelters him and releases him. (55)

The comforting aspect of maternal imagery looms in dynamic comparison/contrast with the poster girl who mesmerizes the battle-dirtied, sexually deprived males. The poster image comforts too, but is too delicate and sensuous to be life sustaining. Yet, like the other sexual symbols in the text (the women with whom Paul and others have brief sexual encounters and the women that officers "get"), the poster girl offers the soldiers affirmation of their maleness so necessary to their survival. Paul and his companions fantasize about sexuality to avoid emotional breakdown, which would be their demise in facing the physically brutal reality of war.

Only those soldiers who have repressed the feminine can survive in the masculine frontlines. Paul labels recruits "infants": They come to the front less hardened; they weep; they are innocent to the potency of shelling; they hold to the delicacy of their civilian youth. To Paul, they are childlike and thus feminized by cultural standards.

> It brings a lump into the throat to see how they go over, run and fall . . .
> a man would like to spank them . . . they have no business to be [here]
> . . . their shoulders are too narrow, their bodies too slight. (130)

Herein lies the greatest irony in the war against the feminine. On one of the days when the masculine war world is described as "quiet," when Paul feels free to release some of his ironness, he is killed.

All Quiet on the Western Front provides the opportunity to examine the military and the role of women in armed forces. Contemporary students are not far removed from controversies over females enrolling at the Citadel, or from claims of sexual harassment by female or homosexual officers. Also: How do qualities of the feminine and masculine relate in military training? Are both welcomed? In particular, Paul left at home an original play and "a bundle of poems" (19); what is the place of artists or of creative or sensitive personalities in war or other experiences demanding destruction? This novel, like *Red Badge of Courage*, like Hemingway's short story "Soldier's Home," and the war-movie genre, insists that readers weigh the necessity of having a strong military against the costs of war, and especially those costs that forever distort and diminish the human spirit.

WORK CITED

Remarque, Erich Maria. *All Quiet on the Western Front* [1929]. New York: Fawcett Crest, 1975.

FOR FURTHER READING

Hunt, Nigel. "*All Quiet on the Western Front* and Understanding Psychological Trauma." *Narrative Inquiry* 9.1 (1999): 207–12.

O'Neill, Terry, ed. *Readings on* All Quiet on the Western Front. San Diego, CA: Greenhaven, 1999.

Ulbrich, David J. "A Male-Conscious Critique of Erich Maria Remarque's *All Quiet on the Western Front.*" *Journal of Men's Studies: A Scholarly Journal about Men and Masculinities* 3.3 (February 1995): 229–40.

"Doctor She!" Helena and Sisterhood in William Shakespeare's *All's Well that Ends Well* (ca. 1602–1603)

Terry Reilly

Based in part on a tale from Boccaccio's *The Decameron*, Shakespeare's *All's Well that Ends Well* traces the adventures of Helena, a poor physician's daughter, as she pursues and ultimately wins the object of her desires, young Bertram, the Count of Rousillon. In sharp contrast to other dominant female characters in Shakespeare's comedies, Helena succeeds by flouting rather than following many of the conventions normally gendered "feminine" in early modern English comedy—cross-dressing, passivity, silence, and an emphasis on virginity and chastity. Instead, calling attention to Helena's sexual desire and tremendous facility with both language and logic, Shakespeare also presents in *All's Well that Ends Well* a unique group of female characters—the Countess, Diana, the Widow, and Mariana—who work collectively to help Helena achieve her ends. This sisterhood of characters and Helena's insistence upon presenting herself as unflinchingly and unquestionably female make *All's Well that Ends Well* unique among Shakespeare's comedies.

Unlike other heroines such as Portia in *The Merchant of Venice*, Viola in *Twelfth Night*, or Rosalind in *As You Like It*, all of whom dress in male attire for various reasons, Helena does not disguise her gender as she pursues Bertram. When she leaves Rousillon for Paris, for example, she travels simply as what she is; a poor physician's daughter. Later, when she sets out for the shrine of St. Jacques in Compostella, Portugal, and arrives inexplicably in Florence, she dresses as a female pilgrim. Moreover, in rebuttal to Parolles' clumsy attempts to seduce her by constantly calling attention to her virginity, Helena silences him by responding, "How might one do, sir, to lose it to her own liking?" (1.1.151). Helena's comment here reinforces our sense of her subjectivity.

Helena pays a price for her overt sexuality and her refusal to cross-dress as a male. When she arrives at court to attempt to cure the King of France, Lafew introduces her parodically as "Doctor She!" (2.1.79), and when he jokingly refers to himself as Pandarus—"Cressid's uncle" (2.1.97)—he underscores the implied sexual nature of the scene. (In the tale from the Greeks, Pandarus arranged the sexual liaison between Troilus and his niece Cressida.) Moreover, when Helena is left alone with the King, she understands full well not only what she is wagering, but also what those outside the room will think of her:

> Tax of impudence,
> A strumpet's boldness, a divulged shame,
> Traduc'd by odious ballads; my maiden's name
> Sear'd otherwise . . . (2.1.170–73)

When Helena cures the King, the courtiers waiting outside the room unanimously agree that his recovery has something to do with sex and/or witchcraft—no one even considers that Helena is simply a competent doctor who has cured her patient.

Helena's reward for her success, of course, is her choice of a husband, but when she chooses Bertram, he refuses her, first because of class difference:

> I know her well;
> She had her breeding at my father's charge—
> A poor physician's daughter my wife? Disdain
> Rather corrupt me forever! (2.3.113–16)

After being pressured by the King to acquiesce, Bertram flees, leaving behind a cryptic letter with a series of challenges reminiscent of the labors of Hercules:

> [Reads] "When thou canst get the ring upon my finger, which shall never come off, and show me a child begotten of thy body that I am father to, then call me husband; but in such a 'then' I write 'never.' " (3.2.57–60)

As Helena travels to Florence to fulfill the conditions of the letter, she enlists the aid of the Widow and her daughter Diana, a young maid whom Bertram is trying to seduce. Helena persuades Diana to agree to have sex with Bertram if he will give her his ring. Bertram at first refuses, prompting Diana to make one of the great speeches about the value of a woman's chastity in early modern English culture:

> Mine honor's such a ring,
> My chastity's the jewel of our house,
> Bequeathed down from many ancestors,
> Which were the greatest obloquy i' th' world
> In me to lose. Thus your own proper wisdom
> Brings in the champion Honor on my part,
> Against your vain assault. (4.2.45–51)

Here, as Diana uses Bertram's language against him, she establishes a complex system of values based on the relative worth of Bertram's ring and her chastity. After Diana's speech prompts Bertram to part with his heirloom much too quickly ("Here, take my ring!" (4.2.51)), Diana then sets the liaison for midnight in her darkened room with the understanding that Helena will substitute for her as Bertram's sexual partner.

The end of *All's Well that Ends Well* presents us with an image of a matriarchal system in that Helena becomes Bertram's wife and replaces his mother as the Countess of Rousillon. Earlier in the play, Helena refused to call the Countess "Mother," since that would imply an incestuous relationship with Bertram and preclude Helena's marriage to him. Now, as she greets the Countess as "my dear mother," (5.3.319), Helena underscores the multivalent nature of her newly found and newly consolidated power; as wife, daughter, mother, and Countess.

In short then, *All's Well that Ends Well* includes a number of representations of gender bias which remain issues today: the problems women encounter working in what have been traditionally male professions; the problems a woman encounters when she portrays herself as a sexual being in a world which privileges female chastity; and finally, the problems that occur when a woman foregoes a passive role and actively pursues the object of her sexual desires.

Conversation about these problems and issues in a classroom setting often leads to heated and fruitful discussions that not only reveal the rich texture of this often overlooked play, but also give the play currency and value with both female and male members of young modern audiences.

WORK CITED

Shakespeare, William. *All's Well that Ends Well* [ca. 1602–1603]. *The Riverside Shakespeare*. 2nd ed. Boston: Houghton Mifflin, 1997, 533–78.

FOR FURTHER READING

Asp, Carolyn. "Subjectivity, Desire, and Female Friendship in *All's Well that Ends Well*." *Literature and Psychology* 32 (1986): 48–63.

Hodgdon, Barbara. "The Making of Virgins and Mothers: Sexual Signs, Substitute Scenes, and Doubled Presences in *All's Well that Ends Well*." *Philological Quarterly* 66 (1987): 47–72.

Snyder, Susan. "Naming Names in *All's Well that Ends Well*." *Shakespeare Quarterly* 43.3 (Fall 1992): 265–79.

Mother, Wife, Fallen Woman: Marital Choice in Leo Tolstoy's *Anna Karenina* (1877)

Lucy Melbourne

From the famous opening—"All happy families are like one another; each unhappy family is unhappy in its own way" (17)—Tolstoy's classic novel *Anna Karenina* announces its theme of marital relationships. In a nineteenth-century aristocratic Russian world where men keep mistresses but "fallen women" (56) are ostracized, Anna and the sisters Dolly and Kitty represent three different responses to difficulty in marriage: self-sacrifice, partnership, and adultery. Through rich characterization and divergent plot structures, Tolstoy vivifies their unions as choices in morality that include feminist concerns. Anna's alienation, her renunciation of maternity, and her suicide contrast with Dolly's self-sacrifice for her children's sake, in the face of her husband's adultery, and Kitty develops from self-abnegation into fulfilled woman, wife, and mother.

At first, 18-year-old Kitty is "in love" (80) with Dolly's sister-in-law, Anna Karenina, who mediates between Dolly and her unfaithful spouse. Observing their problem, "Your wife is getting old and you are full of life" (56), Anna exposes men's unfair rationale for infidelity when a wife has sacrificed the prime of life for domestic obligations. Threatening divorce, financially independent Dolly expresses outrage that her sexual service and responsibilities for five children have robbed her of youth. Anna, with ominous foreshadowing, pleads for her brother, Stiva, explaining to Dolly that men distinguish "between their families and those women" (84–85). Dolly's choice to forgive for the sake of an intact family reflects maternal resignation to patriarchal double standards. Ironically, Anna herself soon becomes one of "those women" when a loveless marriage pushes her into an affair with the wealthy Count Vronsky, Kitty's anticipated suitor. Discussing Dolly's choice—and taking into account

Anna's plight—students will have strong opinions about what constitutes "right" action when maternal responsibilities constrain self-fulfillment.

Unlike Dolly and Anna, Kitty achieves fulfillment and self-integration in marriage. When Vronksy flatters her, Kitty initially rejects Levin, an idealist whose country manners lack urban polish. Disillusioned by infidelity in Anna's and Dolly's marriages, an "emaciated" (132) Kitty renounces sexuality, condemning female objectification "as a shameful exhibition of goods" (225). After attempting religious self-abnegation, Kitty decides she is no "angel" (238) but a woman with her own identity and natural desires, and chooses to accept Levin along with farm life. Eventually, Kitty finds spiritual and physical wholeness in partnership with Levin, but only after a difficult period that requires the couple to compromise and communicate openly. Since Tolstoy contrasts the Levins' marriage to other amorous relationships in the novel, students might consider their own estimations of successful unions. What remains the same and what has changed since Tolstoy's depiction of relations between upper-class wives and husbands?

In contrast to Kitty's difficult but ultimately successful marriage, Anna's affair with Vronsky sunders her corporal from her moral self, leading to fragmentation, betrayed maternity, and suicide. Unlike the amoral Princess Betsy or the self-satisfied Vronsky, Anna is tortured by moral awareness; ironically, Anna's quest for a more genuine life and identity propel her into an affair that only reinforces her alienation.

Initially, financially dependent, provincial Anna accepts her marriage to the older Karenin, sublimating physical and emotional needs into the enjoyment of aristocratic city life and caring for their son, Seryozha. A *grande dame*, beautiful in body and spirit, Anna's youthful vitality animates her smiling eyes. Anna considers herself a dutiful wife, loving mother, and morally irreproachable woman. Yet, on a train, after meeting Vronsky, Anna's self-perceptions are irrevocably altered. Amidst a blizzard mirroring her inner turmoil, Anna questions her life and identity with new urgency: "What am I doing here? Is it me or someone else?" (115), gradually acknowledging the hypocrisy of her loveless marriage and hollow social identity.

Anna's affair, however, cannot answer her fundamental existential questions. Although seeking authenticity and purpose in love, Anna is humiliated by deceit; she becomes ashamed of her unchecked passion and paralyzed with maternal guilt. She enacts her divided self in a recurring nightmare, making love to both men, signifying her impossible desire to simultaneously please husband and lover—both named Alexey. Near death in childbirth, Anna fleetingly glimpses an authentic self and tells Karenin, "I am the real one now, all of me" (418). Recovered from her illness, Anna nevertheless cannot sustain wholeness and remains haunted by dreams of a gnome-like railway man, demonic harbinger of her death. Loathe to accept Karenin's offer of divorce that would forfeit Seryozha to him, she chooses to live openly with Vronsky and their baby daughter, whom she cannot nurture. No longer a wife and thus a socially outcast "fallen woman," Anna renounces motherhood, explaining to Dolly that she uses birth control to retain her figure—and Vronsky. Learning about reproductive choice, Dolly is appalled at Anna's betrayed maternity and self-image as sexual object. Without family and financial support, and terrified at losing the increasingly resentful Vronsky, who had abandoned a promising career for her, Anna concludes: "[who] could be more of a slave?" (634). When Karenin denies her now desperate request for divorce, Anna realizes, finally, that she is trapped: Her search for authenticity has been overwhelmed by her being identified as "fallen woman," and Anna confronts her failed choices as wife, mother, and lover.

A poignant conclusion reunites the three women: At Dolly's Kitty "held out her hand" (750) to the embittered Anna, who rejects feminist solidarity and life-affirming compassion. Driving to the train station, Anna's obsessive stream-of-consciousness expresses only self-destructive nihilism—and her decision to end her suffering. But, at this final, pitiable moment of hatred and imminent death, Anna assumes tragic dignity, again posing metaphysical questions: "Where am I? What am I doing? Why?" (760). Out of existential silence seconds before her death beneath the rails, Anna's appeal elicits a voice of faith: "Lord, forgive me everything!" (760).

Like Edna Pontellier, Emma Bovary, and Lily Bart's suicides, Anna's tragedy indicates romantic passion cannot resolve women's quest for identity and purpose. Students might ask what options women in *Anna Karenina* have, given the constraints of hypocritical patriarchy in its demand for women's sacrifice.

WORK CITED

Tolstoy, Leo. *Anna Karenina* [1877]. Trans. David Magarshack. New York: New American Library, 1961.

FOR FURTHER READING

Mandelker, Amy. *Framing* Anna Karenina: *Tolstoy, the Woman Question, and the Victorian Novel.* Columbus: Ohio State UP, 1993.

"Young Lady" or "Slut": Identity and Voice in Jamaica Kincaid's *Annie John* (1983)

Lucy Melbourne

Jamaica Kincaid's autobiographical novel *Annie John* presents an Afro-Caribbean girl's struggle for individuation and cultural identity on British colonial Antigua. Annie's narrative covers the formative period of transition from girlhood through adolescence, from age ten to seventeen. In mesmerizing poetic style, interconnected incidents trace Annie's distinctive voice as it emerges from an initially paradisiacal then claustrophobic bond with her mother. Students readily identify with Annie's rebellion and grasp the pain of maternal separation seemingly necessary for this character's growth toward adulthood. Teachers may want, however, to also develop the novel's analogies between feminist and post-colonial identity by discussing Annie as she constructs both maternal and colonial imposition of "mother" and "mother country." Just as Annie struggles to overcome female gender stereotypes, so, too, does she incorporate her colonial heritage to discover her emerging identity and autobiographical voice.

Initially, Annie experiences an undifferentiated union with her all-powerful mother. In blissful images of innocent paradise, Annie swims naked on her mother's back and mimics her domesticity. At this point, the daughter's voice is subsumed into maternal stories of Annie's infancy and early childhood, symbolized by memorabilia collected in the mother's trunk. At ten, however, Annie's curiosity about death foreshadows adolescent separation, which begins when her mother prepares her to be a "young lady." To foster Annie's individuation, her mother withdraws from their cocoon, insisting that Annie do so, too. Feeling abandoned and betrayed, Annie suddenly sees her mother as the "serpent" (52) in their paradise: beautiful, even seductive, but dangerous. Later, the resentful 12-year-old perceives her mother as "a crocodile" (84) ready to engulf her. These threatening images reveal not only an adolescent's fear of change, but also her need to demonize her mother.

In her search for autonomy and nascent self-definition, Annie defies her mother's prescribed standards of female propriety: She plays the boys' game of marbles, lies, steals, and sabotages her dancing and piano lessons. Students might expand on the labels "young lady" or "slut" to identify other gender stereotypes and rigid parental messages about "proper" behavior to which they have been subjected as girls and boys. In a multicultural classroom, students might explore significant commonalities and differences among these "assigned" behaviors.

Annie's friendships with the Red Girl and Gwen—forged just after her mother imposes distance between her and Annie—vivify the dichotomy of "young lady"/"slut." Impassioned relationships with peers encompass Annie's love-hate feelings about her mother, enacted in pinching-and-kissing bouts with the unkempt, slovenly, and socially outcast Red Girl, Annie's alter ego and an amusingly caricatured image of the "slut." Annie tries to imitate the Red Girl, especially her skill at playing marbles and climbing trees "better than any boy" (56). When confronted with her mother's angry rejection of her behavior, however, Annie returns to her friend Gwen, whose tender caresses partially replace lost maternal affection and allow Annie to fantasize adulthood as regained domestic paradise with Gwen, thereby avoiding a "future full of ridiculous demands" (53).

Annie's emerging sexuality is linked to the key discovery of her own voice, which finally destroys her illusions of wholeness. As the relationship with her mother deteriorates into the palpable, unbridgeable animosity Annie describes as the "frightening black thing" (101), Annie increasingly relies on supportive friends at her British-run girls' school. In a striking image capturing adolescent girls' anticipation and dread of imminent maturity, Annie sits with a band of girlfriends on churchyard tombstones sharing concern about her as-yet-undeveloped breasts and soliciting admiration for her first menstrual period. This female environment is also an enraptured audience to Annie's story about maternal separation anxiety. Annie discovers that words give her power over others and over the emotional pain she feels toward her mother; later, the written word also helps her articulate her cultural identity despite colonial pretenses: "we, the descendants of the slaves, knew quite well what had happened" (76). Significantly, Annie is punished for her writing—an irreverent caption in her history textbook—and, ironically, forced to copy lines from *Paradise Lost*. The sexually developing, rebellious, and increasingly articulate Annie now understands that the timeless, idyllic union with mother or mother country is irrevocably gone.

Annie's female quest for individuation continues, reinforced by meaningful water images. In the intense, climactic battle between mother and daughter, Annie's mother calls her a "slut," and Annie feels as if her whole being "were drowning" (102), filled with her mother's judgment. During her subsequent nervous illness, paralleled by a three-month deluge, Annie hallucinates water-related acts of self-assertion. After drinking all the water in the sea, "with a loud roar . . . I burst open" (112). In another surreal episode during her illness, Annie washes photographs, erasing reflections of herself as schoolgirl, bridesmaid, and First Communicant. Eventually, Annie is revived through the African traditions of her grandmother, Ma Chess, whose ritual baths and devoted care restore Annie, now grown into physically striking adult stature carrying the strong voice of self-awareness.

As the novel ends, it is clear that Annie John has become the narrator of her own life. In an extended concluding soliloquy, Annie affirms her identity: "My name is Annie John" (132). Ironically, she thereby also names her mother and her town, St. Johns. Thus, although Annie's goal is to reject mother and mother country, she remains tied to both. Students may therefore disagree about the novel's conclusion, alternately viewing it as innovative self-affirmation, irresolvable ambivalence, or as capitulation to maternal and colonial tradition. As she sails to England—now with her own trunk full of potential stories—Annie hears the lapping waves "as if a vessel filled with liquid had been placed on its side and now was slowly emptying out" (148). This concluding image of emptiness already anticipates the self-generated inner life ultimately fulfilled in *Annie John*'s narrator's powerful, poetic, and wise autobiographical voice.

WORK CITED

Kincaid, Jamaica. *Annie John* [1983]. New York: Plume-Penguin, 1986.

FOR FURTHER READING

Simmons, Diane. *Jamaica Kincaid*. New York: Twayne, 1994.

Righteous Activist or Confrontational Madwoman: Sophocles' *Antigone* (441 B.C.E.)

Karen Bovard

Antigone's defiance of her uncle Kreon's order provides one of the earliest stories of radical resistance to state power in Western literature. Such direct challenge of a kingly decree might provoke crisis in any regime, but because Antigone is female, and her act so public and vocal, the offense becomes particularly heinous. The play was quite topical in its time: several generations earlier, the statesman Solon had written laws that were generally regarded as precursors to democracy in Athens but which explicitly restricted women's rights by forbidding them to lament in public at funerals or leave their homes without escorts, lest they forfeit their respectability.

Why does Antigone break with the expectations for her gender so radically? Is it to honor kinship bonds, which the Greeks viewed as central to the city-state? Antigone actually buries Polyneices twice: When the guards clear away the ritual dust, she audaciously repeats her act. She performed these rites for each of her parents, too (56, 1052–53). She chooses loyalty to the dead over her impending marriage to Haimon, and equates her tomb to her marriage bed (55, 1040; 57, 1102). She never mentions her feelings for Haimon directly, but bemoans that she will never bear children, as the etymology of her name predicts (Antigone means "against generation [motherhood]" with "-gone" deriving from the same root as "gonad"). Students are likely to hold varied opinions as to whether her familial loyalty seems inherently female in some way—is it a socialized response or an innate gendered trait?

Antigone claims another rationale for her defiant act, as well: fidelity to a higher law of the gods "which are not for now or for yesterday, they are alive forever." She argues that such laws take precedence over Kreon's legal decree, since it is human and fallible (39, 555–65). Readers often debate whether this represents principled action—above the immediate concerns of political expediency—and, perhaps, resistance of a particularly female kind. Whether Antigone is a passionate political activist motivated by deep spiritual conviction or whether she is suicidal and obsessed by death (or both) can generate lively classroom debate.

Close gender analysis of other key characters is fruitful. Ismene serves as a foil to Antigone: Her compliance to prevalent gender norms points up how radical her sister is. Ismene says, "we are women, born unfit to battle men" (23, 74) and proposes a compromise: She will participate in the protest if Antigone will act secretly. But Antigone remains adamant: "No, shout it, proclaim it. I'll hate you the more for keeping silence" (24, 107–8). The rebellious act of burial is insufficient for Antigone. She craves public confrontation with Kreon.

Ismene retreats into the palace, the proper domestic sphere, and into hysteria. Later she will lie and connive, plying Kreon with her feminine wiles in a vain attempt to save her sister's life. Clearly, Kreon favors Ismene over Antigone, which suggests the marriage between Haimon and Antigone had his blessing only as a guarantee of dynastic succession—the age-old pattern of using women as exchange items in men's negotiation of power. Dismissing Ismene, Kreon orders: "Take them both inside. Now they will have to be women and know their place" (44, 715–16). The sisters reconcile before Antigone goes to her death but only after Antigone castigates Ismene, rejecting her sister's hyper-feminine attempts to work within the system. Ismene's behavior can serve as a case study of the different means that people, and women in particular, use to garner influence when they are denied legitimate access to power.

Eurydice, Kreon's wife, the only other female character, emerges from the palace just once, to pray to Athena. Silently, she endures the details of her son Haimon's violent suicide. Without speaking, she leaves the stage and kills herself. Obeying prohibitions around women's speech and public action leaves her no alternative but suicide. Death or oblivion claims all the women: Antigone hangs herself in the cave where she has been buried alive; we never are told Ismene's fate.

That Antigone's defiant act radically destabilizes gender roles is particularly clear in Kreon's response to it. He says, "I'm no man—she is a man, she's the king—if she gets away with this" (40, 529–31). Stubborn independent action is manly; listening and changing one's mind are womanly. In his view, if he alters his decree, he emasculates himself. He becomes as intransigent as Antigone. The prophet Tiresias urges him to back down, but Kreon regards him with derision, initially: Might this be because Tiresias is a gender-bender, not a "manly man?" Although Tiresias' story is outside the scope of the play, all Greeks would have known that the gods made him female for a time and male for a time in an experiment to determine who derives more pleasure from sex.

When Haimon also argues that his father reconsider, Kreon reacts explosively, in a father–son confrontation that reads as astonishingly modern to many adolescents and young adults. Certainly, Haimon's skillful rhetoric reveals a much more flexible attitude toward gender roles than any other character displays. He voices the support for Antigone that he has heard amongst the commoners who fear the King. Earlier, Kreon reveals his crass sense of women as interchangeable playthings when Ismene begs for her sister's life on the grounds that Haimon loves her. Kreon answers: "There are other fields for him to furrow" (44, 703). Now he tells Haimon, "Don't throw out principle for a little fun, for the sake of a woman. Remember a treacherous wife turns cold in your arms. . . . Send that girl off like any other enemy" (47, 789–94). When Haimon persists, arguing that unilateral action is dangerous and that wise leaders listen to advice, Kreon determines to kill Antigone in front of his son, disowns him, and taunts him: "You're no man. You're a slave, property of a woman" (51, 914–15). Clearly, Kreon's rigidity around gender roles is part of what leads to disaster, multiple deaths, and his own exile. Haimon's efforts to mediate—to speak as a man from a feminist position, without enraging his father—fail and lead to the young man's self-destruction.

Antigone won the festival prize the year it was presented. In Sophocles' time, women were not permitted to attend theater festivals, whereas attendance was required of male citizens. The role of Antigone (and all women characters) would have been played by men in mask. That men debated issues of gender and power amongst themselves suggests how central such issues were then. Many modern treatments of Antigone's story exist, evidence that interest in questions about gender, political protest, and family loyalty remain strong today. Particularly notable are Jean Anouilh's version, written during the Nazi occupation of France, and one by Athol Fugard in which prisoners on Robben Island (where Nelson Mandela spent so many years) perform a drag version in their cells.

Ideas about a higher law provided the legal reasoning used to define war crimes during the Nürnberg trials after World War II. Students might research connections between modern human rights movements and *Antigone*, tracking states where women's rights have been dramatically restricted (e.g., the Taliban regime in Afghanistan) and instances of public resistance by women to state-sanctioned violence, such as that practiced by the Mothers of the Plaza de Mayo in Argentina.

WORK CITED

Sophocles. *Antigone* [441 B.C.E.]. Trans. Richard Emil Braun. Oxford: Oxford UP, 1973.

FOR FURTHER READING

Holst-Warhaft, Gail. *Dangerous Voices: Women's Laments and Greek Literature.* London: Routledge, 1992.

Female Resistance to Gender Conformity in Kate Chopin's *The Awakening* (1899)

Dana Kinnison

The turn-of-the-century world of Kate Chopin's *The Awakening* is one in which women eat bonbons at home while men smoke cigars and talk business at the club. However clichéd these gender images have come to be, there is veracity to them in the novel's sociohistorical setting, and they serve a central purpose. The story, that of Edna Pontellier's struggle against rigid conformity, juxtaposes two key characters alongside Edna to illustrate the few and fixed opportunities available to her.

Adele Ratignolle is the ideal wife and mother who never experiences an impulse that deters her from the sole concern of caring for her family. She embodies "every womanly grace and charm" (9). The description of her beauty has the colorful ring of traditional, romantic poetry: golden, unrestrained hair; "blue eyes that were like nothing but sapphires"; pouty, crimson lips (9). Dressed in pure white and often bathed in the warm glow of light, she is poised, serene, and loved by all. At the other extreme, Mademoiselle Reisz has devoted her energies not to husband and home but to the development of her own abilities. Although appreciated for her talent at the piano, the little musician is depicted as a homely and disagreeable older woman who lives alone. Mademoiselle Reisz's apartment is dingy, her clothing shabby, her gait shuffling. Black lace and artificial flowers mark her appearance. These two characters represent Edna's options: the reward of complete self-sacrifice versus the reproof of female self-assertion. No middle ground exists, only these extreme contradictions.

Although already a wife and a mother of two young boys, to Edna's awakening sensibilities a life like Adele Ratignolle's appears hopelessly flat and dull. Edna is drawn to Adele's beauty like everyone else, but the "mother-woman's" domestic contentment does not satisfy the passionate desires of a soul Edna is only beginning to recognize, a soul characterized by a hunger for selfhood and sensual experience. The vitriolic criticism hurled at this novel and the censure Chopin received, forever damaging her personal and creative life, indicate how threatening was the author's characterization of Edna, whose rebellion against female conformity profoundly offended moral sensibilities. Reading early reviews of the novel ("It is not a healthy book," reported the *St. Louis Globe*; "It leaves one sick of human nature," contended *The Mirror*; "overworked . . . sex fiction," described the *Chicago Times-Herald*, all in 1899 [Culley 163, 166]), students will get a sense of how deeply extended into the fabric of the times were public feelings against women's autonomy. Rather than Adele's contentment, the independence and music of Mademoiselle Reisz stir Edna's imagination. But Mademoiselle Reisz warns: " 'The bird that would soar above the level plain of tradition and prejudice must have strong wings' " (79).

Male power eclipses female prerogative in this upper-class, Louisiana Creole community. Leonce Pontellier, though considered a model husband, orders his wife about and perceives her "as one looks at a valuable piece of property" (4). In particular, three images richly interwoven into the text communicate Edna's experience of oppression. Like the parrot that opens the novel, owned and caged, Edna is also possessed by her husband and restrained by his and others' expectations. Throughout the work the ability or inability of birds to soar unfettered represents the avenues and obstacles to Edna's own freedom. So, too, does the sea. After overcoming the fear and futility she feels in the water, Edna suddenly swims with confidence. The quality of movement and the scope of the space she finds in this natural, limitless medium offer an appealing contrast to the confining cultural spaces that pattern and thwart her developing self. And while actual awakenings from sleep, as suggested by the title, intimate the discovery of new states of awareness, their counterparts are equally significant. Edna often lingers in drowsy reveries (7; 31; 34; and 97, for example), and one may question whether she ever achieves the consciousness needed to realize a transformation. These images of birds, sea, and sleep are satisfyingly complex while remaining accessible to adolescent readers.

The contemporary feminist classroom will likely be cognizant of minor female characters whom Chopin draws less sensitively than she does Edna. For example, it is among the chaste yet uninhibited Creole women that Edna begins to evaluate her own reserved disposition. Mariequita, a barefooted Spanish girl, brazenly makes eyes at men and is described as saucy. And the quadroon nurse who serves as primary caretaker for Edna's children is a slighted, neglected anonymity. Classroom discussion will be necessary to bring awareness to Chopin's stereotypical portraits of women who, by virtue of their race and class, only illuminate but do not share the protagonist's choices and her worries. Teachers might ask: How much a product of privilege is Edna's search for freedom?

Like Mariequita and the quadroon nurse, male characters in the novel, beyond Leonce, primarily play a role in Edna's sensual awakening. However, Edna's love for the youthful Robert and her involvement with the rakish Alcee Arobin cannot free her of the psychic repression from which she suffers. Indeed, Edna comes to recognize that Robert is as conventional as her husband, and that her intoxicating attraction to Arobin is disturbingly fleeting. She says, " 'To-day it is Arobin; tomorrow it will be some one else' " (108). Thus, Chopin suggests neither male companionship nor seduction as key to a woman's search for self.

For the most part, the novel strikes chords of interest and relevancy even though a hundred years, and differences in personal and cultural experience, separate today's young women from Edna Pontellier. For example, female readers are especially engaged by Edna's attitude toward motherhood, which is the conundrum at the core of her self-conflict: "I would give my life for my children; but I wouldn't give myself" (46). What does it mean to *give oneself*, students might ask? Edna's bonbon-eating existence may have gone the way of her parasol, but the domestic confinement that accompanies motherhood even today continues to be a dilemma for many women.

Similarly, Edna's suicide by drowning remains a source of controversy. Students may not agree upon why she killed herself, much less share a response. Is the act romantic and irresponsible or a conscious assertion of strength and autonomy in the face of intolerable limitations and unyielding circumstances? Some students, influenced by the realism of the novel, see suicide as defeat, while others appreciate Edna's death as a metaphorical rebirth. Chopin's character also introduces students to a female literary heritage in which creative and impassioned women, real and imagined, usher in their own deaths. Research into Virginia Woolf and Edith Wharton's Lily Bart, for example, would allow students a broader examination of this tradition.

WORKS CITED

Chopin, Kate. *The Awakening* [1899]. 2nd ed. Ed. Margo Culley. New York: Norton, 1994.

Culley, Margo, ed. "Editor's Note: History of the Criticism of *The Awakening*—Contemporary Reviews." Kate Chopin, *The Awakening*. 2nd ed. Ed. Margo Culley. New York: Norton, 1994, 159–73.

FOR FURTHER READING

Koloski, Bernard, ed. *Approaches to Teaching Chopin's* The Awakening. New York: Modern Language Association, 1988.

Martin, Wendy. *New Essays on* The Awakening. New York: Cambridge UP, 1988.

Mothers and Children in Barbara Kingsolver's *The Bean Trees* (1988)

Mary Jean DeMarr

In her first novel, *The Bean Trees*, Barbara Kingsolver brings to life a variety of characters in a variety of relationships, some by blood and some by choice. Most characters represent female types, from assertive and independent to passive or disabled. Family and motherhood figure centrally in their presentation and are crucial to their values. This likeable gallery, especially Taylor, the protagonist, accounts for the novel's strong appeal to female readers of all ages.

Taylor, a determined young woman, undertakes a cross-country drive to seek a future for herself. Along the way, she acquires a Native American child who has been physically, sexually, and emotionally abused. Taylor and the child, whom she calls "Turtle," soon are living the lives of single mother and daughter in Arizona. To her surprise, Taylor discovers in unsought motherhood a new kind of love and a new focus.

Against Taylor's courage and assertiveness, Kingsolver sets the passivity of Lou Ann. Deserted by her husband and rearing her son Dwayne Ray alone, Lou Ann differs sharply from Taylor, but the two bond quickly and help each become stronger and more complete. Taylor demonstrates that assertiveness and self-confidence are possible for a young single parent; eventually, Lou Ann becomes motivated to get a job, which she loves. Taylor learns mothering skills from Lou Ann. Together they exemplify strong friendship and on the basis of that friendship they form a healthy relationship, almost like a family.

Mattie, a middle-aged businesswoman, serves as a role model for Taylor and Lou Ann. Loving and nurturing, Mattie employs Taylor and acts as her surrogate mother. Politically active, Mattie works clandestinely with the sanctuary movement that brought illegal immigrants into the United States, sheltering them and helping them find permanent, safe homes. Mattie protects the refugees at legal risk to herself: an expression of mothering carried into the political arena.

At the other extreme from the active and assertive female characters are Turtle, the helpless and abused child, and Esperanza, an illegal whom Mattie shelters. Esperanza values motherhood and the love of children highly. Still grieving for her little girl, who had been taken from her and Estevan in Guatemala, Esperanza attempts suicide, but finally begins a slow return to normal life through Turtle. Turtle and Esperanza function as examples of victimization, Turtle by child abuse and Esperanza through political oppression. Each has suffered greatly and withdrawn into her own sad world, and each is restored to life through the nurturance of others. In Esperanza's case, the recovery is complex, for it comes about through her mothering of Turtle as well as through her being mothered.

A background character, Taylor's own mother has provided well for her daughter: Her hard work as a domestic has given Taylor knowledge of maternal strength, courage, and enduring love. Other nurturers include Mrs. Parsons and Edna Poppy. While Kingsolver does not present these two mature women in obviously maternal roles, they enjoy a remarkable, strong friendship with each other, and by caring for Turtle and Dwayne Ray, they thereby take care of Taylor and Lou Ann.

The one important male figure in the novel is Estevan, a strong, wise, masterful male, who represents a type of romantic hero. Taylor falls in love with him, although she knows he belongs to Esperanza. Friendship with and concern for Esperanza as well as a strong sense of fairness outweigh Taylor's physical and emotional attraction to Estevan. Their lives are separate, and the affection they develop for each other must, of necessity, end. Instead of playing the role of the fairy-tale princess who finds romantic fulfillment with a dashing lover, Taylor accepts with composure that her true commitment is to her foster daughter. There can be no conventionally happy ending in this narrative, but the actual ending is more real than any fairy-tale ending could have been. In this way, Kingsolver brings a kind of feminist resolution to what might have, in other hands, been contrived as a typical romanticized plot line. Instead, Taylor, generous and sacrificing, lives happily and self-sufficiently (if not "forever after") without a prince.

Reading this novel centered on motherhood, girls and women will appreciate each of the adult female characters: Even the passive Lou Ann models much that is positive. Love and nurturing can be present in many different, often untraditional, relationships, and women, the novel shows, can find fulfillment in ways they had not expected. Taylor had fled Kentucky because the only life she saw for young women there included early pregnancy, marriage, poverty, and lost opportunities. Ironically, she acquires a child and falls into the motherhood she had been evading. Her love for Turtle becomes fiercely protective, and by the end of the novel she takes desperate steps to normalize and legalize their relationship through adoption. Taylor's spunk and optimism, her sensitivity and ability to make friends, her independence and tolerance—students will find all these qualities worth emulating.

Both male and female students can deepen their understanding of Taylor and her world through certain research assignments: for example, political oppression in Guatemala; the sanctuary movement in the United States; regulations for immigration (especially as applied to women and families from Latin America). Such study will enable students to see the political context from which Estevan and Esperanza have escaped and within which they live with Mattie. Teachers may find comparisons with the Underground Railroad helpful to illuminate both the risks faced and hopes embraced by Esperanza and Estevan, as the runaways, and by Mattie and Taylor as the "conductors" to safety.

Single parenting is another issue about which students can learn from their reading of *The Bean Trees*. Also of interest is controversy surrounding the adoption of Native American children outside their tribes; while not presented as a source of tension in this book, it is more important in *Pigs in Heaven*. With their interest in Taylor and Turtle sparked by *The Bean Trees*, students might be challenged to read the later novel and consider how its treatment of adoption might affect their view of related issues, themes, and maternal characterizations in *The Bean Trees*.

WORKS CITED

Kingsolver, Barbara. *The Bean Trees*. New York: HarperCollins, 1988.
———. *Pigs in Heaven*. New York: HarperCollins, 1993.

FOR FURTHER READING

DeMarr, Mary Jean. *Barbara Kingsolver: A Critical Companion*. Westport, CT: Greenwood, 1999.

William Faulkner's Male Myth: *The Bear* (1942)

Kim Martin Long

William Faulkner's novella *The Bear*, from his work *Go Down, Moses* (1942), chronicles Isaac McCaslin's coming of age as he learns to hunt the mythical bear "Old Ben." This difficult tale about men, men who take to the big woods to hunt and to escape the society of women, fits into the category of other male epics, such as Homer's *Odyssey* or Dante's *The Divine Comedy*.

Divided into five parts, like a drama, *The Bear* presents Ike McCaslin's development from age ten when he first goes to the woods with his cousin McCaslin, Major de Spain, General Compson, Boon, Ash, and his mentor, Sam Fathers. Faulkner describes the setting of the camp and the ubiquitous bottle of liquor present: "that brown liquor which not women, not boys and children, but only hunters drank, drinking not of the blood they spilled but some condensation of the wild immortal spirit" (184). Even the description of the food is masculine: "for two weeks he ate the coarse rapid food . . . which men ate, cooked by men who were hunters first and cooks afterward" (188). This decidedly male setting prepares the reader for the description of Old Ben himself: "the old bear, solitary, indomitable, and alone; widowered childless and absolved of mortality—old Priam reft of his old wife and outlived all his sons" (186). The bear's greatness partly comes from his being alone, not shackled by a wife and children. The narrator Ike says that the bear has given him his education—outside any female sphere, outside society: "the wilderness the old bear ran was his college and the old male bear itself, so long unwifed and childless as to have become its own ungendered progenitor, was his alma mater" (201–2). Faulkner's work glorifies singular maleness, represented by the old bear Ben.

As Ike witnesses and partakes in the death of Old Ben, he becomes more fully the classic hero, possessing unknown abilities and accomplishing feats derived from his masculinity. Students might be reminded of the stereotypical "Hemingway hero" in the descriptions of Ike's hunting abilities—courage, endurance, sensitivity, the need for no woman. Ike tells the stories of his own heroes: Sam Fathers, son of a Negro slave and an Indian chief; Old Ben, creature of nature who cannot be killed but by almost supernatural means; and Lion, the great blue dog, who serves as a fitting adversary for Old Ben. Faulkner says through the voice of Ike: "only Sam and Old Ben and the mongrel Lion were taintless and incorruptible" (183) in their perfect maleness.

Part 4, the most enigmatic of the novella because of Faulkner's use of the stream-of-consciousness technique, breaks from the narrative and relates the McCaslin family history, Faulkner's history of the South in miniature. Faulkner places the narrative of the struggle with Old Ben and the wilderness in a larger context of history, slavery, and family. Ike relates, through the ledgers of his grandfather, the miscegenation present in his family, always reminding readers that gender distinctions separated people more strongly than racial ones. His cousin McCaslin reminds Ike that he is the only male descendent in the male line of McCaslins, his cousin being "derived through a woman" (245). Ike learns that the name of his grandmother Beauchamp came through a black line, albeit a male one, and that the name Edmonds was pure white but derived from a woman. Faulkner takes special care in part 4 to emphasize patriarchy over race.

Also in part 4, McCaslin refers to a childhood memory, "an instant, a flash, his mother's soprano 'Even my dress! Even my dress!' loud and outraged in the barren unswept hall" (289). In this description of a lost memory, Faulkner presents the male fear of primitive, natural female sexuality, something that many of Faulkner's heroes fear: Quentin in *The Sound and the Fury* and Joe Christmas in *Light in August*, for example.

The novella returns in part 5 to the wilderness for a kind of epilogue to the tale. When he visits the site of the previous hunts—now being harvested by a lumber company—Ike flashes back to the "glory days" of hunting with the others. In fact, Ike feels that the wilderness has formed both him and Sam: the

> deathless and immemorial phases of the mother who had shaped him if any had toward the man he almost was, mother and father both to the old man born of a negro slave and a Chicasaw chief who had been his spirit's father if any had. (311)

Although the idea of motherhood surfaces occasionally throughout the book, Ike emphasizes that hunting, male comradeship, the quest, and knowledge of the earth and nature have created him, the hero.

Critics argue that Faulkner's women are either "madonnas or whores," that Faulkner either raises women to a pedestal which makes them unreachable, or he brings them down to the base, sexual level. In *The Bear*, however, female characters play only a minor role. Women such as Tennie Beauchamp, the slave; Ike's wife, who wants to trade sex for a farm; or female animals, such as the "injured bitch" or the "frantic mare" serve only to elevate the male characters. The positive maternal image of the woods gives way often to images of female deceit or weakness. Even the description of the dying Sam Fathers as a self-made man of the woods emphasizes the absence of the female presence: "the old man, the wild man not even one generation from the woods, childless, kinless, peopleless" (236). In this Faulkner tale (and in much of Faulkner's fiction), men are stronger and better men without women to entangle them or weaken them.

Students wanting to explore further Faulkner's views on women should contrast this story to another one of his works, *Light in August*, which contains a very strong female presence, or *The Sound and the Fury*, a novel in which Caddy Compson seems to survive the family events more easily than her brothers. Although *The Bear* presents a strongly male perspective—given the subject of the hunt and the desire to create a classically mythical quest story—many of Faulkner's works portray fully realized female characters in control of their circumstances. If teachers want to compare this work to a second novella, they might try Ernest Hemingway's *The Old Man and the Sea*, another male quest story, this time in a boat rather than with a gun. Both works present a hero who survives because of his abilities, his courage, and his endurance, but without any help from women.

WORK CITED

Faulkner, William. *Go Down, Moses* [1942]. New York: Random House/Vintage, 1990.

FOR FURTHER READING

Fowler, Doreen and Ann J. Adable, eds. *Faulkner and Women/Faulkner and Yoknapatawpha, 1985*. Jackson: UP of Mississippi, 1986.

More Than Skin Deep:
Robin McKinley's *Beauty:*
A Retelling of the Story of Beauty and the Beast (1978)

Ellen R. Sackelman

Robin McKinley's *Beauty: A Retelling of the Story of Beauty and the Beast* examines the life and education of the title character as she resolves issues of self-image and self-worth. Set somewhere "once upon a time," McKinley's text redefines the role of the fairy-tale heroine and allows the protagonist, the youngest of three motherless sisters, to narrate her story in a matter-of-fact manner and explore her identity within the structure of her family, alone in captivity, and in the company of her lover. Beauty's numerous self-defining gestures help her recognize the difference between physical attractiveness and integrity, and resolve the discrepancy between the way she sees herself and the manner in which others do.

After her father is unable to provide 5-year-old Honour with a satisfactory explanation of what it means to be honorable, she renames herself Beauty and thus sets up the first of many contrasts to her gorgeous siblings. When she suffers from acne and oversized hands and feet during adolescence, Beauty admits that her self-chosen appellation had evolved into something of a gentle family joke. These and other wry observations engage even the most reluctant male readers, who may approach this novel with their own bias against the genre of fairy tales. Indeed, Beauty's subsequent refusal to allow her father to escort her past the gates to the Beast's castle and her nightly rejections of the Beast's marriage proposals distinguish her as a heroine not often encountered by young readers: a female voice negating male desires.

Prior to these instances when Beauty negotiates with male authority, McKinley reverses other familiar aspects of characterization within the genre. Instead of passively awaiting marriage, sequestering herself indoors, or perceiving herself as "a weak woman," as one sister does, the intrepid protagonist dreams of attending the university and reads voraciously. In addition, unlike her sisters, Beauty communicates with her father, and her affectionate exchanges with her brother-in-law foreshadow her own healthy, romantic relationship. Despite her obvious rejection of the roles her sisters occupy, Beauty does not reject or demean them, a welcome development to the way females interact with one another in fairy tales. Encouraged to closely contrast McKinley's depiction of familial relationships and gender roles to those in other well-known fairy tales, students begin to recognize their own conditioned, sexist expectations. Such realizations elicit reactions of surprise and heighten students' awareness of how deeply entrenched and frequently reinforced in everyday life gender stereotypes truly are.

McKinley's Beauty embodies a delightfully rebellious spirit as well as some traditional aspects of the female role. Functioning as nurturer, for example, Beauty has raised her own horse, even bottle-feeding it after the death of its mother. Her labor in the garden establishes her as an integral member of the family. However, like others who perform domestic duties in their own homes, Beauty is unable to recognize her value to her family. After her father attempts to fulfill her request for rose seeds, another symbol of the vitality that Beauty brings to her surroundings, she easily exchanges her life for his as a result of his bargain with the Beast.

She attributes her decision to leave her family and live with the Beast to what she believes is her worthlessness, namely, her looks. Of her sisters, she says she is the "ugliest." More than once in the course of the text, she refers to herself as having masculine—or unfeminine—attributes. For example, she claims that her household responsibilities can be maintained by "any lad in the village" (78). At the Beast's castle, she sees herself as a "poor plain girl," not worthy of dressing like a princess. Interestingly, Beauty refuses repeatedly to succumb to the elaborate wardrobe her invisible handmaidens make available to her, an assertive act not only emphasizing Beauty's determination to do as she pleases, but also serving as a reminder to the reader how paralyzing an obsession with looks can be. Yet, even after her declaration of unconditional love for the Beast releases him from his enchantment, Beauty questions whether she is attractive enough to be the wife of such a handsome man. Only in his company does she gain a sense of her comely appearance, and because of this, Beauty's moment of actualization may be perceived as a troubling one. In a text lacking an obvious villain, Beauty's poor self-image makes her her own worst enemy.

Strikingly, the relationship between Beauty and her Beast offers an alternative to love affairs in other pieces of fiction usually assigned to the teenage reader. Theirs is not as impulsive or as tragic a union as Romeo and Juliet's, nor is it as torturous as Pip's devotion to Estella. Rarely is Beauty described as powerless or passive. More than once, she is reminded that "she's stronger than she knows" (173). In fact, she determines the pace and nature of her interaction with her Beast, inviting him to share a sunset or a walk in the garden when she wants company. Additionally, with the Beast, Beauty is able to renew her education. Her thirst for knowledge, a trait her sisters disparaged, brings Beauty closer to him. They read together and often. McKinley's unconventional use of a flower to serve as a metaphor for the male protagonist's health and his misgivings about his appearance can propel discussion relevant to both sexes regarding literary characterizations and symbols typically associated with gender.

By the novel's close, Beauty is reunited with her family and set to marry a prince. In the final paragraphs of the text, she must name her husband, a task that recalls her earlier decision to name herself. The privilege in giving a human name to the Beast makes final and more significant Beauty's sense of control over her world.

Using *Beauty* in the classroom allows students to detect the pervasive gender bias in literature and/or video for young "readers" on which they have been raised. Asking them to analyze whether McKinley's text fulfills the criteria of the traditional fairy tale, or complies with parameters set forth by male-dominated quest legends, serves as an introduction to feminist literary theory. Thus, *Beauty* occupies an important place in the gender-balanced curriculum.

WORK CITED

McKinley, Robin. *Beauty: A Retelling of the Story of Beauty and the Beast*. New York: HarperCollins, 1978.

FOR FURTHER READING

Fisher, Jerilyn and Ellen S. Silber. "Fairy Tales, Feminist Theory and the Lives of Women and Girls." *Analyzing the Different Voice: Feminist Psychological Theory and Literary Texts*. Ed. Jerilyn Fisher and Ellen S. Silber. Lanham, MD: Rowman and Littlefield, 1998, 67–95.
Heinke, Jill Birnie, Diane Zimmerman Umble, and Nancy J. Smith. "Construction of the Female Self: Feminist Readings of the Disney Heroine." *Women's Voices. Feminist Visions*. Ed. Susan M. Shaw and Janet Lee. Mountain View, CA: Mayfield, 2001, 376–80.
Zipes, Jack. *Don't Bet on the Prince: Contemporary Feminist Fairy Tales in North America and England*. New York: Routledge, 1987.

Sylvia Plath's *The Bell Jar:* Trapped by the Feminine Mystique (1963)

Laurie F. Leach

Published in the same year as Betty Freidan's *The Feminine Mystique* but set a decade earlier, Sylvia Plath's novel explores the very problem that was Friedan's subject. *The Bell Jar* traces the mental breakdown and recovery of a talented girl at a time when marriage and motherhood were held out as the only appropriate avenues for women seeking fulfilling lives. Like the windows of the Amazon hotel, which were "fixed so that you couldn't really open them and lean out" (20), working women's options were similarly narrow, giving only an illusion of access to the professional world. The working women who reside at the hotel are "secretaries to executives and . . . simply hanging around in New York waiting to get married to some career man or other" (4). Despite Esther's academic and artistic achievements, her own career prospects seem no brighter. Her mother advises that if Esther would only learn shorthand "she would be in demand among all the upcoming young men, and she would transcribe letter after thrilling letter" (83). Esther, however, wants "to dictate [her] own thrilling letters" and hates the thought "of serving men in any way" (83).

If careers for women seem uninspiring to Esther, the alternative of becoming a housewife is even less appealing. She imagines marriage as an endless cycle of cooking and cleaning, "a dreary and wasted life for a girl with straight A's" (93), and assumes that motherhood conflicts with her aspiration to be a poet (84). Her horror over a possible loss of self in motherhood is symbolized in the scene where she watches a woman give birth and observes the woman's face obscured by her enormous stomach (72). Just as Esther expresses outrage at the male medical establishment drugging the mother so that she would forget her obvious pain and willingly submit to the "torture" of another childbirth, likewise, Esther fears that motherhood itself involves "brainwashing" women so that afterward they "went about numb as a slave in some primitive totalitarian state" (94).

Esther's distress is compounded by the many mother figures in the story—her actual mother, her potential mother-in-law, her editor, and her benefactress, as well as the sadistic nurses—who encourage her to play the role of dutiful daughter and who view her dissatisfaction with the choices open to her as a sign of illness. While very real, her breakdown seems to symbolize her repudiation of her culture's standards of femininity and acceptable domestic roles for women. For instance, she discards her fashionable clothing and then stops washing her hair or changing her clothes, thus rejecting the magazine's imperative to keep up a sexy, well-groomed image so that she can attract a mate. Her explanation for abandoning hygiene echoes her fears about becoming trapped in an endless cycle of housework: "It seemed silly to wash one day when I would only have to wash again the next" (143).

But if, as narrator, Esther can sometimes articulate her protest to herself, she has also internalized cultural standards of proper behavior voiced by her peers, popular magazines, and the older women who try to fashion her in their own image. Despite her certainty that she does not want to marry Buddy Willard, she dreads others' incomprehension of her refusing "a perfectly solid medical student for a husband" (148). Although she decries the sexual double standard, she remains, like many women of her time, obsessed with purity.

The strongest indication that Esther has internalized her culture's expectations is the prevalence of punishment in Esther's world. Her attempts to experiment with sex frequently end in pain or humiliation, culminating in a life-threatening hemorrhage. Both her mother's reaction to her breakdown (urging Esther to behave herself and assuming that Esther can choose not to be mentally ill) and the pain of the initial shock treatment reinforce Esther's fear that her mental illness and confinement are the penalty for failing to be a good girl. Punishment is not always inflicted by others. Esther and other mental patients also turn their anger inward, punishing themselves with self-destructive behavior. Dr. Nolan, the only positive woman character in the novel, helps Esther begin to break this cycle when she doesn't scold or castigate Esther for admitting she hates her mother.

Esther's story can demonstrate why the women's movement was necessary in the first place to students who are apt to take its gains for granted. For instance, finding a female therapist who empathizes with her distress and gives her permission to challenge the gender norms of her society plays a crucial role in Esther's recovery. Students will want to discuss the tremendous advances women have made in the workplace since the time of Plath's novel and the difference this has made in women's lives and in the professions themselves. On the other hand, students can also discuss employment problems that persist for women today. If women are no longer expected to be secretaries rather than executives, or nurses rather than doctors; if women today are not urged to abandon their careers when they become pregnant; they are still underrepresented in top management and are expected to balance work and family responsibilities without significant accommodations from their employers or their husbands.

To explore the role of media in reflecting and enforcing cultural norms (and exploiting them to sell products), students could compare and contrast advertisements and articles in women's magazines of the 1950s with those of today. What has changed and what remains consistent about the images of women and the assumptions and values behind advertising pitches? Advice columns, then and now, in teen magazines and newspapers would make for another worthwhile assignment in which students can examine messages of gender-role expectations. Students may be intrigued to find less far-reaching change than they had imagined, attesting to the continuing relevance of the novel.

WORKS CITED

Friedan, Betty. *The Feminine Mystique*. New York: Norton, 1963.
Plath, Sylvia. *The Bell Jar*. New York: Harper, 1971.

FOR FURTHER READING

MacPherson, Pat. *Reflecting on* The Bell Jar. New York: Routledge, 1991.
Wagner-Martin, Linda. The Bell Jar: *A Novel of the Fifties*. New York: Twayne, 1992.

Toni Morrison's *Beloved* (1987): Maternal Possibilities, Sisterly Bonding

Monika M. Elbert

Although published in 1987, Toni Morrison's most widely acclaimed and Pulitzer Prize–winning novel *Beloved* may just as well have been written in the nineteenth century. A modern-day rendition of the nineteenth-century genre of the slave narrative, it is a fictional account based on the true story of Margaret Garner, an escaped slave. Escaped slaves were never safe in the United States, especially after the Fugitive Slave Act was passed in 1850, a law which permitted slave masters to pursue runaway slaves across state lines. It would be foolhardy to discuss gender roles in this novel without taking into account the "peculiar institution" (as slavery was called in the nineteenth century) of slavery as the framework. It is helpful to juxtapose Morrison's novel with Frederick Douglass' *Narrative of the Life of Frederick Douglass: An American Slave* (1845) and Harriet Jacobs' *Incidents in the Life of a Slave Girl* (1861), although Morrison's account shows a more gender-balanced attitude toward the suffering of both male and female slaves. Morrison is concerned with the suffering inflicted upon both sexes; the oppression or suffering under slavery has no gender preference. The injury to slave men and fathers, like Paul D. or Sethe's husband Halle, is just as egregious as the sacrilege to slave mothers and daughters, like Beloved, the one daughter Sethe manages to murder when Schoolteacher comes to retrieve the escaped mother and children.

Morrison's *Beloved* falls in the tradition of Harriet Beecher Stowe's *Uncle Tom's Cabin* (1852): They both explore maternal possibilities that will effect radical social change. Stowe's readers were the sympathetic Northern mothers, who would react emotionally to the violence done to family life under slavery and then use their influence over their husbands to change the system. Morrison points to the influence of the mothers and grandmothers, the guardians of the community, to exorcise "124" of its ghost. Both authors know that the past needs to be exorcised or healed for there to be a future or for there to be a reconciliation of the sexes (in the case of *Beloved* through a happy marriage between Sethe and Paul D.). The haunted "124" Bluestone Road needs to be put in order—on both a familial and a national level—for Sethe to be reborn and have another chance at finding peace. Tellingly, *Beloved* opens with the ghosts of the past still haunting "124" even though it is 1873, well into Reconstruction and 18 years after Sethe's murder of Beloved.

The quintessentially strong Morrison female protagonist, Sethe withstands the atrocities to herself and to her children and still survives. Spurred on by Schoolteacher's Nephews' desecration of her maternal milk, Sethe is resolved to see that her children find safety and freedom. At the end of the narrative, all the injured mothers, alive and dead, exorcise the ghost of Beloved, representative of all lost children, and come to terms with any sense of guilt for their aborted motherhood by uniting in spiritual communion and song, the words of which resist any white patriarchal framework, represented by the "Word." Sethe and the community are cured by the singing women: "the voices of women searched for the right combination, the key, the code, the sound that broke the back of words. . . . It broke over Sethe and she trembled like the baptized in its wash" (261).

Sethe's personal odyssey involves a rediscovery of the community and of her own power. Initially, she can only identify herself in her maternal role; she proclaims that her children are her "own best thing." Paul D. ("a singing male"), the healing male energy, teaches her about her value as an individual and guides her toward autonomy, as he asserts, "You your best thing, Sethe." But Sethe, too, is able to heal Paul D. through her love, "Only this woman Sethe could have left him his manhood like that. He wants to put his story next to hers" (273). Sethe recovers from the victim role of wounded mother and daughter through Paul D.'s love. In fact, Sethe has learned that, as Paul D. claims, her maternal love is "too thick" and that she needs to replace that with self-love and self-respect. The middle of the text, comprising a dialogue between Sethe, Beloved, and Denver, shows the real danger of merging identities, as it ends with a cacophonous and frenzied pitch (so different from the final cleansing tone of the community), "Beloved/You are my sister/You are my daughter/You are my face; you are me" (216). This attitude shows both Sethe's narcissism and her vulnerability; after all, the devouring demon child returned from the dead also tries to possess Sethe.

Morrison's canon favors women who find emotional equilibrium, and even before Sethe reaches this point, there are two positive female role models: Baby Suggs and Sethe's last child, Denver. Baby Suggs, Sethe's mother-in-law, as a wise woman preacher, provides the community with food for the soul, until the terrible day upon which Beloved is killed. She understands the value of self-love and communal nurturance, and her legacy is passed down to Denver. The granddaughter Denver knows about the dangerous boundaries formed by overidentification as well as the limitations of sisterhood. When Beloved threatens to destroy both her mother and herself, Denver reaches out to the community and works outside "124" to find self-sustenance and to provide for her family. Fully integrated in the neighborhood, Denver begins to bring the healing process home to her mother. The key to happiness for the Morrison protagonist, regardless of one's gender, is a spiritual celebration of oneself, which then makes possible acts of kindness and love to one's family and one's larger community. The beloved is finally oneself.

Students might want to discuss what makes the quintessential Morrison female protagonist so strong. Self-sustaining women with great fortitude, wisdom, and self-respect are revered in the Morrison canon, and she draws much of her inspiration from strong women she has known in her own life. Celebrating generations of strong, capable women in her family, Morrison proclaims, "they believed in their dignity. They believed they were people of value, and they had to pass that on" (Moyers 59). Even though the novel's ending ironically belies the fact, *Beloved*, too, is a story to pass on—as a triumph of the human spirit, students should try to answer the riddle of why the story is so important to pass on, what that means in terms of the American awareness of the past, or in terms of a characteristic historical amnesia among Americans.

WORKS CITED

Morrison, Toni. *Beloved*. New York: Plume, 1987.
———. Interview. "Toni Morrison, Novelist." With Bill Moyers. *Bill Moyers: A World of Ideas, II, Public Opinions from Private Citizens*. Ed. Andie Tucher. New York: Doubleday, 1990, 54–63.

FOR FURTHER READING

Henderson, Mae G. "Toni Morrison's *Beloved*: Re-Membering the Body as Historical Text." *Comparative American Identities: Race, Sex, and Nationality in the Modern Text*. Ed. Hortense Spillers. New York: Routledge, 1991, 62–86.
McKay, Nellie and Kathryn Earle, eds. *Approaches to Teaching the Novels of Toni Morrison*. New York: Modern Language Association of America, 1997, 77–85.

Richard Wright's *Black Boy* (1945, 1991) and Black Women

Kenneth Florey

Reader response to Richard Wright's *Black Boy* is, to a degree, framed by which version of the text is read. The original 1945 edition, truncated by an agreement with the Book-of-the-Month Club, focused exclusively on Wright's early years in the South prior to his departure to Chicago in 1927. In 1991 the Library of America restored to the book the excised Chicago portion of the manuscript entitled "The Horror and the Glory," which revealed that the North, while embodying a culture distinct from that of the South, still actively repressed attempts of "Black Boy" to become "Black Man."

In his journey toward self-discovery in both portions of the book, Wright is often discouraged and impeded by women whose lives touch his. These women, including his mother, his Granny, his Aunt Addie, Mrs. Moss, her daughter Bess, and Wright's neighbors, can be powerful, nurturing, protective, and kind, although many are indifferent to his dreams, and some are even cruel. As a collective gender in *Black Boy*, women, even more than men, affirm the conforming, traditional values of family, tribe, and religion, and accept limitations imposed by society, even when those limitations are inimical to their self-interest. They are perplexed generally by Wright's need to rebel and his "hunger" for a self-definition that is independent of his culture. Some, such as Mrs. Moss and Bess, exhibit what Wright ultimately terms "a peasant mentality," having "no tensions, unappeasable longings, no desire to do something to redeem themselves" (252). Still, it is their presence in his life and the protection they offer that enables Wright at times to survive the brutalities of a hostile, poverty-stricken, racist environment.

One of the few strongly positive women characters to emerge in *Black Boy* is that of Richard Wright's mother, Ella, but even she, in her well-meaning attempts both to shield her son from racial angst and to turn his thoughts to religious and material well-being, often discourages the imaginative and the individualistic within him. Trying to bring up her two sons alone, she is forced by poverty to move in with Wright's Granny, a very light-complexioned and illiterate woman, who imposes a rigid and uncompromising religious structure on the family. Distrustful of anything not directly connected with her church, Granny characterizes Wright's first published story in a local Black newspaper as "lies," since it was the product not of biblical "fact" but of secular imagination. Wright's mother does intercede at times to protect her son from the more violent members of her family, such as her sister Addie, who tries to whip Wright into submission. It is obvious that she loves him. Still, her efforts to be his primary caregiver are ultimately ineffectual as symbolized by her recurrent paralytic attacks. And even she does not escape entirely from Wright's criticism. When the 4-year-old Wright sets fire to the family curtains and nearly burns the entire house down, she beats him, which he expects and perhaps deserves, but so severely that his life is in danger. In his resultant delirium, his fears toward his mother are reflected in his anti-feminist vision of "huge wobbly white bags, like the full udders of cows" (7), suspended from the ceiling above him.

One woman, a schoolteacher living with the family, who is named Ella like his mother, encourages Wright's early passion for the imaginative world of literature. His love of reading and his ambition to become a writer, however, perplex many of the other women he comes in contact with. He proudly shows his first story, not to his relatives who "would think that I had gone crazy" (141), but to the woman next door, who, baffled by his effort, challenges, "What's that for?" (141). Bess, who is seventeen and still in the fifth grade, wants to marry Wright after having known him less than a day, but, fearful of his different ways, demands of him, "What's them books in your room?" (256). A poor, illiterate woman in Chicago, who is sexually exploited by Wright, holds one of his books upside down and can't understand what is in there that attracts him so much. Even Wright's "gentle" mother, whose ideal was "Christ Upon the Cross" (376), cannot understand his fascination for the Communist magazines in his apartment.

Because Wright's exposure of the brutality of racism is so graphic and compelling, students can fall into the trap of accepting all of Wright's characterizations of women at face value. In criticizing American society for damning those it cannot understand, "who look different," Wright points out that he, too, shares "these faults" (321). Teachers should note that Wright's acknowledgment of his alienation from those around him often results in his ignoring the complexities and shattered dreams of women. Robert Stepto argues that an "honorable response" to Wright may be seen in the fiction of such authors as Toni Morrison and Alice Walker, who portray Black women with more going for them in their lives than "a false church, a whiskey bottle, and . . . a peasant mentality" (70–71). Teachers, accordingly, might develop a unit on images of Black women in literature and compare Wright's depictions of women with such characters as Celie in Walker's *The Color Purple* or Pecola in Morrison's *The Bluest Eye*. Moreover, students should be encouraged to "see through" the negativity that often surrounds Wright's portrayals of such characters as Granny and Mrs. Moss and discuss their strengths, even though Wright may minimize them. Critics often characterize Wright as an existentialist, one whose quest for individual identity finds him in a state of alienation from the universe. Does Wright's antipathy at times toward the bonding values of tribe and community cause him to undervalue the nurturing, protective influences of women in his life? Wright was brought up in a household controlled by women. Students might discuss the implications of a strong female environment in shaping Wright into what he was ultimately to become.

WORKS CITED

Stepto, Robert. "I Thought I Knew These People." *Richard Wright*. Ed. Harold Bloom. New York: Chelsea House, 1987, 57–74.
Wright, Richard. *Black Boy* [1991 version]. New York: Harper, 1993.

FOR FURTHER READING

Gates, Henry Louis and K. A. Appiah, eds. *Richard Wright: Critical Perspectives Past and Present*. New York: Amistad, 1993.

Culture, Tradition, Family: Gender Roles in Rudolfo Anaya's *Bless Me, Ultima* (1972)

Montye P. Fuse

Given the frequency with which it is taught and anthologized, *Bless Me, Ultima* seems well on its way to becoming a classic in Mexican American literature. The novel tells of the relationship between 6-year-old Antonio Marez and the *curandera* (female spiritual healer) Ultima. Antonio realizes that a special bond exists between himself and Ultima when he learns that she assisted his mother, Maria, at his birth. Increasingly, this relationship holds importance for Antonio, as he witnesses several deaths and begins to question the existence of God while preparing for his First Communion. Ultima—her powers rooted in Indigenous spirituality and the natural world—is everpresent in addressing Antonio's questions and satisfying his spiritual concerns. At the novel's conclusion, Antonio seeks and receives Ultima's deathbed blessing, implying that he will continue forth in the ways of *curanderismo* (spiritual healing).

While Antonio forms his most important relationship with a woman, readers will immediately recognize that *Bless Me, Ultima* primarily concerns the young protagonist's initiation into manhood. Consequently, the novel centers on Antonio's life choices: Will he become the priest that his mother wants him to be, or will he be a man of the *llano* (the New Mexican plains) after his father? Antonio has other male role models, including his typically male, older brothers, who leave to fight in World War II, and his friend Florence, an atheist, who courageously questions God's ultimate power. Among these, Ultima represents a middle ground: She does not view life through a pragmatic lens like his father nor does she rely completely on spiritual forces beyond her control like his mother. The story suggests that Antonio will follow Ultima's maverick path as he forms his own values.

In pursuit of Ultima's calling, Antonio incurs his father's fear that his youngest boy will heed his mother's wishes and become a priest, a "sissy's" occupation. Indeed, Anaya presents Maria as a woman grounded in her faith while Antonio's father, Gabriel, is a man of action. Thus, Maria's sphere and focus go no further than the family home, and she appears satisfied with her role as wife and mother. For Antonio, Maria's role has always been that of keeping the family functioning; he remarks that she most often appears in "the heart of our home . . . [her] kitchen" (1). Today's students may see Maria as particularly powerless, given that her usual response to family crises is to retreat to a quiet *sala* (room) in prayer; additionally, readers might also see passivity in her remaining a faithful, loving wife despite the well-known fact that her husband frequents the local whorehouse. Although Anaya presents Antonio's mother as conventional in her priorities and interests, readers will note, nonetheless, that Maria's constancy has a steadying influence on her impressionable son.

Ultima plays a maternal role for Antonio, but quite differently from that of his mother. Unlike Maria, who seldom leaves her home, Ultima will not be contained by any physical dwelling. Perhaps Anaya presents an implicit critique of Catholicism in characterizing Maria as spiritually enlightened, but incapable of taking action in the everyday world. By comparison, Ultima exercises power in the real world through her practice of Indigenous healing. By having Ultima heal Antonio's uncle and then defeat the insidious Tenorio and his three *bruja* (witch) daughters, Anaya makes this point clear. For Antonio and his family, Ultima's powers serve as protection against evil forces and evil people around them.

Anaya's depiction of Ultima can promote interesting discussion from a feminist perspective, especially when she is compared to other female characters. In addition to Ultima and Maria, there are only Antonio's sisters, Deborah and Theresa; Rosie and the prostitutes who work in her brothel; and Tenorio's sinister daughters, none of whom is a fleshed-out character. Instead, they all play minor, conventionally female roles. Readers might expect Deborah and Theresa to occupy a more significant place in that they grow up together with the protagonist. However, the two sisters, both flat characters largely indistinguishable from one another, seldom appear in the narrative and have little, if any, influence on Antonio's development. Further, unlike Antonio's older brothers, who are expected to make something of themselves, Deborah and Theresa are raised only to be good wives and mothers. Barely seen and rarely heard in a man's world, these sisters convey believable depictions of female invisibility within a patriarchal Mexican family.

"Real" women in *Bless Me, Ultima* slide neatly into three categories: (1) those who are silent and/or inconsequential to Antonio's development (i.e., Deborah and Theresa), (2) those who are virginal and/or who emulate qualities of the Virgin Mary (i.e., Maria), and (3) those who are evil and/or of ill-repute (i.e., Rosie and Tenorio's daughters). Given that Ultima does not fit into this framework, readers may conclude that although Ultima is female, she is cast as "other-worldly," more like a spirit than a "real" woman. Perhaps, if Anaya had depicted Ultima as a "real" woman (more like Maria or other women in the novel), she would not have been as convincing in her supernatural powers as she appears—and likelier still, as a conventional woman, she would not have been considered powerful by the men around her. While Catholicism's teachings generally situate women as secondary within Mexican American culture and the family, the world of *curanderismo* allows women a position from which they can act with influence.

Why did Anaya portray women (except Ultima) narrowly, relegated strictly to one side of the madonna/whore dichotomy? Any analysis of gender images in this novel should take into account that, most often, Mexican American women's lives have revolved around their roles as wives, mothers, homemakers, or as in the case of Tenorio's daughters, evildoers bent on destruction. Keeping in mind Mexican American women's traditional status, readers should appreciate, especially, Anaya's dynamic, empowered, and unconventional characterization of Ultima.

WORK CITED

Anaya, Rodolfo. *Bless Me, Ultima* [1972]. New York: Warner Books, 1994.

FOR FURTHER READING

Stevens, Evelyn P. "Marianismo: The Other Face of *Machismo* in Latin America." *Female and Male in Latin America*. Ed. Ann Pescatello. Pittsburgh: U of Pittsburgh P, 1973, 89–102.

Girls into Women: Culture, Nature, and Self-Loathing in Toni Morrison's *The Bluest Eye* (1970)

Barbara Frey Waxman

The year is 1941, the place small-town Ohio, in Toni Morrison's coming-of-age tale of a poor, powerless Black girl, Pecola Breedlove. *The Bluest Eye*, Morrison's first novel, describes Pecola's miserable youth, mainly through the sympathetic eyes of her more sheltered friend, Claudia MacTeer. Pecola's pathetic fate becomes a symbol of the vulnerability of all young girls and of the devastating effects of sexism and racism.

Going through puberty may fill the average girl with painful self-doubts. However, Pecola's rite of passage, recorded through four seasons, is much worse, for she contends with a toxic environment at home, at school, in the neighborhood, and in the mainstream white culture. She endures emotional neglect from her mother, whose energies are devoted to her job as housekeeper for the white Fisher family; abnormal sexual attention from her alcoholic father; taunting from her classmates, who, like her parents, deem her ugly; and marginalization by a culture whose Master Narrative defines whiteness as beautiful and lovable. Pecola tries to find an answer to the poignant question, "how do you get somebody to love you?" (32). The answer, she decides, is to have blue eyes, the book's metonym for white beauty. As the novel's title ironically suggests, even when Pecola insanely believes she has obtained blue eyes, she is assailed by doubts about whether she is pretty enough not to be outshone by another female with bluer eyes. Her desire for blue eyes suggests white society's central construct of ideal physical beauty as the source of love, attention, and power for American girls during the 1940s. Pecola's obsession, the rape by her father, and white society's hatred together drive her into madness—escape from an unbearable girlhood. This theme of madness as a remedy for constricting female roles may already be familiar to students in a feminist work such as Charlotte Perkins Gilman's "The Yellow Wallpaper."

As Morrison acknowledges in her Afterword to the novel, Pecola's wish for blue eyes represents an extreme example of "racial self-loathing" (210). And her madness suggests the traumatic effects not only of "even casual racial contempt" (210) but also of women's subjugation and "female violation" (214). Morrison argues that while Pecola's case may be extreme, "some aspects of her woundability were lodged in all young girls" (210).

Teachers will want to help students observe the differences between the reactions of Pecola and of her brother Sammy to their dysfunctional family life. When their parents fight, Pecola responds by simply enduring, by trying to disappear, or by praying that one parent will kill the other (45); in contrast, Sammy either curses, tries to intervene in the fight, or runs away from home—twenty-seven times (43). Pecola's passivity and Sammy's activist behavior represent stereotypical male/female roles during the 1940s. Students can consider whether these stereotypical roles persist today. Pecola's powerlessness is most evident in her rape by Cholly and subsequent beating by her mother. At least Sammy avoids such abuse. Students may be disturbed by the novel's portrayal of dangers within the nuclear family. If the class first reads Kay Gibbons' *Ellen Foster*, which contains a near-act of incest, they may be more prepared for Morrison's powerful story.

Pauline's distaste for her pathetic daughter suggests her embrace of the Master Narrative. She rejects Pecola because "I knowed she was ugly" (126), but adores the little Fisher girl. Pauline yearns to belong to the Fishers' white, middle-class, Dick-and-Jane world of the grade-school primer; recurring lines from this primer punctuate the novel and symbolize its themes of race and class. Her white values operate in Pauline's perfect maintenance of the Fishers' home, which starkly contrasts to her own sordid storefront abode. Pauline has also been influenced by the movies, their depictions of romantic love and physical beauty—"probably the most destructive ideas in the history of human thought" (122), according to Morrison. White actors like Jean Harlow build envy and self-contempt in Pauline; she longs to have Harlow's hair and skin. Her desire to appear other than as nature intended represents, in critic Barbara Christian's view, an unhealthy inversion of the natural order in our society (57). Pauline's self-destructive feelings are also symbolized by her loss of a rotten tooth in the movie theater (123).

Another example of racial self-loathing is in Geraldine's story. Geraldine works hard to purge herself of "the dreadful funkiness of passion, the funkiness of nature" (83), as she builds a clean, artificial nest for her son and husband. She sanitizes out of herself not only her blackness but also her sexuality (84), and there is just enough maternal affection remaining in her to nurture a pet cat. Her racism, sexism, and classism come together when she ejects Pecola from her home with a curse (92).

This grim portrayal of African-American females contains one bright spot: the narrator Claudia, who resists white culture's hegemony. Students dismayed by Morrison's other female characters may be gratified by Claudia's interrogation of her community's values. She and her sister Frieda have the courage to be different from other girls, to befriend and defend Pecola, in part because they come from a loving, stable home. A feminist pedagogy would also emphasize Claudia's distaste for blue-eyed baby dolls, for "old squint-eyed Shirley [Temple]," and for the popular light-skinned Black girl Maureen Peal. Claudia's rejection of these cultural icons and possession of devoted parents protect her from the self-loathing that consumes Pecola.

Using Claudia as a model of cultural critique and Pecola as a model of captivation by the Master Narrative, teachers might encourage students to interrogate their own cultural icons, to consider how the twenty-first century's hegemonic values still control females' self-images. Our penchant for unnatural thinness and perfection and the widespread use of cosmetic surgery and lasers reveal how physical beauty is still worshipped. Students might fruitfully consider what in our culture can build a girl's self-esteem—besides physical perfection. Teachers should allow time for a close reading of Claudia's final comments about Pecola and the marigold seeds that never sprouted. This passage epitomizes one central conflict of *The Bluest Eye*: between the dominant white culture's dictates and a natural order where marigolds and Black girls can grow without the presence of human toxins, especially racism and sexism.

WORKS CITED

Christian, Barbara. *Black Feminist Criticism: Perspectives on Black Women Writers.* New York: Pergamon, 1985.

Morrison, Toni. *The Bluest Eye* [1970]. With a New Afterword by the Author. New York: Alfred A. Knopf/Penguin, 1994.

FOR FURTHER READING

McKay, Nellie Y. and Kathryn Earle, eds. *The Novels of Toni Morrison.* New York: Modern Language Association, 1997.

Founding Women's History:
Christine de Pizan Writes *The Book of the City of Ladies* (1405)

Ellen S. Silber

Christine de Pizan is, by all reports, France's first " 'professional woman of letters' " (Quilligan 1), the first to make her living by the pen. Born in Venice around 1364, Christine moved to Paris at the age of four, as her father had received an appointment at the court of Charles V, King of France (Willard 2). While Christine's mother preferred that her daughter learn the womanly art of spinning, her father supported Christine's intellectual pursuits (de Pizan 154–55). In 1390, after the birth of three children and her husband's death, Christine's literary career began, and between that date and 1429, she produced more than twenty works in verse and prose. *The Book of the City of Ladies*, Christine's most celebrated work today, is one of several she wrote in defense of women, her answers to their many literary detractors.

Sitting in her study surrounded by books, an unusual setting for a medieval woman, "Christine," the narrator, picks up a volume that she has heard praises women. To her surprise and chagrin, the opposite is the case, and her reading precipitates a deep crisis of consciousness. "Christine" is overwhelmed by her memories of the many famous male writers who speak ill of women. While she attempts to give weight to her own positive experiences with women of all castes and classes, in the end she surrenders her ego to male-scripted authority and laments, "If it is so, fair Lord God, that in fact so many abominations abound in the female sex, . . . why did You not let me be born in the world as a man" (de Pizan 5).

Three crowned ladies appear to the narrator. Named Reason, Rectitude, and Justice, qualities rarely associated with women, they have come to give "Christine" a lesson in reading. These three allegorical figures, who may stand for aspects of "Christine" herself, will serve as her muses in a task they have designed for her: to build a literary city of ladies whose foundation and buildings will consist of "Christine's" descriptions of exemplary women, past and present. The remainder of the book consists of a series of women's portraits: examples of political and military accomplishment, learning and skill, vision and prophecy, filial piety, marital love, chastity and repugnance to rape, constancy and faithfulness, integrity, and generosity. There is also a section on the lives of women saints. These women's stories, told by the crowned women to "Christine," and based by Christine de Pizan on her rereading of texts by ancient and modern writers, refute the words of male writers that have so damaged women's reputation. Rather than reinscribing stories of women written from a male point of view—many told through a distinctly misogynist lens—or simply accumulating examples of exceptional women, she does what feminist poet Adrienne Rich defines as "re-vision, the act of looking back, of seeing with fresh eyes, of entering an old text from a new critical direction" (35).

An example of Christine's re-visioning of a literary text is her representation of Medea, the powerful wife of Jason, the Greek warrior. According to Boccaccio in *Famous Women* (Christine's source), Medea fell in love with Jason after "a simple glance" (75), helped him capture the Golden Fleece, and later killed his new bride and his two sons for revenge at his deserting her. Boccaccio begins his story calling Medea "the cruelest example of ancient treachery" (75). He places her in the tradition of Eve, of women who are responsible for evil toward men; and the better part of his portrait details the foul deeds she did both for and to Jason. Boccaccio's Jason is nowhere criticized for deserting his wife.

Christine de Pizan represents Medea as a remarkable woman before her tragic fall at the hands of a famous man. Presented in two different sections of *The Book of the City of Ladies*, among women of outstanding learning and as one of those women who showed extraordinary love for their husbands. Christine's Medea has "a noble and upright heart" and "a pleasant face" (69). Both brilliant and powerful, Medea "knew the powers of every herb and all the potions which could be concocted." She could cause the "air [to] become cloudy or dark . . . confect poisons [and] create fire to burn up effortlessly whatever object she chose" (69). Christine de Pizan lauds Medea for her undying love for and fidelity to Jason. Far from impulsive in her love for Jason, this Medea carefully considered his qualities as a future husband. Christine criticizes Jason for the breaking of his sacred marriage vows to Medea, who had used her powers to help him win the Golden Fleece. She stresses that Jason's desertion caused Medea to end her life in despair, never again feeling "goodness or joy" (190).

Comparing these and other portraits by Christine de Pizan with their sources in works by male authors raises questions for students about the authority of traditional versions of myth and history. Is there a "correct" representation of Medea? Or do we always have to take account of a writer's perspective? Contrasting portraits of women by Boccaccio and Christine de Pizan and other pairs of writers can provoke valuable discussions about gender, reading, and writing. Students might try their hand at "re-vision" by reading and rewriting classical fairy tales. Analyzing the situations of women and men in tales such as "Cinderella" and "Snow White" can help students identify messages about sex roles they may have heard in their own lives. Students may begin to reflect upon the sources of their own "received" ideas and think about how much influence parents, peers, the media, and history have on their views about the roles of the sexes.

WORKS CITED

Boccaccio, Giovanni. *Famous Women*. Ed. and Trans. Virginia Brown. Cambridge, MA: Harvard UP, 2001.

Pizan, Christine de. *The Book of the City of Ladies* [1405]. Trans. Earl Jeffrey Richards. New York: Persea, 1982.

Quilligan, Maureen. *The Allegory of Female Authority: Christine de Pizan's* Cité des dames. Ithaca, NY: Cornell UP, 1991.

Rich, Adrienne. "When We Dead Awaken: Writing as Re-Vision" [1971]. *On Lies, Secrets, and Silence: Selected Prose, 1966–1978*. New York: W. W. Norton, 1979, 33–49.

Willard, Charity Cannon. *Christine de Pizan: Her Life and Works*. New York: Persea, 1984.

FOR FURTHER READING

Richards, Earl Jeffrey, ed. *Reinterpreting Christine de Pizan*. Athens, GA: U of Georgia P, 1992.

A Dystopic Vision of Gender in Aldous Huxley's *Brave New World* (1932)

Cristie L. March

In *Brave New World*, Aldous Huxley presents a global society entirely dependent on biotechnology. In this world, the pleasure principle reigns, and fetal chemical interference combined with infant sleep-conditioning dictate social strata (through a cloning process that has replaced pregnancy and childbirth). The opening passage's tour of the Central London Hatchery and Conditioning Centre explains the genetic manipulation that creates the different social classes, the encouraged use of *soma* (a recreational drug), the governmental and social promotion of promiscuity and sexual games, and the complex athletic activities that occupy adults in Huxley's entertainment-focused world.

The genders appear equal within the social order; both men and women work at the same jobs, have equal choice in sexual partners, and participate in the same leisure pursuits. Yet the system seems flawed when genetic manipulation errs, as in Bernard's case, or when we compare this "utopia" to life on the Reservation, which has preserved familial structure and has produced John, whose education via a volume of Shakespeare reflects more traditional expectations of gendered behavior. While Huxley acknowledges the advantages of a world free from disease, hunger, and class discontent, he questions the moral emptiness of a materialistic, sexually charged society that devalues individuals through its enforced focus on entertainment and its prohibition of close personal relationships between men and women. The novel reinforces traditional gender norms by inciting readers' disgust at the vacuous Lenina, whose sexual promiscuity and social freedom horrifies John (the Savage) and frustrates Bernard, the novel's "enlightened" characters.

Bernard chafes against the social system, particularly the sexual structure that denies him a monogamous relationship with Lenina. His relative introversion, caused by a suspected fetal chemical imbalance, allows him to step outside of the system and criticize it. He objects to his colleagues' discussion of Lenina's sexual enthusiasm, for example, thinking that they talk "about her as though she were a bit of meat" (38). Although he seizes the opportunity to strike out against the system by bringing John back from the Reservation, he falters when presented with the option of actually fighting back. When the Controller transfers him to an island for individually minded citizens, a terrified Bernard is literally dragged away.

While Bernard struggles and then succumbs, John suffers the most from the upheaval of traditional gender roles. He lusts after Lenina, couching his desire in romantic turns of phrase from his Shakespearean education. Yet he also sees her promiscuity as threatening and immoral, disallowing him the opportunity for an exclusive sexual relationship. Frustrated in his attempts to find a middle ground between his perceptions of honor and chivalry and his sexual desire, he unsuccessfully retreats from the society and eventually commits suicide.

Lenina represents the "brave new" womanhood of Huxley's world. She indulges in all the government-endorsed pursuits, although she is less sexually active than her friends and co-workers would like. Her initial leanings toward sexual monogamy leave her open to Bernard's advances, but her awkward encounters with John send her speedily back to the comforts of *soma* and promiscuity. Her seeming superficiality facilitates Huxley's warnings about the impact of mass consumerism and sexual liberty—she acts out the familiar "dumb blonde" stereotype. Yet Lenina also fulfills many goals for liberated women—she chooses sexual partners, is not trapped in a domestic role, has a successful career, and need not fear pregnancy and abandonment due to effective birth control. Lenina strikingly contrasts to Linda, John's mother, whose life on the Reservation has left her unattractive and desperately unhappy. Students might consider the ways in which Lenina and Linda represent the positive and negative impacts each social structure has on women's lives.

While describing the cloning process and birth control that have rendered pregnancy obsolete, Huxley explains the elimination of the concept of "mother" and "motherhood." Whereas procreation was once encouraged and "sacred," now mass sexual activity has become permissible. Words such as "baby" and "mother" are unmentionable, eliciting shock and horror. As June Deery and Deanna Madden explain, this replacement of procreation with sexual activity both liberates and confines women. Women are no longer tied to the household or seen as life vessels, nor are they repositories of family ideas in a non-familial world. Yet they are no longer valued for the same reasons. Bernard's feeling that his colleagues, and Lenina herself, think of her as a piece of meat indicates this devaluation. In addition, the abolition of motherhood allows the patriarchy of Ford's system to run unchecked without family needs displacing community affiliations. Although the genders are equal, no women occupy leadership positions—the men such as the Controller lead, usurping the guiding maternal hand and replacing it with paternal authority.

Students might discuss *Brave New World* in light of their own knowledge about the pervasive influences of popular culture on social values, comparing their experiences with the dangers Huxley envisions. The impact of cloning technology and the idea of Ford's assembly line, consumer-focused social manifesto as a replacement for God, as well as the substitution of drugs, sex, and entertainment for literature and "culture," provide entries into gender discussion. For example, the focus on youth and sexuality means sexually autonomous men and women devote equal attention to appearance, as opposed to the beauty and fashion world's focus today. Students can compare Huxley's dystopia with the "free love" counterculture movement of the 1960s and the present-day sexual climate. A more complex discussion involves questioning the roles of women when divorced from reproductive imperatives—why does Huxley see this as threatening? Students also can think about the dilemma of women who are cherished though restricted in John's chivalrous vision of the feminine, and threatening yet "castrated" in a sexually permissive world.

WORKS CITED

Deery, June. "Technology and Gender in Aldous Huxley's Alternative(?) Worlds." *Extrapolation* 33.3 (1992): 258–73.

Huxley, Aldous. *Brave New World* [1932]. New York: Harper & Row, 1946.

Madden, Deanna. "Women in Dystopia: Misogyny in *Brave New World*, *1984*, and *A Clockwork Orange*." *Misogyny in Literature: An Essay Collection*. Ed. Katherine Anne Ackley. New York: Garland, 1992, 289–313.

FOR FURTHER READING

de Koster, Katie. *Readings on* Brave New World. San Diego: Greenhaven, 1999.

An Immigrant Girl's Quest for the American Dream in Anzia Yezierska's *Bread Givers* (1925)

Norah C. Chase

In Anzia Yezierska's popular novel *Bread Givers*, those who financially support the family, who provide the "bread," are the daughters. The men, for a variety of reasons, fail to provide for their families. Rare among classical Jewish novels in its focus on women, *Bread Givers* describes how an immigrant Jewish family with four daughters tries to survive and prosper in America during the beginning of the twentieth century. The story's primary conflict is clear in the novel's subtitle, "A Struggle Between a Father of the Old World and a Daughter of the New." Each daughter wants to escape the father's tyranny, but only the youngest succeeds. While writing about such themes as the alienation between generations, the trauma of the immigrant, poverty and its destructiveness, the harshness of the ghetto and the sweetness of its communal life, Yezierska brings to life immigrant women's work experiences, their struggles to free themselves from traditional approaches to love and marriage, and shows how gender roles are changed with Americanization.

A Jewish *Little Women*, the richness of this novel comes through in its character development. In typical sibling order, the eldest daughter, Bessie, is the responsible one, the "burden bearer" (39), who toils for the family without complaint. The second daughter, Masha, narcissistically spends her time and some of her money on polishing her beauty. The next, Fania, is more normal. Called "Blood-and-Iron" by her father (20, 23), the youngest, Sara, adapts best to the new world and refuses to submit totally to her father.

He was raised in the old country in Eastern Europe where religion was very important, and the religious scholar was considered the greatest of men. This was no longer true in America, where all men were expected to earn a living for their families, and the best was the richest. Rejecting assimilation, Sara's father prays all day and expects his daughters to earn money for the family. The mother adores his spirituality but curses his contempt for responsibility and his arrogant assumption of superiority as the man of the house. A woman of her time, caught between the old- and new-world values, she does what she can to support her daughters, convincing her husband, for example, to give up the room in which he studies so she can take in boarders to help pay expenses. But this immigrant mother, like many others around her, cannot protect her daughters from their father's misguided, imperious decisions about their lives.

Believing that women will get to heaven only through serving men, the father selfishly wants his daughters to marry rich men who will support him. When his three eldest fall in love with good men who are creative but poor, their father forces them to marry suitors of his choosing, men who seem to be rich but turn out to be crooks and charlatans. Bessie and Fania are trapped in poverty; Fania is lonely and miserable although draped with jewels and beautiful clothes: a hollow status symbol of her husband's ill-gotten wealth. While poverty is poisonous, the latter example shows that money by itself is not the path to the real American Dream, for either women or men.

The three older sisters, limited by their circumstances and by the role each assumes within the family, show support for each other in small ways: For example, they help Bessie clean up the house before the long-awaited suitor she desires comes for supper and then they make themselves scarce when he arrives (37–38). On her own and her sisters' behalf, only Sara courageously confronts patriarchal authority in her father and her sisters' husbands; yet she cannot ameliorate her sisters' lives. She can only save herself.

Telling her father, "I've got to live my own life. It's enough that Mother and the others have lived for you" (137), Sara bravely runs from her father's grasp to live on her own, slaving by day in a laundry and studying by night. At a critical moment, her mother sneaks behind her husband's back and brings sustenance to Sara, indicating the older woman's caring and, perhaps, vicarious pride in her daughter's ambitions. Sacrificing all to her studies, Sara manages to acquire American English, manners, and habits as well as her degree; ultimately, she finds satisfying work as an Americanized teacher, a goal only a few exceptional women immigrants reached in those years.

Symbolically, both the book's title and the transitions in Sara's life are grounded in references to food which, at each step, are emblematic of her economic and social class. With so many scenes set in kitchens, one could consider food or the lack thereof as almost a character in this novel. Indeed, in all of Anzia Yezierska's writings, the hunger for food also represents the hunger for a meaningful life in the new world, for a life with satisfying work and love which is her definition of the American Dream. To be successful, Sara has to find both.

Her sisters and the reader come to see that Sara, despite her rebellion against the tyranny of the Old World (178), in fact shares much in common with her father. When Sara refuses to marry a man who thinks that "money makes the wheels go round" (199), she identifies her rejection of wealth in favor of education with her father's rejection of "worldly success to drink the wisdom of the Torah" (202). They share not only strong wills and their pursuit of learning, but also their conviction that a woman without a man is unfulfilled. Sara says that joy goes out of the work of teachers who do not marry. Fortunately, she finds the perfect mate in her school's principal, Hugo Seelig, a fellow immigrant Jew, but one who is thoroughly Americanized and functions in the novel as a foil for her father. In contrast to the father, Hugo is a learned man who has adapted to America and earns a good living as a school principal. Again in contrast to the father, Hugo is a giving, joyous person who sees Sara not as "blood-and-iron" but as a "spruce tree" (279), the kind of wood that is chosen for the masts of ships because it is both strong and flexible. His own accomplishments and his egalitarian approach to women make it possible for him to value her strengths.

Despite the novel's seeming simplicity, it raises many complex questions. What should the American dream be and how do women participate in that dream? Is the father's psychological makeup and/or conservative background an adequate explanation for his abusive behavior? What choices did immigrant women have in that time, place, and culture? How should one choose a husband? What does a daughter owe her parents? How did immigrant status, class, religious values, and gender intersect to affect each woman's life then and, by implication, now?

Readers, especially those who are immigrants themselves, love this poetic novel. A perfect companion to it is the half-hour video "Heaven Will Protect the Working Girl" (The American Social History Project/CUNY).

WORKS CITED

Yezierska, Anzia. *Bread Givers: A Struggle Between a Father of the Old World and a Daughter of the New* [1925]. Intro. Alice Kessler Harris. New York: Persea, 1975.

FOR FURTHER READING

Bloom, Harold, ed. *Jewish Women Fiction Writers*. Philadelphia: Chelsea House, 1998.

Levin, Tobe. "Anzia Yezierska." *Jewish American Women Writers: A Bio-Bibliographical and Critical Sourcebook*. Ed. Ann R. Shapiro et al. Westport, CT: Greenwood, 1994, 482–93.

As My Mother's Daughter: *Breath, Eyes, Memory* by Edwidge Danticat (1994)

Eileen Burchell

Edwidge Danticat dedicates her first novel to "the brave women of Haiti, grandmothers, mothers, aunts, sisters, cousins, daughters, and friends, on this and other shores." This coming-of-age narrative told in the first person by Sophie Caco celebrates the bonds linking four generations of women. In its psychological and political dimensions, the novel explores the centrality of the mother–daughter relationship to self-identity and self-expression. It is a trope that also stands for the complex relationship of country (mother-land, mother-tongue) and individual. Adolescent readers might compare *Breath, Eyes, Memory* to *Annie John* (Kincaid) or *Miguel Street* (Naipaul) to appreciate how gender influences the patterns and politics of growing up.

Sophie recounts her passage from girlhood to womanhood in a circular narrative of recurring separation-reunion with important mother-figures. At twelve, Sophie leaves Tante Atie and Grandmè Ifé to join her biological mother in Brooklyn. Martine had fled Haiti to escape the nightmare of rape by a *Tonton Macoute* thug. Sophie is conceived through this act of sexual violence in the cane fields, a metaphorical space where the economic and political exploitation of Haiti, the mother-land, also occurs.

Sophie derives identity and strength from the nurturing community created by Caco women, a name referring to a scarlet bird and to Haitian guerrillas who fought foreign occupation. Through their storytelling, Caco women transmit a heritage of survival and resistance to oppression. Tante Atie creates a myth of origin for Sophie in "the story of a little girl who was born out of the petals of roses, water from the stream, and a chunk of the sky" (47). Grandmè Ifé teaches her to endure hardship through ancestral tales: "if you see a lot of trouble in your life, it is because you were chosen to carry part of the sky on your head" (25). Sophie also identifies with Erzulie, goddess of love in Haitian *voudoun*, the "healer of all women and the desire of all men" (59). In her many manifestations, Erzulie suspends antithetical constructions of masculinity and femininity and subverts archetypal male images of women as virgin/mother/whore. These oral and religious traditions empower Sophie to preserve her deepest sense of self. Students might interview elders or ask them to relate a family story to understand how gender roles influence identity formation across generations.

Sophie greets life in New York as her "mother's daughter and Tante Atie's child" (49). She learns that Martine and Atie "always dreamt of becoming important women" (43), but they "had no control over anything. Not even this body" (20), an allusion to men's power over women individually and collectively. Martine provides Sophie the formal education she and Atie never enjoyed and recalls her sister's unrequited love for the village schoolmaster who marries a literate, lighter-skinned woman. Students might analyze what factors make Martine's relationship with Haitian lawyer Marc Chevalier possible in New York but not in Haiti. They might examine the implications of displacement and exile for personal growth.

The narrative of Sophie's adolescent years introduces themes of sexual awakening, the cult of virginity, and incest. Martine discovers Sophie's innocent relationship with Joseph Woods, a Creole-speaking musician from Louisiana. She forces her to submit to a virginity test, just as Ifé had tested her daughters. Sophie is traumatized by this generational ritual that suppresses female sexuality and treats women's bodies as sources of male gratification in marriage (Chancy 121). Sophie resists by "doubling" and finally self-mutilates to stop the testing. Her elopement with Joseph begins a new cycle in her struggle for independence. Students should expose androcentric standards implicit in the cult of female virginity. They also might analyze how gender influences strategies for gaining independence from parental figures.

Themes of memory, reunion, and reconciliation are introduced as Sophie and her mother remain estranged for two years, during which Sophie bears a child, Brigitte. She returns to Haiti with Brigitte and is reunited with surrogate mothers. Atie has learned to read and write with her friend Louise's assistance, an important metatext in the novel about the empowerment of women who overcome silence through language. Through Louise and Atie's relationship, Danticat also subtly explores proscribed love and desire between women. Martine's arrival to reconcile with Sophie and to plan her mother's funeral foreshadows her own imminent death. Students might explore love in the novel among women and between women and men. They might also read for other strategies of survival and resistance that result from Haiti's legacy of slavery and colonialism.

Sophie's struggle to overcome frigidity and bulimia parallels Martine's struggle to bear a child by Marc to term. However, while Sophie seeks the healing presence of husband and women friends, Martine descends into psychosis and suicide. Sophie defies convention by burying Martine in symbolic scarlet, then charging through the cane fields beating the stalks. Her grandmother shouts, "Are you free, my daughter?" (234), a refrain of Haitian market women putting down a heavy burden. Students might explore how each Caco woman liberates herself while remaining linked to other Caco women as daughters of the land.

The power of *Breath, Eyes, Memory* to engage adolescent readers came across in a very personal way during a first-semester college seminar I taught on Caribbean literatures and cultures. In her final project, a young Haitian-American student shared that *Breath, Eyes, Memory* had helped her understand and accept herself. "I am Sophie," she said quietly. She explained that she was born to a teenage mother raped in Haiti who had come to the United States to begin a new life. She too was raised by surrogate Haitian mothers and reunited with her biological mother in New York to work through adolescence in a different country, culture, and language. Danticat's novel was the first she had ever read that mirrored her experience. We were profoundly moved by her courageous self-affirmation that conveyed strength, compassion, and hope to a new circle of women on another shore.

WORKS CITED

Chancy, Myriam J. A. *Framing Silence: Revolutionary Novels by Haitian Women*. New Brunswick, NJ: Rutgers UP, 1997.
Danticat, Edwidge. *Breath, Eyes, Memory*. New York: Random House/Vintage Books, 1994.

FOR FURTHER READING

Dayan, Joan. "Erzulie: A Women's History of Haiti?" *Postcolonial Subjects: Francophone Women Writers*. Ed. Mary Jean Green et al. Minneapolis: U of Minnesota P, 1996, 43–60.

Non-conformists and Traditionalists: Buchi Emecheta's *The Bride Price* (1976)

Osayimwense Osa

Buchi Emecheta's *The Bride Price* depicts the struggles of a teenage girl to assert herself in a conservative and reactionary environment. The Ibo, one of the multitudinous African ethnic groups in which Aku-nna is raised, looks on young girls and women as either commodities that bring wealth in the form of bride price, or as pawns who should accept, without question, the husbands chosen for them.

Early in the novel, Emecheta's narrator establishes how entrenched is the insignificance of the African woman in this culture: "Your mother is only a woman, and women are supposed to be boneless. A fatherless family is a family without a head, a family without shelter, a family without parents, in fact a non-existing family" (28). Since a family "does not exist" after the death of the paterfamilias, the widow and her children are inherited, as material goods, usually by the uncle of the deceased. This nearly disappeared custom, preserved in the past by some African communities, inarguably degrades African women and their children but enhances male privilege.

Notwithstanding the far-reaching inequities promoted by such commerce or trade in women, readers must consider *The Bride Price*'s critique of the distorted practice of dowry. Western readers should be helped to understand that dowry or bride wealth was not a selling price. It was a bond made holy by ancient custom and therefore valued by the ancestors. To scorn the idea was to rebuke the ancestors (Mphahlele 31). Emecheta's story shows how this custom has been abused, rendering the suitor a mere "buyer," and the girl an acquisition. For example, old Uncle Richard, a veteran with army money to spend, "purchases" himself a wife, "too beautiful, too young" for him, whom he then feels free to beat, with impunity, allegedly "for making eyes at other men" (35). Similarly, Dogo, another veteran of some status, marries young

Auntie Uzo whose selling point is the likelihood that "she will give [him] tall sons" (22).

The more wives a man has, the higher his social standing. By inheriting Ma Blackie, after her husband Ezekiel Odia's death, Okonkwo, brother of the deceased, glories in increasing the number of his wives to four. Whereas Okonkwo enhances his status with an additional wife, his other three wives resent Ma Blackie as an intruder competing for their husband's attention. Besides resenting Ma Blackie, Okonkwo's other wives hate and envy Aku-nna, Ma Blackie's daughter, because she attends school. In *Things Fall Apart*, Chinua Achebe depicts a male-dominated society in which women are contented even in a polygamous setting, but in *The Bride Price* Buchi Emecheta paints a completely different picture—a polygamous setting where rivalry among wives makes home life less than ideal. Students could be asked to contrast Achebe's and Emecheta's attitudes toward polygamy and traditional family life.

As Ma Blackie immerses herself in the politics of Okonkwo's home and becomes pregnant with his child, she stops encouraging Aku-nna's love for the gentle Chike, instead bemoaning her bad fortune in having a daughter who prefers the son of a slave to more "worthy" suitors. Chike, an *osu* (outcast), is forbidden to Aku-nna. Thus, she desperately hides the onset of menstruation, knowing that her family will marry her off quickly, now that she is considered "fully grown" (92). Menstruation means that Aku-nna must relinquish whatever small freedoms she enjoyed as a child: Now, she could be kidnapped, and thus claimed, by a suitor; now, she could be taken out of school. Among female students, in particular, Aku-nna's transition might be a springboard for discussing the various, more subtle ways they may have been treated differently—or felt differently—once parents and friends took note of their physical development. Similarly, male students might be coaxed into discussing how their self-perceptions and social relations seemed to change during early adolescence.

Traditional Ibuzza courtship behaviors may startle some students. Among Aku-nna's many suitors, only Chike treats her romantically: He is different from the "rough boys" who subject her to the custom of "night games" in which she must tolerate sexual "squeezing" and "not be bad-tempered about it" (97). Learning that she has matured, Okoboshi, a youth embittered by his physical deformity, kidnaps Aku-nna for the purpose of forcibly taking sexual possession of her and thus, in effect, marrying her—an action sanctioned by the Ibuzza community. Defying her culture's silencing of women, Aku-nna finds the strength to "stand up for herself" (136); by lying to Okoboshi about her sexual innocence, she paradoxically sacrifices her good name in an attempt to save her purity. Successful in rebuffing his sexual aggression, Aku-nna must yet suffer the consequence of her lie: She must endure Okoboshi's beating and being cast as a disgrace to her family and friends. By lying, Aku-nna resists rape and effects her escape, but this act of courage ultimately seals her tragic fate since "nobody goes against the laws of the land and survives" (141).

Of all the relationships Emecheta portrays in this novel, only that of Aku-nna and Chike shows a man and woman committed to mutual respect and egalitarianism. Noting the unusual joy with which an "outcast" couple experiences their love, students will find it interesting to discuss this exceptional relationship. In what ways do Aku-nna and Chike live as equals? How is Chike portrayed differently from the other men? What must women and men overcome if they are to forge relationships of equality, especially in a traditional society?

Teachers of literature will want their students to examine the tone with which Emecheta ends this novel. Emecheta's narrative statement, "if a girl wished to live long and see her children's children, she must accept the husband chosen for her by her people, and the bride price must be paid" (168), seems literally to accommodate male privilege, snuffing out women's power of choice. But this statement should not be taken literally. The balanced relationship between Aku-nna and Chike, their brief, sweet marriage founded not on material gain but on human gain, brings them more fulfillment than an arranged or polygamous marriage. Asking students what they would risk and sacrifice for true love may make for compelling discussion. Teachers may also direct students to consider why Emecheta constructs a plot in which her brave protagonist, Aku-nna, and her child named Joy, must die at the novel's end. (For this, see Emecheta, *Head Above Water*, 154–56).

WORKS CITED

Emecheta, Buchi. *The Bride Price*. New York: George Braziller, 1976.
Mphahlele, Ezekiel. *Father, Come Home*. Johannesburg: Ravan, 1984.

FOR FURTHER READING

Emecheta, Buchi. *Head Above Water: An Autobiography*. Oxford: Heinemann, 1994.
Ezeigbo, Theodora Akachi. "Tradition and the African Female Writer: The Example of Buchi Emecheta." *Emerging Perspectives on Buchi Emecheta*. Ed. Marie Umeh. Trenton, NJ: Africa World Press, 1996, 5–26.

The Symbolic Annihilation of Women in Jack London's *The Call of the Wild* (1904)

Michelle Napierski-Prancl

The Call of the Wild traces the adventures of Buck, a St. Bernard–Scotch Shepherd mix who is unwillingly removed from the comforts of an aristocratic family to live as a working sled dog in the snowy Arctic Circle. Buck soon learns that the North is a rough, uncivilized land where the "law of club and fang" (18) rules. Survival means becoming "the dominant primordial beast" (31).

London makes it clear that the North is no place for a female, human or canine; of the six female characters in the novel, all are represented as weak and in need of protection. The judge's daughters depend on Buck, and Mercedes relies on her brother and husband. In contrast, the more than twenty-five male characters move about independently.

The main female character, Mercedes, a proper lady ill prepared for the North, has been taken care of her entire life by men and naively expects to receive the same chivalrous treatment in the tundra. London creates Mercedes as the embodiment of men's worst view of woman: helpless, bossy, ignorant, and selfish. He makes it clear that he considers this behavior as natural to her gender: she "nursed a special grievance—the grievance of sex" (76). To further emphasize women's helplessness, London's plot sets up situations in which all female characters who migrate north die, indicating that women should not venture far from home. For example, Mercedes meets her demise by falling through the ice; Curly (a female dog) is killed because she oversteps her bounds, trying to befriend a male husky. Indeed, she is attacked in a scene grotesquely similar to gang rape.

> Thirty or forty huskies ran to the spot and surrounded the combatants in an intent and silent circle.... This was what the onlooking huskies

had waited for, they closed in upon her, snarling and yelping, and she was buried, screaming with agony, beneath the bristling mass of bodies. . . . She lay there limp and lifeless in the bloody, trampled snow, almost literally torn to pieces. (19)

In *The Call of the Wild*, fatal consequences ensue when a female dares venture into men's domain.

The deaths of the dogs in this novel also carry gendered significance. Male dogs Dave, Dub, and Billie work themselves to death; in contrast, Dolly goes mad and Skeet faithfully follows her master to her own watery grave. As with humans, male dogs are essentially characterized as workers and warriors, whereas female dogs are portrayed as ruled by emotion and dependency.

Buck embodies masculinity. Unlike Mercedes, he does not need the feminine comforts of home and instead relies on his primitive instincts and masculine strengths. He intuitively knows to refuse to continue the trek with Hal's team. In a battle to the death with his nemesis, Spitz, he confirms his status as a combatant and becomes a sled team leader. And by saving Thornton from drowning and losing a bet, Buck demonstrates his heroism. In the end, Buck becomes a legend by fighting off a wolf pack, becoming its leader and fathering a new kind of animal, a wilder and stronger breed.

The Call of the Wild represents what Tuchman argues is the symbolic annihilation of women in mass media: their exclusion, underrepresentation, and sexist portrayal. Likewise, in London's text, the few female characters play second-class, stereotyped roles. For instance, Buck's mother suffers lower status for being a small dog, a Scotch Shepherd; thus her genes prevent Buck from achieving the grand size of his St. Bernard father. The other female characters are depicted either as helpless, mad, or faithful followers and all face annihilation in the end. Even Buck's feminine traits of gentleness and taking care of others, associated with his past life in the judge's family, disappear as he answers the call of the wild. The book misogynistically insinuates that the feminine must be eliminated for the sake of survival.

London's novel, written in 1902, responds to Darwin's then-popular theory espousing the idea of the survival of the fittest. Students should consider the male bias of Darwinism as well as the anti-emancipation bias of this same pre-suffrage period. Although the denigration of women in this novel can be attributed, in part, to time-specific gender roles, the stereotypical characterization of female dogs cannot.

This novel encourages boys to seek adventures and girls to stay close to home. *The Call of the Wild* should be read in conjunction with adventure novels that challenge rigid gender roles, such as Jean Craighead George's *Julie of the Wolves*, where a young Eskimo woman flees an arranged marriage and gets lost but survives in the tundra. Titles of other novels with female protagonists can be found in the reference book *Once Upon a Heroine* by Alison Cooper-Mullin and Jennifer Marmaduke Coye.

Students also might be encouraged to conduct research on real women who participated in the Klondike gold rush and the exploration of the Arctic Circle. They will discover expeditions by women who were more able than the inept Mercedes. Students also may consider how gender, a social construct, applies to literary animals in children's picture books. How are they drawn? What activities do animals typically participate in? Which animals are more likely to be male and female? Do differences within the animal kingdom account for these findings, or are the depictions an extension of stereotypical social constructions of gender?

WORKS CITED

Cooper-Mullin, Alison and Jennifer Marmaduke Coye. *Once Upon a Heroine: 400 Books for Girls to Love.* Lincolnwood, IL: Contemporary Books, 1998.
George, Jean Craighead. *Julie of the Wolves.* New York: The Trumpet Club, 1972.
London, Jack. *The Call of the Wild* [1904]. New York: Macmillan, 1963.
Tuchman, Gaye. "The Symbolic Annihilation of Women by the Mass Media." *Hearth and Home: Images of Women in the Mass Media.* Ed. Gaye Tuchman, Arlene Kaplan Daniels, and James Benet. New York: Oxford UP, 1978, 3–38.

FOR FURTHER READING

Mayer, Melanie J. and Robert N. DeArmond. *Staking Her Claim: The Life of Brenda Mulrooney, Klondike and Alaska Entrepreneur.* Athens: Ohio UP, 2000.

Geoffrey Chaucer's *Canterbury Tales*: Gender in the Middle Ages (ca. 1388–1400)

Michael G. Cornelius

Chaucer's *Canterbury Tales* provides a unique opportunity for exploring issues of gender from both a historical and a contemporary perspective. Chaucer's stories told on pilgrimage provide readers with numerous views of medieval women, and many of the gender issues that are debated in these pages still claim relevance today. Chaucer's social satire thus ensures lively classroom discussion while offering fresh glimpses into a society often considered antifeminist by the standards of modern culture.

There are three women on Chaucer's pilgrimage to Canterbury: the Second Nun, the Prioress, and the Wife of Bath. "The Second Nun's Tale" tells the story of Saint Cecilia, a Roman martyr. The tale is simple and straightforward, befitting a character upon whom Chaucer bestows one line in his "General Prologue." With the Prioress, Chaucer presents the reader with a more developed character. In the "General Prologue," he seems to generously praise the Prioress: She is "so charitable and piteous / That she would weep if she but saw a mouse / Caught in a trap" (lines 143–45). If the author's exacting descriptions of her clothing and eating habits seem puzzling at first, it is important to remember that Chaucer was a master of sly criticism; in this case, the Prioress' expensive, well-tailored clothes and extravagant foodstuffs alert the reader to her materialism and overindulgence, two qualities unbecoming a medieval nun. With this in mind, teachers should have students closely examine the "General Prologue" for insights into the pilgrims that are not revealed through their tales.

Despite these flaws, or perhaps because of them, the Prioress is in many ways the typical caricature of a medieval woman. A strong mix of both good and bad features, she is matriarchal and pious, greedy and snobbish, kindhearted but materialistic. Her tale, the story of a small Christian boy murdered by the Jewish population of an Asiatic city, is widely regarded as being anti-Semitic. It is certainly possible to dismiss this anti-Semitism as a product of the time and place in which the tale is written, but as with all of the *Canterbury Tales*, we must acknowledge a dual-level of narration: The Prioress is telling a tale that Chaucer, as author, creates. Thus, teachers should ask their students to whom the anti-Semitism belongs: Is it Chaucer's, and is he relaying common thinking of his age, or, as modern critical sources indicate, does it belong to the Prioress?

The Wife of Bath, however, remains the central female pilgrim. Chaucer seems to have intended the vibrant, frank, and appealing Wife of Bath as a proto-feminist, a woman espousing ideals of female strength and independence long before these qualities were considered by general society as appropriate descriptors of women. In her prologue, the Wife of Bath states that "Experience, though no authority / Were in this world, were good enough for me, / To speak of woe that is in all marriage" (lines 1–3). From this beginning, the Wife of Bath questions male and ecclesiastic authority regarding issues of re-marriage and virginity, and challenges strongly held stereotypes of women, including the notion that they are carnal, rancorous, and materialistic. Ironically enough, the Wife is considered to possess all three of these qualities. As such, while she must be read as a zealous defender of her gender, critics have often considered her representative of that which she preaches against.

Yet this view curbs the limitless appeal of the Wife of Bath, and negates the intelligent arguments she is making. Many students cannot conceive of a woman making as strong a case for liberation in the Middle Ages as she does, nor can they imagine a woman who boasts of throttling her husbands with her sexuality in order to get what she wants. In her tale, the Wife relates an Arthurian romance of a knight convicted of raping a maiden. He is spared execution only at the request of the queen, and she promptly sends the knight on a quest to seek "What thing it is that women most desire" (905). After searching fruitlessly, the knight meets a loathsome old lady who reveals the answer: "to have the sovereignty / as well upon their husband as their love" (1038–39). Having saved the knight's life, the old lady secures his promise to marry her and offers the lamenting knight a choice: she can remain loathsome during the day but become beautiful at night for him, or vice versa, thus presenting a picture of beauty to all society but not to him alone. The confused knight says: "I put myself in your wise governing; Do you choose which may be the most pleasing" (1231–32). Thus, the story ends with the old woman's assurance of domestic power, which, Chaucer suggests, is the answer to the question after all.

For the most part, Chaucer's male pilgrims ignore the Wife of Bath, or react to her with mock horror, and at one point she is forced to partly recant her prologue, telling the Pardoner, "My intentions only but to play" (192). The male pilgrims react more strongly to the Clerk's Tale of Griselda, a wife who suffers tremendous abuse at the hands of her husband Walter, all designed to test her loyalty to him. Counterpoint to the Wife of Bath, Griselda is meek, obedient, and loyal to a fault, so much so that her husband takes away their children and tells his wife he has had them destroyed, all to gauge her loyalty to him. Eventually, Walter turns his wife out, and willingly, she departs. Her service to him thus proving her fidelity, he returns her to his castle and their now grown children, and she rejoices, never once becoming angry with Walter for his years of constant abuse and mental torture.

While the Clerk warns that Griselda is meant as an allegory for man's relationship to God, the other male pilgrims respond to Griselda by wishing their wives were more like her. The Host's remarks are typical: "I'd rather than receive a keg of ale / My wife at home had heard this legend once" (1212c–12d).

Wives abound in the *Canterbury Tales*, both the good ("The Man of Law's Tale," "The Franklin's Tale," "The Second Nun's Tale," "The Nun's Priest's Tale," and "The Clerk's Tale," for all her subservience), and, overwhelmingly, the bad ("The Miller's Tale," "The Reeve's Tale," "The Merchant's Tale," "The Shipman's Tale," and the "Monk's Tale," a collection of stories of men whose falls were precipitated by women, representing a popular genre in the Middle Ages stemming from a long tradition of decrying and blaming women for the deeds and fall of men). While the adulterous wives and the honorable wives tend to be balanced in number, it is certainly the former that leave a lingering impression. Teachers may advise students to keep a tally of the women in the *Canterbury Tales*, and at the end of the text, allow debate about gender bias in both quantitative and qualitative terms, considering the work as a whole.

WORK CITED

Chaucer, Geoffrey [ca. 1388–1400]. *Canterbury Tales*. Trans. Nevill Coghill. New York: Penguin, 2000.

FOR FURTHER READING

Martin, Priscilla. *Chaucer's Women: Nuns, Wives, and Amazons*. Iowa City: U of Iowa P, 1990.

Sex, Violence, and Peter Pan: J. D. Salinger's *The Catcher in the Rye* (1951)

Paul Bail

Teenager Holden Caulfield is troubled on several levels. On the most obvious level, he concerns himself with "phonies." In Holden's shorthand, "phony" stands for a shallow materialism, an elevation of form over substance, a worship of superficiality, and a manipulative attitude toward others.

Next, Holden feels quite anxious about sexuality, particularly sexual exploitation. And finally, the deepest undercurrent in the novel: his concern about aggression and brutality. All of these issues are interrelated. A "phony" attitude toward others can easily shade into some degree of sexual exploitation. And the most toxic form of sexual exploitation involves violence and brutality.

Sexuality in itself disturbs and threatens Holden. He complains that "when you're coming pretty close to doing it with a girl—a girl that isn't a prostitute or anything . . . she keeps telling you to stop" (92). Confused about what to do at that point, he stops. As a result he is still a virgin, with mixed feelings about his inability to be more sexually ruthless. Interestingly, Holden, unlike the girls who say "stop," is rather passive. Holden even feels inhibited about disturbing a virgin landscape of fresh snow by hurling a snowball (36). In aggression there is always a winner and a loser, and sexuality seems the same from Holden's view. In Holden's words: "most girls are so dumb. . . . After you neck them for a while, you can really *watch* them losing their brains" (92). The reader can infer that Holden is disturbed by the demand their excitement places on him. But instead of directly experiencing his insecurity, Holden compensates by experiencing himself "in role" as a male and therefore by cultural definition the one who, unlike the girls, is supposed to stay "in control" of the situation.

To escape the confusing world of raw adolescent sexuality, Holden consoles himself with treasured memories of Jane Gallagher. Even though he was attracted to Jane, the main "game" he and Jane played was checkers. And losing was not at issue; Jane unthreateningly left her kings in the back row. In this Never-Never Land of memory, sexuality intrudes only as a kind of menace, represented by Jane's alcoholic stepfather, who seemed to take an incestuous interest in her.

When first published, Salinger's novel was refreshing in its honest portrayal of adolescent sexual confusion. From a contemporary perspective, its 1950s morality seems dated, steeped in simplistic dualisms. Nice girls say no; the others are whores. To get laid you have to act like a cad because nice guys never get any. Mutuality doesn't seem to be an option in this Manichean world view. Neither does diversity: Being "flitty" is unthinkable. And guys who aren't getting laid—or who can't at least convincingly lie to their peers about their exploits—may very well be ostracized as "flitty."

In the aftermath of the 1960s sexual revolution and the feminist critiques of it, the old social-conceptual framework is in disarray. At one end of the spectrum, some feminists have argued that all heterosexual intercourse inescapably mimics dynamics of dominance/subordination and therefore can be considered an act of rape. At the other end is the macho myth that the least dominant males in the pecking order are less than fully heterosexual and therefore deficient. This is illustrated in its rawest form in popular beliefs about all-male prison settings, where the weaker or less dominant are made into sexual objects of the stronger. Teenage boys are particularly susceptible to this confusion of sexuality and violence—more so than adult males; and if they are less dominant, boys can question their sexual orientation.

When Holden becomes involved in violence, sexuality consistently comes into play. The image of Stradlater having sex with Jane Gallagher in the back seat of a car causes Holden to throw a punch at him. Later, Holden wants to smash the head of the "perverty bum" who wrote "Fuck you" on the wall of his sister's elementary school (201). The very phrase "Fuck you" is emblematic of the way sexuality can be turned in the service of aggression. And, after his unsuccessful tryst with a prostitute, Holden—wearing his pajamas—has a confrontation with her pimp who flicks his fingers painfully against Holden's genitals.

The most violent incident in the narrative is Holden's memory of the death of James Costa, who jumps out a window after being beaten by a pack of bullies. Holden is impressed by the actions of his teacher, Mr. Antolini, who cradles Costa's lifeless body, unconcerned about getting blood on his clothing. Therefore, it is to Mr. Antolini that Holden turns in his current crisis, because there are no other nurturant males in his life. His father is an absent presence. His idealized older brother, D. B., has moved away, geographically and spiritually. And his beloved younger brother, Allie, is dead.

But when a slightly tipsy Mr. Antolini begins tenderly patting Holden's head, Holden panics. In his adolescent worldview, tenderness from a man is unacceptable, and he concludes—rightly or wrongly—that Mr. Antolini is a "pervert," a "flit." And by implication, perhaps Holden has these tendencies as well. As he says, "That kind of stuff's happened to me about twenty times since I was a kid" (193).

Mr. Antolini is not the only character whose behavior is ambiguous. To the jaded eye of a contemporary observer, the "innocent" relationship between Holden and his kid sister is suspect. Holden dances with her, holding her "close as hell" (175), and pinches her buttocks. Phoebe in turn invites him to sleep in her bed with her. The image of the child-savior, mature beyond her age, is, according to his daughter's memoir, a favorite of Salinger's, and has raised questions about his own proclivities. In Salinger's case, as *Dream Catcher* suggests, his preference for younger women seems to be about his need for unqualified adoration. Because of his fears about intimacy, Holden too likes being around females who are in some way less threatening or easier to control, like celibate nuns, his prepubescent sister, and the imaginary deaf-mute girl he fantasizes about marrying.

Students could discuss to what degree sexual attitudes have changed, and which gender issues don't simply go away with the passing of decades. They could bring in examples of contemporary rock or rap lyrics that express heterosexist, misogynist, and homophobic attitudes. Researching survey data on teen attitudes toward non-consensual sex and physical coercion can reveal to what extent dominance and sexuality are still a potent mixture in the culture. Students could also research the story of John Lennon's assassin, Mark David Chapman, who used elements of *The Catcher in the Rye* to fuel his pathological fantasies.

WORK CITED

Salinger, J. D. *The Catcher in the Rye* [1951]. Boston: Little, Brown & Company, 1991.

FOR FURTHER READING

Salinger, Margaret A. *Dream Catcher: A Memoir*. New York: Washington Square Press, 2000.

Paths to Liberation in Alice Walker's *The Color Purple* (1982)

Ernece B. Kelly

Alice Walker's epistolary novel, *The Color Purple*, depicts African-American women in the early twentieth century striving to realize selfhood. Focusing on her protagonist's development, Walker shows Celie's progression from sexually abused child to less passive spouse to outspoken equal partner. Ultimately, Celie finds inner strength through the letters she writes, and through the influence and support of the women around her. Dramatizing the capacity for growth and redemption that comes from both self-expression and female bonding, Walker creates several characters who, in following their unique paths toward personal fulfillment, guide Celie to explore and honor her own.

After being raped and bearing her stepfather's two children, 14-year-old Celie fearfully heeds Alphonso's warning to "not never tell nobody but God" (1) and vents her troubles by writing letters addressed to an imagined white deity. For Celie, writing helps compensate for loss. At first, her letters to God ease her loneliness: when the cruel older man she is forced to marry, Mr. ———, makes sexual advances toward Nettie, her sister, Nettie runs away. Before she and Nettie part company, Celie says to her, " 'Write!' " Nettie responds: "Nothing but death can keep me from it" (19), foreshadowing the vital role that letters will play in these sisters' lives. Although she doesn't hear from Nettie for many years, Celie immediately takes pen to paper. Thus valuing her innermost thoughts, Celie eventually moves from being ashamed and silenced to living proud and in full possession of her voice.

As she records what she sees and knows, Celie also befriends Shug, Sofia, and Mary Agnes—each of whom insists on egalitarian love relationships. Fundamental to Celie's emergence is the self-assured Shug, an entertainer whose lifestyle contrasts vividly with Celie's. Shug urges Celie to "git man off [her] eyeball" (204), and so disrupts Celie's narrow world, consisting entirely of meeting her husband's excessive demands. Notwithstanding their differences, Shug sympathizes with Celie's abusive situation and her helplessness, insisting that Mr. _____ , known to Shug as Albert, treat Celie with respect, preparing Celie to assert her rights against his abuses.

Perhaps most importantly, Shug offers Celie emotional support and sincere declarations of love. Their physical intimacy seems natural, not controversial. Indeed, their caring sexual interactions, full of mutual admiration, enhance Celie's sense of self-worth, bolstering her resistance to Albert's domination. While Celie's distrust of men ("whenever there's a man, there's trouble" [212]), and Shug's bisexual orientation may be part of classroom discussion, students should observe that Walker eschews categories—thereby questioning social constructs such as heterosexuality, monogamy, and marriage—and instead delineates a relational universe in which the ability to give and experience love is more important to one's growth than *whom* one loves.

Most students become readily involved in debating Walker's depiction of Black men. Critics argue (for example, George Stade) whether Celie "redeems . . . men by releasing the woman already in them . . ." ultimately, depicting "the rejection of men and all their ways" (381–82). Certainly, as he sews in Celie's pants factory, Albert does sound and act sweet, utterly different from the brutal Mr. _____ . His son, Harpo, also softens; he has "learn something in life" (289), according to his no-nonsense, first wife Sofia. In the words of Trudier Harris, Walker has created "born again male feminists," redeemed by the novel's end (388). Sparking controversy, teachers may ask: Does Albert seem "feminized" or desexualized or genuinely "liberated" as he learns to sew, and for the first time becomes Celie's partner and friend?

Sofia, the first woman Celie meets who retaliates against anyone who tries to dominate her, responds to her own husband's ineffective attempts to rule by beating *him* up. While initially Harpo accepts the role reversal in their marriage, he eventually feels enfeebled by it, anxious about his manly image as he compares the indomitable Sofia to Celie, his father's obedient, and therefore enviable wife. Like Shug, Sofia rejects traditional female roles; with aplomb, she does the heavy domestic tasks—expertly repairing the roof and cutting wood. Here, Walker makes an important point about a woman's abilities as equal to a man's, critiquing men's resistance to women's competence. Depicting tough-minded Sofia as perhaps the most courageous woman in the novel, Walker nonetheless has Sofia learn from Celie, using her friend's meekness as a model of how to behave in prison: "Every time they ast me to do something, Miss Celie, I act like I'm you. I jump up and do what they say" (93).

Mary Agnes—who becomes Harpo's wife when Sofia leaves him—finds her own voice when she intervenes to release Sofia from prison. Influenced by

Mary Agnes' growth, Celie first sees her as "a nice girl, friendly and everything, but she like me. She do anything Harpo say" (83). Stronger than Celie, however, Mary Agnes fights for her man; symbolically, after acting on Sofia's behalf by satisfying her jailer's sexual demands, "Squeak" triumphantly discards her diminutive nickname. As Mary Agnes, she feels free to sing publicly with Shug. Letting loose her "funny" voice, she "come to life" (103). For both Mary Agnes and Celie, self-expression through the channel of musical or narrative voice augurs each woman's emancipation.

In the latter part of the novel, Walker uses Celie's sister's return from West Africa to advance Celie's liberation and Nettie's liberation as well. Shug's discovery of Nettie's unopened letters that Mr. _____ has vengefully stolen from the mailbox over many years, offers Celie an intimate audience to whom she can direct her correspondence. Writing to her sister, Celie begins to lay claim to her own authority: She no longer writes anonymously, as she did to God; now, Celie proudly signs her name.

Meanwhile, Nettie's letters allow her to gather and convey her understanding of cross-cultural gender parallels and differences that students are generally eager to discuss. During her years in West Africa, Nettie, on her own path to liberation, labors alongside the missionary couple Samuel and Corrine. In exchange, she requests—and receives—an education. In contrast, Olinka girls are denied education since "A girl is nothing to herself; only to her husband can she become something." Moreover, the Olinka maintain divisions between men's and women's work, and Nettie, who works hard and likes to learn, is considered a "drudge" (162). But from Nettie's viewpoint, the Olinka women are unhappy and "work like donkeys" (163). An Olinka man explains: "Our women are respected here. . . . There is always someone to look after the Olinka woman" (167).

Teachers may want to examine these paradoxes: In what ways can being well educated and "smart" sometimes create difficulties for girls and women in the supposedly progressive United States? What does it mean for a man to "look after" a woman in the Olinka culture and what does it mean in our culture? What are the costs of such protection? Interrogating Olinka and North American cultures by analyzing gender roles can help students of *The Color Purple* shape not only "womanist" (Walker's term, quoted in Abbandonato 297) but also multicultural, non-Western perspectives.

WORKS CITED

Abbandonato, Linda. "Rewriting the Heroine's Story in *The Color Purple*." *Alice Walker: Critical Perspectives Past and Present*. Ed. Henry Louis Gates, Jr. and K. A. Appiah. New York: Amistad, 1993, 296–308.

Harris, Trudier. "*The Color Purple* as Fairy Tale." *Emerging Voices: A Cross-Cultural Reader*. Ed. Janet Madden-Simpson and Sara M. Blake. Fort Worth, TX: Holt, Rinehart and Winston, 1990, 386–88.

Stade, George. "Womanist Fiction and Male Characters." Madden-Simpson and Blake, 379–83.

Walker, Alice. *The Color Purple*. New York: Pocket Books, 1982.

FOR FURTHER READING

hooks, bell. "Writing the Subject: Reading *The Color Purple*." *Reading Black, Reading Feminist*. Ed. Henry Louis Gates, Jr. New York: Meridian, 1990, 454–70.

The Women in Fyodor Dostoevsky's
Crime and Punishment (1866)

Sydney Schultze

Although nearly every chapter in *Crime and Punishment* focuses directly on Rodion Raskolnikov, the crime he commits, and the punishment he suffers, a surprising amount of the material in the book can be read as an illustration of women's roles in Russian society in the 1860s. As the novel begins, the student Raskolnikov is planning to kill an old pawnbroker, Alyona, who operates out of her apartment. He wants to kill her because he needs money and because he wants to prove that he is a superman, a person who is above human laws. Unfortunately, when he kills Alyona, her sister Lizaveta, a sweet, harmless seamstress, shows up unexpectedly, and Raskolnikov is forced to kill her as well.

Raskolnikov's spiritual punishment begins almost immediately. He has an urge to tell someone what he has done, but of course he cannot. Raskolnikov's mother Pulkheria and his beautiful sister Dunya arrive in town. Dunya plans to help her family by marrying the parsimonious Luzhin, in hopes that he will hire Raskolnikov who will then relieve his family of their poverty. Raskolnikov, however, has no intention of letting his sister sacrifice herself in this way for his benefit.

Although women of the time like Dunya were expected to marry and their social and economic position depended largely on their husbands, Dostoevsky shows that women did not always find a safe harbor in marriage. Svidrigailov's wife Marfa was beaten by her husband which may have contributed to her death. Raskolnikov's father left his wife debts when he died. Katerina, the wife of Marmeladov, ran away and married her first husband for love, but he gambled and beat her, leaving her with small children and no money when he died. She has come down socially from the days when she danced for the governor, a reward for being a good student, and she married Marmeladov out of desperation. When he is trampled by a horse and dies, Katerina is left destitute and takes her children out in the streets to perform for money.

Sonya, Marmeladov's daughter from a previous marriage, takes to the street as a prostitute to earn money for her stepmother's children. Dostoevsky shows how Sonya, a spiritual, kind, and humble girl becomes a prostitute out of need. There is no stigma in Dostoevsky's eyes, although some characters delight in insulting her. Raskolnikov is very sympathetic to the enormous sacrifice this young girl is making and gives the family the little money he has.

Russian women at the time had few rights, and there was no safety net for those who fell on hard times. Women's jobs were generally connected to their traditional functions of caring for the home, bringing up children, making clothes, cooking, entertaining, and acting as sex partners to men; most paid poorly or were not quite respectable. Women occupy a range of occupations in the novel. Both Raskolnikov and Marmeladov have female landladies. Raskolnikov's mother sews to add a little to her dead husband's pension. His sister Dunya has been working as a governess for Svidrigailov. Natasya serves as cook and sole servant in Raskolnikov's building.

Feminism was an issue in Russia in the 1860s. Russian women could own property, unlike women of many other countries at the time, but they lacked access to higher education in most areas and were cut off from prestigious, high-paying occupations and government positions. These issues and the question of sexual freedom were widely debated. People discussed whether women were purer than men and whether they were as intelligent. Dostoevsky has fun with us when he mentions that Razumikhin, Raskolnikov's best friend, is translating an article discussing whether a woman is a human being. Dostoevsky parodies some of the ideas of his time in the liberal Lebezyatnikov, who talks of setting up communes and encouraging married people to take lovers out of principle. Lebezyatnikov says kissing women's hands degrades them, much as women in 1970s America objected to men's opening doors for them. But other characters have a more traditional idea of proper behavior for women. Some men plan to smear Dunya's door with pitch when she is suspected of making advances to Svidrigailov.

One idea widely discussed at the time and mentioned in the novel is that a certain percentage of women have to be prostitutes to satisfy men's desire for sex, so that other women can remain virgins until marriage and stay faithful to their husbands. Dostoevsky uses Svidrigailov as an example of a man who pursues and victimizes women. Dostoevsky's sympathies are with the girls, who often turn to prostitution out of a desperate need for money or because they have been driven from their homes. In one scene, Raskolnikov keeps a drunken teenage girl out of the clutches of a well-dressed man who hopes to take advantage of her. Raskolnikov knows that if her family turns her out after being with this man, she may become a prostitute and take up drinking. Her life will be over before she is nineteen.

As the novel progresses, Dostoevsky uses women as the key to Raskolnikov's salvation. Most of the women are spiritually pure beings, meek and ready to sacrifice themselves, who do their best to make ends meet under trying circumstances. This is especially true among the poor, whose lives are filled with drunkenness and violence, but who deserve our compassion rather than condemnation, and social justice rather than punishment. Raskolnikov finally confesses what he has done to Sonya the prostitute, and it is she who finally leads him to confess his crime, and she who accompanies him to prison in Siberia, where he finally finds spiritual peace.

Students might compare the lives of women today with those in *Crime and Punishment* to see what has changed and what has not. They might also consider whether women are still seen as purer and more self-sacrificing than men.

WORK CITED

Dostoevsky, Fyodor. *Crime and Punishment* [1866]. Ed. George Gibian. New York: Norton, 1975. (Has very good background materials for teachers.)

Witch-Hunting, Thwarted Desire, and Girl Power: Arthur Miller's *The Crucible* (1953)

Karen Bovard

Arthur Miller intended *The Crucible* to critique the witch-hunting mentality of McCarthyism and to expose a disturbing chapter in our colonial history: the Salem witch trials of 1692. It also invites analysis of gender roles, then and now, especially around the dynamics of girls in groups, competition among women for men's attention and for power, and problematic issues of sexual desire. Although John Proctor is unquestionably the play's protagonist, a rich array of female characters permits the exploration of women's behavior under the stresses of a rigid and repressive society.

Abigail Williams, the strikingly beautiful orphan who is the ringleader of a sizeable group of adolescent girls, propels the action. How the girls close ranks against outsiders, terrorize potential turncoats, and use hysteria to deflect doubts about their veracity provides a case study of peer group dynamics. Mary Warren's efforts to stand up to this cohort, and her eventual failure to do so, exposes some ways power can be wielded in groups. Do boys (and men) in groups behave similarly? Did McCarthy and his followers?

Abigail's natural leadership ability and boldness are attractive traits to the reader even as her absolute lack of moral scruples is repellent. It is her genius at manipulation which propels the girls from a position of powerlessness to the pinnacle of importance as "officials of the court" (60). This is a radical disruption of Salem's norms, where male ministers and judges hold all the seats of civic power.

Abigail's illegitimate desire for Proctor fuels her actions against innocent townspeople. Whether there is any desire that would be seen as legitimate for a girl in her position is a question worth raising. It is striking that there are no young male characters in the Salem of the play: only older married men. What's a girl to do, in the Salem of 1692? In Miller's play, fundamental frustrations (which are arguably worse for women than men, given the smaller range of social roles permitted to them) lead to slanderous and vindictive behaviors.

Miller mercilessly delineates the way Proctor's consummated desire for Abigail costs him deeply, both in the loss of his wife's trust and in self-loathing. Today's reader might ask about harassment since the affair begins when Abigail is in Proctor's employ and living under his roof. She is seventeen and he is in his thirties. There is no textual evidence that she resists his advances; rather, the contrary seems true. How do gender differences, as well as power and age variables, influence how we assign responsibility for sexual relationships?

Elizabeth, Proctor's wife, has her own complex relationship to desire. She understands Abigail sooner and better than does Proctor—"she wants me dead!" (61)—and tells him, "You have a faulty understanding of young girls. There is a promise made in any bed" (62). But she also comes to accept some responsibility for his straying: "It needs a cold wife to prompt lechery" (137). The very self-effacement Puritanism required of women robs Elizabeth of the ability to voice her own desire, even within the legitimacy of marriage: "I counted myself so plain, so poorly made, no honest love could come to me! Suspicion kissed you when I did; I never knew how I should say my love." (137).

Thwarted sexual desire is not the only kind Miller examines. Ann Putnam, embittered by the loss of seven children in childbirth, is among the first to level accusations of witchcraft at her neighbors. One of these is Rebecca Nurse, mother of eleven and grandmother of twenty-six, a figure renowned for integrity. The grief Ann Putnam feels at her thwarted motherhood is toxic, and she turns her resentment on Rebecca Nurse.

Basic to the events in the play is a profound puritanical mistrust of the body. It is the discovery that the girls have been dancing in the woods at night, perhaps naked, that precipitates the witch-hunt. Caught in scandalous behavior in a society that provides no outlet for exuberance, much less sexual exploration, several of the girls fall ill. Teachers might ask whether eating disorders today, or other related dysfunctions, could be similar last-ditch strategies for girls facing dilemmas to which they see no healthy solutions. Students of American history may want to consider what legacy our puritanical heritage has left in contemporary society around girls' struggles with desire and their bodies.

Presiding over the illicit gathering was Tituba, a slave from Barbados with knowledge of voodoo, whose "slave sense has warned her that, as always, trouble in this house eventually lands on her back" (8). Racial difference and Tituba's powerlessness make her the safest scapegoat for the disruptions—she is the first accused. Other differences mark early targets: The homeless Goody Good and mentally ill Goody Osburn are quickly named as witches. It has long been dangerous to be different in America, despite our rhetoric of inclusion. That far more women than men are accused and executed in Salem demonstrates that male privilege offers some protection from persecution: The more marginal one is—by race, gender, and class—the more vulnerable at times of social upheaval.

In addition to the McCarthy period, this play suggests study of witch trials during the Middle Ages and Renaissance in Europe, and raises questions about the gendered nature of that violence: Why were women so much more often accused of witchcraft than men, historically? Miller argues that the events in *The Crucible* are rooted in the demise of theocracy in New England (7, 146) and takes pains to document property disputes behind some of the accusations in Salem. That women could not *own* property but rather *were* property until relatively recently is fertile terrain for research. The play's title refers to an ordeal where one's true mettle is tested. Asking students to identify such moments in their own lives (or to interview parents and other adults about this) and compare lists of the events named by men and women may be revealing, as well.

WORK CITED

Miller, Arthur. *The Crucible* [1953]. New York: Penguin, 1953.

FOR FURTHER READING

Conde, Maryse. *I, Tituba, Black Witch of Salem*. Trans. Richard Philcox. New York: Ballantine, 1992.
Nelson, Mary. "Why Witches Were Women." *Women: A Feminist Perspective*. Ed. Jo Freeman. Palo Alto, CA: Mayfield, 1979, 451–68.

"A Nice Girl Ought to Know!"
Henry James' *Daisy Miller* (1878)

Laurie F. Leach

Henry James' *Daisy Miller: A Study* invites discussion of sexual double standards and the harsh penalties exacted for transgressing gender norms. The title character, a "young American flirt," earns the derision and condemnation of a group of Europeanized Americans by such "offenses" as walking in public with men and arriving at parties with a male escort and no chaperone. Considered too delicate to concern themselves with business, politics, or other intellectual activities, middle- and upper-class women in nineteenth-century Europe and America looked to marriage for security and social status. In Europe, unmarried women were strictly chaperoned; however, according to William Dean Howells, only "a few hundreds of families in America [had] accepted the European theory of the necessity of surveillance for young ladies" (quoted in Stafford 111). Daisy is not only accustomed to the American standard, but she also refuses to defer to those who urge her to conform so as to protect her reputation.

While young women's behavior was carefully scrutinized, men enjoyed greater liberty. Thus Daisy's public flirtation with Giovanelli, though innocent, leads to her social disgrace, while Winterbourne's liaison with an older woman in Geneva is condoned, occasioning only mild gossip. Furthermore, Winterbourne remains on Mrs. Walker's guest list and retains his aunt's esteem despite his continuing association with Daisy, while both of these older women feel they must reject Daisy in order to reaffirm their own standards of respectability.

Unlike the other older women in the story, Daisy's mother does little to curb her behavior. Touring Europe only at her husband's insistence, she uses her ill health as an excuse to avoid seeing much of it. Faintly aware that Daisy is not behaving appropriately, she can only protest weakly, for she misunderstands the nature of Daisy's transgressions and commands obedience from neither of her children. Lynn Barnett points out that the illnesses of both Winterbourne's aunt and Daisy's mother are a response to "the paucity of meaningful activity" in their lives (284).

Although told in the third person, the story is filtered through the consciousness of Winterbourne, who is initially both delighted and scandalized by Daisy. He becomes obsessed with trying to classify her: Is she a "nice girl" or "a designing, an audacious, an unscrupulous young person"? (12). Finally deciding that she is "a young lady whom a gentleman need no longer be at pains to respect" (37), he regains his belief in her innocence only after her untimely death.

In James' story, gender issues are closely bound with those of class. The Millers represent the new wealth that accrued to Americans as a result of the Industrial Revolution; Winterbourne and his circle are people of leisure with inherited wealth. Winterbourne observes that Giovanelli is a "spurious" gentleman and faults Daisy for not recognizing this. "Would a nice girl . . . make a rendezvous with a presumably low-lived foreigner?" (27). A nice girl, then, is not only one who observes sexual mores but one who is aware of class distinctions. Yet even before Daisy's flirtatious behavior scandalizes the American colony in Rome, the Miller family is condemned for treating their courier "like a gentleman" (14).

Teachers will want to have students look at gossiping and the withholding of invitations as a means for the women of this American colony to assert social superiority and exercise authority in the one sphere in which they have power.

Moving from this issue to a broader examination of gender dynamics, the instructor may wish to point out that faulting those who don't conform to gender norms serves to reassert one's own position when one is threatened with losing status. James points out that the Americans in Rome take pains to "express to observant Europeans" (35) their disapproval of Daisy's behavior, lest they, too, be considered lax. Winterbourne, who has not made his fortune in business and thus, as Robert Weisbuch points out, has failed to prove himself in the arena of "American competitive manhood" (74), is disconcerted by Daisy's apparent interest in other men. Disdaining to compete with Giovanelli, he consoles himself by feminizing his rival, who is described in terms of physical beauty, impeccable dress, politeness, deference, and charm. Winterbourne insists that Giovanelli is not a "real gentleman," meaning that he lacks the social stature to aspire to Daisy's hand, but perhaps also implying that he is not "man enough" to win her.

Twenty-first-century readers growing up in a world saturated with sexual images may at first have trouble understanding why Daisy's behavior is so shocking; on the other hand, given Daisy's death, they may see her death as punishment, and take the story as a warning to women against transgressing gender norms. Instructors will want to ensure that students realize that the text invites sympathy for Daisy even if she is not wholly admirable. Although attitudes toward sexuality have changed, students will be able to identify the persistence of a sexual double standard and see that their contemporaries who transgress gender norms in other ways also risk teasing and ostracism, often from same-sex peers.

The story also underscores the point that gender-appropriate standards of behavior are culturally dependent. What is permissible in Schenectady is intolerable at Rome. Yet Daisy sees no reason to "change her habits" to suit the local customs, and most of those who speak against Daisy see no need to make allowances for her different upbringing. *Daisy Miller* points to the need for tolerance of and respect for human differences: those based in culture, gender socialization, economic class, and family background.

WORKS CITED

Barnett, Louise K. "Jamesian Feminism: Women in *Daisy Miller*." *Studies in Short Fiction* 16 (1979): 281–87.

James, Henry. *Daisy Miller: A Study* (1878). *Henry James's* Daisy Miller: *The Story, the Play, the Critics* by William T. Stafford. New York: Scribner, 1963, 7–39.

Stafford, William T. *Henry James's Daisy Miller: The Story, the Play, the Critics*. New York: Scribner, 1963.

Weisbuch, Robert. "Winterbourne and the Doom of Manhood in *Daisy Miller*." *New Essays on* Daisy Miller *and* The Turn of the Screw. Ed. Vivian R. Pollock. Cambridge: Cambridge UP, 1993, 65–89.

FOR FURTHER READING

Bell, Millicent. "Daisy Miller." *Meaning in Henry James*. Cambridge, MA: Harvard UP, 1991, 54–65.

Redefining Female Absence in Arthur Miller's *Death of a Salesman* (1949)

Dana Kinnison

Male characters dominate Arthur Miller's *Death of a Salesman*. Their presence and concerns take center stage, literally and figuratively. In both those scenes that occur in the present time of 1949 and those relived through memory of the past, Willy Loman and his sons reveal their dreams and desires, their successes, and especially their failures. Willy is admired by his wife and two young boys, who have a blind faith in his authority and who loyally follow his lead. In the early years, he is competitive and confident, even a braggart, who anticipates fighting his way to the top of the business world just as he encourages his son Biff to aggressively overwhelm opponents on the gridiron. Willy assumes a sense of entitlement, which he in turn engenders in his sons. The aging Willy is bewildered by his inability to realize his dreams and clings even more desperately to his authoritarian, patriarchal ways.

Overshadowed by Willy's grandiose nature is Linda, long-suffering wife and mother. Linda epitomizes the notion of female passivity, caretaking, and self-sacrifice. She stands by her man, seldom questioning and never opposing him. Linda occasionally notices the discrepancies between Willy's exaggerated claims and the reality of their circumstances, but she seems to have neither the desire nor the force of will to counter his distorted perceptions. She is not without insight at times, but her worthwhile observations go unheeded. Although her husband and sons love and even admire her, they do so while simultaneously disregarding her as a full person. Unlike Willy's character, the reader does not know Linda's dreams and desires or, worse, suspects she has none that extend beyond what is in this case a limiting role as wife and mother. Miller affords her less complexity than Willy or Biff, and her lesser status is tied to her gender. If Willy is the magnificently plumed male peacock, loudly proclaiming his sense of self, Linda follows suit and is a plain, quiet pea hen, in attendance but little noticed.

Adolescent readers don't always fully appreciate Miller's flawed and tragic hero. However, it is at least apparent to them that his suffering is worthy of academic discussion, and that he is an ironically forceful figure, a powerful dreamer though not an effective executor of those dreams. Linda, in contrast, lacks any power. Most students are scornful of her gullibility and non-assertion. Willy may be a pathetic as well as a sympathetic character, but Linda is a pitiful "doormat," trod upon by husband and sons alike. Understandably, female students not only resist identification with Linda but sometimes resist full interaction in the classroom if Linda's secondary status is not adequately addressed.

The few other representations of women only serve to compound the problematic messages that the play sends about gender. The character known as The Woman accepts and, indeed, expects Willy's gifts of new hosiery after she spends time with him in a hotel room. The image of The Woman and her new silk stockings is juxtaposed with the image of Linda mending her worn stockings. The old, mended stockings symbolize not only Linda's life of toil and self-sacrifice but also the ignorance and betrayal that mark her existence. These two female figures demonstrate the limited and stereotyped options advanced in many artistic and cultural depictions of women, the polarized madonna/whore syndrome. The other son, Happy, helps to illuminate this point. He wants to marry a good woman like his mother but dates a different sort of woman, as he sees it. Furthermore, he speaks of women in disparaging ways, lies to them, and treats them like sport, winning them away from other men as trophies. If such simplistic and invalidating representations of women go unchallenged, all students suffer, but especially formative young women who need female complexity and potential reflected in literature to aid personal development and esteem.

Is, then, *Death of a Salesman* to be avoided at all costs in the gender-conscious classroom? The answer is no, although to avoid explicitly engaging the abuses and omissions of women in the play is to reinforce sexual inequality. The (non)role that women enact may instead serve as a catalyst for discussions that speak directly to students' lives and to the central concerns of the play itself. First, gender issues may be used as a way of drawing students to the text rather than alienating them. Miller's characters illustrate the elemental power imbalance between the sexes which is at the heart of all varieties of women's marginalization and oppression, large and small, historical and contemporary. If students naively see Linda's domestic subjugation as passé, have them consider Happy's dating practices (his objectification and sexual exploitation of women), which may be closer to young readers' experiences. Also, students might list examples of the madonna/whore syndrome from contemporary popular sources, beginning with the pop star Madonna. Her name calls forth the venerated mother of God, saintly and, well, like a virgin. However, her erotic image and shameless antics are more worthy of a Jezebel. Madonna purposefully exploits the sharply divided choices that have marked female experience.

Next, the play's theme may be addressed. The play is a critique of values embodied in the American Dream: consumerism, competition, and frontierism—including freedom, the acquisition of wealth, and dominance. To be sure, acknowledge that women's subordination in the play parallels their minor role in the dream itself, which is the emanation of a white male ethos. But also critique this very omission as the basis of extended discussion. How might the American Dream have been different if it were influenced by a female ethos? To what extent is the dream's failure (as it is presented in the play) the result of the absence of these traditionally female values? Is the American Dream different today and, if so, how has it been influenced by the changing roles of women? The reading becomes more accessible and more worthwhile for students of both sexes if the absence of forceful female characters is addressed and thus redeemed.

WORKS CITED

Miller, Arthur. *Death of a Salesman*. New York: Viking, 1949.

FOR FURTHER READING

Roudané, Matthew C., ed. *Approaches to Teaching Miller's* Death of a Salesman. New York: Modern Language Association, 1995.

Black and White Womanhood in Sherley Anne Williams' *Dessa Rose*: Mammies, Ladies, Rebels (1986)

Beverly Guy-Sheftall

Analyses of women's lives in fictions of the American South have been sparse but critical to our understanding of the significance of race in the American body politic. In *Dessa Rose*, historically set primarily in the antebellum South, Sherley Anne Williams helps us understand the bi-racialism of the region, its polarization along racial lines—Black and white—and the exaggerated forms of racial and sexual stereotyping—the "Southern lady" and the Black mammy—which emerged during slavery and persist through the modern era. Because of regional peculiarities—the legacy of slavery, strong family ties, rural economies, entrenched poverty, strict religious values—Southern women, Black and white, have a unique, entangled history which Williams helps to illuminate in this powerful story of love, bravery, friendship, and loyalty, inspired by two real-life incidents. In 1829, a pregnant Black woman in Kentucky was sentenced to death for her involvement in a slave uprising, and in 1830, a white woman living on an isolated farm in North Carolina provided sanctuary to runaway slaves. Williams imagines the unimaginable—that these two women meet and somehow discard the racial scripts and stereotypes both learned and embraced tenaciously as Southerners.

Two paradoxical constructions of Southern womanhood emerged during slavery in the United States and continued to coexist for decades: Black women as immoral, promiscuous, and sexually insatiable; and white women as innocent, chaste, and sexually inaccessible. Williams would create more complex portraits of Southern Black and white women and unmask the limitations of these stereotypes in her portraits of Dessa Rose, the fugitive slave; Rufel, the wife of a plantation owner and slaveholder, Master Bertie Sutton; and their mammy, Dorcas, unnamed during most of the novel. Williams is perhaps most transgressive in her portrayal of Rufel, the antithesis of the mythical "pure," asexual, Southern white lady. The anti-virgin Rufel, free from the scrutiny of her absent husband, willingly engages in a sexual liaison with runaway slave Nathan, now living in the Quarters on the plantation with Dessa and the rest of her rescuers. Dessa Rose also disrupts the pervasive stereotype of the promiscuous slave woman; instead, she is devoted to her first love, Kaine, and finds it difficult, even after he has been killed by Master Wilson, to let go of his memory and begin a new life.

Teachers may wish to have students explore both the differences between the two women and their finding common ground by observing shifts in narrative perspective which Williams accomplishes throughout the book. Each of three sections names Dessa distinctly, indicating through whose eyes the protagonist primarily is being seen. Students might be asked to examine when and why the author has a different character's point of view dominate the storytelling: Nehemiah, the racist, sexist, myopic "scholar," desperately trying to entrap "The Darky"; Rufel, who first approaches Dessa condescendingly as "The Wench," yet soon relates to her with admiration, sympathy, and friendship; Dessa herself speaking in the third section, "The Negress," and in the epilogue, both parts of the novel that take readers through the women's triumph.

Despite the potential of their bonding on the basis of common womanhood, many Southern Black slave women distrusted white women because of their inhumane treatment at the hands of mistresses on Southern plantations. In the novel's mid-section, entitled "The Wench," we enter Rufel's consciousness at the beginning of her encounter with the ailing Dessa, and are struck by the chasm between these two women despite Rufel's unbelievable violation of racial taboos, which would have prohibited her from wet nursing Dessa's newborn son. In a remarkable reversal of roles, Rufel, also a new mother, offers her breast to save Dessa's baby, but this act of mercy does not change how she's been conditioned to see Dessa, nor does it obliterate the power imbalance which locks them into the roles of mistress and slave. Dessa continues to be a "wench" and "darky" in Rufel's imagination and the gulf between them remains.

> The wench [Dessa Rose] began to sit up, to take notice of her surroundings, though she said little to Rufel and that in a voice barely above a whisper, eyes downcast. The darky's diffidence irked Rufel and she was offended by the way the girl flinched from her when she reached for the baby, by the girl's surreptitious examination of the child when Rufel returned him after nursing. For all the world like she was going to find some fingers or toes missing, Rufel thought indignantly. Exasperated, she told the wench, "Just because one mistress misused you don't mean all of us will." (140)

From Dessa's vantage point, Rufel is "the white woman" whose behavior she is unable to fathom given what she knows of Southern white culture.

> Dessa knew the white woman nursed her baby; she had seen her do it. It went against everything she had been taught to think about white women but to inspect that fact too closely was almost to deny her own existence. (117)

In order for her to penetrate the mystery of Rufel's identity, Dessa would have to re-imagine herself which, given Dessa's subordinate position, is simply too complicated to pursue.

Williams explores this theme of distrust during the entire course of Dessa Rose and Rufel's intricate and evolving relationship, and creates a set of circumstances which enables them to bond on the basis of their aversion to a patriarchal social order rendering them—each differently but both, fundamentally—victims of their gender. Rufel reflects upon her cloistered marital life in the Quarters and the freedom she would lose when her husband returns: "She would have no more rights than they [their slaves] when Bertie came back" (150).

Clearly, Rufel defies the passive gender role she's been assigned as the white wife of a slaveholder. She also rebels as a race traitor in her disloyalty to the racial norms of the region. She shelters runaway slaves and secretly harbors a liking for Dessa's rebelliousness. While Rufel tells herself that she isn't supposed to admire or

> of course, approve any slave's running away or an attack upon a master—still, something in her wanted to applaud the girl's will, the spunk that had made action possible. The wench was nothing but a little old colored gal, yet she had helped to make herself free. (147)

Finally, it is their common sexual vulnerability where white men are concerned that forces Dessa to rethink her relationship to Rufel, following a near rape by Mr. Oscar. Dessa reflects on the victimization the two women share:

> The white woman was subject to the same ravishment as me . . . I hadn't knowed white mens could use a white woman like that, just take her by force same as they could with us. . . . I slept with her after that, both of us wrapped around Clara. And I wasn't so cold with her no more. (201)

What enables Dessa to transcend her distrust of Southern white women is her awareness that racist, patriarchal gender norms had enslaved both Black and white women. In their quest to be free, of slavery and patriarchy, Dessa and Rufel discover the joys of sisterhood, and herein lies Sherley Anne Williams' bold invitation to readers to imagine a new South and the possibilities of a common bond of womanhood, no matter how elusive.

WORK CITED

Williams, Sherley Anne. *Dessa Rose* [1986]. New York: Quill/HarperCollins, 1999.

FOR FURTHER READING

McDowell, Deborah E. "Negotiating between Tenses: Witnessing Slavery after Freedom: *Dessa Rose*." *Slavery and the Literary Imagination*. Ed. Deborah E. McDowell and Arnold Rampersad. Baltimore, MD: Johns Hopkins UP, 1989, 68–75.

Williams, Sherley Anne. "Some Implications of Womanist Theory." *Reading Black, Reading Feminist: A Critical Anthology*. Ed. Henry Louis Gates, Jr. New York: Penguin, 1990, 68–75.

Anne Frank's *The Diary of a Young Girl*: Writing a Self—The Female Adolescent Voice (1952)

Hedda Rosner Kopf

Most often taught in history or social studies courses on the Holocaust, Anne Frank's *The Diary of a Young Girl* is an especially valuable text for exploring female adolescent gender issues. Hidden away with her family and four other Jews in a secret annex in Amsterdam from July 1942 until their discovery in August 1944, Anne Frank wrote constantly. However, most of her diary is not about what is occurring outside the secret annex in war-ravaged Europe. Instead, in *The Diary of a Young Girl* the reader witnesses the unfolding of a female self as Anne navigates from the exuberances of childhood and comfort of physical freedom toward a much more complex, yet limited, female adolescent persona of self-questioning and self-censorship.

She begins writing shortly after her thirteenth birthday by declaring that her diary will be the "one true friend" (Definitive Edition 6) to whom she can write everything in her heart and mind. Already aware of her need for emotional intimacy and self-revelation, Anne cannot trust others to understand her deepest thoughts and feelings. Her diary, whom she names Kitty, will be her confidante. Not long after Anne begins writing, the Franks go into hiding, and Anne's need to communicate her interior world becomes even more acute. Cut off from friends and classmates, she is desperate to describe her adolescent terrors, delights, and conflicts, all of which remain intense in the secret annex.

Amazingly, Anne Frank's physical isolation from her peers does not change the dynamics of her psychological development. Her emotional needs and reactions continue to change during the more than two years in hiding, and these changes reflect the gender issues which become most pressing for "ordinary" young girls as they move into adolescence. In *Meeting at the Crossroads*, feminist psychologists Brown and Gilligan describe the treacherous loss of self girls often experience: "a giving up of voice, and abandonment of self, for the sake of becoming a good woman and having relationships" (2). Throughout the *Diary*, Anne comments on this problem precisely, constantly frustrated by how the others in the secret annex react to her "sauciness." She writes on one occasion: "They keep telling me I should talk less, . . . and be more modest" (42). She compares herself to her older sister Margot, considered perfect by the rest of the family, but whom Anne sees as too "passive." This conflict between being herself and being admired by others lies at the heart of the female adolescent's struggle to find (or abandon) a voice that will be acceptable to others and yet reflect her true being. Many girls fail in this negotiation.

The private act of writing is a powerful tool for the young female who fears judgment by others, yet needs to express herself fully. Writing is Anne's work and therapy as she endures countless hours in silence and dread. Going inside herself and pouring that self onto paper gives her the strength to grow under horrific conditions. Teachers may want to use this occasion to point out to both males and females in class that diary or journal writing—not to be considered a gendered activity!—can help them find their authentic voices and resolve inner strife intensely felt during the tumult of adolescence.

Yet, Anne's attempts at autonomy are by no means completely successful. One of the most valuable and fascinating aspects of the *Diary* is the fact that Anne began revising her entries after March 1944, with hopes of publication after the war. Teachers could refer to *The Diary of Anne Frank: The Critical Edition* to compare Anne's original version A (uncensored and uncut) with her later version B (written almost two years after the first entry). A comparison of these revisions dramatically reveals a female adolescent's self-censorship as she reconsiders how *others* will view her outpourings. No longer comfortable with her own expressions of anger toward her mother, and her own emerging sexuality, Anne deletes those passages from her diary. Her authentic self is suppressed for the sake of being seen as good and "proper."

Anne's descriptions of a complicated relationship with her mother must be considered as another important gender issue. Anne often becomes frustrated by her mother's insensitivity to her feelings. While Mrs. Frank protects and tries to comfort her daughter throughout their ordeal in hiding, Anne's harsh responses to her mother reflect the growing girl's ambivalence between remaining a child or, alternately, breaking away from maternal protection. Moreover, Anne also criticizes the role that women are forced to play as mothers. Only after Anne resolves this conflict, admitting in her diary to her own complicity in the difficult relationship, can she free herself to turn to another relationship, her romance with Peter van Daan.

Students will easily appreciate how remarkable and wonderful it is that

Anne Frank managed to live out her first (and only) love "affair" while in the secret annex. At first tentatively, and then with great courage and energy, Anne explores the limits of emotional and physical intimacy with Peter. They talk about male and female sexual anatomy (232–34), and Anne records the conversations in her diary. She goes even further by describing her genitalia in great detail (235–36); indeed, Anne insists on claiming her body as a worthy subject of exploration and writing. Teachers can have students discuss the reasons Anne was so forthcoming at a time when it was "unladylike" to even think about such subjects. Her feminism also makes itself strongly felt throughout the diary in passages about the roles women play (318–19) and her own goals as a journalist (249–50; 294–95).

Peter van Daan, the object of Anne's longings, remains a "character" in Anne's highly subjective accounts of their time together. Teachers can ask their students to imagine Peter's version of the relationship. Does he seem to be as incapable of intimacy as Anne claims (276)? What would he write in his diary about their relationship? What would it be like for a 16-year-old male to be confined for more than two years with his parents and five others? Would his fears and issues about confinement be similar or different from Anne's? Students can write diary entries from the point of view of different inhabitants of the secret annex, paying particular attention to ways that each person's gender and age seem to affect his or her perspective.

Finally, throughout the diary Anne refers to the "two Annes"—the public, cheerful, feisty girl, and the private, sensitive, and insecure Anne who is in hiding not just in the annex but also within herself (334–36). Anne Frank's timeless *Diary* provides its readers with a poignant portrait of a vibrant, complicated female voice whose brilliant potential was brutally destroyed. Thankfully, the *Diary* remains, resonating for students of our own era with Anne's probing, honest reflections about the uncertainties, thrills, and risks of teenage girlhood.

WORKS CITED

Brown, Lyn Mikel and Carol Gilligan. *Meeting at the Crossroads: Women's Psychology and Girls' Development*. Cambridge, MA: Harvard UP, 1992.

The Diary of a Young Girl: *The Critical Edition Prepared by the Netherlands Institute for War Documentation*. Ed. David Barnoun and Garrold Van Der Stroom. Trans. Arnold J. Pomerans and B. M. Mooyart. New York: Doubleday, 1989.

Frank, Anne. The Diary of a Young Girl: *The Definitive Edition* [1952]. Trans. Susan Massotty. New York: Doubleday, 1995.

FOR FURTHER READING

Holliday, Laurel, ed. *Children in the Holocaust and World War II: Their Secret Diaries*. New York: Simon and Schuster, 1995.

Kopf, Hedda Rosner. *Understanding Anne Frank's* The Diary of a Young Girl: *A Student Casebook to Issues, Sources, and Historical Documents*. Westport, CT: Greenwood, 1997.

Muller, Melissa. *Anne Frank: The Biography*. New York: Metropolitan, 1998.

The Slammed Door that Still Reverberates: Henrik Ibsen's *A Doll's House* (1879)

Ann R. Shapiro

When *A Doll's House* begins, it appears that both Nora and Torvald are happy assuming traditional, circumscribed gender roles within their middle-class marriage, but it soon becomes clear that Nora is not the frivolous plaything that Torvald thinks she is. As Nora awakens fully to her own needs, which are incomprehensible to her husband, she concludes that she must leave what now strikes her as a false marriage. The slammed door that concludes *A Doll's House* has been a subject of controversy since the play's early performances in Germany and England, where the final scene was changed so that husband and wife happily reconcile. Even now students will argue whether or not it is ever acceptable for a mother to leave her children. Since Ibsen's day, this and other questions about gender roles in marriage have not been resolved, so students can be encouraged to see the play not only in the context of late-nineteenth-century emerging feminism but also in relation to contemporary marital issues.

There is ample evidence that Nora does not change in the course of the play but rather comes to understand who she is. The masquerade costume that Nora wears metaphorically represents her role as doll wife, and when she removes it in the final scene she finally steps out of her submissive self. Although in the opening scenes she cheerfully accepts Torvald's patronizing pet names and admonitions, Nora soon proudly confides in Kristine, telling her friend how she, Nora, heroically saved her husband's life by borrowing money despite legal prohibitions and Torvald's certain disapproval. Working to repay the debt, she says, was "fun" because it "was almost like being a man" (832). Thus Nora reveals that she understands the pleasure of economic independence.

Her reasons for lying to Torvald are less clear-cut, however. When Kristine asks whether she will ever tell Torvald the true story, Nora responds by embracing patriarchal assumptions. First she claims, "Torvald would find it embarrassing and humiliating to learn that he owed me anything." Then she adds that she might tell him "many, many years from now, when I'm no longer young and pretty" (831). At this point, Nora happily accepts the lie that keeps together their marriage: that Torvald is the stereotypical master of the house while she is little better than a prostitute, trading youthful beauty for economic support.

Ibsen challenges the idea that husbands must be breadwinners upon whom wives depend, not only by examining Nora's life but also in revealing Kristine's past. Forced to marry a man she didn't love because she needed money to support her family, Kristine, now widowed, is free to earn her own living and thereby take charge of her life. Ultimately, she will save herself and Nora by proposing marriage to Krogstad, whom she will presumably support. Their pairing, based on mutuality and friendship, serves as a foil for the Helmers' false marriage.

In addition to questioning stereotypical social roles, Ibsen raises gender-related moral issues. Deciding to forge her father's signature, Nora acted in the belief that saving her husband's life justified breaking the law. In contrast, Torvald views her as a criminal. Ibsen seems to have anticipated ideas about distinct male and female values which were later articulated by Virginia Woolf and Carol Gilligan. Woolf wrote: "the values of women differ very often from the values which have been made by the other sex" (76). Gilligan interprets this to mean that women's "moral concerns" are defined by a "sensitivity to the needs of others and the assumptions of responsibility for taking care" (16). Nora's choice to save her husband's life can be seen as explicitly related to female values. Students might discuss whether the play suggests that there is a difference between male and female values, and also whether laws made mainly by men still privilege male interests.

With Dr. Rank's entrance, other issues surrounding patriarchy are introduced. Nora reveals that she prefers Dr. Rank's company to that of her husband, thus indicating that role-playing prevents friendship between husband and wife. She shocks Dr. Rank and Kristine when she declares that she would like to say "Goddammit" in front of Torvald, but when he appears, she figuratively dons her costume and continues to dissemble (834)—a weakness that Torvald accuses Nora of having inherited from her father. Dr. Rank's father, too, is accused of having afflicted his son with the father's "sins." Dying of a hereditary disease—unnamed but clearly syphilis—Dr. Rank declares, "My poor, innocent spine is suffering from my father's frolics" (851). Later Nora will come to understand that, like Dr. Rank, she too has been damaged by her father, who treated her as a doll just as Torvald treats her.

Through Act II Kristine works diligently to repair Nora's costume; in this, she symbolically perpetuates the masquerade of Nora's marriage. The play's turning point occurs when Kristine realizes that the masquerade must end and that Nora and Torvald must be forced to address each other truthfully. Torvald's reactions to Krogstad's letters show Nora that Torvald, governed by patriarchal cliches, fails to understand that she is a human being just as he is. The issues Nora articulates about marriage are as familiar to contemporary students as they were to Ibsen's audience: Is a woman first and foremost wife and mother, or does she have equally important duties to herself? Can a man who acts as a woman's protector also regard and treat her as his equal? Must women earn money of their own to assume independence in marriage?

While Ibsen claimed that he knew little about women's rights and feminism, he clearly understood the basis of the nineteenth-century women's movement: that a patriarchy which turns women into dolls clearly denies their humanity. Finally, students might consider whether today's mass culture, presided over by Barbie and media moguls, still idealizes the doll-like woman as large numbers of women, like Nora, are slamming the door on conventional sexist values in order to create their own lives.

WORKS CITED

Gilligan, Carol. *In a Different Voice*. Cambridge, MA: Harvard UP, 1982.

Ibsen, Henrik. *A Doll's House* [1879]. *Introduction to Literature*. Ed. Alice S. Landy and William Rodney Allen. Boston: Houghton Mifflin, 2000, 822–78.

Woolf, Virginia. *A Room of One's Own*. New York: Harcourt, 1929.

FOR FURTHER READING

Deer, Irving. "Nora's Uncertainty." *Approaches to Teaching Ibsen's* A Doll's House. Ed. Yvonne Shafer. New York: Modern Language Association, 1985, 86–90.

Rogers, Katharine M. "A Doll House in a Course on Women in Literature." Shafer 81–85.

Frozen Lives: Edith Wharton's
Ethan Frome (1911)

Melissa McFarland Pennell

In Edith Wharton's *Ethan Frome*, the cold, inhospitable climate of Starkfield, Massachusetts, mirrors the emotional environment within the Frome farmhouse. A tightly focused narrative, the novella portrays three characters as seen by an unnamed narrator, an outsider working temporarily in the area. The central conflict occurs in the past as the narrator relates his version of Ethan's story and the accident that has left Frome maimed physically and emotionally. The three main characters, Ethan, his wife Zeena, and her cousin Mattie Silver, form a triangle of frustrated hopes intensified by the gender codes and expectations of their day.

Early in the novel a local resident remarks to the narrator: "Most of the smart ones get away" (6), suggesting the entrapment felt by those who remain. Ethan briefly escapes, attending engineering school in Worcester. His parents' declining health and filial duty call him back: As an only child his parents' care falls to him. Never prosperous, the family farm continues to decline, underscored by the dismantling of the "L" that connected the house and barn, a sign of Ethan's diminishing prospects. When Ethan's mother sickens, becoming depressed by her isolation, Zenobia Pierce, a cousin, comes to nurse her. Ethan feels indebted to Zenobia, especially for freeing him to "go about his business and talk with other men" while she manages with "household wisdom" (70). After his mother's death, Ethan proposes marriage to Zeena (Zenobia), more out of fear of loneliness than out of feeling for her. Their situation affords teachers an opportunity to discuss nineteenth-century concepts delineating separate spheres of action for men and women. For example, teachers can ask how a man who does "women's work" might be viewed in Ethan's community. They can also encourage students to consider Wharton's use of irony as she shows Ethan, the bachelor, feeling himself freed by Zeena's presence, and then Ethan, the married man, feeling himself entrapped.

Zeena believes she is owed marriage as compensation for having tended Ethan's mother. An aging, single woman in a small, rural village, Zeena has no social status and few prospects for initiating her own escape. Only through marriage can she achieve a secure place in the community and a household to call her own, even if it is a farmhouse she hopes will be sold so that she can move on to better things. When the farm attracts no buyers, Zeena realizes that she too is trapped and resents her situation. The relationship between Ethan and Zeena, never warm or caring, becomes a cold battle for power. Acutely conscious of public opinion, Zeena knows that a respectable wife is supposed to support her husband and accept his decisions. Because she cannot openly challenge Ethan under these expectations, Zeena uses her invalidism as a means of wresting from him what little money he has and what little sympathy he manages to show her. By exploiting female frailty, Zeena gains power over Ethan while preserving her respectability in the public eye.

The uneasy stability of the Frome household is further threatened by the arrival of Zeena's young cousin, Mattie Silver. Students are usually sympathetic to Mattie, drawn to her youth and warmth of feeling, much as Ethan is. While he waits for her outside the dance and when he pictures her in the kitchen, Ethan reveals his romantic view of Mattie as an ideal woman. He believes that her youthful gaiety and attractiveness can free him from the stifling condition of his life. Teachers, however, can emphasize the similarities between Mattie and Zeena by considering the struggles of a single woman attempting to survive at a time when few employment opportunities are open to her. With no training or skills, Mattie can find only physically exhausting work until she is forced to care for Zeena, much as Zeena had cared for Ethan's mother. Less shrewd than Zeena, Mattie believes that Ethan will provide for her security, but she does not perceive Ethan's passivity or Zeena's resolve. When Zeena leaves for a night, Mattie makes the most of her opportunity to "play house" with Ethan. Raiding Zeena's treasures, both literally and figuratively, Mattie uses the red pickle dish, which falls from the table and shatters. Although Ethan thinks he can conceal the damage, this betrayal sets in motion the final power struggle within the Fromes' marriage.

Exerting her right to run the household as her sphere and to protect her marriage, Zeena orders Mattie's departure. Although Ethan resists Zeena's will for as long as he can, he sees no real possibility of circumventing her plans. Instead, he and Mattie opt for a final sled run, hoping to crash into the great elm and achieve a final, romantic escape in death. Charged with an undercurrent of sexual tension, this episode ends in unexpected disaster. As in his other attempts to flee, Ethan's gesture proves futile, underscoring his impotence.

The last section of the novella allows the narrator to reveal the effects of the accident and the intervening years. Mattie, whose voice is heard as a "querulous drone" (173) has come to resemble Zeena with "her hair as grey as her companion's, her face as bloodless and shrivelled" (173–74). Through this transformation, Wharton suggests that only when both women embody the bleakness that surrounds them do they find a common bond, one that underscores their imprisonment. Another burden for Ethan, Mattie's crippled body and "soured" spirit serve as constant reminders of his failure. Zeena has cared for both Mattie and Ethan while Ethan continues to eke out a scant living from the farm, all three bound by unending routine, their roles still defined by gender divisions.

Mrs. Hale (one of the townspeople who speak with the narrator), sympathetic to Ethan's plight, sees little difference between the living Fromes and those buried in the nearby graveyard, except that among the dead "the women have got to hold their tongues" (181). Her final remark reinforces a perception of Ethan as beleaguered, unable to escape his nagging wife or his dismal fate. Teachers can invite students to consider the implications of this comment as it exposes one of Wharton's themes: conditions of dependency that force perceptions of women as sources of entrapment. Students can further explore how neither Ethan nor the female characters break free of the limits that poverty and nineteenth-century gender roles have placed upon them.

WORK CITED

Wharton, Edith. *Ethan Frome*. New York: Scribner's, 1911.

FOR FURTHER READING

Farland, Maria Magdalena. "*Ethan Frome* and the Springs of Masculinity." *Modern Fiction Studies* 43 (1966): 707–29.
Lagerway, Mary D. and Gerald E. Markle. "Edith Wharton's Sick Role." *Sociological Quarterly* 35 (1994): 121–34.

Catherine Barkley: Ernest Hemingway's *A Farewell to Arms* (1929)

Suzanne del Gizzo

Ernest Hemingway, a writer best known as a celebrant of masculinity, has often been criticized for his inability to create fully dimensional female characters. Critics have argued that "Hemingway's women" are generally caricatures who fall into two categories, determined by their relationship to the men in the novels: bitches and sex kittens. His female characters have been understood so frequently as mere reflections of male fear or fantasy that critic Leslie Fielder once suggested that there are "no *women* in his books" (quoted in Whitlow 13).

Since the publication of *A Farewell to Arms*, Catherine Barkley has been regarded as one of Hemingway's more complex and contradictory female characters. Nonetheless, most critics agree that Catherine's desire to satisfy Frederic Henry's every whim places her squarely in the sex-kitten category. Roger Whitlow, however, has argued that the main problem with critical approaches to many of Hemingway's female characters, including Catherine, is that they "too often merely adopted a posture toward the women held by the male characters" (13). Since the narrative of this novel is told largely from Frederic's point of view, the reader sees Catherine largely through his eyes. For Frederic, a young soldier in World War I, his relationship with Catherine is, at least initially, a simple sexual conquest. Even as their relationship grows, Frederic continues to focus on Catherine as a beautiful and willing lover who makes few demands of him. As a result, he fails to recognize that her nurturing is also a form of strength that is slowly changing his own perspective on the world and the war.

The challenge of reading the character of Catherine Barkley is to focus directly on information and evidence provided about her within the text—her history, her actions, and behavior. Catherine is a young, Scottish woman serving as a nurse in Italy who has been traumatized by the death of her fiancé. Recognizing the significance of this trauma helps explain Catherine's strange behavior in her first meetings with Frederic as well as her willingness to enter into an intimate relationship with him so precipitously. Catherine is, as both she and Frederic will later admit, "a little crazy" when she first meets him. She is not only in mourning for her fiancé, but also suffers from guilt for having refused to marry him (and thus, have sex with him) before he left for the war. Her odd behavior and speech, such as when she asks Frederic: "Say, 'I've come back to Catherine in the night' " (30), suggests that she is substituting Frederic for her dead fiancé. At least in the beginning, then, Catherine is using her relationship with Frederic as a form of therapy to help move back from the brink of psychological disintegration.

The images associated with Catherine throughout the novel emphasize the contradictory sides of her personality. When Frederic meets Catherine, she is wearing her nurse's uniform, but she is also carrying a "thin rattan stick like a toy riding crop, bound in leather" (18) given to her by her dead fiancé. While the uniform signals her nurturing nature, the stick suggests that she is a woman whose loss has forced her to discover her strength and has given her discipline and determination to save herself and those she loves. It is Catherine's hair, however, that provides the richest symbol of the book. Catherine's hair is associated with her femininity and sexuality; her desire to cut it off at various points in the novel suggests that she is frustrated by the markers and limits of traditional femininity.

Catherine's frustration with conventional gender roles is also expressed by her willingness to have Frederic's child out of wedlock. Other women in the novel are presented almost exclusively in terms of their sexual relationship to men—the whores at the front, the virgins on the retreat, and wives of male characters. Catherine, however, resists such categorization. When Frederic asks the pregnant Catherine to marry him, he is surprised by her refusal, explaining that he thought "all girls wanted to get married" (115). Catherine's war experiences, however, have disabused her of any romantic notions or sense of obligation to conventional morals. This episode exemplifies the main irony of the novel—the fact that the same world that has sanctioned mass murder in the trenches would condemn their intimate relationship as unlawful.

Catherine's adamant desire to create a separate, private love with Frederic as demonstrated by her continual effort to create "homes" for them—in the hospital at Milan and later in the Swiss Alps—reflects her determination to exert control in a world that seems wildly out of control. Her attempts to escape the world are not acts of weakness, but examples of her ability to cope with feelings of powerlessness and disconnection. Unlike Catherine, Frederic is largely uncritical of the war and remains bound to conventional behavior throughout most of the novel. In this way, Catherine is the more mature and thoughtful character. The story of *A Farewell to Arms*, then, is largely the story of Frederic's ability, through his relationship with Catherine, to arrive at a similar realization and make his "separate peace" (243).

Still, the image of Catherine as a weak and somewhat too obliging woman is a powerful one in the novel where she is seen principally from Frederic's point of view. Gender bias occurs not only on the narrative level itself, where Frederic presents his immature and limited view of Catherine, but also in many readings of the novel which accept Frederic's position without question. Students might discuss how the narrative point of view affects readers' impressions of Catherine, and seek out support for alternate readings of her. They may also discuss how "traditional" feminine qualities, such as caring and nurturing, can be understood as a form of power.

WORKS CITED

Hemingway, Ernest. *A Farewell to Arms* [1929]. New York: Collier Books, 1986.
Whitlow, Roger. *Cassandra's Daughters: The Women in Hemingway*. Westport, CT: Greenwood, 1984.

FOR FURTHER READING

Donaldson, Scott, ed. *New Essays on* A Farewell to Arms. New York: Cambridge UP, 1990.

The Invisible Black Female Artist in Alice Childress' *Florence* (1950)

Nassim W. Balestrini

Florence, a young, widowed Black mother from a small town in the racially divided South, never appears on stage. In a segregated railway station waiting room, Childress juxtaposes four female characters, exposing their differing attitudes toward the rights and responsibilities of Black women, particularly during the pre–Civil Rights era. Florence, the aspiring and talented actress struggling for dramatic roles on New York's stages, contrasts with her younger, more conservative and pessimistic sister Marge, who wants Florence to return to her maternal duties and to accept the restrictions imposed on Blacks; their thoughtful, sensible, open-minded mother, Mrs. Whitney, clashes with Mrs. Carter, a white, patronizing liberal on her way back to New York. While originally intending to travel to New York to take an unsuspecting Florence home, Mrs. Whitney ultimately responds to Mrs. Carter's sugar-coated condescension toward Black women and men by deciding instead to send Florence money and so encourage her daughter to reach for artistic success. The play climaxes in Mrs. Whitney's final, moving insight that Florence "can be anything in the world she wants to be! That's her right. Marge can't make her turn back, Mrs. Carter can't make her turn back" (120), thus promoting a Black woman's prerogative to pursue her ambitions unhampered by others' prejudicial views of her proper "place." Interestingly, not only racist, limited Mrs. Carter but also the socially accommodating Marge represents fearful, biased attitudes that have caused many a young, gifted mother like Florence to sacrifice self-fulfillment.

At the beginning, Mrs. Whitney (Mama in the stage directions) and Marge discuss Florence's predicament. Knowing that Black actresses are humiliated by playing domestics rather than "serious" characters (111), Marge concludes that "Them folks" will prevent Florence's success, as "there's things we can't do cause they ain't gonna let us" (112). Although being on the "white" side of the waiting room "Don't feel a damn bit different" (112), Marge does not expect anything to improve. Using family values as moral arguments against artistic, that is, unconventional and (thus) futile, aspirations, Marge urges Mama to appeal to Florence's maternal instinct. In contrast to the forced separation of families during slavery, Florence seems to have "abandoned" her child to her mother's and sister's care; however, we understand Florence's motivation better as we learn that her husband was killed, probably lynched, when trying to vote. Thus, she attempts to prepare a better future in an environment that would save her son from his father's fate and may offer possibilities that the South has denied African Americans.

The conversation between Mama and Mr. Brown, the elderly porter, reveals that whereas a Black mother is criticized for pursuing an artistic career, a Black man is encouraged to seek self-fulfillment. After mentioning that his brother Bynum saw Florence "in a Colored [moving] picture" (113), he proudly reports that Bynum is studying to become a writer and that his (Mr. Brown's) son will attend Howard University. The double standard applied to women as opposed to men engaging in the arts becomes even clearer because Mr. Brown also draws attention to Florence's son's minor acts of misbehavior (113) and thus bolsters Marge's view that her ambitious sister "got notions a Negro woman don't need" (111). Whereas Florence's absence from her maternal duties taints her artistic quest, Mr. Brown's brother's and son's efforts induce pride without considering their performances as husband, father, and provider.

Moreover, Childress juxtaposes two other pairs of characters: Mr. Brown's brother set against Mrs. Carter's novelist-brother Jeff—and the mulatto protagonist of Jeff's novel, *Lost My Lonely Way*, implicitly compared with Florence. While a Black writer like Bynum may project genuine images of his people, Jeff perpetuates stereotypes detrimental to the public image and self-perception of African Americans. The protagonist, Zelma, "wants to be a lawyer" (115) but commits suicide because she is only "almost white" (116). This melodramatic plot illustrates white people's inflated fears concerning Blacks—and especially Black women—entering white-dominated fields. Zelma's professional aspirations and senseless suicide contrast with "brown-skin" (112) Florence's determination to succeed.

The remaining dialog then sharpens all juxtapositions by cementing Mrs. Carter's racism and by preparing Mrs. Whitney's ultimate support for Florence. When Mrs. Whitney debunks Jeff's novel by enumerating successful "near-whites," Mrs. Carter blames Jeff's sudden writer's block on the people whose characteristics he misrepresents. This foreshadows her final condescension toward Florence and exposes her conviction of white superiority and fear of competition. Although Mrs. Carter praises her brother for "generously" mentoring a Black male poet (giving Jeff credit for everything Malcolm ever wrote!), she dismisses Florence's artistic aspirations by offering her "security" (120) as a white actress's maid; accordingly, having addressed Mr. Brown as "Boy!" (114) earlier on, she now reduces Florence to a "girl" (119).

In contrast, Mrs. Whitney's final insight about Black women's rights reveals the necessity of pursuing goals according to one's talents. Although Mama's life circles around her family and her community, Childress presents her neither as a "mammy" type living for the well-being of white employers nor as a tyrannical matriarch. Mama cannot help but address Mrs. Carter as "mam," but her pride as a Black woman supersedes any deference she might feel for whites. Mama knows of Blacks demanding their civil rights (112); she reads the newspaper (113), and appreciates the achievements of her community (116)—and her daughter.

Students may want to compare the play with depictions of women in sociological studies (such as the controversial Moynihan report). They could also compare the "mammy" stereotype in the novel or movie *Gone with the Wind*; images of Black female domestics in Douglas Turner Ward's play *Happy Ending*; notions of "lost" versus "ideal" Black womanhood in Childress' play *Wines in the Wilderness*. Such comparisons raise questions concerning the roles of mothers, homemakers, daughters, working women, and artists within the Black and white communities. How do employment conditions and social status influence women's choices? Which social structures still restrict mothers, women artists, and educated women? Students will realize that Florence's struggle for self-definition and emancipation is doubly difficult: She faces not only white prejudice against Black people's talents, but also the demands of both white and Black notions of women's role.

WORKS CITED

Childress, Alice. *Florence* [1950]. *Wine in the Wilderness: Plays by African American Women from the Harlem Renaissance to the Present*. Ed. Elizabeth Brown-Guillory. New York: Praeger, 1990, 100–121.

———. *Wine in the Wilderness* [1969]. Brown-Guillory, 122–49.

Ward, Douglas Turner. *Happy Ending*. *Happy Ending* and *Day of Absence*. New York: Dramatists Play Service, 1966, 5–25.

FOR FURTHER READING

Brown-Guillory, Elizabeth. "Alice Childress." Brown-Guillory 97–108.

Dressner, Zita Z. "Alice Childress's Like One of the Family: Domestic and Undomesticated Humor." *Look Who's Laughing: Gender and Comedy*. Ed. Gail Finney. Philadelphia: Gordon and Breach, 1994, 221–29.

Daring Creation: Mary Shelley's *Frankenstein* (1818, revised 1831)

Lucy Morrison

Mary Shelley's first novel both endorses and challenges the traditional gender roles of its late-eighteenth-century time period. Set principally in Switzerland, *Frankenstein* depicts women firmly entrenched in the domestic sphere, their focus conventionally invested in children and household, while men are more active, more powerful, and encouraged to study and explore the world. Caroline Beaufort, Elizabeth Lavenza, Justine Moritz, and Agatha De Lacey are fixed in roles expected of women at this time—wife, mother, daughter—and are somewhat idealized. However, as Anne K. Mellor suggests, Shelley presents these rather passive characters as if, through their secondary status, she could express her frustration with and resentment of the bourgeois, patriarchal family model so prevalent in her own day. For the most part, *Frankenstein*'s women (all minor characters) and men exemplify the roles and limitations imposed upon both genders during the era. Only with Arabian Safie does Shelley step outside those societal boundaries which ensured female submission to parental direction and to dutiful, retiring domesticity. Taught by her mother "to aspire to higher powers of intellect and an independence of spirit" (108–9), Safie is uniquely independent: Courageously, she defies her father to marry the man she loves.

Shelley complicates *Frankenstein*'s representation of typically accepted gender attributes with Victor Frankenstein's act of creation; many critics see the creature as Victor's offspring, and, indeed, he uses the term himself. It takes Victor nine months to construct and then to bring the creature to life, so that Shelley clearly identifies Victor's preparations as a form of pregnancy. Shelley thus feminizes Victor, and his lack of care for his "child" is one of the novel's central themes. Victor flees from his creature as soon as it awakens (when it becomes an autonomous self) and does not provide him with any of the love or guidance expected of a responsible father; in fact, Victor sees the life he has spawned as an abomination and, throughout the text, fails to acknowledge any parental responsibility. As a "mother," Victor is deficient, a man without the inherent nurturing qualities usually accredited to women. Thus, the author identifies stereotypes of the "mother" and simultaneously questions the stereotype of the providing "father" since those cast in the latter role are shown to be either ineffectual (Alphonse Frankenstein) or cruelly controlling (Henry Clerval's and Safie's fathers). Advanced for its time, Shelley's literary investigation of traits that society attributes to each parental role implies that such traits have been incorrectly fixed, principally in biology.

In defying God and nature by creating this being, Victor disturbs the "natural" order—men and women creating children together. His experiment results in an "abortion" or an unnatural being. Not only Victor but other humans encountering the creature reject or abuse him, and he leads a solitary existence. Longing for membership that he is repeatedly denied, this abnormal creature represents the disenfranchised. As such, the creature's experience can be contrasted and compared with Safie's: both are social outsiders, and have punishing fathers and unusual physical appearances. While Safie's unfettered spirit enables her to overcome others' prejudices, it is the creature's repellent looks which disbar him even though he shows compassion and in his eagerness for acceptance has learned, clandestinely, along with Safie. Teachers will want to lead students through a consideration of "otherness" by drawing parallels and contrasts between the Arabian and the creature as outsiders eliciting very different responses.

From reading Milton's *Paradise Lost*, the creature discovers humanity's need for companionship, and specifically that men need women; he subsequently asks Victor to make him a mate. Victor initially agrees, but destroys the female before completion. The creature's desire for female companionship seemingly threatens Victor as he seems to realize fully the import and independence of the being he has created. Victor worries that the female might "become ten thousand times more malignant than her mate, and delight . . . in murder and wretchedness" (150). Above all, Victor fears that she would reject his male creature, turning "with disgust" from him "to the superior beauty of man"; with this, Shelley highlights Victor's fear of the "female" (150). The creature's acts can be read as those of Victor's double, since the creature—which Shelley termed her "hideous progeny"—appears to be enacting Victor's subconscious desires. Seemingly without sexual desire (evinced by his hesitation to marry Elizabeth and his consistent lack of passion), Victor stands in stark contrast to the creature, who is passionate and urgent in his desire for a mate. The creature, then, in killing Elizabeth before she and Victor consummate their marriage, expresses Victor's subconscious fear of and alienation from the feminine realm. With this powerful metaphoric rendering of Victor's dread-of-the-female-turned-murderous, Shelley implicitly considers whether gender differences may prove irreconcilable while fear and loathing dominate men's deeply held attitudes toward mothers, wives, and daughters. Certainly, Shelley suggests that men fail to understand women.

Readers react strongly to the ways that Shelley's novel treats gender roles and socially assigned behaviors and traits. In particular, teachers will want to point to the minor female characters, helping students recognize the limits their historical and cultural contexts place around them; such reflection includes scrutinizing their stereotypic roles and exploring how—and why—such stereotypes may still be prevalent in our society. Identifying the creature as "other" by virtue, initially at least, of his physical appearance, and later by virtue of his lethal vengeance, readers can see the damage done by prejudice based on nothing more than variations in human appearance or circumstance. In addition, discussing how *Frankenstein* challenges conventional notions of "natural" ties and responsibility, students can engage with nature versus nurture debates as relevant then as now. Moreover, Victor's act of creation can be used to initiate ethical debates concerning controversial developments in modern science: gene therapy, test-tube babies, parthenogenesis, and genome mapping. Finally, considering Shelley's own experiences (her mother's death soon after Shelley's own birth deeply affected her) provides further avenues for dialogue, especially about *Frankenstein*'s apparent rage against the maternal.

WORKS CITED

Mellor, Anne K. *Mary Shelley: Her Life, Her Fictions, Her Monsters*. New York: Routledge, 1989.

Shelley, Mary. *Frankenstein* [1818, 1831]. New York: Bantam, 1991.

———. *The Journals of Mary Shelley 1814–1844*. Ed. Paula R. Feldman and Diana Scott Kilvert. 2 vols. Oxford: Clarendon, 1987.

FOR FURTHER READING

Gilbert, Sandra M. and Susan Gubar. *The Madwoman in the Attic: The Woman Writer and the Nineteenth-Century Literary Imagination*. New Haven, CT: Yale UP, 1979, 213–47.

Homans, Margaret. *Bearing the Word: Language and Female Experience in Nineteenth-Century Women's Writing*. Chicago: U of Chicago P, 1986, 110–19.

Shattered Rainbows in Translucent Glass: Tennessee Williams' *The Glass Menagerie* (1945)

Nassim W. Balestrini

The irreconcilable contrast between Amanda Wingfield's pre-Depression Southern genteel youth and her subsequent unsuccessful marriage determines this nostalgic mother's dreams for her grown-up children's success. Assessing life from her cramped apartment in Depression-ridden St. Louis, Amanda finds that women of the lower middle class have few options: They either find a husband/provider, get training to earn a meager salary, or become spinsters dependent on other people's "grudging patronage" (1556). Attempting to save her daughter from the economic hardship and social disgrace she herself has suffered, Amanda counterplots Laura's predicament with outdated gender roles—even at the expense of disregarding Laura's introverted sensitivity.

Tom and Laura reject their mother's desire to uphold her Southern ideals of genteel society. Amanda's unceasing advice to Tom concerning eating habits expressive of a pleasure-oriented lifestyle indicates her wishful view of her children's upper-class calling. Similarly, she wants Laura to conform to antebellum gender roles: a woman must attract a husband by being beautiful, charming, and vivacious. On account of her slight handicap and her painful shyness, Laura escapes from her mother's nostalgia concerning "gentleman callers" into the dream worlds of her estranged father's sentimental old records and her "menagerie" of perfectly shaped, tiny glass animals. These fragile glass creatures symbolizing Laura's sensitivity must necessarily collide with Amanda's notions of coquettish affability.

Despite her nostalgic strain, the years without her husband and the humiliating experience of selling magazine subscriptions have alerted Amanda to the predicament of single women without marketable skills. Thus, Amanda enrolls Laura in a typing class, attempting to combine her own high-brow sense of decency with a keen awareness of material necessity. But self-conscious Laura cannot cope with the competitive environment and nervously vomits during class. Just as her records and her glass menagerie offer an imaginary world at home, she escapes the unpromising fate of a young, unmarried, lower-middle-class woman in the Depression by visiting the park, the zoo, the museum, and the movies. When Amanda inadvertently finds out about Laura's absence from her classes, Williams contrasts the similarity of the two women's experiences (i.e., being forced by economic necessity to attempt work they do not feel suited for) with their different personalities: Amanda focuses on her own embarrassment while discounting Laura's sense of humiliation.

Amanda's motherly, yet suffocating anxiety concerning Laura's material well-being bars her from understanding her daughter and prompts her to transform Laura into a feminine-looking glass figurine, thus—ironically—removing her further from the real world. Ignoring the incongruity of the Southern belle's feminine "charm" in a lower-middle-class St. Louis tenement, Amanda projects her outdated courtship experience onto the urban predicament: deprived of a mansion and a porch for displaying Laura, she pushes Tom to invite a "gentleman caller"—who, by definition, should have come voluntarily to see the young lady he desires. By stylizing Laura into a woman resembling "a piece of translucent glass touched by light, given a momentary radiance, not actual, not lasting" (1574), Amanda forces her daughter to repress her own personality for the sake of conforming to the traditional woman's role.

The clash between Laura's superficial femininity and her sensitive character then reveals the danger in trying to trick reality with the help of illusions. Fascinated by Jim, her former high school idol whom Tom invites as the supposed "gentleman caller," and excited by Jim's pseudo-psychological encouragement of her dormant abilities, Laura momentarily believes in Amanda's fairy-tale prince. While Amanda and Tom are in the kitchen, Jim's and Laura's encounter recalls the pattern of contemporary romantic movies: They chat, exchange compliments, dance, then kiss. However, reality destroys the dream when Laura learns that Jim—who did not know the purpose of the dinner—is engaged. Unable to avoid pain in real experience the way she averts it in her fantasy worlds, she is crushed. In the scene during which Laura verbally excuses Jim's accidental breaking of the glass unicorn's horn, she states that it will now "feel less—freakish" and "more at home with the other horses" (1592). Symbolically, Williams shows that Laura's excursion into the supposed normalcy of romantic love has not removed her "freakish[ness]." The already limited professional and personal choices of women in strained economic circumstances leave little room for accommodating the needs of a slightly handicapped and painfully shy young woman.

Tom, the narrator of this memory play, implicitly summarizes Laura's fragility in a final image which recalls Laura's surface transformation for the fateful dinner with Jim and again stresses the danger of reducing women to decorative assets: "tiny transparent [perfume] bottles in delicate colors, like bits of a shattered rainbow" (1597). Williams effectively juxtaposes Laura's "drifting" with Tom's "restlessness"—as insightfully described by Amanda—and thus contrasts the siblings' shared insecurity with their differing gender-based options: the more restricted, domestic female sphere and the larger (perhaps global) male sphere. Tom escapes his provider role by joining the merchant marine, but remains haunted by Amanda's and Laura's imprisonment in dismal economic circumstances. Williams both evokes empathy for Tom's decision and makes Amanda's attempts to force her ideals on her children appear tragically (rather than deliberately) destructive.

Today, accommodation to socially acceptable gender roles, often defined by one's parents' generation, as well as the urge to escape them remain pressing concerns. Students could compare gender-related notions of physical beauty, success, wealth, and good character expressed in the play with their own and their parents' ideas. How are women today confronted with idealized femininity? Have the personal and professional choices for single and/or married women changed? How do romantic love (in fiction, movies, or personal experience) and notions of idealized worlds influence a young woman's choices? For contrast, one could read Williams' play alongside the brutal depiction of a young secretary fighting the potentially dehumanizing constraints of poverty, marriage, and childbearing in Sophie Treadwell's *Machinal* (1928).

WORKS CITED

Treadwell, Sophie. *Machinal* [1928]. London: Hem, 1993.
Williams, Tennessee. *The Glass Menagerie. Literature: An Introduction to Fiction, Poetry, and Drama.* Ed. X. J. Kennedy and Dana Gioia. New York: Harper-Collins, 1995, 1548–97.

FOR FURTHER READING

Blackwell, Louise. "Tennessee Williams and the Predicament of Women." *South Atlantic Bulletin* 35.ii (1970): 9–14.

What It Means to Be a Lady: Margaret Mitchell's *Gone with the Wind* (1936)

Jane Marcellus

Critic Anne Jones has called *Gone with the Wind* "a study in gender roles, in what it means to be a man or a woman in the South" (105). One of the few stories set on the home front of a war's losing side, the novel subverts the male-as-conquering-hero myth as it describes the dissolution of Southern culture during and after the Civil War. That culture was distinguished by aristocratic gentility that masked a patriarchy organized around property, class, lineage, and white supremacy. To ensure the continuation of that ideology, gender roles were tightly prescribed. White women were put on pedestals; Black women were sexually exploited or expected to fulfill their owners' needs for mother figures. White men saw themselves as gallant rulers, and Black men, as slaves, were treated contemptuously.

The Southern belle was central to this social structure. Bound physically by whalebone stays and emotionally by taboos against individuality, she was a socially constructed object for whom appearance was everything. This type of woman is best exemplified by the book's matriarch, Ellen O'Hara, a "great lady" who accepts "woman's lot" and knows "how to carry her burden and still retain her charm" (61). Melanie Wilkes is gentle, maternal, and self-effacing. Neither, however, survive in the New South after the war.

Gone with the Wind's main character, Scarlett O'Hara, flourishes in the role of belle even as she rails against it. Proud of her seventeen-inch waist, she nevertheless tells her Mammy, "I'm tired of acting like I don't eat more than a bird, and walking when I want to run and saying I feel faint after a waltz, when I could dance for two days and never get tired" (81). Scarlett's power has been restricted, but events force her to claim it. She delivers a baby during a Yankee siege, nurses dying soldiers, picks cotton, kills a Yankee soldier, runs a lumber mill. Hers is a female strength that she gets from "the red earth of

Tara." It is as if the war forces her to shed the false femininity of the belle in order to reach her true feminine strength.

Although perceived as a proper belle, Melanie, too, subverts Southern femininity. Often read as a weak character who dutifully represses her own needs, hers is a strength that Scarlett (and many readers) fail to note. Melanie sees the good in everyone, even people rejected by the Southern aristocracy. She accepts not only the disreputable Rhett Butler but also the golden-hearted prostitute, Belle Watling.

Mammy exemplifies the stereotype her name implies. Although a slave, she is a strong maternal figure who wields considerable, if covert, power. She schools Scarlett in the proper behavior for a belle, helping to perpetuate the system that represses them both. The product of a white fantasy, Mammy is loyal to the oppressive system that denies her freedom.

Although members of a powerful patriarchal elite, many of the male characters cannot, as individuals, outlive the destruction of their culture. Neither Scarlett's blustery father Gerald nor the idealistic Ashley Wilkes, whom Scarlett loves, has the necessary strength to survive in the reconstructed South. Only the roguish and independent Rhett Butler matches Scarlett for staying power. A social outcast who is "not received" in polite society, Rhett endures in the new world because he refuses to capitulate to Southern ideals. As the maverick, Rhett alone survives with his masculinity unquestioned.

This may strike the reader as a dubious distinction, for near the end of the novel Rhett rapes Scarlett, who has become his wife. Scarlett's terror is sexualized: "Suddenly she had a wild thrill such as she had never known; joy, fear, madness, excitement, surrender" (929). She wakes up realizing she "had gloried in it" (930). Scarlett's denial of her husband's violent effort to control and humiliate her reveals her core belief that women find their meaning as objects of male desire. Students might discuss rape as a sexual crime and/or one which draws on a person's desire to dominate and control another.

Focusing on race and gender in the novel will make students aware that beneath a tale of gallant men and beautiful women there is much to be learned about how privilege functions in people's lives. Students can discuss how today's gender expectations are both like and unlike those in the novel; how even women with economic and social advantages do not share power with men. Students might question whether there exist today traces of *Gone with the Wind*'s racist sterotypes: African Americans thought of as children who do only menial work and Black women contentedly taking care of white children. Students might investigate why the novel was so popular when it was published near the end of the Great Depression, and view the widely acclaimed film by the same name made in 1939. In addition, they might want to read *Uncle Tom's Cabin* by Harriet Beecher Stowe, *The Color Purple* by Alice

Walker, or *Beloved* by Toni Morrison, books that portray both African Americans and the South differently from *Gone with the Wind*.

WORKS CITED

Jones, Anne. " 'The Bad Little Girl of the Good Old Days': Sex, Gender and the Southern Social Order." *Recasting*: Gone with the Wind *in American Culture*. Ed. Darden Asbury Pyron. Miami: Florida International University, 1983, 105–15.

Mitchell, Margaret. *Gone with the Wind* [1936]. New York: Warner Books, 1993.

FOR FURTHER READING

Bridges, Herb and Terryl C. Boodman. Gone with the Wind: *The Definitive History of the Book, the Movie and the Legend*. New York: Simon and Schuster, 1969.

Taylor, Hellen. *Scarlett's Women*: Gone with the Wind *and Its Female Fans*. New Brunswick, NJ: Rutgers UP, 1989.

Patriarchy and Property: Women in Pearl S. Buck's *The Good Earth* (1931)

Eleanor Pam

The Good Earth, based on Pearl S. Buck's personal experiences in China, describes a world in which women are property, thereby melding class and gender. In the rigid and severely restrictive patriarchal society of early twentieth-century China, females are forever locked into a caste system of their own; they are de facto slaves, no matter how high born or privileged, nor however much the family to which they belong may have evolved economically and socially. For them, gender *is* class, the ultimate glass ceiling.

Although Buck's Pulitzer Prize–winning saga is set almost a century ago in the backward rural province of Anhwei, she anticipates themes which resonate today, including male mid-life crisis and cultural preoccupation with female body image. These and related issues of extreme gender bias are embedded in clear narrative prose as Buck compellingly relates the story of a peasant couple, Wang Lung, a poor illiterate farmer, and his homely wife, O-Lan, a former slave.

The book begins on the day of their wedding, then traces their lives of hardship and poverty. It is only when they prosper that their marital partnership splinters and the gender gap deepens, allowing Buck to contrast their diverging and disparate destinies. For Wang Lung has changed his class, but O-Lan cannot; as property she has no real agency and no authentic future. Reaching the outer limits of her possible achievements by acquiring a husband and birthing three sons, she is still not safe. As the passing years erode youth, relevance, fertility, and erotic power, her value continues to diminish with the inexorability of age, making her even more unequal than before.

Time treats Wang Lung differently, precipitating what today's reader will recognize as male mid-life crisis. Restless, irritable, now too rich to work, he addresses his growing sense of dislocation by satiating his personal needs while ignoring O-Lan's. He owns his life—and hers. *The Good Earth* is an intense and unsentimental novel that provocatively illustrates Sigmund Freud's observation, "biology is destiny."

When poor, Wang Lung is admirable and compassionate, disdaining the sloth and decadence of the rich, their casual cruelty. But when Wang Lung becomes wealthy his kindness changes along with his perspective, and he loses his moral authority. He even exhibits a strong sense of male entitlement. Bad things happen, as Buck repeatedly reminds us throughout the book, when "the rich become too rich." In this instance, class and upward mobility are determinative of gender behavior. Students might consider and discuss well-known couples in the media whose rags-to-riches marriages parallel problems faced by the male and female protagonists in this book.

One of the author's most memorable characters is Lotus, a young and beautiful singsong woman Wang Lung meets in a teahouse and with whom he becomes passionately involved. This relationship might be perceived by young readers as Buck's version of today's trophy wife, and a productive focus for discussion about class and gender implications surrounding the phenomenon of older men seeking relationships with younger women for show and sexual pleasure.

Wang Lung moves Lotus into the marital home, showers her with luxuries and jewels, even giving her O-Lan's most treasured personal possession—two pearls. This is the author's first signal to the reader that he has erased his wife. Past childbearing years, O-Lan has no more value for him and so she deserves nothing of value from him. "Her breasts had grown flabby and pendulous with many children and had no beauty, and pearls between them were foolish and a waste" (171). Wang Lung has begun the process of objectifying women by concluding, in effect, that those who are not ornaments should not *have* ornaments. When he instructs his wife to decorate his concubine's bedroom, he is thereby de-sexing O-Lan as a wife and demoting her as a woman. Predictably, Lotus will herself be supplanted by a younger rival, Pear Blossom. Considering Wang Lung's intimate relationships from a feminist point of view will enable students to see the double standard with respect to aging and sexual conduct.

An intergenerational saga, *The Good Earth* provides Wang Lung's father with a prominent place in the story but readers never hear anything at all about his mother. By this omission Buck might be signaling the general invisibility of females in that society. Daughters are portrayed as commercial properties who do not belong to their parents, but are born and reared for other families. Thus, they are sold into marriage or slavery, or murdered by the family if it is too poor; but in all events they are treated as inconsequential or transient characters. Ironically, it is Wang Lung's educated sons and heirs who eventually betray him. At the end of the book Buck strongly hints that his descendants will not keep faith with his values, presaging the coming changes in China itself.

The main focus of this intergenerational novel, however, is Wang Lung's three intimate relationships, which highlight and distinguish stereotypical roles of females in Confucian society: O-Lan performs the procreative function, his working-class partner who founds and sustains the family and home. Lotus provides sex and pleasure; she is pampered and excused from work because of her disabling bound feet, a status symbol for Wang Lung. Pear Blossom, a very young and pretty girl, provides solace and companionship in his old age, but is sexually undemanding.

Within their respective castes each is at the top: O-Lan derives her identity through marriage to an affluent man; Lotus, the singsong girl, occupies the highest position in the hierarchy of Chinese prostitution Pear Blossom's assets are youth and beauty, enabling her to become the mistress of a Master rather than be sold to a fellow slave. But in that milieu none can achieve independent success; all have one function—to serve the man.

This book can be assigned as an example of multicultural literature since Buck commonly described herself as "culturally bifocal." Her message about poverty and its special effect on the women of early twentieth-century Chinese society is relevant and transferable to the heterogeneous populations of modern civilization.

WORK CITED

Buck, Pearl S. *The Good Earth* [1931]. New York: Washington Square Press Publication of Pocket Books, 1994.

FOR FURTHER READING

Conn, Peter. *Pearl S. Buck: A Cultural Biography*. New York: Cambridge UP, 1996.

No Expectations at All: Women in Charles Dickens' *Great Expectations* (1861)

James R. Simmons, Jr.

Charles Dickens' *Great Expectations* was published near the end of a long and illustrious career, the thirteenth of the fourteen novels the writer completed before his death in 1870. In the novels prior to *Great Expectations*, women typically embody the extremes represented by Eve and Mary. Like Eve, they are villainous, tempting, and corrupt, often responsible for the downfall of men; or, like Mary, they are perfect, idealized women, good wives and mothers. In *Great Expectations*, the lines are similarly drawn.

The "good" female characters in the novel are easy to identify. Biddy and Clara Barley fit the mold of the ideal Victorian woman: both are caregivers. Biddy takes care of Joe after his wife's death and Clara takes care of her alcoholic father. Biddy marries Joe and has a child and Clara is married by the end of the novel. Like many of Dickens' model women, often referred to as "hearth angels," Biddy and Clara are rewarded for taking their place in the domestic sphere. After marriage they will be further affirmed as the Victorian ideal of womanhood when they become perfect wives and mothers.

The fate of the "bad" women is quite different (and much more interesting). Mrs. Joe, Miss Havisham, and Estella do not fit the Victorian standard of the good wife and mother. Consequently, when these women step outside of what is considered the norm, and, especially if they become assertive in any way, they have to be punished—often severely—in order to "save" or "correct" them. Mrs. Joe Gargery (who does not even have the benefit of an identity separate from that of her husband) is frequently referred to negatively. Dickens writes that Mrs. Joe has brought Pip up "by hand," stressing not the fact that she unselfishly raised her orphaned brother by dry nursing him. Dickens instead uses the term as a pun to mean that she frequently beats Pip as a form of discipline. Dickens depicts Mrs. Joe as a bad wife and a bad mother, reinforcing this characterization for the reader when he has her tell Pip, "It's bad enough to be a blacksmith's wife . . . without being your mother" (9). A feminist reading of Mrs. Joe, however, notes that Dickens "never focuses on [her] deprivation and expectations," never asks the question " 'Why does not society allow her to have any great expectations?' " (Ayres 89). Ultimately, it seems the only way to correct this woman who does not conform is to beat her into submission—as Orlick does.

Miss Havisham, a wealthy woman of property and great influence, is an anomaly in Victorian society. Growing old in her wedding gown, she is a gross distortion of spinsterhood whose development stopped the moment she was left at the altar. Because she can no longer reach her desired objective of marriage, dictated for women by her culture, she attempts to revenge herself on men through Estella, her adopted daughter. Like other non-traditional women in Dickens' novels, especially women who attempt to compete in a male-dominated world, Miss Havisham is punished in the end, dying unloved and alone.

Estella is "corrected" from "bad" woman to "good." Groomed by Miss Havisham to be a femme fatale, she will clearly not easily become a "hearth angel." According to Brenda Ayres, Estella is not "gentle, kind, and tender, she is calculating, malicious and hard. . . . Instead of internalizing her suffering, as was expected of a good Victorian woman, she inflicts suffering on men" (90). Estella marries Bentley Drummle, not for love, but instead to torment him. For this perversion of Victorian ideals she is repaid in kind. After her marriage, Pip hears that she has led a "most unhappy life," that her husband has used her "with great cruelty" (482). However, in the end, Estella acknowledges to Pip that her suffering has become "stronger than all other teaching"; she has "been bent and broken, but—into a better shape" (484). Estella, the only one of the three, gets a second chance. Finally, the humbled and reformed young woman has the possibility of marrying for love.

Examining the female characters in *Great Expectations* in light of Victorian ideals for women provides us a useful way to understand Dickens' women. Good women—wives, homemakers, and caregivers, those who adopt the accepted feminine role, are portrayed favorably. Those who defy the stereotype usually come to an unhappy end. Students may want to discuss the ways in which some of Dickens' female characters do not conform, what expectations they might have, and what options women had during the nineteenth century outside of marriage. If students have read additional novels by Dickens and other nineteenth-century authors, they might compare the roles of women in these works with those in *Great Expectations*. Although Dickens was the most popular author in England and perhaps the world during the nineteenth century, *Great Expectations* unfortunately conforms to and perpetuates the stereotypes that good women were wives and mothers, and women who wanted something more were aberrant. Students might also try to find traces of the Victorian mentality in current literature, films, and television programming.

WORKS CITED

Ayres, Brenda. *Dissenting Women in Dickens' Novels: The Subversion of Domestic Ideology.* Westport, CT: Greenwood, 1998.
Dickens, Charles. *Great Expectations* [1861]. London: Penguin, 1996.

FOR FURTHER READING

Schor, Hilary M. *Dickens and the Daughter of the House.* Cambridge: Cambridge UP, 1999.
Slater, Michael. *Dickens and Women.* London: Dent, 1983.

Beautiful Fools and Hulking Brutes: F. Scott Fitzgerald's *The Great Gatsby* (1925)

Linda C. Pelzer

Midway through the dinner party with which *The Great Gatsby* opens, Daisy Buchanan makes a rather startling confession to narrator Nick Carraway. At the birth of her daughter three years before, she confides, she had wept upon learning her child's sex. "I'm glad it's a girl," she had then asserted. "And I hope she'll be a fool—that's the best thing a girl can be in this world, a beautiful little fool" (24). Daisy's perspective, despite its self-consciously cynical sophistication, provides a focus for analyzing gender in Fitzgerald's American classic. The postwar world of the 1920s may have been discarding outmoded values and customs, embracing new freedoms and attitudes. But as Daisy's remark and Fitzgerald's novel testify, the power dynamics of gender were largely unchanged in the aftermath of World War I. Sexual and social freedoms, *The Great Gatsby* reveals, did not really translate into significant differences in men's and women's roles and expectations.

In Fitzgerald's novel, women remain prisoners of patriarchy. They are either commodities to be possessed and discarded by brutish louts such as Tom Buchanan or embodiments of an ideal for romantics such as Jay Gatsby. Either status essentially denies women their integrity. Daisy, for instance, has been purchased with an expensive pearl necklace, the promise of the comfortable white life of privilege that she desires more than Gatsby. A woman of limited emotional and intellectual resources whose "What'll we plan?" (18) and languid repose on the sofa during that first dinner party are emblematic of an essential passivity, she relies upon others to care for her, and her money assures her that they will. Thus, at her moment of crisis and with Gatsby exposed as a fraud, she retreats into the safety of the Buchanan life. Tom may be a brute who betrays their marriage vows and physically abuses her, but he can and will protect his property. As the violent scene at the Plaza Hotel attests, Tom will fight to retain what he owns.

Around Daisy cohere the novel's floral images and its color symbolism, including the green light at the end of her pier and the white freshness and golden radiance emblematic of her name, which suggest to Gatsby the possibility of achieving a dream. To possess Daisy is to possess "some idea of himself . . . that had gone into loving" her (117). But Daisy is neither a dream nor an ideal; much to Gatsby's surprise, she actually has a daughter. So she will "[tumble] short" (103) of his illusions. A real Daisy inevitably must.

Despite her cynical understanding of their place in the world, Daisy evinces little genuine concern for the other women in *The Great Gatsby*. Jordan Baker, for instance, Daisy tolerates because she can be of use, but looks for neither depth nor sincerity in their friendship. For Myrtle Wilson, who is likewise the victim of Tom Buchanan's possessiveness, Daisy has nothing but contempt. While Myrtle's affair with Tom might justify such feelings, it does not excuse Daisy's callous disregard for the other woman's life. Neither does it excuse her selfish escape from the scene of the hit-and-run accident that leaves Tom's lover lying, heart exposed, on the road that connects West Egg to New York, the locus of Myrtle's own pathetic dreams.

Survivors in the *Gatsby* world must be tough. They can safeguard no illusions: not the tawdry sort that constitutes Myrtle Wilson's; not the enchanted ones that transform a James Gatz and sustain a Jay Gatsby. Illusions make people vulnerable to the brutish realities of Tom Buchanan, whose sheer ability to possess constitutes his invulnerable strength. His Georgian colonial mansion affords him the permanence and place that justify his sense of "Nordic" superiority, so he can rail with utter conviction against people of color and the threat they pose to the civilization that he believes he represents and upholds (19–20). Everything about him, from his "arrogant eyes" to the "great pack of muscle shifting" beneath his clothing to the note of "paternal contempt" in his voice, makes him the very image of patriarchy. Against this "hulking" (18) specimen of man and his institutions, romantics such as Gatsby, and women, even those such as Daisy with their own hard patina, dependent as it is on male prerogative, are doomed.

Tom's aggressive masculinity and appropriation of power, quintessentially patriarchal, provide a starting point for discussing gender in *The Great Gatsby*. Both racist and sexist, this masculine presumption is also class-bound. Working people such as the Wilsons have no significance in the *Gatsby* world, and even Gatsby's wealth cannot confer respectability because it is self-made. Readers must then consider traditional patriarchal values and attitudes within the context of the Jazz Age, the period of American social and cultural history that the novel documents. The Roaring Twenties mounted a challenge to tradition, but the decade's changes provoked a wave of anxiety and a backlash of conservatism that the novel's elegiac tone reflects. Women may have won the vote in 1919, but they were well-represented in the Ku Klux Klan and among religious fundamentalist groups. Their criticism of Margaret Sanger's pioneering efforts to promote reproductive freedom also suggests that modernism's mantle lay uneasy on their shoulders.

The novel's background also provides a context for discussing the period's New Woman and its flapper. Both images reflect the new sexual and social freedoms that have defined Daisy's and Jordan's sense of self. Yet the women's own attitudes about men, especially Daisy's, paradoxically belie the depth of any real change in gender roles and expectations. In a patriarchal world, Daisy's insight holds much weight: A woman's only advantage resides, strategically, in being a "beautiful little fool."

Finally, readers must consider *The Great Gatsby*'s critique of the American Dream as a fragile web formed by intersecting threads of gender, race, and class. Despite the seeming fluidity of its social world, embodied in images of chauffeur-driven African Americans (75) and Gatsby's gay parties, even Gatsby, a man capable of reinventing himself in pursuit of a dream, is denied admission to East Egg and possession of the "golden girl" (126) who there resides. East Egg's denizens, Gatsby's fate suggests—its privileged white men— and the women they possess, have always been and remain still the owners of the American Dream.

WORK CITED

Fitzgerald, F. Scott. *The Great Gatsby* [1925]. New York: Scribner's Paperback Fiction, 1995.

FOR FURTHER READING

Fryer, Sarah Beebe. *Fitzgerald's New Women: Harbingers of Change*. Ann Arbor and London: UMI Research Press, 1988.

Reading between the Lines: Connecting with Gertrude and Ophelia in William Shakespeare's *Hamlet* (ca. 1600)

Elizabeth Klett

William Shakespeare's *Hamlet* is considered one of the world's greatest literary works. Yet women readers may find it difficult to connect with this play: There are only two female characters, Hamlet's mother Gertrude and his girlfriend Ophelia, who have important roles in the overall plot, but they are given very little to say, and therefore can seem frustratingly one-dimensional. While it is easy to dismiss them as a product of Shakespeare's time, it *is* possible to see Gertrude and Ophelia as more complex than they appear at first glance. If students become skilled at reading between the lines, these women can develop into the most interesting characters in *Hamlet*.

Traditionally, critics have scorned Gertrude as a weak-willed, silly woman. Certainly, she poses some interpretive problems: Hamlet is upset because a mere two months after Gertrude's husband the King dies, she marries his brother Claudius, who takes the throne. In Shakespeare's day, marrying one's husband's brother was considered incest; therefore, Hamlet feels that his mother's actions are morally reprehensible on several levels. When he finds out that Claudius killed his father, he is forced to ask—and the reader wonders—whether Gertrude knows and was involved, as well. According to Hamlet, Gertrude is a "most pernicious woman" (1.5.105), who lacks loyalty and selflessness, the qualities that make a good wife and mother, which are a woman's only roles in this patriarchal world. Teachers might have students look at what various characters (such as Hamlet, Claudius, and the Ghost) say about her. From these different perceptions of the Queen, students might analyze Gertrude's supposed failure as a wife and mother in light of what she actually does or says. This kind of comparison/contrast exercise would help raise awareness of how Gertrude's actions are perceived according to expectations for women in that culture.

Ophelia plays a similarly constrictive role: the young, beautiful, and obedient daughter of Polonius, the Lord Chamberlain. She stands for everything an adolescent girl was expected to be in the seventeenth century. After her father dies, she goes mad and commits suicide. She has often been read as a tragic casualty of the oppressive male-dominated court who is driven to destruction because she is deprived of autonomy by her father and used as a pawn in Claudius' efforts to control Hamlet. Her madness and suicide have a long history of representation in art, literature, and on the stage, and Ophelia has become an icon of attractive suffering: a girl with long trailing hair in a white nightgown garlanded with flowers. Even today, "Ophelia" remains emblematic of the troubled teenage girl. Teachers might bring in artworks that depict Ophelia (which usually show her dead or dying) and have students compare them with contemporary fashion magazines, to see how much these images of idealized beauty and suffering are still part of our culture's ideas about young women.

Critics have argued that Ophelia serves as a mirror for Hamlet, since they both go through similar crises over their fathers' deaths, and they both exhibit some degree of madness. Yet this criticism invariably uses Ophelia to foreground Hamlet, emphasizing in the comparison how we can understand *him* better, not her. *Hamlet* is a perfect example of a male-centered narrative: Hamlet, with the most lines and stage time, has cornered critical and public attention for generations. That we are expected to identify with him can present a problem for the woman reader, since Hamlet is contemptuous of both Gertrude and Ophelia, summing up their sex dismissively by saying, "Frailty, thy name is woman" (1.2.146).

Neither woman needs to be confined by Hamlet's depiction of her, however. If we look at Gertrude based on the evidence of what she says and does in the text, she emerges as a practical, intelligent woman who speaks her mind. When Claudius and Polonius puzzle over the cause of Hamlet's supposed "madness," Gertrude offers, simply, "I doubt it is no other but the main, / His father's death and our o'erhasty marriage" (2.2.56–57). And, of course, she's right. In the same scene, frustrated by Polonius' verbosity, she boldly asks him to use "more matter with less art" (96). Gertrude clearly loves and cares about both her son and her husband; as Claudius tells Laertes, she "lives almost by [Hamlet's] looks" (4.7.12). Indeed, there is no textual evidence indicating that she knows about or was involved in the murder of her first husband.

Young women readers might find it easier to connect with Ophelia, since they themselves may feel conflicted by parental and amorous relationships in similar ways. Interestingly, her character can be read as one who resists the role of perfect daughter. For example, when she tells her father, "I shall obey, my lord," Ophelia need not say that line meekly (1.3.136). Also, her madness presents a very real threat to the royal court, as stated clearly in Act 4, Scene 5: "she may strew / Dangerous conjectures in ill-breeding minds" (14–15). Her two mad scenes are disruptive to those around her, and she expresses a keen awareness of male sexual exploitation of women, showing herself to be neither silent nor merely obedient. Her riddling speech in these scenes uncovers Claudius' deceitfulness and Hamlet's betrayal of her. Madness, therefore, grants her access to "voice"—perhaps by the only means available—to expose duplicity and sexual double standards characterizing male/female relationships.

Although it is important to consider *Hamlet* as a text, it is also worth remembering that Shakespeare wrote his plays for performance. In performance, students actively engage with various interpretations of language and characters. Playing Gertrude and Ophelia, they will readily see that actions and gestures speak volumes about Shakespeare's women. By having to consider these characters' motivations and choices, students will draw a deeper understanding, perhaps seeing unexpected connections in Gertrude's and Ophelia's lives and their own lives. Film clips also work extremely well: Franco Zeffirelli's 1990 *Hamlet* has Glenn Close as a young and vibrant Gertrude, and Helena Bonham Carter as a rebellious Ophelia; Michael Almereyda's 2000 version presents a very young, resistant, and accessible Ophelia (Julia Stiles). As they examine different representations of these women on stage as well as in the text, students will come to appreciate this play as more than just a one-man show.

WORK CITED

Shakespeare, William. *Hamlet* [ca. 1600]. Ed. Susanne L. Wofford. Case Studies in Contemporary Criticism Series. Boston: Bedford, 1994.

FOR FURTHER READING

Lenz, Carolyn Ruth Swift, Gayle Greene, and Carol Thomas Neely, eds. *The Woman's Part: Feminist Criticism of Shakespeare*. Urbana: U of Illinois P, 1980.

Neely, Carol Thomas. " 'Documents in Madness': Reading Madness and Gender in Shakespeare's Tragedies and Early Modern Culture." *Shakespearean Tragedy and Gender*. Ed. Shirley Nelson Garner and Madelon Sprengnether. Bloomington: Indiana UP, 1996, 75–104.

Rutter, Carol Chillington. "Snatched Bodies: Ophelia in the Grave." *Enter the Body:*

Women and Representation on Shakespeare's Stage. New York: Routledge, 2001.

Showalter, Elaine. "Representing Ophelia: Women, Madness, and the Responsibilities of Feminist Criticism." *Shakespeare and the Question of Theory.* Ed. Patricia Parker and Geoffrey Hartman. New York: Methuen, 1985, 77–94.

Freedom Reconsidered: Margaret Atwood's *The Handmaid's Tale* (1985)

Magali Cornier Michael

Margaret Atwood's *The Handmaid's Tale*, set in the not-too-distant future, presents a dystopia in which the U.S. government has shifted to a military theocracy, Gilead. Although at first glance this new society might seem far-fetched, the first-person narrator's detailed examination of her present surroundings and her memories of the takeover and life immediately prior to it make clear that Gilead only exaggerates rather than creates anew certain aspects of late-twentieth-century American culture. Through these exaggerations, the novel forces its readers to look more carefully at their present culture and in particular at the precariousness of the advances made in the rights, status, and roles of women. For young women today, who are often reluctant to claim themselves as feminists but nevertheless support and take for granted the changes brought about in American culture as a result of the brave and tireless work of dedicated women over the course of the past century and a half, Atwood's novel conveys a sharp reminder of the continued need to guard and develop more fully women's rights and positions.

During the Gileadean takeover, for example, those in power all too easily freeze the bank accounts of women. Consider that all information in present-day America remains marked by gender—what official form exists that does not make one circle that "F" or "M"? Within Atwood's novel—as in contemporary America—women robbed of economic independence are immediately thrust into complete dependence on men, raising questions about the close relationship between freedom and money in the United States and about how access to money remains gendered. Both these topics would make for good classroom discussion—especially given the continued differences in wages earned for the same jobs by men and women, and for jobs traditionally male dominant (doctors, lawyers, corporate leaders) as opposed to those associated with women (e.g., day care workers, nurses, teachers).

More specifically, the novel warns of the dangers inherent in all forms of extremism and fanaticism, so that both right-wing anti-feminist and radical feminist notions about gender roles and women's positions are depicted as flawed and potentially dangerous. Gilead takes to its extreme the right-wing position that women should stay home and focus solely on childbirth and raising children. Women are relegated to the home forcefully—women who refuse must clean up toxic waste—and organized into classes all aimed at the successful reproduction of the human race, a goal made particularly urgent given the high rate of sterility resulting from unspecified ecological disasters. The narrator belongs to the class of Handmaids, young fertile women selected out and assigned to Commanders' households to conceive and bear children. As older infertile women, the Commanders' wives are assigned to rule over the internal workings of the household. Offred, named to mark her position as a possession of her Commander "Fred," and her fellow handmaids are objectified, reduced to the status of "two-legged wombs" (76). Her narration of the monthly fertilization ceremony is particularly chilling: it depicts the dehumanization of both handmaid and wife, who are made to participate as passive objects and victims in a sex act robbed of sensuality, desire, and love. The novel thus lends itself to discussing the dangers of reducing women to their reproductive functions and how primary biological sex characteristics have been and continue to be used to control and oppress women.

Atwood's novel also demonstrates how the radical feminist position against pornography is co-opted by Gilead, which engages in a wholesale ban on reading and reading materials—except for the Commanders. Censorship thus surfaces as a complex question: It necessarily entails a suppression of freedom and thus always has the potential of turning into a means of oppression. Moreover, given the historical link between literacy and power in the Western world, denying literacy to particular groups of people becomes a method of controlling and thus subordinating them—this certainly was true of slavery in the United States. Indeed, the novel forces the reader to acknowledge that "freedom from" is not necessarily an improvement if it means giving up "freedom to." In other words, although in Gilead Offred can walk down the street and "no man shouts obscenities at us, speaks to us, touches us" (33), the cost seems too high: an oppressive system that dictates all aspects of her life. Teachers can productively use this part of the novel as an excellent springboard for gender-related examination of censorship, individual versus societal freedom, and literacy as a form of power.

Although *The Handmaid's Tale* depicts a dystopia, its lengthy first-person narration also highlights how those who are oppressed can use the power of language themselves. Indeed, Offred asserts herself as a person by telling her story. Much like American slave narratives, her story not only points to the oppressive structures that victimize her but also allows her to move beyond the role of victim, creating herself as an individual with whom the reader can sympathize and identify. Teachers might ask their students to explore how language shapes identity. They will also want to encourage students to think about what it means to find that Offred's narrative is framed by the "Historical Notes" chapter—written by archive director Professor James Pieixoto. With this frame, the novel shows how personal narratives, particularly oral ones, have traditionally been devalued in a culture dependent on written and signed documents. After having read and thus vicariously lived through Offred's harrowing experiences, most readers will take offense at the professor's attitude toward her story, which he presents and trivializes as a transcription of an oral tale from centuries past. This last chapter provides insight into the biases inherent in white, male-dominated records of the past, including how some stories get left out of official histories and how those omissions distort received histories.

WORK CITED

Atwood, Margaret. *The Handmaid's Tale* [1985]. New York: Fawcett Crest, 1987.

FOR FURTHER READING

Wilson, Sharon, Thomas B. Friedman, and Shannon Hengen, eds. *Approaches to Teaching Atwood's* The Handmaid's Tale *and Other Works*. New York: Modern Language Association, 1996.

When Women Shape the World: Charlotte Perkins Gilman's *Herland* (1915)

Jerilyn Fisher

Republished in 1979 after disappearing for decades, the utopian novel *Herland*, (with both predecessor and sequel entitled, respectively, *Moving the Mountain* and *With Her in Ourland*) playfully and earnestly communicates Gilman's vision of a nearly perfect society that owes its success to its nurturing the fullest range of women's capacities. Living harmoniously with each other and with nature in remote mountain country, the all-female inhabitants of Herland give birth parthenogenetically to daughters only; a devastating war eliminated all men and boys from this civilization two thousand years before the story begins. Over time, this virgin, cooperative society has flourished based on principles that valorize, above all else, motherhood, community, and the individual's freedom to develop according to her greatest talents, uninhibited by custom or law. While Gilman elevates women's nurturing above men's propensity to conquer, she also contends that the two sexes, given equal rights and opportunity, would, as parents, produce the ideal world.

Contrasting "our" land, as seen through the eyes of liberated women, and Herland as seen through the eyes of conformist North American men, Gilman presents a cogent argument in literary form, decrying gender stereotypes and misguided notions of "civilization." To make this point, the narrative satirizes sexist attitudes and practices that, then and now, generally escape incisive questioning: from women's name exchange upon marriage (75, 118) to women's impractical fashion (38, 73) to generic male word choice that ignores the existence of women and girls (52, 60, 67). Fundamentally, by freeing women of Herland from assigned behaviors and by ridiculing men's need for control, Gilman exposes the artificial split between masculine and feminine behaviors as counterproductive to "the interest of us all" (Lane xxiii). Class differences among women, economic injustices, and even carnivorous dietary practice come under scrutiny as the novel, replete with irony and wit, vivifies destructive tendencies we tend to regard as "normal" in a society arranged by patriarchal design.

Highlighting three explorers' distinctive responses to a country formed and ruled by women alone, Gilman positions the narrator Van as her delegate. He is—like the author herself—a sociologist who reasons scientifically. Freethinking and objective enough to appreciate the miracle of this country, Van steadily grows into an observer who views the citizens of Herland as simply people: a frame of mind from which the other two men depart. Jeff, the physician, idealizes females and tends toward chivalry, an attitude neither understood nor generally desired by the women he woos. More stubborn and pitiable is Terry, a "macho" mechanic by avocation, whose inherited wealth funds the trip but also inflates his perceived right to dominion. Terry cannot shake his heightened expressions of masculinity, which result, ultimately, in his attempting rape and being expelled from the land.

Adding dimension to discussions of idealized motherhood in *Herland*, teachers may wish to assign excerpts from the author's autobiography. There students will learn that the author suffered a poor relationship with her mother and that, once a mother herself, Gilman reluctantly gave up caring for her young daughter. With this in mind, readers may become especially interested to observe that in *Herland* motherhood is the most honored role anyone can perform. But Gilman doesn't prescribe this function universally: Not every woman gives birth and Herlanders understand that not every woman will reach her greatest potential as a biological mother; indeed, "mother-love has more than one channel of expression" (71). Participating in the care of babies born to other women is considered a meritorious social contribution that women make if they don't wish to have children of their own. In this civilization founded on the principle of mother love "raised to its highest power," children are the "raison d'être" (57, 51). Thus, the countrywomen of Herland, living *sans* men, have gradually lost interest in destructive competition because it conflicts with their communal concern for children, a concern which they believe improves every aspect of daily life and every social institution.

Underlying the social criticism in *Herland* is Gilman's socioeconomic treatise, *Women and Economics*. In this lucid, far-ranging study, Gilman shows that men and women, as a species, are more similar to than different from each other. Further, she claims that women's so-called feminine traits have evolved as a result of "excessive sex distinction": " 'a feminine hand' " or " 'a feminine foot' "(45) develops not because it is needed to preserve the race, but because a woman's heightened femininity increases the possibility of her attracting a protective mate. Consequently, in the human species—unlike any other—the sex-relation becomes a dependent, economic relation. This results in "the over-sexed condition of the human female" which "reacts unfavorably upon herself, her husband, her children, and the race" (47). Excessive sex distinction not only disturbs the natural capacities of women's bodies and minds; it also curbs the evolutionary progress of the species by limiting human potential. Here, narrator Vandyck Jennings conceives this theory as he mulls over his changing perceptions:

> These women . . . were strikingly deficient in what we call "femininity." This led me very promptly to the conviction that those "feminine charms" we are so fond of are not feminine at all but mere reflected masculinity— developed to please us because they had to please us, and in no way essential to the real fulfillment of their great process [which is] . . . how to make the best kind of people. (58–59)

Van's ideology, supported by excerpts from *Women and Economics*, can give teachers and students fodder for examining the social construction of gender as well as heterosexuality, which Gilman posits as normative. In both the novel and in her non-fiction, Gilman emphasizes gender and class distinctions that leave many women disadvantaged, but she is strangely silent when it comes to exposing racial bias. The women of Herland are both dark and light-complected, but nowhere does Gilman hold up to scrutiny racial differences as they affect women's status. Teachers may want to point out that while Gilman reaches ahead of her time in treating sex discrimination, as a late-nineteenth-century radical feminist, she stops short of questioning assumptions of whiteness as the cultural norm.

Yet readers today usually agree that *Herland*'s didactic political messages about these thoroughly female but not "feminine" women are quite sophisticated. Conversely, the novel's story line is simplistic and predictable—the males invade; two try to learn from their liberated teachers, one does not. His expulsion for attempting rape occasions the men's departure. On the final pages, Van's romantic interest, Ellador, equally enamored of him, decides to leave along with the men to investigate their world as she follows her love. One critic takes Gilman to task as a feminist writer who has been seduced, for the sake of popular appeal, into adopting deeply entrenched structures of patriarchal literature which centralize male sexual intrusion and conflict (299). Noting what strikes her as a conquest-focused, sex-focused plot, Kathleen Lant claims that Gilman allows "masculinist values of the patriarch" to "impose themselves on the feminist values of the novel" (292). This controversial response can spark discussion of what makes a novel "feminist." Readers will find challenge in reconciling Lant's ideas about the book with prevailing views (see Lane and Degler) that Gilman has produced a revolutionary work of feminist fiction.

WORKS CITED

Degler, Carl. Introduction. *Women and Economics* [1898]. By Charlotte Perkins Gilman. New York: Harper and Row, 1966, vi–xxxvii.

Gilman, Charlotte Perkins. *Herland* [1915]. New York: Pantheon, 1979.

———. *Women and Economics* [1898]. New York: Harper and Row, 1966.

Lane, Ann J. Introduction. *Herland*. By Charlotte Perkins Gilman. New York: Pantheon Books, 1979, v–xxiii.

Lant, Kathleen Margaret. "The Rape of the Text: Charlotte Perkins Gilman's Violation of Herland." *Tulsa Studies in Women's Literature* 9.2 (1990): 291–308.

FOR FURTHER READING

Gilman, Charlotte Perkins. *The Living of Charlotte Perkins Gilman: An Autobiography* [1935]. Madison: U of Wisconsin P, 1990.

Girls and Women in Sandra Cisneros' *The House on Mango Street* (1984)

Darlene Pagán

Sandra Cisneros' *The House on Mango Street* consists of a series of vignettes set in a Chicago suburb that poignantly, and often painfully, reveal the joys and difficulties for young girls approaching womanhood. From observation and experience heightened by her coming of age, the narrator, Esperanza, begins questioning the distinctive situation of girls and boys and how this is reflected in and elaborated by the actions and interactions of women and men in her neighborhood. Through Esperanza's eyes, Cisneros provides teachers with a wealth of material for discussion of gender roles and issues that are often inextricably connected to race, class, power, and violence; the social construction of sex; female empowerment; and the feminization of poverty.

Esperanza recognizes immediately, in "Boys and Girls," that boys and girls live in separate universes where communication, particularly name calling and humiliation, maintains that separateness. From experience, however, Esperanza begins to recognize how gender distinctions continue into adulthood, for young girls, in a guise that appears to be both the object of their dreams—marriage and family—and the source of their pain and domination. In "Hips," for example, Esperanza and her friends imagine the day they will have hips and learn to move them to attract men, to dance, and to rock children to sleep; but, in "Rafaela Who Drinks Coconut & Papaya Juice on Tuesdays," the girls are saddened by the fate of a young bride who arrives at womanhood only to be physically locked inside, isolated from family and friends, by a possessive husband.

The most important symbol in the novel is the titular house which represents young girls' dreams for their own happy homes but also the prison that many homes are, guarded first by domineering fathers, and second by domineering husbands. The house also indicates a gender trap fortified by the cycle of poverty from which women and children suffer in their economic dependence on men. And while there are young women who cast off the passive role relegated to them, they must endure resulting difficulties and costs. In "Alice Who Sees Mice," Alice's mother has died and it is the daughter who must assume the household chores and care of her father, but her role as both her father's primary caregiver and a university student proves exhausting. At the end of the story, the narrator lauds Alice for being a good girl, for studying, and for seeing the mice her powerful father insists do not exist. In a parallel to David and Goliath, the mice symbolize Alice's persistence as she attempts to escape her father's domination and control. At the same time, she must also deal with her real potential for failure as a young woman entirely responsible for full-time work in and out of the home, in addition to her responsibilities to herself at the university.

One threat to young girls that Cisneros does not shy away from is the reality of violence against women. Two stories specifically address this subject in vivid though not graphic terms: "Minerva Writes Poems" and "Sally." In the former, a young girl refuses to leave her husband, even though he beats her, because he is the father of her children. In the latter, the narrator is raped by a group of boys near a carnival. As if the violence alone were not difficult enough, we learn that one of the boys had whispered about his victim, the narrator, being Spanish, conveying racist as well as sexist domination. Teachers will want to prepare readers before pursuing these particular stories by sharing the subject matter beforehand and perhaps also by asking readers about their understanding of and ideas about violence in women's lives. Such a discussion will help teachers recognize what their students do and do not know about violence against women, how they might react to the fiction, and what their multiple cultural contexts of violence are. Equally important is that teachers not fear addressing the subject of racism, but also not reinscribe stereotypes of brutish, Mexican men and passive, Mexican females. Cisneros' short story, "Woman Hollering Creek," as companion to the novel, presents possibilities for a young married woman resisting a husband who treats her badly.

To help articulate issues of race, class, and gender, but also of language and identity formation vivified by the metaphoric and geographic U.S./Mexican border, teachers can utilize any number of resources in Chicano/a studies and literature. Rafael Pérez-Torres specifically cites Cisneros' use of irony and humor to elaborate the tensions and ironies of men expected to claim power and women expected to relinquish theirs (198–200). Pérez-Torres also addresses symbolism in Cisneros' earlier fiction, including mythical and legendary females to exemplify power, which finds parallels in *Mango Street*, though not equivalents. In another vein, Cisneros' wealth of symbols in general might be compared among her works and also with the work of other authors who use common cultural symbols. The house as a symbol of confinement and liberation, for example, can be found in writers from Virginia Woolf (*A Room of One's Own*) to James Joyce (*Araby*). The recurring portrait of women physically and psychically immobilized as they sit in their houses, looking out of windows, and of girls' and women's sense of self as represented by shoe-imagery might respectively encourage creative classroom exploration as well as interesting parallels to classical literary texts (i.e., *Jane Eyre*, "The Yellow Wallpaper") or to folktales and children's stories ("Old Mother Hubbard," "Snow White," "Cinderella," *The Wizard of Oz*).

Despite the occasionally difficult subject matter, the narratives in *The House on Mango Street* are carried primarily by brave women who fight and succeed, and who love and laugh with an abandon that can inspire. Esperanza's name translates as hope in English; it thus signifies young girls' hopes for womanhood, but expressly for womanhood that represents empowerment as opposed to oppressiveness. Ultimately, that hope for empowerment extends not solely to women but to humanity in general.

WORKS CITED

Cisneros, Sandra. *The House on Mango Street*. New York: Vintage Contemporaries, 1984.

———. "Do You Know Me? I Wrote *The House on Mango Street*." *The Americas Review* 15 (Spring 1987): 77–79.

———. "Woman Hollering Creek." *Literature and Society*. 3rd ed. Ed. Pamela Annas and Robert Rosen. Upper Saddle River, NJ: Prentice Hall, 2000, 1168–77.

Pérez-Torres, Rafael. *Movements in Chicano Poetry: Against Myths, Against Margins*. New York: Cambridge UP, 1995.

FOR FURTHER READING

Anzaldúa, Gloria. *Borderlands/La Frontera*. San Francisco: Aunt Lute Books, 1987.

Behar, Ruth. *Translated Woman: Crossing the Border with Esperanza's Story*. Boston: Beacon, 1993.

Sánchez, Marta Ester. *Contemporary Chicana Poetry*. Berkeley: U of California P, 1985.

Living in a Borderland: Cultural Expectations of Gender in Julia Alvarez' *How the García Girls Lost Their Accents* (1991)

Karen Castellucci Cox

In her first novel, *How the García Girls Lost Their Accents*, Julia Alvarez explores the difficulties four sisters face as they assimilate into modern American life. The novel is made up of fifteen interrelated stories that chronicle the coming-of-age of Carla, Sandra, Yolanda, and Sofía, who flee the Dominican Republic with their parents to seek a new life in New York City. Students will find the novel relevant in its handling of contemporary female adolescent issues, its discourse on gender stereotypes, and its attention to the influence of class and culture on girls' and women's gender identity.

The narrative of the García family's journey, from a privileged existence in the politically troubled Dominican Republic to a modest life in the Bronx, is grouped into three time periods. The stories move backward through the family's years in New York, finally returning to their pre-exile life in an increasingly unstable Dominican Republic. The divided narrative highlights the conflict between two competing visions of ideal womanhood from which these daughters must choose—either the restrained domestic mistress of the Island or the politicized, independent woman of the United States. The first story opens with the Americanized, adult Yolanda (Yo or "I" in Spanish) enviously admiring her Dominican cousins "with households and authority in their voices" (11). Yo's *antojo* or deep craving here, ostensibly for ripe mango, is in actuality her desire for the defined gender roles that make life simpler for her female counterparts. Hoping the Island will "turn out to be [her] home" (11), Yo discovers instead that spending years abroad has shaped her feminist beliefs to such an extent that she can never reintegrate satisfactorily into her previous life, even as its straightforward gender roles attract her. The rest of the novel serves to underscore the impossibility of return for all four sisters, as they precariously straddle two disparate cultures in the undefined border-land that is the immigrant's legacy.

Growing up in the counterculture of the 1960s, the García sisters' initiation into adulthood seems deceptively "American" despite their Island roots. Like stereotypical American teenagers, they rebel against parental control, experiment with marijuana, explore their sexuality, and struggle with eating disorders; as grown women, they suffer mental collapses, and marry and divorce with frequency. While their crises are in many ways conventionally North American, the sisters face a unique problem as immigrants, in that their every choice as maturing women positions them in a complex cultural tug-of-war. Each time these daughters behave in a predictable American manner, they act against Dominican cultural standards that value familial devotion, sexual purity, and feminine deference. Sofía's transformation in the sixth story exemplifies this conflict. Exiled to the Island for her teenage misbehavior, Sofía horrifies her sisters when she capitulates to tradition, becoming a twin of her "hair-and-nails" cousins (108) and acquiring a macho boyfriend who monitors her activities and discourages her from reading. Using the sexist double standard of the Island to their advantage, the García girls deliberately leave their once-feminist sister unchaperoned, thus damaging her "good reputation" and exacting her permanent release from the upper-class *dominicana*'s circumscribed fate. The girls' liberty is dubiously won, however, in that the sisters are required always to enact double lives, those of self-reliant Americans, on the one hand, and obedient Island innocents, on the other, if they are to gain any portion of personal independence.

The transplanted García daughters must grapple daily with the irreconcilable cultural and gender messages that confound their identities. The eldest, Carla, retreats into psychological study, cloaking her confusing dualities with protective, clinical names. Sandi, the only child to have inherited blue eyes and light skin from Swedish ancestors, wishes only to blend in with her transplanted family, to be "darker complected like her sisters" (52), and she suffers from anorexia and bouts of anxiety. Sofía, the youngest and most rebellious of the four, chooses sides early: Defying her traditional upbringing and Catholic background, Sofía behaves promiscuously and elopes with the blondest German she can find. Yet even this mutinous act does not resolve the split antagonisms she feels, as Papi ignores the granddaughter of the union, only extending his approval when a subsequent son's "fair Nordic looks" promise to guard the family's European blood against "a future bad choice by one of its women" (27). The cultural breach widens as the daughters reject Papi's sexist ideology that treasures male heirs but restricts and impedes its females.

Yolanda suffers most deeply from the cross-cultural balancing act of expatriation. Experiencing herself as a divided person, first as a *"writer-slash-teacher"* on official documents (46) and then as a *"head-slash-heart-slash-soul"* in a goodbye note to her husband (78), Yo struggles throughout her adolescence and early adulthood to locate a whole, authentic self. Invited to give a speech at her middle school assembly, Yo stumbles upon Walt Whitman's "Song of Myself" and constructs a loose plagiarism of self-aggrandizement that she believes finally "sounded like herself in English" (143). When her father tears up the speech in a fit of rage, overcome by shame at her egotism and haunted by fears of political retribution for her outspokenness, Yo bitterly flings dictator Trujillo's hated nickname "Chapita" at her father and thus begins a painful defection from the patriarchal social structure that has demanded she submerge her truest self.

In addition to examining cultural influences that shape these women's roles, students should also analyze the insidious effects of patriarchy on class-consciousness. They may start by debating why the wealthy *dominicanas* choose to participate in women's oppression, patronizing and overworking their maids whose sole purpose is to deliver creature comforts to others. Interrogating American culture, teachers might encourage students to conduct interviews or otherwise consider the lives of Dominican girls and women not so materialistically fortunate as the García sisters. How does economic hardship differently affect assimilation and gender relations for Dominican female immigrants who come to this country with little English, little education, and little money?

WORK CITED

Alvarez, Julia. *How the García Girls Lost Their Accents*. New York: Plume/Penguin, 1991.

FOR FURTHER READING

Alvarez, Julia. *Something to Declare*. Chapel Hill, NC: Algonquin, 1998.
Rosario-Sievert, Heather. "The Dominican-American Bildungsroman: Julia Alvarez' *How the García Girls Lost Their Accents*." *U.S. Latino Literature: A Critical Guide for Students and Teachers*. Ed. Harold Augenbraum and Margarite Fernández Olmos. Westport, CT: Greenwood, 2000, 113–22.

A Song of Freedom: Maya Angelou's *I Know Why the Caged Bird Sings* (1969)

Yolanda Pierce

As the first volume of a five-volume autobiographical series, Maya Angelou's *I Know Why the Caged Bird Sings* is the triumphant account of several Black women raising a young Black girl in a racist and sexist society. This book reveals how Black women love themselves and each other despite living in a world that does not love or value them. Angelou's autobiography describes a collective identity of Black women who support each other and still remain individuals, free to sing their own songs of freedom.

Angelou writes: "if growing up is painful for the Southern black girl, being aware of her displacement is the rust on the razor that threatens the throat. It is an unnecessary insult" (4). Her autobiography deals with the painful double strikes of growing up Black and female. As a young girl, Marguerite Johnson longs to be white, to be a member of what she perceives as the more favored race. She wants to wake up out of her "ugly black dream" and instead find herself with long blond hair and blue eyes (2). She understands, even as a little girl, that her "nappy black hair" and dark skin are not prized. She begins her life with the pain of not being "good enough," since she could not find girls who looked like her in any books or movies.

Marguerite experiences the pain of racism as she watches her beloved paternal grandmother endure humiliation when white girls call her "Annie" instead of respectfully addressing her as "Mrs. Henderson." As a teenager, Marguerite has a similar experience in which she is "called out of her name" by a white female employer who attempts to rename her "Mary" (108). Momma Henderson's bitter experiences have prepared Marguerite for her own confrontations with racist America. The refusal of a white dentist, to whom Momma Henderson has lent money, to perform badly needed dental work on Marguerite is another example of the humiliation these two generations of

Black women face together. Told by the dentist that he would "rather stick [his] hand in a dog's mouth than in a nigger's," granddaughter and grandmother are forced to travel twenty-five miles to the nearest Black dentist (189). The repercussions of Jim Crow, even eighty years after slavery, place Black women at the very bottom of a white patriarchal system.

And yet despite the pain and humiliations of racism, Angelou's autobiography is a tale of triumph and a celebration of the strength of Black womanhood. Momma Henderson is a strong, self-made, economically independent woman who has learned to operate and succeed in a world that believes women should be submissive and dependent. Despite demeaning confrontations with those who attempt to humiliate her, Momma Henderson is always the victor because she never relinquishes her self-respect—and she teaches Marguerite to do the same. Likewise, her maternal grandmother, "Grandmother Baxter" raises her "six mean children" in an effort to prepare them to deal with a mean world (62). It is she who is responsible for punishing Mr. Freeman after he rapes 8-year-old Marguerite. Knowing that the legal system often does not protect Black people, Grandmother Baxter takes the law into her own hands.

Vivian Baxter, Marguerite's mother, is a woman of great resourcefulness, like her own mother. She takes joy and pleasure out of life, despite life's pains. From her, Marguerite learns the joys of being a woman, delighting in the feminine, and being proud of her Black body. Mrs. Flowers, the "aristocrat" of Stamps, Arkansas, also encourages Marguerite to be "proud to be a Negro" (95). She helps Marguerite regain her voice after the rape; she teaches her about the importance of language; she exposes her to great literature; and she gives her "lessons in living" so that Marguerite would learn to listen "carefully to what country people called mother wit . . . couched in the collective wisdom of generations" (100). All of these women teach Marguerite to love herself, and to love the generations of Black women who have come before her and helped pave a road of freedom in a restrictive world.

At sixteen, Marguerite becomes the first African-American street car conductor, due in large part to the tenacity that her mothers, grandmothers, and "other mothers" have taught her. At the end of her autobiography, Marguerite herself becomes a mother, and in that role she has to draw upon all the collective wisdom taught to her. Angelou writes that Black women are often "assaulted in [their] tender years" by male dominance, white hatred, and powerlessness, so the fact that adult Black women survive and emerge as formidable human beings is deserving of respect (272). Feminist historian Elizabeth Fox-Genovese echoes these sentiments, suggesting that Angelou deliberately "links herself to the Southern roots and history of her people" and to those

"American Negro female survivors whom she implicitly credits with laying the foundation for her own survival" (23).

Students should pay particular attention to the themes and definitions of motherhood within this book; an important exercise would be to list the multiple "other mothers" and discuss why Black motherhood is not dependent on the presence of an actual biological mother. Students must also examine self-definition as a continuous theme in *I Know Why the Caged Bird Sings*; and central to the text is Angelou's search for a place in which both blackness and womanhood can be celebrated.

Finally, despite its controversy, neither students nor teachers should be intimidated by the sexual content of Angelou's autobiography. What makes her work particularly powerful is her discussion of the vulnerable sexual positions in which all girls and women are placed. As the issue of childhood sexual abuse continues to be silenced within our society, Angelou's autobiography is a starting point in shattering that silence and finding a place of healing.

WORKS CITED

Angelou, Maya. *I Know Why the Caged Bird Sings*. New York: Bantam Books, 1969.
Fox-Genovese, Elizabeth. "Myth and History: Discourse of Origins in Zora Neale Hurston and Maya Angelou." *Black American Literature Forum* 24:2 (Summer 1990): 221–35.

FOR FURTHER READING

Braxton, Joanne M. *Maya Angelou's* I Know Why the Caged Bird Sings: *A Casebook*. New York: Oxford UP, 1999.

Good Mother, Bad Mother in Joanne Greenberg's *I Never Promised You a Rose Garden* (1964)

Paul Bail

In the nineteenth century the male physician/female invalid supplanted the old dyad of male confessor/female penitent that characterized the Age of Faith. Women's interest in relational connectedness historically was pathologized as "dependency" (Ehrenreich and English 18), while masculine norms of independence and autonomy were held up as the ideal of psychological health—as they still are! So, it is no coincidence that women have penned some of the most famous literary memoirs of madness. One thinks of *The Yellow Wallpaper*, Charlotte Perkins Gilman's story about her "rest cure," poet Sylvia Plath's *The Bell Jar*, and, more recently, novelist Susanna Kaysen's *Girl, Interrupted*. Similarly, *I Never Promised You a Rose Garden* is Joanne Greenberg's fictionalized account of her treatment by psychoanalyst Dr. Frieda Fromm-Reichmann in 1948. Greenberg and Fromm-Reichmann had planned to co-author her case history, but the latter's death intervened. *Rose Garden* was Greenberg's way of completing the project and of paying homage to her psychiatrist, whom she depicts as Dr. Clara Fried.

Deborah Blau's strange inner world, with its detailed visions and altered states, was both fascinating and frightening to readers in the psychedelic 1960s. But, as Dr. Fried sees, Deborah's florid mental creations are not the fundamental problem, but are camouflage for Deborah's true dilemma—a failure of intimacy. Undeniably, both genders need intimacy, but women particularly have been socialized to be more expressive emotionally, and to draw psychological strength from their relational connectedness to others. Deborah is unable to do this because she must conceal her "true" nature, which she sees as fundamentally bad. Also, she is particularly afraid of contaminating other women with her inner "poison" (146). Her fear of intimacy with women as destructive (142) seems as panicked as a homophobic's abhorrence of same-sex love.

The nature of Deborah's "badness" is never clearly defined, although the author leaves clues that it relates to the teenager's emerging sexuality. Greenberg's discrete hints might have seemed revelatory by conservative standards of the 1950s, but in the current "tell all" climate they seem frustratingly elusive and cryptic. One revealing episode occurs when Deborah discovers her camp friend Eugenia in the woods, naked and perspiring, exuding an urgent, palpable "need." The exposed girl hands Deborah a heavy leather belt, pleading with her, "You know what I am . . . beat me" (145). As if confronted by a frightening reflection of herself, Deborah rejects Eugenia in horror and runs away.

The notion that women whose behavior is considered deviant should be made to suffer is embedded within Western culture, as evidenced by the burning of witches and branding of adulteresses. Deborah seems to have internalized these misogynistic strictures. After seeing an immobilized female patient being slapped by Ellis, the "pacifist" orderly, Deborah pictures *herself* being beaten while she is "naked . . . in a locked seclusion room . . . simple pictures, explicit and terrifying" (107). No one actually beats Deborah; instead she continually inflicts punishment on her own flesh, cutting and burning it.

Deborah's penchant for suffering is reinforced by her sense of Jewishness. Her grandfather, an Eastern European, was humiliated repeatedly by anti-Semitic aristocrats. Obsessed with hatred, he vowed to become wealthy and successful in America, in order to avenge himself on his oppressors. Although he makes disparaging comments about women to Deborah, and would have preferred a boy to act as his instrument of retaliation, he views her blonde hair and superior intellect as trophies of his victory. To compensate for her being female, he tries to instill in her a warrior's code: "If you are hurt, never cry, but laugh. You must never let them know that they are hurting you" (96). But his old humiliations still sting, and he demands she be perfect in order to support his ambitious pretensions. Telling Deborah, "You're like me," the unsympathetic patriarch cannot see her for who she is.

Because of this experience, Deborah is extremely wary of the male ego of the psychiatrists, who use "icy logic" (160) and see her once again as a trophy in their "ambitious . . . daydream" of success (66). In contrast, Dr. Fried appears unpretentious (23), secure in herself and her status. She reassures Deborah that she will not force her to give up her symptoms. Her motherly qualities provide a welcome contrast to the grandfather's tyrannical demands. But Dr. Fried also shares certain qualities with him. Both are refugees from European anti-Semitism. Both are plain-spoken, strong, determined individuals who have achieved success despite great obstacles—in Dr. Fried's case, prejudice against women in medicine. In this way, Dr. Fried bridges Deborah's past and her present, and combines some positive "male" qualities with positive "female" ones.

Unlike the typical male psychoanalysts, Dr. Fried works at establishing a real relationship with her patients rather than intellectually dissecting them. Instead, she tries to re-mother the patient. In real life, Dr. Fromm-Reichmann viewed severe mental illness as due to a failure in early mothering, and sought to provide a corrective experience for her patients, completing the task that the biological mother supposedly did not do properly. But acknowledging the role of "real" connection in the process of cure comes at a price: that of blaming mothers for what goes wrong with their children. Analogous to the madonna/whore split, Fromm-Reichmann's notion dichotomizes the idealized Freudian mother of perfectly well-adjusted children, versus the bad, "schizophrenogenic" mother, whose unconsciously hostile and domineering style of child rearing induced madness in her offspring.

An independent woman, Dr. Fried is constrained by working in an institutional culture controlled by male psychiatrists. Some male colleagues respect her, but through the distorting lens of their own masculinist values, admiring the analytical power of her intellect. Only Dr. Halle recognizes that intellect is not all-powerful and that Dr. Fried's authenticity and personal engagement with her patients are equally important. Not coincidentally, Dr. Halle is the most sympathetically drawn male psychiatrist.

It is interesting to contrast this novel with its mirror image, *One Flew Over the Cuckoo's Nest*. In *Rose Garden*, the female patient's longing for connectedness is frustrated by impersonal male psychiatrists. Conversely, in Ken Kesey's novel the male patient focuses on maintaining his autonomy and is frustrated by an extremely controlling female character, Nurse Ratched. Students could discuss how these two books illustrate the differing values and behaviors that some researchers claim as typical for males and females socialized in our culture.

WORKS CITED

Ehrenreich, Barbara and Deidre English. *For Her Own Good: 150 Years of the Experts' Advice to Women*. New York: Doubleday, 1978.

Gilman, Charlotte Perkins. *The Yellow Wallpaper* [1899]. New York: Feminist Press, 1973.

Greenberg, Joanne. *I Never Promised You a Rose Garden*. New York: New American Library, 1964.

Kaysen, Susanna. *Girl, Interrupted*. New York: Turtle Bay, 1993.

Kesey, Ken. *One Flew Over the Cuckoo's Nest*. New York: Viking, 1982.
Plath, Sylvia. *The Bell Jar*. New York: Harper & Row, 1971.

FOR FURTHER READING

Shannonhouse, Rebecca, ed. *Out of Her Mind: Women Writing on Madness*. New York: Modern Library, 2000.

Bobbie Ann Mason's *In Country* (1985): A Girl's Quest for Her Father and Herself

Jeanne-Marie Zeck

A *bildungsroman* set in rural Hopewell, Kentucky, Bobbie Ann Mason's *In Country* shows people still suffering from repercussions of the Vietnam War in 1984. Samantha Hughes is an intelligent, persistent, and fiercely independent 17-year-old graduating from high school. Her nickname, Sam, suggests her ability to transcend gender stereotypes. Sam lives with her 34-year-old uncle Emmett, a Vietnam veteran with whom she shares power and responsibility in the household. She knows that before she can make decisions about her future, she must come to know herself better. The first step is to learn more about her father, Dwayne Hughes, who died in Vietnam before Samantha was born.

Through the voices of Sam and her mother Irene, Mason assesses the dangers and costs of America's worship of stereotypical masculinity by examining its institutionalization in military service. Our image of the American fighting man emphasizes aggression and violence while negating the feminine values of empathy, nurturing, and love. Because Samantha has experienced the tragedy of war—not only has she lost her father, but her uncle Emmett suffers from post-traumatic stress disorder—she challenges one accepted rationale for war: Women are weak and dependent; men are their protectors. She berates her boyfriend for his desire to join the military:

> My daddy went over there to fight for Mom's sake, and Emmett went over there for Mom's sake and my sake. . . . If you went off to war, I bet you'd say it was for me. But you might ask my opinion first. The ones who don't get killed come back with their lives messed up, and then they make everybody miserable. (71)

Men make killing "their basic profession," Sam notes later (209). "Women," however, "didn't kill. That was why her mother would not honor the flag, or honor the dead. Honoring the dead meant honoring the cause" (210). Samantha recognizes that the emphasis on violence and power causes an imbalance in people's individual lives and in our culture as a whole. She understands that in order to stop the violence, women's voices must be heard.

Rather than accepting the culture's image of the rugged, hypermasculine war hero, Mason reveals American soldiers to be vulnerable and fully human: more than 58,000 American soldiers died in Vietnam; thousands of others were physically and psychically wounded. Mason presents Emmett and his friend Tom as examples of veterans so damaged by the war that they cannot sustain intimate relationships with women. Buddy Mangrum was exposed to Agent Orange and passes on birth defects to his infant daughter. Pete has serious problems with alcohol abuse and fits of violence. The devastation of these men's lives reverberates through the existence of women and children. Dwayne's death reveals the void a father's absence can leave in his daughter's life.

Mason provides the protagonist with a mother, however, who is a substantial force in her daughter's life. Irene is a feisty, imaginative, nurturing woman who has recovered from the trauma of her young husband's death, raised a daughter, cared for her war-damaged brother, and is entering college in her mid-thirties. Irene offers her daughter sound advice, encouragement, and financial resources. Samantha insists to her mother that mobility is a requisite for taking that giant step into adulthood. Longing for a car, she laments, "Boys got cars for graduation, but girls usually had to buy their own cars because they were expected to get married—to guys with cars" (58). In Mason's novel, the themes of mobility and freedom for girls and women are central. Literature frequently presents women as stationary beings trapped in domesticity, while men are portrayed as travelers and adventurers. However, in *In Country*, the mother advocates adventure for her daughter by buying Samantha a second-hand car that propels the young woman forward in her quest to find her father and know herself.

Each seeking some kind of closure, Samantha, her paternal grandmother, and Emmett travel across the country in Sam's VW Beetle on a pilgrimage to the Vietnam Memorial in Washington, DC. This essential ritual promotes healing and resolution for all three. Samantha finds not only her father's name on the wall, but her own, Sam Hughes. The androgynous name suggests women and children are as much victims of war as the dead soldiers. It also implies that in grief we are all one.

Girls will feel empowered by reading a novel that has such a passionately committed and vocal female protagonist; boys, too, will benefit by seeing a young woman as an active force in her own life. Students may be encouraged to examine messages about gender in films like *Top Gun* and *Rambo*, or more serious films such as *The Deer Hunter* and *Apocalypse Now*. Students can discuss whether the images of manhood in the films coincide with those in Mason's novel. How does each define femininity? Students can compare their own definitions of masculinity and femininity. They might watch films with female heroes: *Norma Rae*, *Sarafina*, and *The Long Walk Home*; and discuss images of courageous women and whether they are common or rare in the media today.

Throughout the novel, Bruce Springsteen's lyrics from "Born in the USA" illuminate scenes. Using the CD in class, students can analyze several songs. They may be surprised to learn that songs they assumed were patriotic actually have anti-war lyrics. In "Cover Me," for example, Springsteen uses a military term to request protection and comfort from a woman: The man is vulnerable; the woman provides safety.

Finally, *Maya Lin: A Strong Clear Vision* is a superb documentary on the young Asian American woman architect who designed the Vietnam Veterans' Memorial. The videotape reveals the sexism and racism at the center of the controversy over Lin's design. The documentary is an excellent impetus for discussion regarding prejudice.

WORKS CITED

Mason, Bobbie Ann. *In Country*. New York: Perennial, 1985.
Maya Lin: A Strong Clear Vision (Film). Dir. Freida Lee Mock, 1994.

FOR FURTHER READING

White, Leslie. "The Function of Popular Culture in Bobbie Ann Mason's *Shiloh and Other Stories* and in *In Country*." *The Southern Quarterly* 26.4 (1988): 69–79.

The Invisible Women in
Ralph Ellison's *Invisible Man* (1952)

Yolanda Pierce

Ralph Ellison's 1952 novel, *Invisible Man*, is the tale of an unnamed African-American protagonist who longs to be treated as fully human in a society which only views him as lesser and inferior. The protagonist is literally forced underground by those who deny his individuality and want to keep him nameless and voiceless. As one of the most important fixtures in the African-American literary tradition, *Invisible Man* contains dozens of female characters. Yet, despite the sheer bulk of the novel (almost 600 pages), all the female characters play minor roles; most of these women, like the protagonist, are not actually given names. Of the more developed female characters, it is Mary Rambo, Sybil, and a nameless nude dancer who play vital roles in the protagonist's search for recognition, manhood, and humanity.

During a rite-of-passage ritual, the protagonist and his boyhood friends, all young Black men, are forced to watch a naked "magnificent blonde" dance for an all-male audience (19). As indicated by the tattoo of the American flag on her thigh, the dancer symbolizes the highly valued standards of "all-American" beauty: she is white, blonde, and blue-eyed. The white male sponsors of this event are playing on the taboo of interracial relationships and the notion that all Black men desire white women because white women are "trophies" to be won. These men force the Black teenagers to look at the woman, but they make sure that the boys do not touch her. Implicit in this scene is a clear social message: white female beauty is the ultimate prize, but it is off-limits to all but white men. In the South during the 1940s, the repercussions for the protagonist and his friends even looking at a naked white woman could be death, and thus the young men react with fear at the sight of the dancer. This reinforces the dancer's power; she smiles at the boys, knowing all too well that her beauty and her whiteness are prizes. While she believes that she is in a more powerful situation than the young boys, she ultimately realizes her own vulnerability and powerlessness against her white "protectors," who shield her from Black men, but barely allow her to escape assault at white hands. The dancer comes to realize that she, too, is a victim of white patriarchy.

Mary Rambo is a hard-working Black woman, a community pillar who is "always helping somebody" (253). She is described as a "big dark woman" with a "husky voiced contralto" (251). She nurses the protagonist after his industrial accident and provides him with a place to live. While Mary is the protagonist's only maternal figure, she is depicted as smothering and restrictive. She literally disappears from the text when the protagonist joins the Brotherhood, and does not reappear until hundreds of pages later, when the protagonist is running for his life and seeking a safe haven.

Ellison presents Mary as a typical "Mammy" figure, existing only to serve the needs of others. Like the other female characters in *Invisible Man*, we get very little sense of Mary's interior life: we never learn what motivates her to care for the protagonist. And like the "Mammy" stereotype, Mary is completely desexualized; we do not know if she had children and/or a husband. She is "invisible" to the protagonist as a real person and is, instead, a "stable, familiar force" that can be used and discarded (258).

It is Sybil, wife of one of the members of the Brotherhood, who epitomizes the opposite extreme of a "Mammy" figure; Sybil is a seductress/whore. Her only interest in the protagonist is based on racist assumptions about Black male sexuality. Sybil wants the protagonist to be her "big black bruiser" (522) and pretend to rape her—a game which reinforces the notion that only violence would persuade an honorable white "lady" to defile herself with a Black man.

Literary critic Ann Fowler Stanford points out that all of Ellison's female characters are extremes of a common duality: Women are either "madonnas or whores." Because this duality forces all the female characters to be one-dimensional, they are, in fact, rendered invisible. White women are portrayed as overtly sexual, and Black women, as represented by the "saintly" Mary, are desexualized.

Most all of the female characters in *Invisible Man* are victims of racism, sexism, or both, but there appears to be no space for them to step outside of their victim status. Whether "madonna" or "whore," the female characters are defined by their relationships to men, and thus never operate in an independent fashion. For example, Trueblood's wife Matty Lou and their daughter Kate can only be seen as victims of Trueblood's actions; he commits incest, he impregnates them both, and he insists that they remain with him. The two women are never allowed to tell their own stories.

Unless reading very closely, you can miss the operation of gender roles in *Invisible Man*. The novel is so powerful and the story of the protagonist is so compelling, it is easy to set aside concerns about the female characters. An important exercise for students would be to note all the female characters, and discuss why many of them are nameless. Students might also discuss the clear differences in the way that Black women are portrayed in contrast to the depictions of white women. If one of the major underlying themes of *Invisible Man* is the inability of white America to see/recognize Black men, then an examination of the role of women in the novel may prove the inability of men to see/recognize women. Perhaps, as literary critic Mary Rohrberger suggests, Ellison presents "stereotypes of women in an effort to call attention to the stereotypes" (132). The careful reader must decide in what places Ellison is critiquing the way gender functions and in what places he is falling into the trap of confining women to prescribed roles.

WORKS CITED

Ellison, Ralph. *Invisible Man* [1952]. New York: Vintage Books, 1989.

Rohrberger, Mary. "Ball the Jack: Surreality, Sexuality, and the Role of Women in *Invisible Man*." *Approaches to Teaching Ellison's* Invisible Man. Ed. Susan Resneck Parr and Pancho Savery. New York: Modern Language Association of America, 1989, 124–32.

Stanford, Anne Folwell. "He Speaks for Whom? Inscription and Reinscription of Women in *Invisible Man* and *The Salt Eaters*." *MELUS* 18.2 (Summer 1993): 17–31.

FOR FURTHER READING

Sundquist, Eric J. *Cultural Contexts for Ralph Ellison's* Invisible Man. New York: Bedford/St. Martin's, 1995.

Be True to Yourself:
Charlotte Brontë's *Jane Eyre* (1847)

Barbara Z. Thaden

Jane Eyre is a Cinderella story with a feminist twist. Overwhelmingly, the poor, plain orphan hears that she is entitled to nothing. But Jane insists on her right to make choices and seek satisfaction. With her will, intelligence, and perseverance, along with some good luck, she prevails. For this reason, Charlotte Brontë's most popular novel has been seen as a manifesto of a woman's right to the pursuit of happiness.

During Jane's progress through patriarchy, the women she meets illustrate a range of compromised responses to an unjust, patriarchal social system. Her Aunt Reed, a wealthy, imperious widow, is at the mercy of her 14-year-old son John, future owner of the estate. Georgiana Reed becomes an idle, empty-headed flirt, while Eliza despises pleasure, preferring miserliness and asceticism. At Lowood Institution, Helen Burns sacrifices her "self" completely, in imitation of Christ. To love her enemies, she must punish and deny herself. Miss Temple's actions, like Helen's, seem exemplary of the Christian virtues of temperance and mildness, characteristics expected and admired—then and, arguably, still now—in women much more than in men. At Thornfield, the rich mamas angle to catch the eligible Mr. Rochester as a son-in-law. Indeed, none of the women Jane meets (except possibly Diana and Mary Rivers) seek "to do more or learn more than custom has pronounced necessary for their sex" (96).

When Rochester proposes marriage to Jane, it seems that Jane, as well as Brontë's readers, will be drawn into convention: We enter a fairy-tale romance where the most deserving daughter is chosen by the prince. However, to Rochester's gifts and the suggestion of possession in his smile (236), Jane responds, quite unlike Cinderella, with fear about her anticipated transformation into "Mrs. Rochester": she begins to see that, married and dependent, she endangers her freedom, her integrity, and the inner "self" that originally attracted him.

Further disrupting the Cinderella parallel to this story, Brontë creates a "prince" who is not only already married, but who keeps his mad wife locked in the attic. As the current possessor of the position Jane covets, Bertha represents Jane's subconscious dread of marrying Rochester; Bertha's beastliness represents Jane's fear of sexuality and unrestrained passion; her imprisonment represents Jane's secret dread of being absorbed into Rochester's will. Examining the content and timing of scenes where Bertha appears to Jane (setting fire to Mr. Rochester's bed after he first flirts with the young governess; tearing Jane's bridal veil on the eve of her wedding), students will see other significant parallels between "the madwoman in the attic" and Jane Eyre: both are repeatedly associated with fire, likened to monsters, cast in animal imagery, and identified as "mad" (in its double meaning). As Sandra Gilbert and Susan Gubar speculate, Bertha functions symbolically as "the angry aspect of the orphan child" (360)—Jane's psychological double, whose behavior mirrors Jane's (and Brontë's) forbidden, repressed rage at and rebellion against social inequalities and sexual restraints which prevent women from realizing their fullest expression of self.

Questioning Jane's choosing to be poor and homeless rather than being Rochester's kept woman, students can discuss the extent to which her decision is motivated by Christian virtue and a desire to avoid sin, or by her desire to avoid entrapment at all costs. Yet, when Jane runs away from Thornfield, she becomes the object of another indomitable male will: St. John Rivers wants to own, control, and use Jane for his own purposes, insisting that she marry him for appearances' sake when they go abroad as missionaries. Jane then understands that a loveless marriage is more of a sacrilege to her than passion outside of marriage. St. John's power over her, like Rochester's, leads her almost to the point of capitulation (368). To provide historical context for Jane's dilemma (self-sacrifice or psychic self-preservation), teachers may want to point out that some early critics regarded Jane's desire for equality in marriage as un-Christian.

Rebelling against her "place" in society, and even against patriarchal religion itself when she refuses St. John's proposal, Jane asserts her right to follow her "call" as much as St. John does—her call to return and minister to Rochester. Escaping entrapment once again, Jane returns to Thornfield as a woman of inherited means, thus preparing the way (narratively speaking) for the romantic couple to reunite on terms of social parity. Twice remaining true to her values (turning down Rochester's first proposal, rejecting St. John), Jane is finally rewarded by an equal union with the man she loves. Her sudden wealth and his physical handicap seal their equality and interdependence.

Jane finally achieves her goal: passionate love and true friendship, not marriage to a husband who is only "a giver and a protector" (392) or a man who would mold, influence, and "retain [her] absolutely till death" (357). But students are likely to differ in their reactions to Jane's position at the novel's end: Has Brontë reduced her intelligent, passionate, and courageous heroine to an ordinary wife and mother? Has Jane achieved nothing but a woman's traditional place?

Jane may be considered a feminist for daring to hope for marriage on her terms, but some post-colonial critics have seen her as a white, middle-class woman concerned only with her own rights, despising or ignoring women of other races, cultures, and economic classes. For example, Jane tacitly accepts slavery, failing to protest that Rochester's wealth, and the wealth of the British Empire, flow from oppressed and enslaved colonies; she also suggests that it is degrading for her, but not for other women, to be servants. Students will enjoy discussing Jane's—and Brontë's—positions on social class, marriage, religion, and employment for women. Strikingly, feminists continue to struggle with exactly these issues at the beginning of the new millennium.

WORKS CITED

Brontë, Charlotte. *Jane Eyre* [1847]. 2nd ed. Ed. Richard J. Dunn. New York: Norton, 1987.

Gilbert, Sandra M. and Susan Gubar. *The Madwoman in the Attic: The Woman Writer and the Nineteenth-Century Literary Imagination*. New Haven, CT: Yale UP, 1979.

FOR FURTHER READING

Hoeveler, Diane Long and Beth Lau, eds. *Approaches to Teaching Brontë's* Jane Eyre. New York: Modern Language Association, 1993.

Teachman, Debra. *Understanding* Jane Eyre: *A Student Casebook to Issues, Sources, and Historical Documents*. Westport, CT: Greenwood, 2001.

"Thinking Different" in Amy Tan's
The Joy Luck Club (1989)

Cecile Mazzucco-Than

In *The Joy Luck Club* four pairs of mothers and daughters, An-mei Hsu and her daughter Rose, Lindo Jong and Waverly, Suyuan Woo and Jing-mei, and Ying-ying St. Claire and Lena, split along generational lines to form a cultural divide. E. D. Huntley calls this intersection between race and identity a "biculturalism" that exists in immigrant families and is characterized by the older generation remaining connected to their homeland's ancestral culture, alien to their children. The children, on the other hand, trapped between their heritage and their American upbringing, cannot escape into American culture because their appearance puts them outside the mainstream (70–71). "Thinking different," Suyuan's proud assessment of her daughter's willingness to go against society's conventional wisdom (208), represents a strategy for reconciliation between generations and empowerment of the younger generation to take control of their lives by embracing their bicultural identity.

Jing-mei must "think different" when, two months after Suyuan's death, she is asked to take her mother's place at the Joy Luck Club, the mothers' mahjong/investment club. Jing-mei worries that she cannot "be" her mother (27), but the aunts see her presence as an opportunity to reconnect with their own daughters by helping her realize An-mei's admonition, "your mother is in your bones!" (40). The aunts help her search her "bones," the DNA of her memories of and feelings toward her mother, by helping her reconstruct her mother's life story. Jing-mei brings closure by fulfilling her mother's wish to find the daughters she left behind in China, and her own wish to reconnect with her half-sisters and her Chinese self.

The mothers and daughters speak languages that differ on a metaphorical level, more deeply separated than are broken English and American slang. The daughters' stories are the alienating, materialistic, self-centered speech of young Americans. The daughters reject their mothers and their Chinese ways, as in Lena's ruse to get a metal lunchbox like her American classmates' instead of a worn paper bag (106), or Waverly's challenge to her mother: " 'Why do you have to use me to show off?' " (99). The mothers employ talk story narration, a mystical, fable-like, lyrical translation from their native Chinese, to tell their life stories, always offering morals that will help guide their daughters' lives.

That is, each woman is responsible for finding herself, a variation on Ying-ying's secret desire whispered to the Moon Lady: "I wished to be 'found' " (83). Lindo defines being found as "the day when I finally knew a genuine thought and could follow where it went" (66). Each woman finds herself when she puts her own ideas into words and actions and liberates herself and other women from societal expectations that keep them subservient. For the daughters, being found also means embracing their mothers' voices as sources of wisdom and love.

Each daughter presents a childhood story of defying a bullying mother by not living up to her expectations. This disobedience deepens into guilt and resentment and backfires in the adult daughters' lives as self-destructive behavior, such as marrying men because their mothers have disapproved. However, in the course of the novel, each daughter struggles to gain her mother's approval and their stories end with the possibility of understanding and reconciliation. On her thirtieth birthday, Jing-mei accepts the piano her mother insisted would make her a child prodigy. Rose finds the strength to deny the husband who left her for another woman by embracing the story of her mother, An-mei, who watched her own mother suffer as the concubine of a wealthy man. Readers find in the stories of mothers and daughters that the limitations society placed on women in the mothers' pre-1949 China are remarkably similar to those placed on women in the daughters' 1960s America.

Tan portrays the mothers as stereotypically overbearing until the daughters mature enough to understand them, according to critic Gloria Shen. Students might examine mother–daughter relationships in movies, books, or television shows from several eras and trace how a society's attitudes toward women determine the stereotype of good and bad mothers. The mother of Bette Davis' character in *Now, Voyager* represents the clichéd, domineering mother of the 1930s upper class. June Cleaver of the TV series *Leave It to Beaver* has become symbolic of the 1950s stay-at-home mom devoted to her family. In *Guess Who's Coming to Dinner*, Katherine Hepburn plays a unique upper-class mother bewildered by the 1960s, but tolerant of her daughter's interracial relationship. Students might also examine their relationships with their own mothers and compare and contrast mother–daughter relationships with mother–son relationships.

The mothers in *The Joy Luck Club* worry that language does not facilitate communication between generations, as Maria Heung points out, while Walter Shear makes a related point that the daughters lack the peer relationships that helped their mothers. Students might evaluate the experiences of immigrant women, keeping in mind the potential differences between women of various races, ethnicities, and eras. They might also consider comparing and contrasting the mother–daughter experiences of first- and second-generation Americans.

In *The Joy Luck Club*, mothers and daughters find themselves and each other by embracing their cultural and personal similarities and differences. Students might pick out the lessons from the stories, such as Lindo's "know your own worth and polish it" (254), and evaluate how such advice speaks to the daughters and to themselves. Students might also search their "bones" for signs of their mothers. This search goes beyond Waverly and her mother looking alike to how students have absorbed the gender and/or ethnic lessons their own mothers have transmitted to them.

WORKS CITED

Heung, Maria. "Daughter-Text/Mother-Text: Matrilineage in Amy Tan's *The Joy Luck Club*." *Feminist Studies* 19.3 (Fall 1993): 597–613.

Huntley, E. D. *Amy Tan: A Critical Companion*. Westport, CT: Greenwood, 1998.

Shear, Walter. "Generational Differences and the Diaspora in *The Joy Luck Club*." *Critique* 34.3 (Spring 1993): 193–200.

Shen, Gloria. "Born of a Stranger: Mother-Daughter Relationships and Storytelling in Amy Tan's *The Joy Luck Club*." *International Women's Writing: New Landscapes of Identity*. Ed. Anne E. Brown and Marjanne Gooze. Westport, CT: Greenwood, 1995, 233–44.

Tan, Amy. *The Joy Luck Club*. New York: Putnam, 1989.

FOR FURTHER READING

Braendlin, Bonnie. "Mother/Daughter Dialog(ic)s in, around and about Amy Tan's *The Joy Luck Club*." *Private Voices, Public Lives: Women Speak on the Literary Life*. Ed. Nancy Owen Nelson. Denton, TX: U of North Texas P, 1996, 111–24.

Wong, Sau-Ling Cynthia. "Sugar Sisterhood: Situating the Amy Tan Phenomenon." *The Ethnic Canon: Histories, Institutions, and Interventions*. Ed. David Palumbo-Liu. Minneapolis: U of Minnesota P, 1995, 174–210.

Gender Bending: Ursula Le Guin's
The Left Hand of Darkness (1969)

Marianne Pita

In Ursula Le Guin's futuristic science fiction tale, *The Left Hand of Darkness*, Genli Ai, a man from earth, has been sent as envoy to the planet Gethen, where human beings are androgynous and bisexual. He finds it difficult to relate to the Gethenians because they have no fixed gender. Unable to transcend the categories of male and female, Genli is forced to see a Gethenian as first a man and then a woman. He suffers from culture shock because he is a man among people who are hermaphrodites. His own gender stereotypes are rigid, and he looks down on women as kind, but prying, ignoble, unable to mobilize, and not given to abstraction. In many ways, Genli is caught up in maintaining standards of manliness.

Genli Ai's views expose the rigid gender stratification in our world. When he is asked if women are a different species than men, he answers:

> The most important thing, the heaviest single factor in one's life, is whether one's born male or female. In most societies it determines one's expectations, activities, outlook, ethics, manners—almost everything. Vocabulary. Semiotic usages. Clothing. Even food. . . . It's extremely hard to separate the innate differences from the learned ones. (234)

Teachers might first ask students for examples of how gender influences or determines various aspects of behavior in their own community, starting with Genli's list. Students can also debate whether these differences are due to genetics, socialization, or both. Like the narrator, some students may initially find it difficult to think outside the binary of male and female. To some students, the blurring of customary sexual and gender roles on Gethen may be humorous—as for instance, when the king gets pregnant—or even repulsive, like the physical appearance of Gethenians midway between male and female. Le Guin's provocative fantasy of human sexual interaction devoid of conventional gender constraints invites impressionable readers to examine, along with Genli Ai, some of their own unquestioned opinions concerning "appropriate" male and female behavior.

On Gethen, anyone from seventeen to around thirty-five years old can be tied down by childbearing and breastfeeding, so no one is permanently assigned a caretaking role, physically or psychologically. There is no discrimination based on gender; in fact, "there is no division of humanity into strong and weak halves, protective/protected, dominant/submissive, owner/chattel, active/passive" (95). Students may find this notion liberating.

Because of the nature of sex on Gethen, there can be no rape and even seduction depends on timing. Only two consenting individuals in heat, or *kemmer*, can have intercourse. (Pairing is the most common, but orgies are not unusual, taking place in *kemmerhouses*. At the other extreme, two people may vow *kemmering*, the equivalent of marriage.) Sexuality is latent five-sixths of the time, and then fully indulged, so that sexual frustration is extremely rare. Young adults will probably be extremely interested in the issues of sexuality raised in this book. The vision of a world with no danger of sexual violence is intriguing although the idea that sexual frustration causes sexual violence is debatable. To examine this idea, students might analyze news articles or personal stories about sexual harassment, discussing what social dynamics contribute to such incidents and what are some damaging effects.

To the Gethenians, Genli is a sexual freak because he is a man. On Gethen about 3 percent of adults are perverts, like him. Because of a hormonal imbalance, they are in heat all the time and have a permanent gender. Perverts are tolerated but looked down on, like sexual minorities in the United States. Genli's friend Estraven is baffled by his masculine peculiarities, like the difficulty he has crying. Teachers can exploit this shift in cultural viewpoint to help move students beyond their initial distaste for the bizarre appearance, gender, and sexual behavior of the Gethenians. Perversion depends on point of view, and from the Gethenian perspective, traditional gender and sexual roles are perverse. With this in mind, homophobia and even heterosexuality can be challenged as culturally biased.

Genli Ai goes through a sort of conversion as he gradually begins to accept the Gethenians for who they are, neither male nor female, but human. For example, he recognizes that "the parental instinct, the wish to protect, to further, is not a sex-linked characteristic" (100). On a trip across the tundra, dependent on a Gethenian friend, Genli begins to recognize that he is locked into his own virility and must let go of some of the more competitive aspects of masculinity if he is to survive in this harsh world. From a feminist per-

spective, teachers may want to facilitate an analysis of how adaptive traditional masculine or feminine behaviors are in the novel and in students' own
cultural milieus. For example, in a boys' high school locker room, it may be
adaptive to play the traditional male role, but in what other settings would
the same behavior be ill-suited to the context? Students can explore how they
put on and take off different versions of their identities (speech, appearance,
even beliefs) in different situations, and in particular how they bend their own
gender training to fit a specific occasion.

Genli's final realization is that human beings are both masculine and feminine, like the Chinese symbol for yin and yang. As Ursula Le Guin writes in
her introduction, "If you look at us at certain odd times of day, in certain
weathers, we already are [androgynous]." Reading *The Left Hand of Darkness*
can help teachers and students challenge the notions of "normal" and "perverse" in gender and sexuality in order to question tenacious assumptions and
thus imagine a conception of the human that is deeper than either male or
female.

WORK CITED

Le Guin, Ursula. *The Left Hand of Darkness* [1969]. New York: Ace, 1976.

FOR FURTHER READING

Fayad, Mona. "Aliens, Androgynes, and Anthropology: Le Guin's Critique of Representation in *The Left Hand of Darkness*." *Mosaic* 30 (September 1997): 59–
73.
Rudy, Kathy. "Ethics, Reproduction, Utopia: Gender and Childbearing in *Women on
the Edge of Time* and *The Left Hand of Darkness*." *NWSA Journal* 9.1 (Spring
1997): 22–37.

What a Teacher Learns:
Ernest J. Gaines' *A Lesson Before Dying* (1993)

Elise Ann Earthman

The central question in Ernest J. Gaines' *A Lesson Before Dying* is both simple and profound: What does it mean to be a man? And more particularly, what does it mean to be an African-American man in the Deep South of the late 1940s? Through the struggles of schoolteacher Grant Wiggins—to please his Tante Lou and her friend Miss Emma, to retain his dignity in the face of white oppression, to break through to condemned prisoner Jefferson, to find peace with his girlfriend—students can grapple with the ways in which not only gender but also race has been socially constructed.

Grant, a man in his late twenties, seethes with anger and despair. He hates his job teaching the children of his poor community but sees no other options. Brimming with frustration after six years, believing that his efforts make no difference in these students' lives, he takes out his anger on the children, acting the petty tyrant, terrorizing them with small cruelties. A bad teacher who knows it and hates himself for it, Grant feels powerless to improve his students' prospects or change his situation. Indeed, he fears that the dismal advice of his own teacher may be right: "Just do the best you can. But it won't matter" (66), because sooner or later, the situation "will make you the nigger you were born to be" (65).

Grant's anger grows as his elderly Tante Lou, who raised him, and Miss Emma present him with what seems a near-impossible demand: to go up to the jailhouse and teach the slow-witted young Jefferson, Miss Emma's godchild, to die like a man. Innocent of the crime for which he has been sentenced, in his own despair Jefferson has accepted his defense lawyer's public depiction of him as a fool, "a thing that acts on command" (7), a "hog" whom it makes little sense to put to death in the electric chair. Miss Emma is adamant about what she wants: "I don't want them to kill no hog . . . I want a man to go to that chair, on his own two feet" (13). Grant chafes against the role of teacher that Tante Lou and Miss Emma have defined for him (13), arguing that he cannot undo what twenty-one years have done to Jefferson, but his protests fall on deaf ears. Grant understands what their request will cost his sense of himself as a Black man, and his fears are realized. He endures entering Pichot's house through the back door—to ask permission to see Jefferson in his cell— and being kept waiting, standing—for two and one-half hours until Mr. Pichot brings the Sheriff back to the kitchen to talk to him. His mission becomes the subject of spirited wagering among the white men there, who don't believe Grant can get Jefferson ready to die. He must be searched when he goes to the jail, must humbly say, "Yes, sir," at the appropriate time, must not appear smarter than a Black man "should" be at that time and in that place. He fears that what Tante Lou and Miss Emma want from him will break him, just as the other Black men in his community have been broken. Although he under-stands the desire of women in his community to reverse the cycle of Black men who have "failed to protect [their] women since the time of slavery" (166), he resents their clinging to him, because he is an educated man, because he is *there*.

Turning to Vivian, the woman in his life, Grant cries out, "Do I know what a man is? Do I know how a man is supposed to die? I'm still trying to find out how a man should live" (31). Yet through his struggles with Jefferson, Grant learns to live like a man, even as Jefferson learns to die like a man. Ironically, the "impossible" demands that the older women make enable Grant to finally transcend the limitations that being a Black man in 1940s Louisiana imposes on him. Indeed, the women in the novel set conditions for the growth of both Grant and Jefferson, showing "the direct influence of women on a mature man" (Gaudet 152). Tante Lou and Miss Emma, in getting Grant to go to Jefferson in jail, exert the iron will that has allowed them to survive. Vivian, in a relationship of equals, offers Grant comfort and strength when he feels he can't go on, and a mature love that helps show him the way to peace within himself, to understanding that he is so much more than what the white world has defined him to be. In class, students could examine exactly what it is Tante Lou, Emmy, and Vivian say and do that influences and sup-ports Grant—and enables him to empower Jefferson—"without compromis-ing the dignity or integrity of either gender" (Gaudet 152).

Jefferson's final words in his journal—"good by mr wigin tell them im strong tell them im a man good by mr wigin" (234)—reveal the effect that Grant has had on Jefferson's life, as does the deputy Paul's testimony: "[Jef-ferson] was the bravest man in the room today. I was a witness, Grant Wig-gins" (256). But Grant's life has been positively affected as well; he has learned to focus on the student rather than on himself, to feel and show empathy, to apologize, and to cry. What characterizes a strong man? A strong woman? Teachers might ask this question to elicit students' responses to Grant's gradual transformation and to the women who have supported his growth. Although some of Grant's emotional reactions are stereotyped as feminine qualities, *A Lesson Before Dying* clearly shows that they are an essential part of a man as well.

WORKS CITED

Gaines, Ernest J. *A Lesson Before Dying* [1993]. New York: Vintage, 1997.

Gaudet, Marcia. "Black Women: Race, Gender, and Culture in Gaines' Fiction." *Critical Reflections on the Fiction of Ernest J. Gaines*. Ed. David C. Estes. Athens: U of Georgia P, 1994, 139–57.

FOR FURTHER READING

Auger, Philip. "A Lesson about Manhood: Appropriated 'The Word' in Ernest Gaines's *A Lesson Before Dying*." *Southern Literary Journal* 27 (1995): 74–85.

Jones, Suzanne W. "Reconstructing Manhood: Race, Masculinity, and Narrative Closure in Ernest Gaines's *A Gathering of Old Men* and *A Lesson Before Dying*." *Masculinities* 3.2 (1995): 43–66.

The Foreignness of Femininity in Joseph Conrad's *Lord Jim* (1900)

Laura McPhee

Reading Joseph Conrad's *Lord Jim* with the goal of examining gender roles can at first appear to be a daunting enterprise. Women do not enter the story until Chapter 28, more than two-thirds through the book. The scant attention given to women in this novel and the subservient role of the only major female character can combine to make *Lord Jim* a discouraging text for female readers. Because narrative bias is the key to understanding the foreignness of femininity in the novel, a close look at the telling of the story will help students to analyze the feminine—even in its absence—and to question whether honor, attributed to men only, can have meaning for women as well. A discussion of narrative bias will also provide insight in analyzing themes of racism and imperialism.

While an omniscient third-person narrator frames the text, the story told by Marlow takes up most of the novel. Rather than simply reading the novel as the story of "Lord Jim," readers should identify: (1) the setting in which the tale is told (after dinner where only men are present); (2) the gender of the speaker (male); (3) the gender of the audience (male); (4) the dominant theme of masculine pride and honor. These four elements create a context for male narrative bias and the exclusion of women. Marlow, Jim, and the assumed audience for Marlow's oration are sailors who by occupational choice have chosen the sea over traditional family life. Women are perhaps more foreign to them than the distant lands to which they sail.

Although women are literally absent from the lives of the men, and from most of the novel, there is a metaphorical or figurative female presence throughout the story. With this in mind, the foreignness of femininity can be explored as students examine how the feminine is represented in the near-absence of female characters. For example, the *Patna* and other ships are referred to as "she," and so is the earth itself. Students may wish to consider why the men describe the earth and sea in feminine terms and how it may relate to their attitudes toward women. Other feminine metaphors, such as Marlow's description of the opportunities awaiting Jim in Patusan as sitting "veiled by his side like an Eastern bride" (158), can also be used to construct and define a feminine presence in the absence of women. Students can examine how and why men living apart from women use feminine pronouns to describe such forces as fate and nature. Students will discover power relationships of dominance and subordination that occur throughout the novel: men/women, man/nature, English/native.

Very few women are given significant treatment in this novel: Jewel, who becomes Jim's wife and touches Marlow with her "pretty beauty . . . her pathetic pleading, her helplessness" (200), native chief Doramin's "little motherly witch of a wife" (177), and Jewel's dead mother "with tragic or perhaps only a pitiful history" (142). It is Conrad's Jewel who presents challenges to many twenty-first-century students. Marlow describes her as so devoted to Jim, the man she loves, that she is "ready to make a footstool of her head for his feet" (183). Following this kind of description and Marlow's attribution of weak character to all women, some students may simply dismiss her. However, those who recognize the filter of Marlow's male bias in his characterization of Jewel and are aware of the social and literary history of the "tragic mulatresse" as an exotic and romanticized female archetype may construct an identity for Jewel apart from Marlow's version. In doing so, they can compare Marlow's description of Jewel with her brief appearance at Stein's house near the novel's end, where she demonstrates more power and intelligence than Marlow's previous narrative had given her credit for.

The near-absence of women from the lives of the main characters does not mean that female readers must feel excluded from the novel, despite Joseph Conrad's claim that he made due allowances for the novel's subject "being rather foreign to women's normal sensibilities" (viii). Conrad and, by extension, Marlow, assume that women will not understand the novel's code of male honor. Yet, by comparing Jim's actions and Jewel's reactions as a woman, female and male students alike can resist Marlow's assumption and consider for themselves whether Jewel's ideas are inferior, as Marlow implies. Looking outside of the novel, students may also speculate whether gender differences exist in concepts of honor, deciding whether the distinctions they perceive are rendered fairly in Conrad's novel.

There are striking assumptions about difference in *Lord Jim*. The novel treats both women and people of color as if their differences from white European men are biological in nature. Students can assess the problems that arise when social differences are treated like natural distinctions. Deciding whether

Jim chooses honor over family in coming to Patusan and in choosing to die can also foster a discussion of whether Jim is "one of us," as constantly claimed by Marlow. Students might decide who "us" is—how the distinctions are made based upon gender, race, and occupation—and how the exclusion of others shapes the sailors' attitudes and worldview.

Teachers should encourage students to determine divisions based on gender, race, and other common traits in the novel and in their own lives and communities. Connections to issues of loyalty, honor, work, and family will be relevant as readers discover their own codes of honor, as well as what kinds of choices these codes demand. These types of connections will help in making *Lord Jim* a relevant text to all readers. It may not be easy for most female readers to overcome the near-exclusion of their sex and the hardly compensatory descriptions of the women who do make brief appearances. Students may also struggle with the blatant racist and imperialist attitudes shown by the novel's characters, particularly the narrator Marlow. Engagement will come by equipping readers with an awareness of narrative bias from the outset, and then challenging them to understand the novel's gendered and racist portrayal of honor and family.

WORK CITED

Conrad, Joseph. *Lord Jim* [1900]. New York: Bantam Classic, 1981.

FOR FURTHER READING

Kuehn, Robert E., ed. *Twentieth Century Interpretations of* Lord Jim. Englewood Cliffs, NJ: Prentice Hall, 1969.

Boys' Club—No Girls Allowed: Absence as Presence in William Golding's *Lord of the Flies* (1954)

Paula Alida Roy

William Golding's *Lord of the Flies* is peopled entirely by boys and, briefly, adult men. The absence of girls and women, however, does not prohibit interrogating this text for evidence of sexism/gender bias. We might begin by questioning the implicit assumptions about male violence and competitiveness that permeate Golding's Hobbesian vision. Today's sociobiologists will embrace these boys, whose aggressive reversion to savagery "proves" the power of testosterone-fueled behavior. In fact, one approach to studying this novel could involve research into the rash of books and articles about male violence, about raising and educating boys. Teachers might ask if or how this story would be different if girls had been on the island. Complementary books about girls include *John Dollar* by Marianne Wiggins, and *Shelter* by Joyce Anne Phillips. More interesting, however, is the text itself, in which the very absence of girls or women underscores how *feminine* or *female* stands in sharp contrast to *masculine* or *male* in Golding's island world.

The three major characters, Ralph, Jack, and Piggy, form a sort of continuum of attitudes toward life as it develops on the island in relation to their past memories of "civilized" British boarding school. Ralph and Jack are both masculine boys, handsome, fit, strong. Piggy, on the other hand, is fat, asthmatic, and physically weak. Jack, the choir leader, enters equipped with a gang; the development of this group from choirboys to hunters and Jack's deterioration from strong leader to cruel tyrant offer opportunities to look at male bonding and group violence, especially when we examine rape imagery in the language of the sow-killing scene. Ralph enters the book first, alone, and develops as the individualist who struggles to maintain some sort of order amid the growing chaos.

Piggy is the pivotal character: Not only do his glasses ignite sparks for the signal fire, but it is also he who defines the role of the conch in calling assemblies and he who insists on reminding the other boys over and over again of the world of manners and civility back home. Of the three boys, in fact of all the boys, only Piggy makes constant reference to a maternal figure—his "auntie," the woman raising him. We hear no reference to Jack's mother and we learn that Ralph's mother went away when he was very young. Some of the littl'uns cry at night for their mothers, but in general, only Piggy makes repeated and specific reference to a mother figure as an influence on him.

As Golding sets up the influence of Piggy's "auntie," we see that it is a mixed message about women. On the one hand, Piggy offers important reminders of civilized behavior and serves as a strong influence on and later the only support of Ralph in his efforts to keep order. On the other hand, Piggy's weakness and whining seem to be the result of the feminizing influence of his "auntie." He is, in fact, a somewhat feminized figure himself, in the negative stereotypical sense of physical softness, fearfulness, nagging. The early homoerotic connection between Ralph and Jack is underscored by Jack's jealousy of Piggy, his sarcastic derision of Ralph's concern for the weaker boy. Piggy's nickname, in fact, links him to the doomed pigs on the island, most notably the sow killed in a parody of rape by the hunters "wedded to her in lust," who "collapsed under them and they were heavy and fulfilled upon her" (154). The identification of Piggy with the slaughtered pigs is made explicit in Piggy's death scene: "Piggy's arms and legs twitched a bit, like a pig's after it has been killed" (209). If Piggy and the sow are the only female or feminized creatures on the island, then we can see that the one is useful only for meat and as a totemic figure and the other, the fat asthmatic boy, serves as scapegoat, victim first of ridicule, then physical abuse, and finally murder at the hands of the now savage boys under Jack's command. To the extent that he chooses to remain with Piggy, to hang on to elements of civilization, Ralph too becomes a hunted victim, "rescued" only by the appearance of the naval officer, Golding's ironic personification of adult male violence dressed up in a formal officer's uniform.

Searching the text itself, we find the female pronoun applied only to Piggy's auntie and to the sow. There are very few references to mothers, none to other women such as sisters or grandmothers. There is only one specific and direct mention of girls, quite late in the novel, when Ralph and Piggy and Sam and Eric seek to clean themselves up in preparation for a visit to Jack's camp where they plan to make a reasonable attempt to help Piggy recover his stolen glasses. Piggy insists on carrying the conch with them, and Ralph wants them to bathe: "We'll be like we were. We'll wash" (199). When he suggests they comb their hair "only it's too long," Piggy says, "we could find some stuff . . . and tie your hair back." Eric replies, "Like a girl!" (199). That single reference stands, along with the references to Piggy's auntie and the contrast set up by the absence of all other female figures, to identify the female with "civilization," ineffectual, far away, and dangerously weak. To return to the details of the rape-murder of the great sow, it is important to note that the sow is a mother figure, "sunk in deep maternal bliss," nursing her litter of piglets. The rape/murder of the sow and the final murder of Piggy suggest that the final movement into savagery involves the killing and defiling of the maternal female. Golding would not be the first to identify the female with attempts to control or tame male violence; he concludes that the female is unsuccessful because she is too weak, flawed, flesh-bound to overcome the ingenuity, craftiness, and sheer brutality of male violence.

Golding's Hobbesian view of human nature carries with it a whiff of misogyny or at least a suspicion that what women represent has little impact, finally, on culture or civilization. The island is a boys' club shaped by the theme of "boys will be boys" when left to their own devices. Obviously allegorical, the novel invites the reader to consider the absence of girls as a symbolic presence and the perils of ultramasculinity.

WORK CITED

Golding, William. *Lord of the Flies.* New York: Riverhead Books, 1954.

FOR FURTHER READING

Kindlon, Dan and Michael Thompson with Teresa Barker. *Raising Cain: Protecting the Emotional Life of Boys.* New York: Ballantine, 1999.

Unnatural: Women in William Shakespeare's *Macbeth* (ca. 1606)

Elizabeth Klett

Macbeth has a woman as a leading character, making it unusual among Shakespeare's great tragedies. Often labeled an "unnatural" woman because she manipulates her husband into killing the king and seizing his crown, Lady Macbeth is allied with the three witches: they all represent the feminine forces of darkness that turn Macbeth to murder. Lady Macbeth stands in strong contrast to Lady Macduff, the good wife and devoted mother. But such characterizations are overly simplistic and do not portray the complexities of Shakespeare's script. The women in *Macbeth* are all, to varying degrees, "unnatural," not because they are necessarily evil, but because they critique their roles, either directly or indirectly, in an oppressive patriarchal world.

Set in medieval Scotland, the play depicts a violent society in which gender roles are rigidly defined: men are judged by their ability in combat, and women by their docility and obedience. Conformity to these roles is of utmost importance, as demonstrated by the character progressions of Macbeth and Lady Macbeth. Although a soldier, Macbeth shows himself, initially, to be weak-willed and conscience-stricken about the deadly deed. Lady Macbeth takes the more "manly" role, providing an example of courage and resolve that he must follow if he wants to fulfill his desires. Yet as the play continues, Macbeth becomes cold, remorseless, and emotionally dead, a caricature of the violent warrior-king. Conversely, Lady Macbeth gradually falls apart, consumed by guilt, and eventually commits suicide.

Given the stark split between masculine and feminine behavior in this world, it is not surprising that Lady Macbeth's main persuasive tactic is to question her husband's manhood. "When you durst do it, then you were a man," she rebukes him as he vacillates over the murder, "And to be more than what you were, you would / Be so much more the man" (1.7.49–51). Later, when Macbeth sees Banquo's ghost at the banquet and, in his terror, seems inclined to give away their secret, Lady Macbeth scornfully says, "What, quite unmanned in folly?" (3.4.74). She dares him to remain a coward.

Lady Macbeth herself does not conform to feminine stereotypes. Rather, she renounces her femininity in order to commit the murder. In her first soliloquy, she calls on dark spirits to "unsex" her so that she can be cruel and merciless (1.5.42). Later, she tells Macbeth that she would forsake motherly instincts and murder her own child if necessary to prove her devotion and courage (1.7.54–59). Her famous, uncompromising declaration often obstructs readers' sympathies with Lady Macbeth. Most often, she is considered only as a "fiend-like queen" (5.8.69)—forcing an otherwise reluctant Macbeth into murder. Yet is this common interpretation entirely fair? Certainly, a somewhat sympathetic reader might see Lady Macbeth as the one who can nudge an already eager Macbeth toward the deadly deed. Above all, as a woman of ambition living in a patriarchal world that allows no outlet for her intelligence, she becomes motivated to seize power through her husband. Thus, Lady Macbeth must act and think "like a man" because good women are by definition subservient, and can exert no recognizable authority.

The presence of Lady Macduff echoes this theme. She represents everything feminine and passive that Lady Macbeth is not. Confined to the domestic sphere in her one scene, Lady Macduff cannot prevent either her own death or the slaughter of her young son. Yet in her brief appearance, she offers a meaningful commentary on gender roles: She argues that Macduff "wants the natural touch" that would make him care more about protecting his family than his king (4.2.9). Moreover, she realizes that her only "womanly defence [is] / To say I have done no harm" (79–80), and bitterly articulates the precarious position of women in a world focused exclusively on the acquisition of power through violence.

Lady Macduff and Lady Macbeth can be discussed as "unnatural" women in different ways: the former in terms of her straightforward criticism of patriarchy, and the latter in explicit acts that renounce traditional notions of femininity and her implicit critique of women's powerlessness. Both characters demonstrate the rigid gender roles of medieval Scottish society. The three witches round out the play's "unnatural" female perspectives. They are, quite literally, unwomanly because they have beards (1.3.46), and frightening not only because of their magical powers, but also because their physical sex cannot be determined absolutely. Like Lady Macbeth, the witches have become subject to a major interpretive question: Do they control Macbeth's actions, or do they simply suggest to him what might happen?

Performing scenes can be a useful tool to get students thinking about alternate approaches to imagining these female characters. Doing scene work that includes the witches (see, especially, 1.3.1–88 and 4.1.1–134) becomes particularly challenging if the three parts are played in different ways. Teachers might have students analyze how Shakespeare's witches compare to widely held medieval beliefs about witches as consorts of the Devil, asking how that idea of women's inherently evil nature has influenced the position of women, then and even now. Interested students could also contrast such beliefs that link women and evil with our own culture's reactions to contemporary practices of witchcraft. In performance, students should be challenged to enact these roles so that the characterization moves beyond stereotypical, cackling old crones.

Film clips facilitate comparison of various, well-known interpretations of Shakespeare's lead characters. Most often, Lady Macbeth has been played as either an "Iron Maiden" type (as in Orson Welles' 1946 film) or as young and sensual (as in Roman Polanski's 1971 version). In response, students might consider why these two approaches are most commonly taken, and how opposing interpretations of his wife would affect an actor's playing of Macbeth. The two films also present contrasting witches: Welles' as mysterious figures who control Macbeth with a voodoo doll, and Polanski's as vagrant women whose power is less clearly defined. Additionally, Trevor Nunn's 1979 TV film provides an important interpretive tool, with Dame Judi Dench as a complex and provocative Lady Macbeth. By engaging with the women of *Macbeth* through fresh interpretations in text, film, and performance, students can appreciate their unique perspectives on the story and decide for themselves the degree to which these women seem "unnatural."

WORK CITED

Shakespeare, William. *Macbeth* [ca. 1606]. Ed. Sylvan Barnet. Signet Classic Shakespeare. New York: Penguin, 1987.

FOR FURTHER READING

Adelman, Janet. " 'Born of Woman': Fantasies of Maternal Power in *Macbeth*." *Shakespearean Tragedy and Gender*. Ed. Shirley Nelson Garner and Madelon Sprengnether. Bloomington: Indiana UP, 1996, 105–34.

Lenz, Carolyn Ruth, Gayle Greene, and Carol Thomas Neely. *The Woman's Part: Feminist Criticism of Shakespeare*. Urbana: U of Illinois P, 1980.

Newman, Karen. "Discovering Witches: Sorciographics." *Fashioning Femininity and English Renaissance Drama*. Chicago: U of Chicago P, 1991, 51–70.

Rutter, Carol et al. "Lady Macbeth's Barren Sceptre." *Clamorous Voices: Shakespeare's Women Today*. Ed. Faith Evans. New York: Routledge, 1989, 53–72.

Emma Rouault Bovary: Gendered Reflections in *Madame Bovary* by Gustave Flaubert (1857)

Eileen Burchell

Madame Bovary was published to critical acclaim and public scandal during Second Empire France (1852–1870). Government censors cited the novel for offending public morality and religion, though prosecution and defense both acknowledged the artist's achievement. Flaubert was tried and acquitted for a compelling portrait of his heroine's unhappy marriage, adulterous love affairs, financial ruin, and suicide. The creation of a powerful and profoundly conflicted male imagination, Emma Rouault Bovary is a polarizing figure. She embodies yet challenges archetypal images of women (virgin/mother, madonna/whore, angel/siren) arising from male experience. She calls into question education, marriage, and motherhood, institutions that inculcate these dichotomous views of women. To provide contrast with Flaubert's depiction, students might identify (or teachers might assign) other novels about adultery. Discussion could focus on how the adulterer's gender influences reader response and critical reception, as it does in *Madame Bovary*.

Emma's story is framed by Charles Bovary's story (Prince 88). The title of the novel defines Emma by social function and emphasizes how her identity derives from that of her husband. Susan L. Wolf underscores how "the boy's tale may be held out as the model . . . of childhood experience under which the little girl's story is subsumed and thus erased" (35). It is the men throughout Emma's life who mirror societal norms. She sees herself in the eyes of father, husband, and lovers, internalizing their values and judging her worth accordingly.

The daughter of an improvident, widowed farmer from Normandy, Emma receives a convent education in Rouen, intended for girls well above her social station. Acting to reinforce bourgeois norms, the Ursuline sisters try to socialize her to be an obedient daughter, faithful wife, and loving mother. Her role as housekeeper is idealized to compensate for lack of power in the public realm where she cannot divorce, travel freely, or vote. As Emma's imagination and sensuality develop in adolescence, she is taught to repress sexual desire in imitation of the Virgin Mary. Her surrogate mothers portray marriage as the only outlet for emotional and physical satisfaction. Money becomes a metaphor of forbidden sexual desire, seen later in Emma's consumerism.

After her mother's death, Emma turns to romance novels in search of female role models to mirror her identity and aspirations. "She would have liked to live in some old manor house, like those long-waisted chatelaines who . . . spent their days leaning on the stone . . . watching a white-plumed knight galloping on his black horse from the distant fields" (26). As a young female reader of works written primarily by men, Emma unconsciously identifies with male romantic views of women that legitimize male agency and female passivity. This experience serves to oppress rather than empower her. Adolescent readers of *Madame Bovary* might make a list of women with whom Emma identifies and compare/contrast them with role models for young people today. Similarly, students might be asked to list novels that have influenced them, and then to examine encoded messages about gender roles for men and women.

As daughter, wife, mistress, and mother, Emma continually comes into conflict with men's images of her and experiences guilt for not living up to impossible male-centered ideals. In her father's eyes, Emma is an eccentric girl whose fanciful notions—like the desire for a midnight candlelight wedding—make her a sentimental dreamer of little use for farm work. Marriage to the widowed country health officer Charles Bovary seems to promise escape. Charles sees Emma as a beautiful, accomplished hostess who could manage his household, raise their children, and help build his medical practice. Yet the stark contrast between the wearisome mediocrity of provincial life and the elegant aristocratic ball that Emma and Charles attend at the château of Vaubyessard disillusions her. She wonders bitterly: "Why, for heaven's sake did I marry" (31).

Rodolphe Boulanger and Léon Dupuis play on romantic clichés to seduce Emma. Rodolphe declares, "In my soul you are as a madonna on a pedestal . . . my angel" (115). Emma thinks back to the novels she has read and "adulterous women began to sing in her memory with the voice of sisters . . . she saw herself among those lovers she had so envied, she fulfilled the love-dream of her youth" (117). Emma later turns to Rodolphe in desperation for money to pay her debts, "unaware that she was hastening to offer what had so angered her a while ago, not in the least conscious of her prostitution" (225). Léon Dupuis is flattered to pursue and possess a chic mistress, yet he comes to view Emma as overbearing in her sexual and emotional demands. Léon's mother warns her son against "that vague and terrible creature, the siren, the fantastic monster which makes its home in the treacherous depths of love" (210–11). As the couple wearies of each other, "Emma found again in adultery all the platitudes of marriage" (211).

Many critics have emphasized what a rejecting and inadequate mother Emma is but fail to examine androcentric norms of motherhood and marriage (Danahy 137). When Emma asserts her need for authentic self-fulfillment, she is labeled selfish, hysterical, and extravagant. Her suicide by arsenic attests to her extreme self-denial and desperate sense of failure. Students might search *Madame Bovary* for the "shoulds" and "shouldn'ts" Emma attempts to observe. They might examine how gendered norms shape social roles and how "breaking the rules" has different consequences for men than for women. They might also explore the novel for gender ambiguity. Charles Baudelaire, poet and contemporary of Flaubert, thought that Emma was "almost masculine and that, perhaps unconsciously, the author had bestowed on her all the qualities of manliness" (Baudelaire 340).

Just as Emma is the object of masculine gaze, she also experiences linguistic alienation. Flaubert used a technique called free indirect style, hailed as a remarkable breakthrough in objective narration in the nineteenth-century novel. However, students should examine passages in *Madame Bovary* where the narrator appropriates Emma's voice to the extent that it is impossible to know who is speaking. Flaubert's narrator is neither neutral nor objective in ironically judging the protagonist. Similarly, much of the literary criticism on *Madame Bovary* provides less than a balanced view of this complex protagonist because of its own gender bias and failure to acknowledge the archetypal tensions underlying the gender bias in the text (Danahy 153).

"Bovaryism" denotes the inability to see oneself accurately. Yet, Emma Rouault Bovary's story reflects the dilemma of many women who live with, and die without understanding, the contradictory messages they receive about themselves in a society incapable of resolving them.

WORKS CITED

Baudelaire, Charles. "*Madame Bovary*, by Gustave Flaubert." *Gustave Flaubert*, Madame Bovary. Ed. Paul de Man. New York: Norton, 1965, 336–43.

Danahy, Michael. *The Feminization of the Novel*. Gainesville: U of Florida P, 1991.

Flaubert, Gustave. *Madame Bovary* [1857]. Ed. and Trans. Paul de Man. New York/ London: Norton, 1965.

Prince, Gerald. "A Narratological Approach to *Madame Bovary*." *Approaches to Teaching Flaubert's* Madame Bovary. Ed. Laurence M. Porter and Eugene F. Gray. New York: Modern Language Association, 1995, 84–89.

Wolf, Susan L. "The Same or (M)Other: A Feminist Reading of *Madame Bovary*." Porter and Gray 34–41.

FOR FURTHER READING

Donaldson-Evans, Mary. "Teaching *Madame Bovary* through Film." *Approaches to Teaching Flaubert's* Madame Bovary. Ed. Laurence M. Porter and Eugene F. Gray. New York: Modern Language Association, 1995, 114–21.

The Road to Nowhere: Stephen Crane's *Maggie: A Girl of the Streets* (*A Story of New York*) (1893)

Marsha Orgeron

Stephen Crane's *Maggie: A Girl of the Streets* depicts the struggles of the working poor to survive in an environment that appears determined to trap its inhabitants in eternal ugliness and despair. Crane's portrayal of women is of particular interest; despite its bleakness, the novel is replete with characterizations that will enable discussions of the ways that gender identity has been represented, perceived, stereotyped, and even caricatured. Crane wrote about the kinds of characters that had been neglected in the "polite fiction" of the nineteenth century, affording contemporary readers the opportunity to analyze women who are clearly caught in a cycle of violence and gloom.

The very title of this short novel alerts us to the fact that Crane's central female character, Maggie Johnson, will suffer greatly in the dilapidated world she lives in. Maggie not only ends up "A Girl of the Streets," forced to turn to prostitution as her only means of survival, but she ends up dead, mourned by a mother and brother who showed her little kindness during her brief and tragic life. Maggie is just one of the many beleaguered tenants of this slum, but we almost immediately sympathize with her plight because Maggie alone possesses a propensity toward "better things," even if her aspirations are never realized. When Maggie accidentally breaks a plate toward the beginning of the novel, her mother's disproportionately hostile reaction indicates the regularity of abuse this daughter endures and we cannot help but want improved chances for Maggie, helplessly cast as a "small pursued tigress" (42).

Maggie's mother, Mary, is in fact the most difficult female character to discuss. She is a screeching and destructive mother—known "by her first name" to court officials and police officers (50)—who is more likely to "howl" than to speak, who routinely makes threats and breaks furniture in fits of drunken rage, and who daily strikes terror into the hearts of her children.

Students might read Mary as the villain of the story and blame her for the pathetic fates of her children, but it is worth noting that she lacks sensitivity and warmth in part because her world demands that she fight and scratch to survive. Accordingly, Mary appears as much a hapless victim as Maggie. As the narrator states, "It seems that the world had treated this woman very badly, and she took a deep revenge upon such portions of it as came within her reach" (60). The narrator does not excuse Mary's appalling behavior, yet there is the suggestion that Mary, like many of the characters in this novel, lacks the capacity to see a way out of her dismal lot in life. When she curses her daughter in her roughly drawn dialect, " 'who would tink such a bad girl could grow up in our fambly,' " we as readers are aware of the irony and of the mother's seemingly unforgivable irresponsibility (67). We may curse Mary for forcing her daughter onto the streets as punishment for Maggie's implied sexual relationship with a low-class con-artist, Pete, but we might also pity Mary for her blindness to her own situation.

Thinking about Mary from a feminist standpoint will allow students to address issues of motherhood, starting with questions about what options women seem to have in the New York slums Crane depicts. Students might want to consider "mother Mary" as symbolic of women's historically limited choices—here of marriage and motherhood, or prostitution. It might also be productive to assign this novel in the context of a unit on turn-of-the-century gender and poverty, including works such as Jacob Riis' important photographic study, *How the Other Half Lives*. Mary is an intriguing character with which to enter the debate over whether people can defy the limits of their environment to transcend cruelties and injustice built into the milieu in which they are raised.

Like her mother, Maggie is sentenced to an equally dire, though decidedly quieter, fate. At first Maggie seems a possible exception: "The girl, Maggie, blossomed in a mud puddle. She grew to be a most rare and wonderful production of a tenement district, a pretty girl. None of the dirt of Rum Alley seemed to be in her veins" (49). The author suggests here that Maggie has potential in a world that has no room for virtue or loveliness. Maggie's environment, her naïvete, and particularly the constraints of her position as a woman render her vulnerable to sexual exploitation. Teachers might want to analyze the societal double standards that lead Maggie to prostitution and death while leaving her sexually permissive brother Jimmie in a position of false moral superiority. Even when Maggie tries to react with conventional morality by refusing Pete's first goodnight kiss, without the counsel of a good mother or friend she is left to her own limited devices and, it is suggested, fails to stave off his sexual advances. Maggie needs a female role model, but there are none to be found in the Rum Alley. In fact, with no affirming female communities for Maggie to turn to, with neither confidante nor protector, she is left adrift and ends defeated, never having a trusting friend or an older woman to guide her.

Maggie is about both the absence of hope for the lower classes and the demise of the one character in the novel who manages to have dreams, however humble or naïve: Maggie. Because Crane's novel presents a complex picture of the underclass, despite the decided coarseness of his characters, it would be a mistake to claim that *Maggie* is a book that merely espouses stereotypical beliefs in gender or class; indeed, this novel possesses absolutely no positive representations of either men or women. From a feminist perspective, teachers can discuss *Maggie* with an eye toward raising questions about the ways that female characters—as monstrous mothers, scam artists, and fallen women— are used to dramatize the plight of the hungry and disenfranchised. Boldly and somewhat crudely, Crane exposes his readers to poverty and its particularly deleterious effect on women; more than one hundred years later, we should continue to question the degree to which class and gender produce similar constraints both in imaginative representations and in the real lives of the poor.

WORK CITED

Crane, Stephen. *Maggie: A Girl of the Streets (A Story of New York)* [1893]. Ed. Kevin J. Hayes. Boston: Bedford, 1999, 36–94.

FOR FURTHER READING

Hayes, Kevin J. Introductory essays. *Maggie: A Girl of the Streets (A Story of New York)*. Boston: Bedford, 1999, 195–262.

(Re)surfacing *Main Street* (1920) by Sinclair Lewis

Shirley P. Brown

When *Main Street* first appeared, women had just gained the right to vote. The shift from a largely agricultural economy to an industrial one was accelerating, and the ideal of small-town living was being replaced by the promise of exciting possibilities to be found in large urban centers. Sinclair Lewis, who had a painful history in his small-town birthplace of Sauk Centre, Minnesota, was a product of the time, and *Main Street* has been construed as both an expression of his complicated personal history and a scathing attack on the constraints of small-town life. A contemporary reading, however, reveals how the novel gets beneath the surface of women's lives to illustrate the conflicting pressures they faced.

Most critics agree that Carol Kennicott, the central figure in Lewis' satiric treatment of small-town life in America from 1912 through World War I, represents the author in his uneasy relationship to his home town. Lewis' reconstruction/transformation of his own experience aptly captures the role of the marked other, a role familiar to women. As the "other," Kennicott struggles to see the ugly town of Gopher Prairie, Minnesota, through her husband's loving eyes, while also experiencing what Betty Friedan later analyzed, in the case of white middle-class women in the 1950s, as "the problem that has no name" (11). This emotional emptiness of women who are expected to live their lives through another, usually a husband or a child, is an added dimension of Kennicott's discomfort with her life in Gopher Prairie.

Carol struggles to express herself within the limited options offered by small-town life and the gendered role assigned to her by marriage as Dr. Kennicott's wife. Dutifully carrying out household tasks and social obligations and seldom revealing her inner concerns, Carol chafes against the repetitive routine expected of her and other women of her class who are seen as appendages of their husbands. Even before she meets and marries Dr. Will Kennicott, Carol's predetermined role has been clearly signaled in an earlier marriage proposal proffered by college friend Steward Snyder. When she responded to the offer by saying, "I want to do something with life," he retorted, "What's better than making a comfy home and bringing up some cute kids and knowing nice homey people?" (10). Snyder's assumptions about what is important to Carol and women in general is not idiosyncratic but represents the common wisdom of the time.

Before marrying, Carol follows a pattern common to single women working in the many feminized professions, only to eschew paid work later on as improper for a doctor's wife. Her attempts to find satisfaction in voluntary civic work are doomed both by her yearning for a more cosmopolitan environment and her lack of agency in a community where all power is in the hands of men. It is not until the disruptions in social and economic life occasioned by the World War I war effort that Carol can rationalize leaving Gopher Prairie and her husband to go to work in Washington, D.C., where she feels alive again. However, that feeling quickly fades, and by the time Will visits, she is asking him to tell her whether or not she should return home. To his credit, he refuses and tells her she must decide. Consistent with the mores of the time and her failure to find complete satisfaction in urban life, Carol eventually complies with Will's request to return to Gopher Prairie, but she is no longer the same person:

> Though she should return, she said, she would not be utterly defeated. She was glad of the rebellion. The prairie was no longer empty land in the sun-glare; it was the living tawny beast which she had fought and made beautiful by fighting; and in the village streets were shadows of her desires and the sound of her marching and the seeds of mystery and greatness. (511)

Despite her enhanced sense of personal power, Carol Kennicott is neither a bluestocking nor a radical feminist, and recognizes women's issues solely as they affect her in the private sphere. Her private sphere, however, is governed by public opinion, and she is loath to connect her personal injuries with broader concerns. For example, after being humiliated by having to ask her husband Will for money each time she needs to make a purchase for their home, she is forced to confront him with the need for an "allowance." Will is not mean spirited and finally agrees, but it is the public display of his blindness to Carol as an equal that is demeaning. Carol does not connect her personal dissatisfactions with larger issues that confront women's lack of power in the public sphere. In another example of Carol's dependence on public opinion, Carol's solution to finding space for herself and taking some control over her own life is to claim a room of her own, anticipating, yet with a different agenda from, Virginia Woolf in *A Room of One's Own*. Carol insists on her own room as a place where she can be herself but it is, perhaps, much more a way of holding Will at arm's length than it is a place for self-fulfillment. Unlike Woolf, who saw having a "room of one's own" as symbolic of agency, Carol uses her room as a buffer and cannot really appreciate it until she learns that another woman in the town has also claimed a room for herself. Finally, although the fight for women's suffrage is being waged throughout most of her life, she remains essentially uninvolved in that effort.

Young women today may not feel the pressure of choosing between a life of independence or a partnership, as Carol Kennicott did, but they face the new burden of juggling more roles without corresponding role changes in men's lives and/or in public support. They might want to consider how increased career opportunities for women today have impacted private lives in complicated ways. Students might also find it useful to compare Carol's life with those of middle-class African-American women in Paula Giddings' *When and Where I Enter*, to gain a picture of how women used feminized venues like service clubs to affect public policy.

WORKS CITED

Friedan, Betty. *The Feminine Mystique.* New York: Dell, 1963.
Giddings, Paula. *When and Where I Enter: The Impact of Black Women on Sex and Race in America.* New York: Morrow, 1984.
Lewis, Sinclair. *Main Street* [1920]. New York: Bantam Classics, 1996.
Woolf, Virginia. *A Room of One's Own.* New York: Harcourt, Brace and World, 1929.

FOR FURTHER READING

Bucco, M., ed. Main Street: *The Revolt of Carol Kennicott.* New York: Twayne, 1993.

Critiquing "the We of Me": Gender Roles in Carson McCullers' *The Member of the Wedding* (1946)

Elise Ann Earthman

Teachers looking for texts through which to raise questions about the forces that shape girls into women will find much to discuss in Carson McCullers' *The Member of the Wedding*, whose focus and meaning critics have been debating since its publication. Is Frankie's story, as some 1960s writers argue, one of an awkward misfit's successful transformation into an acceptable young woman (e.g., Gosset 1965)? Do we find in *The Member of the Wedding* a case study of the cost to a free-spirited young "tomboy" of assuming the straitjacket of the traditional female role, as suggested by more recent critics (e.g., White 1986)? Or do we read deeply enough to discover that "Frankie's attraction to her brother is incestuous, whereas her attraction to her brother's bride is homosexual/lesbian," as Thadious Davis has very recently suggested (216, also Adams 1999)? By bringing these critical debates into the classroom, we offer students analytical tools for thinking about both literature and the stereotypical roles that our culture has historically dictated for girls as they turn into women.

Frankie, who until age twelve has been comfortably unconventional, running with the neighborhood kids in her small Southern town, giving shows underneath the scuppernong arbor, now suddenly feels like "an unjoined person who [hangs] around in doorways" (1), who has emotions she cannot put to words, who feels "her squeezed heart beating against the table edge" (4). Displaced and unattached, Frankie belongs to no group that she values and that values her. Too old for her 6-year-old cousin John Henry, resistant to the motherly attentions of the African-American housekeeper, Berenice, Frankie longs to belong to a *we*, the "we" that "all other [people] except her had to claim" (39). The girls with whom she associated in the past have now barred Frankie from the clubhouse where they have parties with boys, telling her she's "too young and mean," "spreading it all over town" that Frankie smells bad (10).

Frankie believes she is a Freak—her mirror reveals a tall, narrow-shouldered, barefooted girl in shorts and an undershirt with a ragged boy's haircut, one who has grown four inches in the past year. Figuring that at this rate she will ultimately be over nine feet tall, Frankie fears that she will soon only be welcomed in the traveling fair that comes to town, where she will take her place with the Pin Head, the Alligator Boy, and the Half-Man Half-Woman, who all seem to look at her "in a secret way . . . as though to say: we know you" (18). Her fears, when combined with the rejection of her former friends, create in Frankie a strong desire to be "normal," though she is not at first clear about how that might be achieved.

She imagines salvation in her brother Jarvis and his intended bride Janice, "the two prettiest people I ever saw" (27). Her decision to improve herself before their wedding, and her resolve to "go with them to whatever place they will ever go" (43) after the ceremony, lead Frankie to remake herself into a more "acceptable" version of womanhood (renaming herself "F. Jasmine" in the process), to enter a bar for the first time, to attract unwelcome sexual attention, and to ultimately see her fantasies come crashing down around her. Yet she seems to rise above these disasters. By novel's end we see Frankie rename herself yet again, as "Frances"—a young woman now interested in Michelangelo and poetry, no longer preoccupied by freaks, devoted to her new friend, Mary Littlejohn. What has Frankie/F. Jasmine/Frances gained and lost in this transition?

Although we can see Frankie at the novel's end as having achieved what some may consider a healthy balance between two extremes (the boy-girl who digs a splinter from her foot with a butcher knife and later hurls the knife across the room in anger; the parody of femininity she becomes in the second section, in a too-big orange satin evening gown, a silver ribbon in her hair). We may also note the price she pays: Individuality that made Frankie unique (if quirky) is now gone. No longer can she dream of being a pilot or a soldier, of hopping a freight, unacceptable goals for "normal" girls in the postwar period; she is now "just mad about Michelangelo" (150), looking forward to having a laundry room in their new house, cutting sandwiches into fancy shapes.

Barbara White has suggested that "*The Member of the Wedding* is less a novel of initiation into 'acceptance of *human* limits' than a novel of initiation into acceptance of *female* limits" (141). Responding to this statement and those of other critics, students can debate the question of whether Frankie is better off at the novel's end than she was at the beginning, and the mature class can even take on the issue of whether Frankie's lesbianism is inscribed in the text (as contemporary critics have suggested), and the role that racial limitations play in the different fates of Berenice as an African-American woman, and Honey Brown as an African-American man. Through these discussions, students will have excellent opportunities to develop skills in textual analysis and critical thinking, as they consider McCullers' coming-of-age novel, which presents feelings and dilemmas that girls today still face as they navigate the often turbulent transition from childhood to adolescence.

WORKS CITED

Adams, Rachel. " 'A Mixture of Delicious and Freak': The Queer Fiction of Carson McCullers." *American Literature* 71 (1999): 551–83.

Davis, Thadious M. "Erasing the 'We of Me' and Rewriting the Racial Script: Carson McCullers's Two *Member(s) of the Wedding*." *Critical Essays on Carson McCullers*. Ed. Beverly Lyon Clark and Melvin J. Friedman. New York: G. K. Hall, 1996, 206–19.

Gosset, Louise Y. "Dispossessed Love: Carson McCullers." *Violence in Recent Southern Literature*. Durham, NC: Duke UP, 1965, 159–77.

McCullers, Carson. *The Member of the Wedding* [1946]. New York: Bantam, 1973.

White, Barbara A. "Loss of Self in *The Member of the Wedding*." *Modern Critical Views on Carson McCullers*. Ed. Harold Bloom. New York: Chelsea House, 1986, 125–42.

FOR FURTHER READING

Davis, Katherine. " 'A Thing Known and Not Spoken': Sexual Difference in Carson McCullers' *The Member of the Wedding*." *Text and Presentation: The Journal of the Comparative Drama Conference* 16 (1995): 39–42.

Beauty and Gender in Alix Kates Shulman's *Memoirs of an Ex-Prom Queen* (1972)

Charlotte Templin

Alix Kates Shulman wrote *Memoirs of an Ex-Prom Queen* after she became involved in the Women's Liberation Movement in the late 1960s. The novel reflects the understanding of the political aspects of personal life that Shulman and other activists developed in so-called consciousness-raising (CR) sessions. Through CR, women came to recognize themselves as an oppressed group. They learned to see their problems as related to entrenched social, cultural, and economic conditions that favored men and disadvantaged women, conditions that stem from basic assumptions about the fixed natures and roles of men and women.

When Shulman wrote this novel, many people did not comprehend situations women face such as sexual harassment, job discrimination, and the sexual double standard. For example, in the 1950s and 1960s, it was considered natural for men in the workplace to make sexual advances toward women, perhaps to even expect sexual favors as a condition of employment. While the inherent sexism in these situations is better understood and less tolerated today, the problems Shulman writes about have not disappeared.

Memoirs tells the story of Jewish American, middle-class Sasha, alternating chapters of her adult experiences with chapters about her childhood. As a young child she is a tomboy, known for climbing the tallest trees. She also loves to read the Little Leather Library of classics that her father gave her. However, in spite of her potential, she succumbs to the strong influences that decree that her beauty is far more important than anything else, that pleasing a man should be her highest ambition. Sasha believes that "there was only one thing worth bothering about: being beautiful" (22). Her dreams and ambitions are narrowed accordingly, even though some part of her is always striving for self-fulfillment. Although the men in the novel appear most often as nuisances, threats, or disappointments, Sasha will do anything to keep their good opinion. For the attention of men, she sacrifices her ambitions again and again, only dimly grasping a sense of herself at the end of the novel.

Shulman shows clearly how gender roles are defined, enacted, and reinforced. Social roles privilege boys and restrict girls: boys throw mud at girls, knock them down or pull their hair, with impunity; teachers at Sasha's school blame girls for going near the boys when girls complain of boys' violence. Like other adults in this white, middle-class world, Sasha's mother also contributes to the narrowing of her daughter's ambitions, communicating how important beauty is by continuously praising—to the exclusion of her other attributes—Sasha's beauty, mentioning many times that Sasha is the prettiest girl in her class.

Sasha's sexual experiences further illustrate cultural practices that sustain rigid gender expectations. As a teen, Sasha accepts that boys will be sexual predators. She comes to dread the struggle that takes place on every date but considers it inevitable. Moreover, she never questions the idea that the best jock is the best date. When she is voted prom queen, she sees nothing remarkable about parading before the judges and the assembled audience while her body undergoes inspection. Broad humor pervades episodes such as Sasha's tussles with boys in parked cars and her arguments with a meat chef who wants sexual favors at the hotel where she waits on tables. Teachers could ask students to play with Shulman's humor by having them prepare skits derived from a few of the comic scenes, such as Sasha the prom queen parading through the gym; Sasha the waitress trying to get her customers' roast beef orders from the sleazy meat chef.

When Sasha moves into her young adult years, her experiences illustrate the narrowness of female roles in the 1950s. As she prepares for a career in graduate school, she also sees that her career opportunities are very limited, that her best option is to marry. She is expected to quit school and support the family while her husband finishes his education. But in a world where employment openings are advertised under "Help Wanted, Female" and "Help Wanted, Male," Sasha qualifies only for jobs that are menial and poorly compensated.

Through Sasha's two marriages, Shulman shows women's position in the family. When Sasha becomes a mother, her life is dominated by that role. Her husband sees her differently when she is a stay-at-home mom, and his romantic interest wanes. Just as in earlier phases of her life, Sasha feels subject to male experts in her role as a mother. The novel quotes from Dr. Spock's book on childcare, implicitly suggesting that his advice does not take into account the actual experience of women who spend entire days with small children. (Shulman says in the introduction to the twenty-fifth anniversary edition of *Memoirs* that Spock revised his advice after reading her novel.)

More than any other sexist code of conduct, Shulman emphasizes the pressure on women to be and remain beautiful. Students might compare today's attitudes toward physical appearance by critically regarding male and female news anchors, or males and females in other visible, public positions. They might compare magazines aimed at teenage girls or women to boys' and men's magazines, examining differences in glamorized personal appearance, hygiene standards, health concerns of both sexes, and which gender-oriented images are associated with power. Students might also be asked to consider beauty product advertisements on television. In particular, Shulman's book can facilitate discussion of aging and gender bias in perceptions of beauty. Even when she is young, Sasha worries that her beauty is fading. What are some of the many social and psychological implications of our culture's contention that women age more quickly than men?

Memoirs exposes how natural gender roles can seem—even while they are enforced by various social practices that teach gender roles. Examining the family, early childhood play, organized school sports, TV sitcoms, or dating practices, students will easily identify ways in which boys and girls are pressured to act. Teachers are likely to find that, while decades old, *Memoirs* is hardly dated: indeed, it has much to say about growing up female and male today.

WORK CITED

Shulman, Alix Kates. *Memoirs of an Ex-Prom Queen* [1972]. Introduction by the author. New York: Penguin, 1997.

FOR FURTHER READING

Templin, Charlotte. "An Interview with Alix Kates Shulman." *The Missouri Review* 24.1 (2001): 103–21.
———. "Alix Kates Shulman: Novelist, Feminist, Twentieth-Century Woman." *The Human Tradition Since 1945*. Ed. David Anderson. Wilmington, DE: Scholarly Resources. Forthcoming.

Where No Role Fits: Maggie's Predicament in George Eliot's *The Mill on the Floss* (1860)

Missy Dehn Kubitschek

A *bildungsroman*, *The Mill on the Floss* tells the story of how Maggie and Tom Tulliver grow up. The novel consciously examines stereotypes as Maggie strives to be a good girl, then a good woman. Set earlier than its publication (1860), it depicts a time and place in which women's opportunities were historically limited. Girls received almost no education. They could work only as servants, seamstresses, or governesses—dismal economic prospects. They were trained to attract and then obey the husbands who would support them. The marriage of Maggie's parents shows these expectations in operation.

In *The Mill on the Floss*, the older generation of women is composed of various stereotypes. Griselda Moss exemplifies the plight of the impoverished married woman. Her strength sapped by constant childbearing, she is too poor to act on her generous feelings. A passive, conventional woman who lacks judgment and relies on others for guidance, Mrs. Tulliver is both stupid and foolish. She and her sisters exemplify the narrow, ungenerous, and unthinking allegiance to social conformity that Eliot calls "the world's wife" (Book 7, Ch. 2).

Temperamentally, physically, and spiritually, Maggie is a bad fit with her social role, which has no use for her intelligence, compassion, or passion. Instead, she must try to be proper, obedient, self-sacrificing and, above all else, chaste. Although she cannot completely repress her true self, Maggie internalizes these stereotypic expectations. For example, she becomes a parody of self-denying virtue when she insists on doing the most tedious, least aesthetic kind of needlework ("plain sewing") as her contribution to family income.

Initially, like most children, Maggie acts directly on her feelings. She is not simply selfish, however, for she deeply loves her father and her brother Tom. Maggie needs love; she cannot cope with rejection from Tom and ridicule from her mother's family. To make matters worse, her cousin Lucy epitomizes the socially perfect little girl—obedient, neat, and pretty. At first Maggie has male protection and support from her loving father. After his death, however, she becomes subject to the judgments of her harsh, self-righteous brother, who succeeds his father as head of the Tulliver household.

As a child Maggie tries to escape her social role by running away to the gypsies; as a young adult she tries to disappear into the role by denying her real self. The comic gypsy episode points up the impossibility of escape. Maggie then decides to play the role perfectly. Misunderstanding Thomas á Kempis' *The Imitation of Christ*, she tries to be good by repressing her desires completely. Thus, misconstrued religion reinforces the social ideal of womanly self-sacrifice.

Maggie's adult conflicts focus on the one area of female choice, romantic love. Even here, Tom tries to control her, insisting that she give up Philip Wakem. At twenty, when she and her cousin Lucy's fiancé Stephen fall in love, she comes to an impasse. She can't bear to hurt Lucy and Philip, to whom she is attached; yet she cannot give up her love for Stephen. Paralyzed by her old conflict of emotional desire and the female duty of self-sacrifice, she makes no conscious choices and simply drifts—literally, when the river current propels her and Stephen's boat too far downstream for them to be able to return before the next morning. Given the social mores, Maggie's reputation is irrecoverably ruined: she is presumed to be Stephen's mistress. Disowned by her brother, she becomes a social outcast, a public example of the fallen woman. Maggie dies in a supremely self-sacrificing way, however, trying to rescue Tom from a flood.

The Mill on the Floss implicitly asks for a feminist approach, since it depicts the female's appointed social role as harmful both to individual girls and women, and to society. The role has no room for Maggie's talents, and it fosters immorality through ignorance and intolerance. In fact, the role seems to encourage the worst in women, as we see after Maggie and Stephen's misadventure. The women of the town are ignorant of all motivation beyond the stereotypical view of Maggie as the "femme fatale," the fallen woman. Disregarding the advice and example of the clergyman who might be their religious guide, they consider it their moral duty to separate themselves from all sexual scandal by condemning Maggie.

A teacher might wish to focus on three areas: (1) nature versus social nurture in the creation of a female's life, (2) the effect of media as part of nurture, and (3) analysis of the novel's ending.

Eliot characterizes Maggie as needing love in a way that her brother does not, by her very nature. A teacher might suggest that Maggie's dependent tendencies are encouraged, that she is *trained* to need love as part of the woman's role. Classes might then find examples of that training and contrast it with the boy characters' training to be active and independent. This text-based discussion is likely to lead smoothly into a consideration of the effects of both kinds of gender training as they apply to students' experiences growing up female and male today.

Americans often discuss the role of the media in giving children stereotypical ideas about violence in movies and television, for example, or pornography on the Internet. In Book 5, Chapter 4, Eliot explicitly mentions literature as creating stereotypes of women. Maggie and Philip discuss a French novel in which a light-haired, conventional woman wins the love of a man away from the dark-haired heroine. Historically, literature often presented light hair and complexion as symbolic of angelic traits (unselfishness and purity); dark hair and complexion often symbolized the opposite (selfishness and active female sexuality that Victorians considered depraved). This pronounced pattern in nineteenth-century American literature is called "the light lady/dark lady dichotomy."

Teachers can use this part of the novel to discuss the extent to which we use art to help us "plot" our lives, to tell us what to expect. They might also guide students' exploration of what the media teach girls and young women now about physical appearance—is the light/dark pattern still present for white girls? For all girls? Can female bodies that are considered sexy belong to "nice" girls, or is sexuality still taboo?

Finally, teachers should encourage students to evaluate whether the novel's ending appropriately resolves the plot's issues: by drowning Maggie, Eliot could avoid both crushing the spirit of her character and condemning sex roles and moral standards to which her audience was still devoted. Teachers can present the biographical fact that complicated Eliot's narrative problem. In an arrangement that made her an outcast among women, this writer lived with a man married to someone else who could never marry her. She was thus particularly vulnerable to charges of writing immoral literature. Students might explore whether/how much social standards for women have changed, and construct alternative endings made possible by these changes.

WORKS CITED

Beer, Gillian. *George Eliot*. Bloomington: Indiana UP, 1986.

Christ, Carol, ed. *The Mill on the Floss* [1860]. By George Eliot. Norton Critical Edition Series. New York: Norton, 1994.

Ermarth, Elizabeth. *George Eliot*. Boston: Twayne, 1985.

FOR FURTHER READING

Gilbert, Sandra and Susan Gubar. *The Madwoman in the Attic: The Woman Writer and the Nineteenth-Century Literary Imagination*. New Haven, CT: Yale UP, 1979, 491–94.

Herman Melville's *Moby-Dick*: Epic Tale of Male Destruction (1851)

Kim Martin Long

Herman Melville's *Moby-Dick*, a most celebrated novel, presents the adventure of Ishmael, the narrator, and his captain, Ahab, as they and the crew members of the *Pequod* chase the great white whale, Moby Dick. Certainly, one of the least female fictional works of all time, the book contains no real women since there were none on board the ship. A few actually appear in the beginning of the novel as Ishmael and his new-found friend Queequeg prepare to set out on their three-years' whaling journey; however, *Moby-Dick* is essentially peopled by male characters. But as students study the novel in depth, they will see that Melville has included many female presences in this novel, and these female presences actually win out over the male-dominated aggression that pervades the story.

Readers come to know Ishmael as a flawed, tolerant, risk-taking, questioning, analytical narrator. He introduces himself to us in the famous first sentence, revealing almost immediately his flaws. When talking about the plight of human beings, he calls Adam and Eve "the two orchard thieves," laying blame for original sin on both progenitors. Ishmael speaks in a most democratic and open-minded way, overcoming his "prejudice" against cannibals and becoming "bosom buddies" with the head hunter Queequeg. As to Ishmael's descriptions of female characters (for example, about his stepmother [33]; Mrs. Hussey [64]; or Aunt Charity [89]), his comments, if in the least bit negative, are designed for a good laugh. Ishmael has a finely honed sense of humor, and he is conscious at all times of a reading audience. Melville cannot be indicted for gender bias only by examining the few images of "real" female characters in *Moby-Dick*.

Once Ishmael begins the voyage, his focus shifts strongly to Ahab, the ultra-masculine character whose monomaniacal quest eventually brings the entire crew (except Ishmael) to destruction. Describing Ahab, Ishmael notes "an in-finity of firmest fortitude, a determinate, unsurrenderable willfulness, in the fixed and fearless, forward dedication of that glance" (111). Even though Mel-ville characterizes Ahab as a romantic hero, the overriding emphasis through-out the novel's action is that of masculinity out of control ("I'd strike the sun if it insulted me" [144]). In fact, Ahab in his patriarchal dominance presents the clearest picture of gender bias in *Moby-Dick*.

One might notice the whale as another male "character" in the book; how-ever, readers' primary view of Moby Dick is the image that Ahab has constructed for his crew, including narrator Ishmael. He is the one who calls the whale a "monster," projecting all the evil of the universe onto one creature. Although other boats purport to have encountered this whale, no evidence exists that Moby Dick was really malicious; the beast seems very much like Faulkner's Old Ben or Hemingway's great fish, a large creature of nature who has avoided capture for a long time. When Ahab's fierce masculinity is pitted against such a creature, masculine power loses in the conflict with the natural.

In "The Grand Armada," Melville presents a large group of whales in their natural habitat, mothers and suckling calves, which Ishmael describes as a "wondrous world," making the ocean "an enchanted pond" (375, 376). Here the "monster" whales are just creatures of nature, conceiving, giving birth, nourishing the young. Elsewhere Melville depicts nature as benevolent and harmonious, male and female in natural union.

> It was a clear steel-blue day. The firmaments of air and sea were hardly separable in that all-pervading azure; only, the pensive air was transpar-ently pure and soft, with a woman's look, and the robust and man-like sea heaved with long, strong, lingering swells, as Samson's chest in his sleep. (442)

Although these representations of the sexes are rather traditional, Melville suggests they form a picture of harmony and balance.

Ishmael, the only crew member to survive the quest for Moby Dick, does so by laying hold of his friend Queequeg's coffin lifebuoy. Throughout the narrative, Ishmael has demonstrated his searching, flexible character. Ending many chapters with philosophical questions, Ishmael's narrative voice differs from Ahab's voice of unchallenged knowledge and unbending surety in his mission. Ishmael's ability to seek answers rather than answer all questions with the same answer—as Ahab does—keeps the character-narrator alive: "through all the thick mists of the dim doubts in my mind, divine intuitions now and then shoot, enkindling my fog with a heavenly ray" (314). Floating on his friend's discarded coffin, Ishmael is saved by the ship *Rachel*, named after the Biblical character who lost her children. From a gendered perspective, one might see Ishmael's character as essentially feminine, relying as he does on his ability to negotiate, network, and adjust to survive—a striking contrast to Ahab's more masculine and deadly linear, fixed, and competitive stance.

In *Moby-Dick* images of the feminine—in Ishmael's own character, in the natural world, in the names of the other ships—contrast with the powerfully destructive masculine force of Ahab's obsession. A feminist approach recognizes that Melville's lack of female characters does not indicate gender bias, yet the presence of such strong maleness brings danger and imbalance. In "The Counterpane," "A Bosom Friend," and "A Squeeze of the Hand," for instance, Melville even hints at homosexuality as an appropriate response to obsessive masculinity: "I found Queequeg's arm thrown over me in the most loving and affectionate manner" (32); "No more my splintered heart and maddened hand were turned against the wolfish world. This soothing savage had redeemed it" (53); "Such an affectionate, friendly, loving feeling did [squeezing my co-laborers' hands] beget" (348). The feminine wins out ultimately over male competition, obsession, and vengeance in what has been considered a story dominated by men and maleness.

Students sometimes approach this novel psychologically, noting that Ahab has been symbolically castrated by Moby Dick, having lost his leg, and that he attacks the whale—a female image—with his harpoon, a phallic symbol. Water, traditionally a symbol of the feminine, eventually swallows the *Pequod* after Moby Dick hits the ship. Moby Dick, then, can be interpreted as an ironic symbol of the feminine—the force in nature that brings down Ahab's overdone masculinity.

Other literary works that students might want to read along with and compare to *Moby-Dick* are Ernest Hemingway's *The Old Man and the Sea* and William Faulkner's *The Bear*. Both stories portray men in search of something, symbolized or realized in a creature of the wild. Santiago, in Hemingway's short novel, looks for the biggest fish of his life, and Ike, in Faulkner's novella, participates with other men in search of Old Ben, a mythical, larger-than-life bear. All three works lack female characters, although the feminine manifests strongly in the form of nature, which ultimately defeats all three of these male questers.

WORK CITED

Hayford, Harrison, and Herschel Parker, eds. *Moby-Dick* [1851]. By Herman Melville. Norton Critical Edition. New York: Norton, 1967.

FOR FURTHER READING

Martin, Robert K. *Hero, Captain, and Stranger: Male Friendship, Social Critique, and Literary Form in the Sea Novels of Herman Melville*. Chapel Hill: U of North Carolina P, 1986.

Weigman, Robyn. "Melville's Geography of Gender." *Herman Melville: A Collection of Critical Essays*. Ed. Myra Jehlen. Englewood Cliffs, NJ: Prentice Hall, 1994, 187–98.

Images of Possibility: Gender Identity in Willa Cather's *My Àntonia* (1918)

Dana Kinnison

The setting of Willa Cather's *My Àntonia* is the American plains during the adventurous days of pioneering. Along with scenes of burgeoning town life, the novel presents a world of cowboys and settlers, of murder and wilderness exploits. Such tales usually privilege male characters, but this one is different. Cather offers instead an appreciation of the female spirit and a bountiful gathering of gender-balanced characters.

The image most indelibly left by the novel is that of the title character: a strong, vibrant, and independent pioneering woman. Àntonia expresses herself boldly against the blank slate of the Nebraska plains. With blazing eyes and sun-browned muscular limbs, she is considered beautiful. But even after time diminishes her beauty she remains a forceful personality. Her adventurous spirit and willingness to work hard, often laboring in the fields wearing men's clothing, are more memorable than a passing youthful attractiveness. When she is warned that outdoor activity will make her manner coarse, Àntonia exclaims that she enjoys working like a man and flexes her muscle in response (133).

Àntonia is proud and opinionated but not immune to cultural influences which place greater value on men. Still, she often disregards the limitations imposed upon her gender, as do Lena Lingard and numerous immigrant girls whose self-reliance leads them to fulfill their various dreams. Within the Harling family, Mrs. Harling exudes an intelligent and forceful energy. Young Sally is wild, strong, and resourceful at all boys' sports. The adult daughter, Frances, is unusually adept at business, knowledgeable about grain cars and cattle, and an important figure in the community. Admittedly, Mrs. Harling is head of the household only during her husband's (frequent) absences, and it is one of her father's offices that Frances manages. Nonetheless, the women in Cather's novel are dynamic individuals who, more often than not, assert themselves in a fashion and with a frequency rare in American literature.

If Àntonia is the heart and soul of the novel, Jim Burden is its consciousness. As with Àntonia, Jim's gender attributes near proportionality. He is an intelligent and rugged fellow who is also reflective and romantic. In fact, the novel is Jim's paean to the loves of his youth, primarily Àntonia but also Lena. Jim, too, is affected by traditional attitudes toward gender roles but also resistant to their potency. Thus, ironically, he resents the power men wield over women, and yet he wishes to partake of it. For example, he bridles at Àntonia's deferment to Ambrosch, her older brother, but wishes that Àntonia would defer to him rather than assuming a protective manner. The opportunity arises for him to right their reversed roles when he kills a large rattlesnake, thus securing Àntonia's safety and becoming her brave knight in shining armor. However, as much as he has wanted this position he can't help but acknowledge that luck and the snake's old age weighted the battle in his favor. He concludes, "So in reality it was a mock adventure; the game was fixed for me by chance, as it probably was for many a dragon-slayer" (48). Cather makes clear to the reader that, far from a verity or an inevitability, many supposed examples of male superiority are merely fairy tales.

Cather's characters offer what is perhaps most important to young readers contemplating gender issues—images of possibility. Transformations to gender role expectations must begin with the capacity to imagine different identities and relationships. *My Àntonia* offers many positive, non-threatening images of males and females who are not drawn according to rigid gender prescriptions. The novel subtly yet persistently invokes new possibilities for human behavior, for men's and women's relationships, and for supportive interconnectedness among women.

The novel's female characters experience mutual bonds of devotion and respect, within and across generational lines. The immigrant girls are proud of each others' accomplishments and work to improve conditions for their mothers. They are appreciative of the sacrifices women of an earlier generation made for them. The relationship that develops between Àntonia and Mrs. Harling exceeds that of employee and employer:

> There was a basic harmony between Àntonia and her mistress. They had strong, independent natures, both of them. They knew what they liked, and were not always trying to imitate other people. . . . Deep down in each of them there was a kind of hearty joviality, a relish of life, not over-delicate, but very invigorating. (174)

Students can discover many instances, obvious and obscure, in which Cather consciously manipulates gender roles: In what ways is Otto Fuchs consistent/ inconsistent with the image of a cowboy? Why does Jim feel disgust when he is beaten by Wick Cutter? However, Àntonia's full significance is not only as a flesh-and-blood figure but as a spirit, a Muse: an inspirational and invigorating life force identified with the new country, clearly feminine and beautiful yet not overly delicate. Classroom discussions intended to heighten students' awareness of gender roles need to recognize this symbolic element, which can serve to complicate—yet enhance—observations about her balanced gender identity made previously in this essay. Are Àntonia and Lena protofeminists or simply Jim's beautiful Muses? Does Cather give in to convention by insisting on the beauty of the immigrant girls, or is she expanding that which is deemed beautiful since their looks are distinctly different from the town girls? Why are the country girls "considered a menace to the social order" (195)? Students might also examine why a female spirit is more common as a Muse than a male spirit, for people of both sexes. (Note that Àntonia is not only Jim's Muse but Cather's as well.) Finally, what dangers are inherent in presenting women in a romanticized or a transcendent light?

WORK CITED

Cather, Willa. *My Àntonia* [1918]. Ed. Charles Mignon. Lincoln: U of Nebraska P, 1997.

FOR FURTHER READING

O'Brien, Sharon, ed. *New Essays on* My Àntonia. Cambridge: Cambridge UP, 1999.
Rosowki, Susan J., ed. *Approaches to Teaching Cather's* My Àntonia. New York: Modern Language Association, 1989.

The Good Woman: Kamala Markandaya's *Nectar in a Sieve* (1954)

Shakuntala Bharvani

Rukmani, Kamala Markandaya's protagonist, is a girl of twelve when her father marries her to Nathan, a "tenanted farmer." This lowly union with a landless farmer occurs for several reasons: her father has lost his position as Headman (probably to a British Collector), she is without beauty and without dowry, and she is a fourth daughter. Her father has already married off and endowed three other daughters with substantial dowries. Thus, it is with reason that Rukmani bends her head low when she leaves her parents' home on a bullock-cart. This is certainly not the kind of marriage a young girl would ever dream of.

Rukmani's dynamic recapitulation of her married life violates no norms of proper feminine virtue. According to her, Nathan, whose name literally means "Lord," is ever and always the kind and considerate husband, for he praises her for whatever she accomplishes. He does not blame her when their first child is "only" a girl, or when Rukmani is barren for the next seven years. Even under the most adverse circumstances—when two of her sons die of starvation—she does not question her harsh peasant life with Nathan, or think of the greater comfort and status of her father's home. Rukmani is a good woman, and a good woman must "look up" to her husband, and always assume her place "with her husband" (111). In this way, Rukmani's narrative is intricately linked with expected feminine correctness and propriety.

Thus, in her eyes Nathan becomes the ideal husband. She dismisses his confession that he has fathered Kunthi's sons with a single comment: "That she is evil and powerful, I know myself. Let it rest" (90). Male desires are privileged. He is the breadwinner because "the land is mistress to man, not to woman: the heavy work is beyond her strength" (131). She never thinks of her own superiority, her literacy, or makes much of her ability to teach her children. The male world cannot be subverted.

Western students might discuss her attitude toward suffering and her adulation of her simple and uneducated husband. These students may undoubtedly find her boneless and weak. Not so the Indian student. Narrative is nation and nation is narrative, and here the nation is articulated in language and text, and the Indian student (one who is a resident of India), will identify with Rukmani, for she is a simple peasant woman located in a specific social and historical context.

According to ancient Indian myth and legend, the good woman accepts her "Lord," and his suffering unconditionally. Thus in the *Ramayana*, when Crown Prince Rama is banished to the forest at the whim of his stepmother, Sita is the exemplary Hindu wife. She insists on accompanying her "Lord" and sharing his exile. In the other Hindu epic, the *Mahabharata*, Gandhari, the wife of the blind prince, blindfolds her own eyes, so she may not enjoy the pleasures of sight. Sufferance is accepted by the Hindu, particularly so by women, who undergo all kinds of penance and fasting for the sake of their families.

Rukmani symbolizes the earth-mother figure. In the earlier stages of Indian writing in English, there was a propensity to associate simplicity, strength, and goodness with this simple, peasant "earth-mother" figure and to romanticize this picture. Patriotic pre-Independence writers always personified India as "Mother India," and its people as her children. (Through continuous usage, this has become a cultural construct.) Sarojini Naidu, an eminent Indian poet, in her poem "The Gift of India," asks the Allies whether they will remember and reward her sons, "priceless treasures torn from my breasts," when the day of victory approaches. The Hindu pantheon of gods and goddesses also reinforces this representation of the goddess as the nurturing and energizing force, and it is because of this that Rukmani, when the rains are over, takes the "seed" to the Goddess to receive her blessings, "and then bore it away to make our sowing" (83).

Nationalist discourse too spoke of India as Mother Goddess. The Empire, represented by the Lion, was an image constructed in male terms. Students may discuss how contemporary women politicians in India have conveyed themselves as Mother India, and mother of the people, in order to further their own ulterior motives of winning votes and popularity.

There are thumbnail sketches of other women too in Markandaya's novel—Irawaddy, Kali, Janaki, Kunthi, Old Granny; and Murugan's forsaken wife, Irawaddy, a sympathetic figure, prostitutes her body, not because of lust, but to alleviate her family's dire needs. Also explicit in Irawaddy's story is the privileged male notion, which crosses cultural boundaries, that a woman must always be blamed for childlessness within a marriage. The story suggests that Irawaddy is punished for her adultery when she later gives birth to an albino child. She has not achieved motherhood in the socially approved time or manner. Kunthi too suffers for her adultery, because her sons refuse to support her. But notice the manner in which Nathan's adultery is neither punished nor questioned. Students can explore the gender bias here, in differing attitudes toward male and female adultery. Kali and Janaki are types of simple village women, one garrulous and the other exhausted with childbearing. Murugan's untidy wife arouses pity. Old Granny must die starving and alone. Only Rukmani receives a tender welcome from her son at the end of the novel: "Do not worry," Selvam says, "We shall manage" (189). This is her reward. Although her life is like nectar in a sieve, with happiness being washed away even before it has come, she has the invincible blessing of hope and comfort from her family, because she is the archetype of the Good Indian Woman.

NOTE

This chapter derives its title from a popular song, taken from a film made in Tamil, one of the main languages of Southern India. The song defines a woman thus: "One who combines Timidity, bashfulness, Implicit acceptance and Physical sensibility—She is (A good woman, a very good woman . . .)."

WORK CITED

Markandaya, Kamala. *Nectar in a Sieve* [1954]. New York: Penguin, 1956.

FOR FURTHER READING

Narayan, R. K. *The Dark Room*. Chicago: U of Chicago P, 1938.

Boyhood Unraveled: Elie Wiesel's *Night* (1960)

Sara R. Horowitz

A slender but powerful volume, Elie Wiesel's autobiographical *Night* recounts the details of life and death during the Holocaust from a teenage boy's perspective. One of the most widely read books about the Nazi genocide, *Night* begins in 1941, when Eliezer was a child of twelve living in the Transylvania region of what was then Hungary, and concludes with his liberation from Buchenwald. The memoir focuses on one year's passage—from the spring of 1944, when Germany invaded Hungary, until the German defeat in the spring of 1945, and liberation.

The German entry into Sighet catapulted Eliezer from an ordinary life into a nightmarish world of ghettos, slave labor, concentration camps, and death. Early on, Wiesel makes clear the role that gender played for Jews during the Holocaust. On the one hand, Jewish men and women were equally targeted by Nazi genocide. Enduring or perishing under inhumane conditions, both faced the privations of the ghetto, the degradation of the camps, and the death sentence. On the other hand, men and women suffered in different ways, with different chances for survival. Upon being herded out from the trains, the Jews are divided according to gender, men separated from women. Abruptly and brutally, the boy loses contact with his mother. As Eliezer's father takes his son's hand, the boy sees her walk off with his younger sister. "I did not know that in that time, at that place, I was parting from my mother and Tzipora forever" (27). Indeed, he later learns, they were taken immediately to the gas chambers and murdered.

This separation by gender begins the process called *selection*, in which Nazi S. S. officials "select" which Jews are to be killed, and which will be subjected to hard labor and unspeakable conditions until they die. Only those arrivals who appear strong enough to endure slave labor are left alive. One's chances of surviving the first selection were linked to both age and gender. A seasoned prisoner tells Eliezer and his father to lie about their ages. Eliezer must say he is eighteen, rather than fifteen, and his father must say he is forty, rather than fifty. Younger boys and girls are deemed not fit for work, and hence not fit for living. They accompany their mothers, and—along with women who arrive pregnant—are sent directly to the gas chambers. Thus, as Eliezer's mother is led away with her youngest daughter, the two elder ones join the women's camp (and survive the war, as Wiesel indicates elsewhere). Ironically, this un-imaginably painful separation saves the boy's life.

In *Night*, segregation by gender plunges the boy into a womanless world, a world where men vie with one another for the scarce resources necessary to survival. Some Holocaust scholars note that writing by women survivors em-phasizes cooperative efforts among women and formation of family-like groups, while men's writing emphasizes individual struggles and competition for survival. They link this difference with the nurturing roles women fre-quently assume, and the competitive behavior men often exhibit. Teachers might ask students to what extent the behavior of Eliezer, his father, and other males in the book uphold, refute, or complicate this idea.

The contrast between traditional gender roles at the opening of *Night*, and the later upheaval of roles, puts into powerful relief the ways in which Nazi atrocity affected its victims on a personal level. Students might reflect on whether life in the camps, as depicted in *Night*, challenges or reinforces con-ventional masculinity. For example, during his childhood, Eliezer remembers his father as a "cultured, rather unsentimental man. There was never any display of emotion, even at home" (2). The elder Wiesel, deeply involved in community affairs, was held in great respect. But clearly, Wiesel's mother was the household's emotional center. Thus, the absence of women amidst the prisoners' extremely harsh realities influences the relationship between father and son. When his son's care is thrust upon him in Auschwitz, Eliezer's father struggles to sustain the boy emotionally, and to protect him from Nazi cru-elties—to be both father and mother, in the book's terms.

Soon it becomes evident that the adolescent is better able than his father to withstand the crushing labor, beatings, epidemics, and starvation. Eliezer watches as the older man deteriorates physically, unable to do what fathers do in his culture: provide for and keep their families safe, ensure religious continuity. In stark contrast to his prior role as community leader, the older man loses control even over his own body, passively accepting beatings and obeying orders. In a reversal of the father–son relationship characteristic of Holocaust narratives, Eliezer assumes the role of protector, sharing his limited food ration with the weakened older man.

As a male in an Orthodox Jewish household, Eliezer has already embarked upon study of sacred texts and daily prayer by the time the Nazi genocide intrudes upon the life of Sighet Jews. For him, the daily torments of the concentration camp not only threaten his life and assault his human dignity; they also challenge his understanding of the workings of God and God's covenant with the Jewish people. Thus, the narrative presents Eliezer's theological struggle—his crisis of faith. Although Eliezer observes that the loss of faith can lead to disabling despair and death, he himself questions God's silence, even going so far as to proclaim Him dead, "hanging . . . on this gallows" (62). The degeneration of the relationship between father and son—Eliezer's frayed trust in the older man's authority and protection, discerning his father's increasing impotence, and finally outliving the elder Wiesel—parallels the progress of Eliezer's relationship with God, drawing on a traditional Jewish Godlanguage, depicting God as Father.

Because women and men were kept separate, few women appear in *Night*. Those who do appear point to an inversion of gender roles typical of war narratives. Conventional war stories depict heroic men braving danger, defending or victimizing passive and beleaguered women, who remain in the background. Since the Holocaust was not a war fought on battlefields, but an attack upon civilian life waged first in the home, women as well as men fell victim, and also had opportunities to show courage and insight. For example, when the Sighet Jews were already in the box cars, well before their arrival at Auschwitz, Mrs. Schächter wildly anticipates what awaits them, screaming in the darkness about "a terrible fire" (22). The others regard her as mad. But in Wiesel's oeuvre, the figure of the mad(wo)man is elided with the figure of the prophet, or the moral visionary. Indeed, as the narrator acknowledges, Mrs. Schächter's vision proves horribly prophetic. Further, several social historians have noted that the gender roles prevalent in prewar society often enabled women to grasp the gravity of the situation. More attuned to the informal flow of information among neighbors and in the marketplace, women frequently understood what was coming earlier than their husbands, who relied on more official sources of information.

In another reversal, Eliezer encounters a young French woman while assigned to a work detail at a warehouse. Assuming that the two had no common language, he makes no attempt to communicate with her. He suspects her of being Jewish, and only passing as an Aryan laborer. Once, after the boy was brutally beaten by the Kapo, or supervisor of the labor detail, the woman surprises him by risking her life to lift his morale, giving him food, cleaning his wounds, and speaking words of encouragement to him in perfect German, a language she claimed not to understand. At a chance encounter in Paris many years later, she confirms Eliezer's suspicions, telling him of her forged papers, and that speaking more than a few words in German to the young boy "would have aroused suspicion" (51). This episode reverses the gender roles: a boy in distress is rescued by a bold woman willing to put her own life on the line.

Wiesel has repeatedly commented that posing the right questions is far more important than finding the answers, particularly since the answers to certain questions may not exist. The cosmic questions Wiesel raises in *Night*—about the nature of humanity, God, history, and human meaning—are crucial not only in thinking about the Holocaust, but about the postwar legacy, the world we inhabit. In today's classrooms, teachers of *Night* will want students to consider not only life, death, and survival under Nazi atrocity but also the roles, treatment, and courage of men and women in contemporary wartime situations and oppressive regimes, all too immediately with us in the twenty-first century.

WORK CITED

Wiesel, Elie. *Night*. New York: Bantam, 1960.

FOR FURTHER READING

Horowitz, Sara R. "Memory and Testimony in Women Survivors of Nazi Genocide." *Women of the Word: Jewish Women and Jewish Writing*. Ed. Judith Baskin. Detroit: Wayne State UP, 1994, 258–82.
Ofer, D. and L. Weitzman, eds. *Women in the Holocaust*. New Haven, CT: Yale UP, 1998.

Sexuality as Rebellion in George Orwell's *1984* (1949)

Paul Bail

1984 is set in a hypothetical future where advanced technology enables a ruling elite to intrude into every aspect of personal life through electronic surveillance. Those who deviate from social conformity are coerced into submission through a combination of sheer brutality and sophisticated mind-control techniques.

The society is strictly hierarchical, with the laboring masses, the "proles," at the bottom. At the apex of the pyramid is Big Brother, the symbolic figurehead whose portrait dominates every public building. To the extent that the upper echelons of the Party are glimpsed in the narrative, they seem to be exclusively and stereotypically male, their sole motive being the quest for power, purely for its own sake.

In this grim pecking order women are at the margins—nameless proletarian housewives, prostitutes, puritanical anti-sex fanatics, and low-level Outer Party functionaries. Personal relationships are taboo, particularly romantic liaisons. The only legitimate purpose of sexuality is for reproduction, a duty owed to the Party for creating new citizens, not an experience in which to take any personal pleasure. With this emphasis on sexual repression, *1984* becomes a feverish Freudian nightmare writ large. In this Oedipal vision, the sons' access to sexual fulfillment is savagely blocked by an omnipotent Big Brother whose image resonates with the repressive patriarchal stereotypes of both anthropomorphic religious monotheism and Freudian psycho-mythology.

To Winston Smith, the protagonist, women—especially young, pretty ones—exist mainly as a source of frustration, irritation, or temptation. He is contemptuous of females, considering them particularly susceptible to Party propaganda. When Winston first encounters Julia, he fears and hates her, and fantasizes about raping her and beating her to death. Although this liaison is supposed to be the novel's love story, the stronger "romance" is between Winston and another man, O'Brien.

As readers we see the relationship with Julia only through Winston's eyes. The couple scarcely know each other when they first have sex, and since they are both Party members their relationship is illegal. What binds them together is the transgressive quality of their act and the danger in which it puts them. By having illicit sex Winston is rebelling against Big Brother and the Party hierarchy.

Winston's relationship to Julia is accidental, and subordinate to his involvement with O'Brien, which seems fated and necessary. From the opening chapter, Winston gravitates strongly to O'Brien, an important member of the Inner Party. O'Brien pretends to join Winston in rebelling against Big Brother but actually works for the secret police, and after Winston is arrested, O'Brien becomes his chief torturer and confessor. It does not matter to Winston that O'Brien dupes and betrays him. Winston had anticipated that possibility from the start, deciding that whether O'Brien proved to be friend or enemy, he was nevertheless the one person who could truly understand him.

O'Brien not only violates Winston's body, through the pain of the torture chamber, but also gets inside his mind. Through drugs, torture, and persuasion Winston eventually comes to see the world much in the way that O'Brien does. Once Winston surrenders to O'Brien and the Party, whatever flame of intimacy existed between him and Julia is snuffed out forever. The climactic moment occurs when Winston, faced with the form of torture he most fears, cries out, "Do it to Julia! Not me! Julia! I don't care what you do to her . . . Not me!" (236).

Some young women may find it difficult to engage with *1984*, finding Winston's misogynistic attitudes and sadistic fantasies repugnant and Julia's character insufficiently fleshed out for reader-identification. In fact, none of the significant women in Winston's life are developed as characters—neither his mother, nor his sister, nor his lover. Other than having sex with Winston, Julia does and says very little in the narrative. Speaking through Winston, Orwell even dismisses Julia as "only a rebel from the waist downward" (129).

Orwell's marginalization of his key female character and his foregrounding of the "serious" concerns of politics and male camaraderie are characteristic of the author's historical era. He deserves credit as a genuine humanist, with a deep aversion to ethnic and class prejudice, who tried to live his personal life according to his political beliefs. But, like most of his contemporaries, Orwell had an ideological blind spot concerning gender politics: he wrote condescendingly of the "pansy left" and in his voluminous political writings he ignored the women's movement, except for a passage where he bemoans how the Left attracts a "disquieting prevalence of cranks" such as the "fruit juice drinker, nudist, sandal-wearer . . . quack, pacifist, and feminist" (206).

Despite Orwell's shallow treatment of Julia, it is possible to imagine her as a three-dimensional character based on the few hints the author leaves in the text. Some of Julia's traits reflect the perspective of "difference" held by theorists such as Carol Gilligan and Nancy Rule Goldberger. For example, Julia bases her judgments on contextualized and experiential knowledge. Having had clandestine sex with scores of Party leaders, Julia sees through the hypocrisy and sham of the official social structure. As a result, she has the pragmatic realism of an outsider. In contrast, Winston, like many males, is enamored of abstract knowledge. Even after he rejects the official ideology of Big Brother, he still remains vulnerable to the lure of bankrupt political abstractions—the "ideals" of the Brotherhood—which O'Brien dangles before him as bait.

While Winston remains intellectually fascinated by Party ideology and is willing to risk all for some purely abstract issue (128–29), Julia believes it is worth taking risks only when one's network of personal relationships is at stake. An enlightening exercise for students would be to take the bits of personal information that are given about Julia and construct an alternate narrative of events from her point of view. Retelling the story from Julia's perspective highlights how Winston's narrative resonates with the psychology of an adolescent boy, focused on power struggles with an all-powerful father figure who is feared, hated, and loved simultaneously. It also suggests currents of closeted, repressed homoerotic attraction.

WORKS CITED

Gilligan, Carol. *In a Different Voice: Psychological Theory and Women's Development.* Cambridge, MA: Harvard UP, 1982.

Goldberger, Nancy Rule. "Looking Backward, Looking Forward." *Knowledge, Difference, and Power: Essays Inspired by Women's Ways of Knowing.* Ed. Nancy Rule Goldberger, Jill Tarule, Blythe Clinchy, and Mary Betenky. New York: Basic, 1996, 1–21.

Orwell, George. *1984* [1949]. New York: New American Library, 1984.

———. *The Road to Wigan Pier* [1937]. New York: Harcourt, Brace & World, 1958.

FOR FURTHER READING

Patai, Daphne. *The Orwell Mystique: A Study in Male Ideology.* Amherst: U of Massachusetts P, 1984.

Homer's *Odyssey*: "The *Iliad*'s Wife" (ca. 700 B.C.E.)

Deborah Ross

Samuel Butler's nickname for the *Odyssey*, "the *Iliad*'s wife," suggests that the poem is *feminine* without being *feminist*; that is, it describes activities like laundry without questioning who is supposed to do it. The poem abounds with female characters of tremendous power, both positive and negative, but they exercise this power only within women's traditional domain. As "wives and daughters of heroes" (XI, 329), the *Odyssey*'s women are defined by their roles in the lives of men.

The life of a Greek epic hero could be said to consist of going out to get treasure, through conquest or gift, and coming back home to add it to his pile. The *Iliad* is a story of going out; the *Odyssey*, of coming back. Both going and coming, the hero encounters many female deities: Olympian goddesses, the Muse, the Fates. Mortal women, however, belong mainly to the return phase, and therefore they are greatly occupied with the storage and maintenance of the hero's property.

Through negative and positive example—treacherous Klytemnestra versus faithful Arete, Helen, and Penelope—the ideal wife is shown to be a commodity, a storehouse, and a gift dispenser. Her influence raises the civilized Achaian home above the level of the savage Cyclopes' caves. However, since she belongs only to the homecoming phase of the hero's life, even the successful wife may become his enemy by trying to hold him when he has to leave. Telemachus, going out to manhood, must break the hold of his worried and uncomprehending mother and nurse (II, 363–70; IV, 732). Odysseus, coming back, must resist the magnetic pull of Circe's and Kalypso's provisional homes. Only the goddess Athene is never left behind.

The poem thus shows that women's domestic attraction can be dangerous—much like their sexual attraction. Part of Odysseus' heroism requires that he steer clear of women's lust and avoid being sucked dry by Charybdis (XI, 105) or devoured in the cave of Skylla (XI, 93–94), which both hides and represents the monster's genitalia (XI, 105). He must also master his own sexuality, which makes him vulnerable to the Sirens as well as to Circe and Kalypso. The decisive battle for mastery takes place on Circe's bed (X, 295–301), from which Odysseus emerges triumphant, to be rewarded with a properly feminine cave, a passive hole where he can stash his goods (XIII, 366–71). Telemachus, too, masters sex by punishing the female bodies where he believes sex resides— in this case by sentencing to torture and death all serving women who, willingly or not, had sex with the suitors (XXII, 457–72).

By thus blaming the victims, the *Odyssey* seems to sanction the most appalling sexism. We're meant to cheer the heroes' victories; yet what reader is not shocked at the "punishment" of serving women whom the suitors "mishandled" (XVI, 108–9)? Who does not pity the abandoned Kalypso, whose "crime" is love (V, 129–37)? Who can miss the injustice of the suitors' calling Penelope a tease, a sneak, and a waverer for not liking them (II, 91–128)? A teacher may bring students to see the ways in which the heroes displace their own desires onto their objects in much the same way Adam casts his sexual guilt onto Eve—a projection that continues to plague victims in rape and sexual harassment cases today.

A teacher may also bring students beyond indignation by noting that the poem draws readers in and empowers them to resist its own masculine, heroic values in several ways. It issues women readers a special invitation when it makes Penelope the ultimate audience for Odysseus' tale, thus overruling Telemachus, who sent his mother to her room for listening to the men's poetry (I, 356–59). Historical research projects might investigate the possibility of a real female audience for the poem in various eras.

The *Odyssey* also encourages readers to identify with Penelope and other women as characters—even with Kalypso, whose interests oppose the hero's (V, 116–44)—by revealing their words and thoughts. A creative writing assignment might ask students to describe events from a female character's viewpoint. (For further discussion of these and other issues, see Cohen.)

Centuries of women have entered the *Odyssey* through these doorways, some even going on to write their own narratives imitating Penelope's plot. Through stories about women faced with a marital choice that is really no choice, early women novelists could show that to the victim, forced marriage is just a respectable form of rape. Imprisoned in her chamber, pondering the suitors' demands, Penelope assumes nearly the same position as the maidservants who are being gang-"mishandled" below. She and the maidservants become literary foremothers to generations of heroines trapped in buildings that symbolize their own bodies, fending off male intruders. From the Gothic heroine in her tower to the babysitter whose crank caller turns out to be *inside the house*, students encouraged to trace their lineage can recognize Penelope's daughters. Broader connections may be made as well, helping students appreciate that love is not a "merely" feminine concern but the fuel that drives the plot in many a comedy and romance, from *Tom Jones* and *Jane Eyre* to the television sitcom.

The influence of "the *Iliad*'s wife" has not been merely literary: as Scheherazade demonstrated, a good story can save a woman's life. The decline in arranged marriages may have come about in part because, after looking through Penelope's eyes for two or three millennia, society began to feel less comfortable selling its daughters into matrimony. With the *Odyssey* as starting point, students can explore the role of fiction in helping to bring about social change—and perhaps even predict the stories and realities of the next thousand years.

WORKS CITED

Butler, Samuel. *The Authoress of the* Odyssey. 2nd ed. Chicago: U of Chicago P, 1967.
Cohen, Beth, ed. *The Distaff Side: Representing the Female in Homer's* Odyssey. New York: Oxford UP, 1995.
Lattimore, Richmond, trans. *The Odyssey of Homer* [ca. 700 B.C.E.]. New York: Harper and Row, 1967.

FOR FURTHER READING

Lefkowitz, Mary R. and Maureen B. Fant. *Women's Life in Greece and Rome.* Baltimore, MD: Johns Hopkins UP, 1982.

Jocasta and Her Daughters:
Women in Sophocles' *Oedipus Rex*
(ca. 430 B.C.E.)

Paula Alida Roy

How are we to view the women in *Oedipus Rex*, an ancient myth about identity, pride, and suffering? Aristotle contends in the *Poetics* that women "are an inferior type of person" (309), and centuries later, the Oedipal theory led Freud and his followers to conclude that women show a morally inferior sense of justice when compared to men. If women were considered inferior in the age of Greek tragedy and if Sophocles' *Oedipus Rex* affirms contemporary stereotypes about women's capacity for moral reasoning, what about Jocasta and her daughters?

Queen Jocasta, wife of Oedipus, sister of Creon, mother to two daughters and two sons, is a figure of some power in that she provides access to the reign of Thebes. As Sarah Pomeroy points out in *Goddesses, Whores, Wives, and Slaves: Women in Classical Antiquity*, the marriage of Oedipus and Jocasta is an example of matrilineal succession to the throne: "The power of the mother's brother and the close bond between brother and sister—common features of matrilineal societies—appear most significantly in the Oedipus myth" (19).

The play opens with Oedipus, the father-king, as he greets the suffering people of Thebes. The citizens are his "children"; he is "Oedipus . . . a man wisest in the ways of God." Thus Sophocles foreshadows the male hubris that oils the wheels of tragedy. It is noteworthy, however, that Jocasta also makes her entrance as a figure of influence. In the midst of an argument in which Oedipus accuses Creon of treachery, Choragos announces with relief that the queen is coming, "and it is time she came for the sake of you both. / This dreadful quarrel can be resolved through her" (32). Her first lines suggest her assumption of power: she reprimands husband and brother as "Poor foolish men." She summons Oedipus into the palace and orders Creon to "go now."

In responding, both men underscore her gender, calling her "woman" and "sister." Each, however, respects her enough to try to explain his side of the quarrel. After Creon leaves, Jocasta hears out Oedipus' anger that Creon should accuse him of killing Laios. She reassures him with the story of how her infant son, fathered by King Laios, was set out in the mountains to die because the infant was prophesized to grow up to kill his father and marry his mother. She tells Oedipus to ignore prophecies. "Have no dread of them." Her bitterness comes through as she explains, "my child—Poor baby!—it was my child that died first" (43). After news of Polybus' death, Jocasta tells Oedipus again not to worry about oracles. When he asks about the danger of sleeping with his mother, she replies, "Have no more fear of sleeping with your mother. / How many men, in dreams, have lain with their mothers! / No reasonable man is troubled by such things" (49). Thus far, Jocasta shows herself to be practical, concerned less with future or past than with present, involved in keeping human relationships smooth.

When the messenger/shepherd unravels the details of how the infant Oedipus survived, Jocasta realizes the truth. She tells Oedipus to "forget it all." She pleads, "For God's love, let us have no more questioning! / Is your life nothing to you? / My own is pain enough for me to bear" (55). She cries, "May you never learn who you are!" before she rushes into the palace to hang herself. Pomeroy notes that suicide in classical mythology "is a feminine and somewhat cowardly mode of death" (101). In that sense Jocasta's death stands in gendered contrast to Oedipus' decision to live in exile, blinded by his own hand. In fact, our last glimpse of Jocasta reinforces a conventional view of women as emotional beings, victims of male power. On the other hand, her stance in the play suggests a commonsense reliance on experience and practical necessity versus prophecy and abstraction. While Sophocles creates the tragic hero mold out of Oedipus' stubborn pursuit of truth and justice, contemporary readers may interrogate Jocasta's emphasis on concrete realities. Jocasta's concern for Oedipus, her warnings to him to stop seeking the truth, may be interpreted to reflect what Carol Gilligan has called "an ethic of care," which she contrasts "with the formal logic of fairness that informs the justice approach" (73).

Women also enter the play briefly in the persons of Antigone and Ismene. Oedipus commends Jocasta's body to Creon—"The woman in there— / Give her whatever funeral you think proper: / She is your sister" (74), his language suggesting that he seeks to distance himself from Jocasta by emphasizing her relationship to Creon. Then he asks Creon to care for "his poor daughters," and begs to be allowed to see them before he goes into exile. As the girls appear, Oedipus weeps over them in a speech that reveals much about the fate of women:

I weep for you when I think of the bitterness
That men will visit upon you all your lives . . .
And when you come to marriageable age,
Where is the man, my daughters, who would dare
Risk the bane that lies on all my children? (75)

While Oedipus acknowledges that his curse lies on all of his children, he specifically makes a distinction between daughters and sons: "As for my sons, you need not care for them. / They are men, they will find some way to live" (74). He emphasizes the importance of marriage for his daughters, while assuring himself that his sons will be self-sufficient as "men." In the classroom, this comparison can raise historical and contemporary questions about parental fears for and decisions about children of either sex.

Indeed, the very antiquity of the play throws into sharp relief the relevance of the issues it raises. Teachers often emphasize how the play illustrates Freud's Oedipal Complex, an example of the power of myth to transcend time. When we introduce gender as a category of analysis, with particular questions about the roles of women and attitudes toward them, we can encourage students to explore historical research into both Greek society and Freudian psychology through the lens of feminist scholars such as Carol Gilligan and Sarah Pomeroy. We can also use the play to explore ancient roots of contemporary attitudes toward marriage and motherhood, power and agency, the raising of sons and daughters. Through these approaches, we invite students to see Jocasta and her daughters as more than stick figures leaning in the doorways of palaces and temples.

WORKS CITED

Gilligan, Carol. *In a Different Voice: Psychological Theory and Women's Development.* Cambridge, MA: Harvard UP, 1982.

Pomeroy, Sarah B. *Goddesses, Whores, Wives, and Slaves: Women in Classical Antiquity.* New York: Schocken, 1975.

Sophocles. *Oedipus Rex* [ca. 430 B.C.E.]. Trans. and ed. Dudley Fitts and Robert Fitzgerald. *The Oedipus Cycle.* New York: Harcourt Brace, 1949, 1–78.

FOR FURTHER READING

Willner, Elinor. "Classical Proportions of the Heart" and "Operations." *Reversing the Spell: New and Selected Poems.* Port Townsend, WA: Copper Canyon Press, 1998, 90–93, 177–79.

Women Stripped of Humanity: John Steinbeck's *Of Mice and Men* (1937)

Lesley Broder

Of Mice and Men portrays the desperation people experienced during the Depression. The novel is set in rural California, and Steinbeck presents people of different ages, races, abilities, and classes, all of whom are subject to isolation. Although loneliness is inescapable in Soledad, as the name of the town suggests, Curley's wife especially suffers because she is the only woman on a ranch where women are treated as nothing more than sexual objects. She therefore develops tactics for surviving loneliness that are markedly different from those used by the men who surround her.

From the outset, women are categorized loosely as either nurturing or troublesome. Lennie, a mentally retarded individual, has fond memories of his Aunt Clara, who took care of him and entrusted his welfare to George before her death. She is the only maternal representation of women; more often women are cast as conduits to misfortune for men. George and Lennie have been forced to find employment in Soledad because a woman at their former job accused Lennie of rape when he tried to feel her dress. Later, George spends the money he is saving for a ranch on prostitutes. Portrayed only as objects of entertainment and forces of destruction, women repeatedly distract men from their goals.

Curley's wife further adds to this portrayal. Entirely devoid of company, she is the one character who remains nameless. The men acknowledge nothing about her true being, but merely that she is married to the boss's son. She wanders the ranch asking for Curley and using her sexuality to get attention. When Lennie and George first meet Curley's wife, she is described unequivocally in sexual terms.

> She had full, rouged lips and wide-spaced eyes, heavily made up. . . . Her hair hung in little rolled clusters, like sausages. . . . She put her hands

behind her back and leaned against the door frame so that her body was thrown forward. (31)

Since her husband pays little attention to her and she has no occupation or friends, to fight desolation she must use her sexual appeal among the ranch hands, whose male camaraderie plainly excludes her.

George puts Curley's wife into the category of "trouble" by warning Lennie that "They's gonna be a bad mess about her. She's a jail bait all set on the trigger" (51). Curley's wife is sensitive to this kind of rejection. When the Black ranch handyman, Crooks, and his white counterpart, Candy, gather with Lennie in the barn, she wants their company and tries to flirt with them. The men respond coolly to her advances and ask that she leave. Discomfited, she responds, "If I catch any one man, and he's alone, I get along fine with him. But just let two of the guys get together an' you won't talk. . . . Think I don't like to talk to somebody ever' once in a while?" (77). Furious and desperate, she attacks each man viciously, but sensing his vulnerability she threatens Crooks in particular: "I could get you strung up on a tree so easy it ain't even funny" (81). Invoking her husband's power when her charms do not work, Curley's wife also draws force from the prevailing racist notion of which laborer she—an utterly powerless white female—could attempt to dominate.

In addition to suffering loneliness as the men do, Curley's wife also lives off dreams as they do. While seducing Lennie, she speaks to him about her unspent potential and a man who wanted to make her a movie star. "Says I was a natural. Soon's he got back to Hollywood he was gonna write to me about it" (88). When this man did not fulfill his promise, she married Curley. In all her dreams, men provide salvation and joy, for happiness is not something she can attain for herself. Ironically and pitiably, the sexuality she uses to cope with her lost dreams results in her death as Lennie pets her hair, then panics and snaps her neck just as Curley's wife confides her cherished fantasies.

Upon her death, Lennie is hunted for destroying Curley's property; thus Curley's wife's death makes George and Lennie's dream of owning land impossible. Predictably, Curley's wife, like the prostitute George visits, serves to lead men astray. As such, Curley's wife is often compared to Eve: unintentionally, her actions bring about the fall of paradise, or in this case, the dream of paradise. While the men mourn the end of their own dream, they have remained oblivious to Curley's wife's fantasies, the dreams she could not easily share with the male companions who so readily dismiss her.

By examining the character of Curley's wife, students may consider what happens when women submerge their identity in that of another person. Additionally, *Of Mice and Men* reinforces the idea that women without access to other forms of power often use sexuality to get what they need from men. Students can debate the legitimacy of this: Was Curley's wife to blame for her own death? Did Curley's wife have any other recourse than using her beauty for attention? This subject can lead to a controversial discussion of date rape or the criminalization of prostitution. Those sympathizing with Curley's wife may also see the destructive effects of judging women solely on appearances, and the sometimes dire consequences women face when they flaunt their sexuality. If Steinbeck's novel were paired with Harper Lee's *To Kill a Mockingbird*, students could further discuss how another lonely woman, Mayella Ewell, uses her sexuality for attention and how this affects an entire town in rural Alabama.

Alienation rings through every page of this short novel. Each character faces the loneliness caused by unmet needs and miserable circumstances. Until her conversation with Lennie, Curley's wife is alone in a hostile world. While the men actively work toward realizing their dreams, Curley's wife has no way even to imagine executing her plans, however unrealistic they may be. Her lost dreams become, perhaps, the most poignant dreams of all because she has no one with whom to share them, except in the moments preceding her death. Like her fantasies, Curley's wife herself is cut down without ever having had a chance to develop.

WORK CITED

Steinbeck, John. *Of Mice and Men/Cannery Row* [1937]. New York: Penguin, 1987, 1–107.

FOR FURTHER READING

Spilka, Mark. "Of George and Lennie and Curley's Wife: Sweet Violence in Steinbeck's Eden." *Modern Fiction Studies* 20 (1974): 169–79.

Role Traps in Ken Kesey's *One Flew Over the Cuckoo's Nest* (1962)

Michelle Napierski-Prancl

One Flew Over the Cuckoo's Nest is set in a male mental ward where gender roles run counter to those in patriarchal society. Here, women are in control and patients, according to Harding, "are victims of a matriarchy" (61). The most powerful person in the ward is Miss Ratched, the "Big Nurse," whose authority is contested by the new patient, Randle McMurphy. The narrator is Chief Bromden, a Native American who feels small despite his great physical size.

Sexism is apparent in *Cuckoo's Nest* as characters are relegated to two types of role traps: those that favor traditional norms of femininity/masculinity and those that challenge them. We sympathize with characters who act gender appropriately and dislike or feel sorry for those who do not. Role traps pigeonhole characters into classes of one-dimensional gendered beings.

Female characters are limited to the roles of "Good Girls," "Whores," "Ball-cutters," and "Iron Maidens." Good Girls are "little." The little, birthmarked nurse wears a cross to represent virginity; another little nurse expresses her femininity by flirting with patients, and the little "Jap" nurse is a compassionate motherly figure. On the other hand, Candy and Sandy portray the unacceptable role of "Whore" by engaging in behavior that is celebrated by men like McMurphy. This condemnation represents the sexual double standard to which women are held.

Miss Ratched, wives, and mothers emasculate men and are "Ball-cutters." Harding's wife belittles him, Bromden's mother dominated his father, Billy's mother never let him grow up, and Nurse Ratched symbolically castrates all men on her ward. The Big Nurse also falls into the category of "Iron Maiden," an asexual powerful woman who dismisses traditional notions of femininity. She carries "no compact or lipstick or woman stuff" (4) and conceals her breasts. The trade-off for power is the loss of femininity; she is "impregnable" (70).

Male role traps include the "Cowboy," "Mama's Boy," "Wimp," and "Homosexual." McMurphy portrays the acceptable role of "Cowboy." He is a tough, broad man with scars and tattoos. He rocks in his boots, swaggers when he walks, and gambles with sexy cards. He even arranges a high-noon showdown. McMurphy proclaims to be a psychopath, a guy who "fights too much and fucks too much" (13). In contrast, Billy Bibbit is a "Mama's Boy." At thirty-one, he would rather die than have his mother disapprove of him. Most other patients, as well as Dr. Spivey, are "Wimps," too weak to challenge the women in their lives, including the Big Nurse. The category which represents the most negative threat to a man's masculinity is "Homosexual." This role trap fits Harding who is refined, effeminate, and possibly gay.

In each role trap, emphasis is placed on size. Femininity has long been associated with being small, frail, and thin, while large size, weight, and strength have corresponded to masculinity. The acceptable female characters are described as "little" while the most ill-favored is "Big." Readers learn that women must be careful not to engage in gender-inappropriate behavior. They can be motherly, virginal, or flirtatious but should not cross over and become stern, asexual, or sexually aggressive. In comparison, to be masculine is to be like McMurphy: larger than life, sexually promiscuous, violent, and resistant to controlling women.

Cuckoo's Nest will affect young readers' understanding of gender because power differentials in this novel are clearly embedded in gender relations. Men gain power through sexual assault while women control men through symbolic castration. McMurphy has a secret family recipe for violence against women and has been arrested for statutory rape of a 15-year-old girl. Disturbingly, this is quickly dismissed because "she was plenty willin' " (42). McMurphy continually attacks Miss Ratched with sexual innuendoes that culminate in a sexual assault. Minor characters also make reference to rape: one orderly witnessed his mother's rape; Ruckly says "Fffffffuck da wife!" (16); and Colonel Matterson lifts nurses' skirts. Kesey posits that "man has but one truly effective weapon against the juggernaut of modern matriarchy" (68), his penis. As in society, rape is a form of social control. Female characters like Nurse Ratched retaliate through castration, making patients into weak rabbits who have no "whambam" (65).

In this novel, presenting a rapist as a protagonist and a powerful woman as an antagonist condemns strength in women and condones violence in men. It reinforces sexist ideas about appropriate behavior and expectations. It promotes the use of sexual harassment and the threat of rape to prevent women from reaching their potential. It limits men's achievements by maintaining that men are defined primarily through their sexuality and physical power.

Gender roles in this novel are best understood if placed in the social context of the time of publication. The 1960s was a period of social turmoil when the drug culture, the Civil Rights movement, and the second wave of feminism occurred simultaneously. While embracing the drug culture, this book acts as a form of backlash against the civil rights and feminist movements.

In order to understand attitudes about racism and sexism students might compare and contrast the 1960s to today. Consider how the portrayal of Chief Bromden, the Black boys, and the little "Jap" nurse would be different if the book were written today. How have subtle and overt forms of racism changed over time? Can the same be said of sexism? Would the portrayals of female characters be different if written today? Consider the issue of weight, size, beauty, and power. In popular culture big women are still regarded as ugly, sexless, and domineering. In contrast, little (i.e., thin) women are celebrated as being attractive, glamorous objects of desire. Students may also consider prevalent views on rape and violence against women. How are sexual harassment, rape, and the threat of rape used to control women?

WORKS CITED

Kesey, Ken. One Flew Over the Cuckoo's Nest: *Text and Criticism*. Ed. John Clark Pratt. New York: Penguin, 1996.

Scully, Diana. *Understanding Sexual Violence*. New York: Routledge, 1994.

Searles, George J., ed. *A Casebook on Ken Kesey's* One Flew Over the Cuckoo's Nest. Albuquerque: U of New Mexico P, 1992.

FOR FURTHER READING

Goffman, Erving. *Asylums: Essays on the Social Situation of Inmates and Other Inmates*. Chicago: Aldine Publishing, 1962.

Under the Burden of Yellow Peril: Race, Class, and Gender in Yoshiko Uchida's *Picture Bride* (1987)

Montye P. Fuse

Yoshiko Uchida's *Picture Bride* depicts the struggles of Hana, a young Japanese woman who exchanges pictures with a man she will marry when she comes to the United States. Uchida shows us the trials, disappointments, and triumphs of an Asian female who immigrates to America in the early twentieth century. According to historian Sucheng Chan, despite restrictions on the numbers of immigrants from Asia who could legally enter the United States between 1908 and 1920, thousands of so-called "picture brides" immigrated under the sponsorship of Japanese men who intended to marry them. Like Hana in Uchida's novel, many of these women traveled thousands of miles to a strange land intending to marry men they had never met. This custom was based on the tradition of arranged matches in Japan, where marriage was a family matter, often orchestrated by relatives (Takaki 248). However, these men often misrepresented themselves. Hana's reaction upon meeting her would-be husband, Taro, was typical: "[Hana was] . . . startled to see that he was already turning bald . . . he looked older than thirty-one" (7).

Asians were the first immigrant group to be excluded from entrance to the United States on the sole basis of race. Asian women were further excluded because it was thought that they often came to work as prostitutes. Because of anti-miscegenation laws preventing Asian males from marrying white women, picture brides served an important social function for Japanese Americans, allowing them to start families and form communities.

Picture Bride effectively describes the impact of gender and race on the quality of life for early Japanese immigrant women. Not only were many disappointed at the sight of their husbands-to-be, but many Japanese men in America exaggerated the extent of their economic success. Although Hana is initially excited by the prospect of marrying a man she believes to be a wealthy merchant, she is dismayed to discover that Taro's is a "shabby" store catering to a Japanese-only clientele. She soon learns that racism limits the Japanese to subsistence levels within the California economy. And although a high school graduate in Japan, Hana finds that her own employment possibilities in America are limited to helping Taro in his shop or cleaning the houses of affluent white families.

Hana must also learn to be a good Japanese wife, as her friend Kiku tells her:

> Just don't have too many big dreams and you're less likely to be hurt . . . you came to America to make Taro Takeda happy . . . just remember that and don't expect too much from him or from America. (25)

Kiku's advice is that Japanese wives must sacrifice their happiness for that of their husbands. She thus reinforces Japanese cultural ideals regarding women's roles. Indeed, such economic, emotional, and spiritual investment was put into making these arranged marriages successful that most women had little choice but to stay with their husbands. In the close-knit Japanese community, shame would surely result for a woman who left her husband.

The message that women must support their husbands unconditionally is consistent throughout *Picture Bride*. Before her arrival in America, Hana imagines that her arranged marriage will be a "means of escaping both [her] village and the encirclement of her family" (4). In other words, Hana exercises forethought in trying to choose her own life circumstances, but she finds she is severely limited when she marries Taro. Hana's gender roles (and those of other Japanese women in the novel) as wife, mother, and homemaker are determined by the circumstances of the arranged marriage. Given the logic of *Picture Bride*, Hana's agency is usurped by the structure of the Japanese family.

Teachers of *Picture Bride* might discuss Uchida's development of Hana's character. Conversations might focus on the ease with which her desires to escape the confinement of societal expectations in Japan lead her into even more strictly determined gender roles in America. Interesting also is the relationship between Hana and Kiyoshi Yamaka. Kiyoshi San is a handsome and charismatic young man who falls in love with Hana. Disappointed with her marriage, Hana is strongly attracted to Kiyoshi San, and the two endeavor to spend private time together. Once, when Taro is away delivering charity to poor Japanese farmers, Hana and Kiyoshi San kiss "with such hunger that she had almost lost control" (53). Yet, despite her desire for Kiyoshi San, Hana cannot continue this "infidelity." Students might discuss Hana's motivation for her "affair" with Kiyoshi San. How does this relationship challenge gendered expectations for Hana? How do such expectations arise? Students may see Hana's actions as a final attempt to subvert the role of a good Japanese wife, especially given her subsequent avoidance of Kiyoshi San.

Hana and Taro's daughter Mary is an interesting character when compared to Hana herself. Like many Asian-American novels, *Picture Bride* portrays intergenerational relationships within Asian-American families. In this regard, Mary's character and her relationship with her parents will facilitate fruitful discussion. Much to her parents' dismay, Mary is unlike other traditional Japanese girls; she is boisterous, outgoing, and completely unlady-like. When she grows up and goes to college, Mary falls in love and elopes with Joe Cantelli, a white American. This disturbs Hana and Taro, particularly when Mary and Joe decide to move to Nevada. Apparently, Mary has cut ties with her parents and the ethnic Japanese community, preferring to live as an American rather than as a "Japanese American." The impact of Mary's decision is clear when her parents are put into internment camp, while she avoids relocation because she and Joe live outside of those areas zoned for internment. Mary's moving away from the Japanese-American community might be compared with Hana's choice to leave Japan. Yet although Mary's decision clearly affects her identity as a Japanese American, her gender roles as wife, mother, and homemaker do not change. In the end, given the constraints of both American society and Japanese culture, *Picture Bride* suggests that few opportunities existed either for immigrant or second-generation Japanese-American women to transcend expectations placed on them by both Japanese and American cultures.

In what seems like a postscript at the end of the novel, Uchida reunites Hana and her old friend Kiku in the internment camp after both have become widows. This friendship has withstood the time and trials of each woman's life. Watching them walk off together, their friend Kenji says, "They each crossed an ocean to come to this country, and they're going to survive the future with the same strength and spirit" (216). Students might talk about the nature of women's friendships in this novel.

WORKS CITED

Chan, Sucheng. *Asian Americans: An Interpretive History*. Boston: Twayne Publishers, 1991, 103–88.

Takaki, Ronald. *A Different Mirror: A History of Multicultural America*. Boston: Little, Brown, 1993.

Uchida, Yoshiko. *Picture Bride*. Seattle/London: University of Seattle Press, 1987.

FOR FURTHER READING

Hune, Shirley. "Doing Gender with a Feminist Gaze: Toward a Historical Reconstruction of Asian America." *Contemporary Asian America: A Multicultural Reader.* Ed. Min Zhou and James V. Gatewood. New York: New York UP, 2000, 413–30.

Woman and Art in James Joyce's
A Portrait of the Artist as a Young Man (1916)

Maria Margaroni

James Joyce's *A Portrait of the Artist as a Young Man* is structured around the key moments in the formation of Stephen Dedalus, a male artist in turn-of-the-century Catholic Ireland. As the novel is narrated through the protagonist's subjective perspective, none of the other characters is significant in his/her own right. They exist as manifestations of Stephen's inner struggles, concerns, and desires. This is especially true of the women that populate Stephen's world: his mother Eileen (his idealized beloved), a prostitute, the Virgin Mary, and a girl he sees at the seaside. All of these women are portrayed in terms of the mind-versus-body opposition that structures Stephen's thinking and that can be traced back to his strict Catholic upbringing in the Jesuit institutions where he spends his formative years.

The world of these all-male institutions is characterized by suspicion toward anything material, anything relating to the body and the senses. As one of the Fathers tells the boys, it is the "immortal soul" that is of value, not the body which, being mortal, is perceived as keeping the soul in bondage (362). Stephen internalizes this suspicion to such a degree that he never frees himself of it, even when he repudiates Catholicism in order to embrace art. Thus, he comes to conceptualize his vocation as a writer in terms of an ability to rise above material life and its sounds, shapes, colors "which are the prison gates of our soul" (473).

From a feminist perspective it is important to understand how this denial of material existence determines Stephen's relationships with women and his view of the female body. The influence of the Catholic institutions he attends needs to be reemphasized, for here young Stephen learns to aspire to a spiritual ideal of masculinity, one represented by the ascetic, pale, mirthless figures of his Jesuit tutors whose sexed bodies are invisible under their long soutanes. It is also in these institutions that he comes to experience the female body as a threat to the asexual spirituality he is striving for. Indeed, soon after his arrival at Glongowes Wood College Stephen is teased for kissing his mother good-night and is forced to deny having any physical contact with her (253–54). Later on he learns to shun the eyes of women (409) and repeatedly links the female body to imagery denoting crude, offensive smells, rotten food, and excrement (336, 353).

Stephen's encounter with the prostitute who is responsible for his first spiritual "fall" is illuminating in this context. Students might discuss Stephen's perception of the woman as a series of body parts (352), which he can only bring together in the lifeless figure of a "huge doll" placed beside the bed, that serves as her metaphorical substitute. It is significant that the doll is described as sitting "with her legs apart," thus flaunting woman's sexual nature. If Stephen resists the prostitute's embrace, then, it is because her body, being the bearer of "earthly beauty" (370), excites within him physical, "base" emotions that reduce him to the state of "a baffled, prowling beast" (351).

Interestingly, Stephen's denial of the prostitute recalls his earlier traumatic experience of having to deny the mother. Students may examine the ways in which the figures of mother and whore merge in this scene. Indeed, for Stephen a woman's sexuality is inextricable from her reproductive function. This is why the more he succeeds in fashioning himself as a disciple of spiritual life, the further away he draws from his mother, whose body has been a haven of comfort to him. In fact, as the novel progresses, Mrs. Dedalus comes to function as the polar opposite to the male world of ideas that gradually absorbs her son (513); hence her disapproval of his decision to enter the university. It is no wonder that the final chapter of the novel centers on Stephen's confrontation with his mother and his growing awareness of a "noiseless sundering of their lives" (426).

It is in this light that the climactic scene of the novel at the end of Chapter IV needs to be interpreted. After his decision not to join the church, Stephen takes a walk to the sea and, in an epiphanic moment, realizes his destiny to "recreate life out of life" (434). Thus, in defining himself as an artist, he comes to reembrace life, if only as the raw material of art. In this scene, however, material reality is no longer embodied in the sexualized, reproductive female body, but in the virginal figure of a girl he sees at the beach. Students will find it useful to compare Stephen's perception of this girl with his perception of the prostitute. While the prostitute is reduced to flesh, the girl is "magically" transformed into "a strange and beautiful seabird," a symbol of pure spirit (433). What is more, whereas the prostitute's body is engulfing, forcing the young man into helpless surrender, the girl's body functions as a neutral mediator through which the artist has a vision and emerges triumphant (this scene marks the birth of Stephen as an artist). Interestingly, this is precisely how Eileen functions throughout the novel. This is why Stephen thinks of her as his muse and repeatedly associates her with the cowled figure of the Virgin Mary (286–87, 316).

Joyce's *Portrait* offers students a unique opportunity to recognize the gender bias of the Catholic privileging of spirit over body. By demonstrating how it results in the devaluation of the female body, constraining women within the stereotypical roles of virgin or whore, a feminist analysis exposes the extent to which Catholicism strengthens the political disempowerment of women within patriarchal society. In doing so, it enables students to keep a critical distance from Stephen's Catholic-inspired theory of art and to question the universal (i.e., *context-free*) validity assigned to it in the novel. To this end, it may be productive to pair *Portrait* with Virginia Woolf's *To the Lighthouse*, a novel that consciously engages with the gender politics of producing and defining art.

WORK CITED

Joyce, James. *A Portrait of the Artist as a Young Man* [1916]. *The Portable James Joyce*. Ed. Harry Levin. Harmondsworth, Middlesex: Penguin, 1976, 243–526.

FOR FURTHER READING

Deane, Seamus. "Introduction." *James Joyce*, A Portrait of the Artist as a Young Man. Ed. Seamus Deane. Harmondsworth, Middlesex: Penguin, 1992, vii–xliii.
Middleton, Peter. *The Inward Gaze: Masculinity and Subjectivity in Modern Culture*. London and New York: Routledge, 1992.

Truths Universally Acknowledged: Stereotypes of Women in Jane Austen's *Pride and Prejudice* (1813)

Missy Dehn Kubitschek

Modern readers may think that *Pride and Prejudice* shows only stereotypes of women obsessed with marriage. Mrs. Bennet and Mrs. Lucas scheme to secure "good" husbands (wealthy and respectable) for their daughters. The young women safeguard their reputations not just to remain moral, but to remain marriageable. The famous opening sentence of *Pride and Prejudice*, "It is a truth universally acknowledged that a single man in possession of a good fortune must be in want of a wife," mocks this preoccupation, but the novel also shows why marriage is an obsession.

Historically, middle-class British women had little choice. Austen's Charlotte Lucas correctly says that marrying nearly any husband is more pleasant than remaining single and poor. Women received little education, and they could get only low-paid employment as servants, seamstresses, factory workers, or governesses. Middle-class women were socially destined to be dependent on men for financial support, to be wives and mothers. Once married, they could be divorced only by an act of Parliament, which only the richest could afford. A woman's decision about marriage must be made early, then, and it is permanent. *Pride and Prejudice* explores its female characters—the Bennet sisters Jane, Elizabeth, Lydia, and their friend Charlotte—through their responses to every woman's necessity to find a husband to provide a home.

These marriage dramas play out within Britain's rigid class society, in which a family's class is determined by the status of its men. Mr. Bennet's inherited money is entailed—it would have gone automatically to a son, but he cannot leave it to his daughters. Even if women had been allowed to earn wages, British society honored hereditary wealth rather than earned income.

The conservative values of *Pride and Prejudice* often baffle modern readers, who expect to find society as the villain and the rebellious individual as the heroine. Of the five Bennet daughters, Jane and Elizabeth (Lizzie) best exemplify the novel's conservative values: female chastity, emotional sincerity, rationality, and loyalty to tradition. (Jane Austen remained unaffected by romanticism, which espoused much that contemporary American culture also honors—experimentation, emotional intensity, imagination, and creativity.) They are "rewarded" with the best husbands—those with good moral character, wealth, and compatible personalities. Yet feminist readers may appreciate Austen's nuanced presentation of Elizabeth Bennet. Unwilling to endorse Charlotte Lucas' position that women must marry any husband rather than live with the material and social deprivation experienced by single women who are not wealthy, Elizabeth refuses to give up her self-respect by marrying the foolish Mr. Collins. Further, she insists that others respect her. She rebuffs Mr. Darcy's first, insulting proposal, which unwittingly reveals his assumption that a woman in her position will of course be grateful for his offer, and she later refuses to answer the intrusive questions of Mr. Darcy's interfering aunt, Lady Catherine.

Other women marry both the people and the situations that their lesser moral characters deserve. In uniting with the foolish, unpleasant Mr. Collins, Charlotte dispenses with any enjoyment of a marriage. However, by marrying, she avoids being an unpaid servant in a brother's household and secures her own home. The most rebellious female character, Lydia, is also the most selfish and immoral. Lydia violates the critical taboo for an unmarried woman when she runs away with Wickham. Her action disgraces not only her but her family. It does not doom her sisters' chances for good matches only because Wickham is bribed into marriage. Lydia will enjoy neither her husband nor their financial situation.

Implicitly supporting both traditional gender roles and this class structure, *Pride and Prejudice* shows that faults belong to individuals rather than to the system. Both sexes and every social class have faulty representatives. If Mrs. Bennet and Lydia are weak and irresponsible, so are Mr. Bennet and Mr. Collins. Both the heroine Lizzie and hero Darcy must correct character flaws to establish and enjoy their marriage. In the class system, Lady Catherine misuses her social power to meddle in others' lives rather than to provide for dependents on her estate (her servants, the clergyman), but is balanced by Mr. Darcy, who embodies the responsible aristocrat. The middle class likewise includes both the villain Wickham, and the genteel, responsible Gardiners.

The teacher should help readers see the novel's system of values before critiquing them as sexist and classist. Identifying stereotypes and more nuanced characterizations may be a start. Mrs. Bennet represents the silly, unreasonable female chatterbox; her daughter Lydia presents a younger manifestation of the same problem, the boy-crazy adolescent. Their opposite, Jane, exemplifies the ideal, the virtuous woman always considerate of others, always reserved in expressing her feelings. Mary Bennet is the ridiculous, half-educated female pedant; Lady Catherine, the bossy, rich, old woman. Teachers may approach the stereotypes by asking how changes in historical conditions would affect these characters' fates. For example, Lydia would be more likely to become a single parent than a bride, and Mary would have a chance for a real education. How might the possibility of financial independence or the expectation that they contribute wages to a family income change women like Mrs. Bennet?

To convince students of the extent to which women are treated as stereotypes by male characters, focus on Mr. Collins' proposal to Lizzie and his refusal to take "no" for an answer. Ask students in what modern situations women may have trouble making "no" understood; consider the possible similarities between Collins' mind-set and young males' attitudes that in the contemporary world can go so far as to lead to date rape. Are young women still as dependent as Lizzie on fathers to defend them from unwelcome or threatening attention? The discussion might compare another of the novel's incidents—perhaps the bargaining that results in Lydia's marriage—with current institutions such as police and court systems. Who controls these institutions? What do they try to achieve for women?

Discussing relationships between/among female characters may help shift focus from male/female relationships while simultaneously clarifying the power dynamics. What are the women's main responsibilities toward one another? What are their main pleasures in one another's company? Why?

Charlotte Lucas offers one of the best opportunities for class discussions: given her options, is she a gold-digger? Does her marriage coarsen her, or her attitudes toward Lizzie? Mr. Collins' last letter to the Bennets indicates that Charlotte is pregnant—how does that affect our understanding of her?

Another strategy would examine how some female characters *pretend* to stereotypical feminine traits because they lack the power to act directly. Here the Bingley sisters and Charlotte (in her dealings with Lady Catherine) offer possibilities.

WORKS CITED

Austen, Jane. *Pride and Prejudice* [1813]. New York: New American Library, 1961.
Lauber, John. *Jane Austen*. New York: Twayne, 1993.

FOR FURTHER READING

Morgan, Susan. *In the Meantime*. Chicago: U of Chicago P, 1980.
Teachman, Debra. *Understanding* Pride and Prejudice: *A Student Casebook to Issues, Sources, and Historical Documents*. Westport, CT: Greenwood, 1997.

Undue Influence in Muriel Spark's
The Prime of Miss Jean Brodie
(1961)

Cristie L. March

Muriel Spark's *The Prime of Miss Jean Brodie* details the intimate relationship between six school-age girls and their teacher and mentor, Miss Brodie, as the girls move from an all-girl primary school and secondary school into their adult lives. In the process, Spark explores both the powerful role of authority figures such as Miss Brodie in the identity formation of young girls, and the development of sexual desire and religious conviction. Spark's non-chronological narrative allows the reader to see how the girls develop into adults, revealing Miss Brodie's eventual betrayal to the school board by her most trusted student, Sandy, and Sandy's entry into a convent. The interaction between Miss Brodie and Sandy explores the ambiguity between right and wrong as Sandy first emulates, then resists, then betrays the influential and possessive Miss Brodie.

Miss Brodie wields great power as an authority figure and role model for her students. A greater presence in their middle-class lives than their mothers are, she recognizes her ability to influence the direction of their futures. "Give me a young girl at an impressionable age, and she is mine for life," she proudly proclaims (9). Through Miss Brodie and her teachings, Spark illustrates larger issues of social unrest afoot in Scotland. While Miss Brodie embraces alternative social models such as the then-young fascist movements of Mussolini and Franco, she clings to romantic images of feminine self-sacrifice and un-requited love. She embodies a first generation of women who attempt to move out of conventional gender roles while at the same time remain confined by their own conservative upbringings.

As a result, Miss Brodie calls on her authority over her "impressionable" students in order to urge them into roles she herself is too afraid to occupy. For example, Miss Brodie convinces Joyce Emily to join her brother in the

Spanish Civil War, where she is killed, out of her own enthusiasm for Franco. She also tries to groom Rose as the married Mr. Lloyd's mistress—a sexual commitment the remnants of her Calvinist upbringing continue to prohibit (although she unreservedly becomes the unmarried Mr. Lowther's lover). As Anne Bower explains, Miss Brodie satisfies "her own sexual, emotional, and psychological needs with almost no regard for her students' real present or future situations" (42). Miss Brodie's lasting effect on Sandy illustrates the subtle and sometimes sinister impact older women can have on young girls. Although Sandy recognizes and resists Miss Brodie's intentions for her, she emerges deeply, if unwillingly, influenced by her experiences under Miss Brodie's tutelage. At the same time, the detrimental outcome of Miss Brodie's plans belies the potentially beneficial impact an involved teacher might have on her pupils. Students can question whether or not Spark is perpetuating gender stereotypes in her negative depiction of Miss Brodie as a megalomaniacal "progressive spinster" and a "great talker and feminist" (43) and might compare her to the other teachers Sandy briefly describes.

Miss Brodie's interest in an affair between Rose and Mr. Lloyd illustrates the novel's focus on sexual development. The otherwise unimportant Mr. Lloyd and Mr. Lowther act as foils for exploring Miss Brodie's and Sandy's sexuality. In fact, Sandy's relationship with sex occupies much of the novel. She often imagines herself the bosom companion of dashing Scottish heroes from Miss Brodie's classroom stories, although her daydream relationships are purely platonic. At one point she considers a passionate encounter with Alan Breck of *Kidnapped* but finds the logistics of clothing removal too confusing to make the experience viable. Later, she sees herself as the companion of Sergeant Anne Grey (a potential counterpoint to Miss Brodie's influence), committed to "eliminat[ing] sex from Edinburgh and environs" (68). Yet Sandy becomes Mr. Lloyd's mistress, acting first as an artist's model (for paintings that always resemble Miss Brodie), then later as his lover (the position Miss Brodie refuses).

Sandy eventually becomes interested in Mr. Lloyd's Catholicism, ultimately rejecting sex and finding a new "mentor" in the convent that can replace Miss Brodie, allowing Sandy to betray her. In effect, Sandy replaces one community of women with another, learning to her chagrin that the undue influence of women such as Miss Brodie exists in all places, even the safety of the convent. Students might consider the resemblance Sandy bears to Miss Brodie through her betrayal—in overturning Miss Brodie's authority she becomes "Brodie-like" herself.

Students can discuss the influence authority figures have on crafting girls' self-images, comparing Miss Brodie to their own female teachers. They can also consider the influences male versus female teachers have on male and female students. In addition, they can examine the dichotomy between Miss Brodie's progressiveness and conservativeness to address the ways in which women are often expected to fulfill (or are caught between) conflicting sociosexual roles.

The 1968 film version of the novel offers an excellent entry into gender discussions of both novel and film. Unlike the novel, which mingles sexual, political, and religious concerns in its presentation of Miss Brodie, the film, moving chronologically, centers almost entirely on the contest between Sandy and Miss Brodie for sexual supremacy. Although the film eliminates Sandy's second women's community in the convent, it does provide scenes such as the school dance, where the girls must needs dance with each other, and a tango between Sandy and Jenny while they discuss the problems of sex—itself a highly sexualized scene—that hint at the women's community Sandy's growing sexual jealousy will disrupt.

WORKS CITED

Bower, Anne. "Tyranny, Telling, Learning: Teaching the Female Student." *West Virginia University Philological Papers* 36 (1990): 38–45.

The Prime of Miss Jean Brodie. Dir. Ronald Neame. With Maggie Smith, Robert Stephens, and Pamela Franklin. Twentieth-Century Fox Productions, 1968.

Spark, Muriel. *The Prime of Miss Jean Brodie* [1961]. Middlesex, England: Penguin, 1984.

FOR FURTHER READING

Lodge, David. "The Uses and Abuses of Omniscience: Method and Meaning in Muriel Spark's *The Prime of Miss Jean Brody*." *Critical Quarterly* 12 (1970): 235–57.

Robb, David S. *Muriel Spark's* The Prime of Miss Jean Brodie. Aberdeen, Scotland: Association for Scottish Literary Studies, 1992.

Exploring the Gender Puzzle of George Bernard Shaw's *Pygmalion* (1912)

Michael G. Cornelius

George Bernard Shaw's drama *Pygmalion* purports to be about class, and the shallow distinctions between the classes in Edwardian society—in this case, dialect Professor Henry Higgins believes that he can transform Eliza Doolittle, a common flower girl, into a duchess by merely reforming her speech patterns, and indeed, he succeeds well enough to pass her off as a member of the upper echelon. In the ultimate scene of the play, Higgins says to Eliza, "The great secret, Eliza, is not having bad manners or good manners or any other particular sort of manners, but having the same manner for all human souls; in short, behaving as if you were in Heaven, where there are no third-class carriages, and one soul is as good as another" (66–67). This seems to be the redeeming moral of the piece, though ultimately, while class distinctions may be blurred, they are never wholly crossed; I've "not forgott[en] the difference between us," Eliza tells Higgins later in that same scene (70). This indicates to the reader that class is more insurmountable than Higgins and his cohort Colonel Pickering realize, and that the play truly deals with another, more complex Edwardian social more: gender, and the still new but increasingly prevalent notion of women's independence and liberation.

The early twentieth century represents a time of enormous social change in England. The Victorian Era over, women's right to suffrage became a worldwide movement; gender issues were moving to the forefront of both society and popular culture. The women in *Pygmalion* are wholly aware of this. Indeed, Mrs. Higgins' exasperated cry, "Oh men! men! men!" at the end of Act II, reveals her frustration at her son and his companion, who fail to comprehend the disastrous impact that their experiment would have on Eliza's psyche (174). When told to consider Eliza's feelings, Higgins replies that she has none, a common refrain throughout this piece; though Higgins concedes that Eliza has feelings, he is indisputably more concerned with his own. In a show of masculine self-centeredness, Higgins bemoans to Eliza, "You never asked yourself, I suppose, whether *I* could do without you" (67).

This scene, in a nutshell, dramatizes the larger question surrounding this play. Does Shaw support the new liberation of women, or does *Pygmalion* demonstrate Eliza herself as a female prototype, the creation of men; and are these two ideas necessarily in opposition, or can female independence exist as a beneficiary of male generosity? Students should consider this question throughout their reading.

As a "draggle-tailed gutter snipe," Eliza hardly represents a feminist icon; she is dirty, incomprehensible, and easily subdued by Higgins and Pickering (16). In transforming her into a lady, though, the two men create a creature less easily reckoned with, a woman who now has the verbal skills to do battle with them: "Don't you dare try this game on me," Higgins roars after one such parry. "I taught it to you; and it doesn't take me in" (62). Nonetheless, Higgins has taught her all too well: "Apart from the things anyone can pick up . . . the difference between a lady and a flower girl is not how she behaves, but how she is treated" (63).

The original Greek myth of Pygmalion concerns a sculptor who creates a piece of art so beautiful that he falls in love with it. Praying to the gods, Pygmalion is rewarded when his sculpture is brought to life; the two are wed, and live joyously together. Rather than acting like an inanimate sculpture, though, Eliza shares more in common with Frankenstein's monster, another creation of an educated but short-sighted man. She has the power to destroy her maker if she so chooses; if not sexually, then emotionally. After Eliza threatens to teach Higgins' phonetic methods to his competitor, he rails, "You damned impudent slut, you!" (71). Quickly, though, he reconsiders: "By George, Eliza, I said I'd make a woman of you; and I have. I like you like this. Five minutes ago you were like a millstone around my neck. Now you're a tower of strength" (71). Higgins' emotional outbursts reveal his loss of control; when Eliza informs him she "shall not see you again, Professor Higgins," she leaves him emotionally dashed in her wake (72). Eliza now has independence within her grasp; all she need do is walk through the door and it is hers.

Yet she cannot do this, and as is typical in *Pygmalion*, the moment of feminine strength is replaced by feminine weakness. At the very conclusion of the play Higgins orders Eliza to complete some menial errands for him; though she says she will not, he has every confidence that she will complete her task. Although she herself realizes the degradation inherent in such utterly dependent acts as fetching Higgins' slippers ("I think a woman fetching a man's slippers is a disgusting sight"), she has performed them, and as Higgins suggests, she may well perform them again (68).

Thus female independence is saddled with gender bias, and becomes the interesting crux in interpreting *Pygmalion*. Students will want to consider whether the play is inherently biased against women, or is it about a society that is? Reading this drama both with and without Shaw's prose epilogue may affect students' reactions to this question, so teachers are advised to address the issue before coming to the epilogue and then again afterwards. Also, teachers should advise students of the two excellent film versions of the work: the 1938 black-and-white version starring Leslie Howard and Wendy Hiller, and the 1964 film version of the Lerner and Loewe musical starring Rex Harrison and Audrey Hepburn. The musical, of course, takes more liberties with the play, and proffers a more conservative ending (with Eliza returning to Higgins' home), but the songs add an interesting element in interpreting the drama.

WORK CITED

Shaw, George Bernard. *Pygmalion* [1912]. New York: Dover, 1994.

FOR FURTHER READING

Berst, Charles A. Pygmalion: *Shaw's Play with Myth and Cinderella*. New York: Twayne, 1995.

Seasoned with Quiet Strength: Black Womanhood in Lorraine Hansberry's *A Raisin in the Sun* (1959)

Neal A. Lester

One might think that Walter Younger is the heroic center of Lorraine Hansberry's sociopolitical drama. Much of the action deals with him and his apparent initiation into Black manhood. His "initiation," however, is orchestrated by Mama's manipulation: allowing Travis to witness his actions with Lindner. Mama embarrasses Walter into making the decision she deems appropriate. Her self-congratulatory comment about Walter to Ruth and Beneatha at Lindner's departure—"He finally come into his manhood today, didn't he?" (151)—signals the play's climax only for Mama as Walter's actions allegedly demonstrate his personal integrity and the cultural dignity of African Americans like his deceased father who, according to Mama, gave his all to provide for his family. This moment and Walter's ranting throughout the play might seem to present Black manhood as the sexist metaphor for communal blackness during the 1960s Civil Rights and Black Power movements: "That is just what is wrong with the colored woman in this world. . . . Don't understand about building their men up and making 'em feel like they somebody. Like they can do something" (34). Attention to Walter's self-centeredness, his selfishness, and his obsession with a get-rich-quick money scheme, however, shows that Walter is not Hansberry's mouthpiece.

Walter's burgeoning Black manhood highlights a white patriarchal cultural script from which he reads and endeavors to follow—providing Travis and Ruth with illusory symbols of living the "American Dream." While these tokens themselves are not problematic, Walter feels less than "a man" without them. His manhood is based on economics and relegating the women in his home to secondary positions of importance in his personal dream: "A man needs a woman to back him up. . . . We one group of men tied to a race of women with small minds!" (32, 35). Walter assumes that his limited socioeconomic position results from having unsupportive Black women. Despite his and the other male characters' sexist attitudes, some see the play as a testimonial for Black manhood and Walter's dilemma as Hansberry's main focus (Lewis 35). However, a reexamination of male–female relationships exposes Hansberry's critique of sexism and male chauvinism within Black culture.

Hansberry's critique of Black manhood occurs on many fronts. Most recognizable are the Black male voices in the play, that like Walter's, relegate women to secondary positions in both public and private arenas. Beneatha's romantic encounters with George and Asagai reveal that male chauvinism transcends cultural, national, educational, and economic boundaries. Beneatha's efforts to discover herself as an independent, thinking Black adult female are challenged by men's desire to force her into traditional gender roles that hinder her creativity and life experience. Not only does Walter think her aspirations to be a doctor senseless—"Who the hell told you you had to be a doctor? If you so crazy 'bout messing 'round with sick people, then go be nurse like other women, or just get married and be quiet" (38)—but her relationships with George and Asagai are equally disheartening. Despite Beneatha's intellect and daringness to consider various avenues toward self-discovery, George's interest in her is solely romantic and sexual: "You're a nice-looking girl. . . . That's all you need honey. . . . Be glad for that. As for myself, I want a nice—simple—sophisticated girl . . . not a poet" (96).

Asagai affords fresh spiritual energy for Beneatha while consoling her about her lost medical school money, but his philosophical challenges prove empty when they undermine her personal possibilities. His sexist, Afrocentric worldview presents men as leaders and thinkers, women not as their partners but their students:

My dear, young creature of the New World. . . . [T]he African Prince [himself] . . . swept the maiden back across the middle passage over which her ancestors had come— . . . Nigeria. Home. I will show you our mountains and our stars; give you cool drinks from gourds and teach you the old songs and ways of our people. (137)

Asagai believes Beneatha can be complete only through marriage to him and becoming his American cultural conquest, a symbol of his own vainglory.

Hansberry complicates her critique of Black manhood through Mama. Just as many readers wrongly make Walter the play's heroic center, many raise Lena Younger to motherly sainthood, failing to see Mama's unquestioning acceptance of the patriarchal values that guide her actions and thinking. Particularly, Mama's treatment of Walter is different from her treatment of Beneatha, reflecting her own gender bias. Mama works to mold Walter into a responsible adult—"a man," attaching little seriousness to Beneatha's move toward adulthood. Although Mama does not oppose Beneatha's dream of becoming a doctor, she focuses more on Walter's life, entrusting her son with a significant portion of the insurance money—"[T]ake this money . . . [B]e the head of this family from now on like you supposed to be" (107). Contrast Mama's inattention to Beneatha when she solicits her responses to Asagai's proposal of marriage and life with him in Africa: "*(Distracted)* Yes, baby—" (150).

To conclude that Mama is a product of a time when men headed households and women remained passive in decision making oversimplifies the play. From subtle comments about Travis' bed making—"[H]e's a little boy. Ain't supposed to know 'bout housekeeping" (40)—to her behavior with Beneatha when Beneatha challenges her beliefs about God—"It don't sound nice for a young girl to say things like that" (51)—Mama supports deeply entrenched gender roles.

Ruth Younger, the play's heroic center, is the most selfless, self-sacrificing, and emotionally balanced character. She is a peacemaker between Walter and Beneatha, a bridge between Mama and Walter. Ruth's strength of character evidences when she is faced with the greatest single moral dilemma in the play: whether to abort her pregnancy. Indeed, our impressions of Ruth come largely in what she does—look closely at Hansberry's stage directions for Ruth—and less in what she says: Her "life has been little that she expected, and disappointment has already begun to hang in her face" (24). About the circumstances of her life, she is neither angry nor disillusioned; rather, she remains hopeful and centered. The ambiguity around Ruth's pregnancy adds thematic and structural complexity in the same way that Langston Hughes' poem "Harlem"—the source of Hansberry's title—provides no single answer to the question of "what happens to a dream deferred?"

At a time when collective Black identity was couched in the values and rhetoric of Black manhood, Lorraine Hansberry challenged such a notion. A study of racial, cultural, and political realities and of universal human experiences—joy, confusion, disappointment, and uncertainty—*A Raisin in the Sun* shows the strength of Black women whose selfless actions speak louder than others' selfish words.

WORKS CITED

Hansberry, Lorraine. *A Raisin in the Sun* [1959] and *The Sign in Sidney Brustein's Window*. Ed. Robert Nemiroff. New York: New American Library, 1987, 21–151.

Lewis, Theophilus. "Social Protest in *A Raisin in the Sun*?" *Catholic World* (October 1959): 31–35.

FOR FURTHER READING

Clark, Keith. "Black Male Subjectivity Deferred?: The Quest for Voice and Authority in Lorraine Hansberry's *A Raisin in the Sun*." *Black Women Playwrights: Visions on the American Stage*. Ed. P. Marsh-Lockett. New York: Garland, 1999, 87–111.

hooks, bell. "Raisin in a New Light." *Christianity and Crisis*, February 6, 1989, 21–24.

Heroism against the Odds: William Shakespeare's *Romeo and Juliet* (ca. 1599)

Lesley Broder

In *Romeo and Juliet*, a broiling Verona summer provides a volatile backdrop for Romeo and Juliet's passion and their families' rancor. Although male aggression fuels the play, Juliet blossoms as a sturdy, intelligent woman whose devotion to her love and her ideals makes her heroic.

The feud between the families is continually described in terms of misogynistic violence. When the Capulets' servingmen discuss how they would fight the Montagues, Sampson declares, "women, being the / weaker vessels, are ever thrust to the wall. Therefore / I will push Montague's men from the wall and thrust his maids to the wall" (9). Here, showing power over enemies is equivalent to sexually mauling women. That this conversation occurs in the opening scene highlights the centrality of masculine power and feminine submission against which Juliet must fight.

Capulet plays the dominant role society has set for him when he shows his aggression toward and power over daughter Juliet. He hesitates when Paris wants to marry her, for mothers "too soon marred are those so early made" (27). Although it was customary for upper-class children to marry at a young age to preserve their families' wealth, he senses thirteen is too young for his daughter to wed. Nevertheless, he reverts to brutality when Juliet refuses to marry Paris. He curses, "Out, you green-sickness carrion! Out, you baggage! / . . . I tell thee what: get thee to church o' Thursday, / Or never after look me in the face" (167). Her disobedience to his will is an egregious and unacceptable affront. Whether or not Capulet even considers her best interests, finally, he makes his decision about Juliet's marriage partner to satisfy his own needs, not her desires.

Unlike Juliet, who resists easy stereotyping and patriarchal domination, the Nurse obeys male authority. After Romeo's banishment, the Nurse advises

Juliet to marry Paris for, "Romeo's a dishclout to him. . . . / Your first is dead, or 'twere as good he were" (171–73). The Nurse believes it is better that Juliet meekly marry someone she does not love than take the risk of meeting secretly with Romeo. Lady Capulet, too, submits to a man's will, as she is the agent for her husband's wishes. She broaches the subject of marriage with Juliet, scolds her when she mourns Tybalt's death too long, and swears, "Do as thou wilt, for I have done with thee" when she refuses to wed Paris (171). Besides the tears she sheds at Juliet's death, Lady Capulet only interacts with her daughter to transmit her husband's thoughts.

Although men are ostensibly the dominant power, Juliet often shows greater sense and strength of character than does Romeo. While Romeo is given to pining for his love with extravagant phrases, Juliet restrains him when he goes too far. She chastises him when he swears his love by the moon, "O, swear not by the moon, th' inconstant moon, / That monthly changes in her [circled] orb, / Lest that thy love prove likewise variable" (77). During this exchange, Juliet takes decisive action to consummate their love through marriage. She is also more reasonable when facing adversity. After Romeo is banished for killing Tybalt, he is insensible. He cannot stop weeping and threatens to stab himself. Friar Lawrence insults him by calling him feminine. "Art thou a man? Thy form cries out thou art. / Thy tears are womanish . . ." (149). While the Friar sees only a man disgracing himself, Juliet is better able to reason, despite her grief: "That villain cousin would have killed my husband. / Back, foolish tears, back to your native spring" (137).

Students should be alerted to Juliet's courage; it may be difficult for them to understand how radical she is for her time. In a patriarchal culture where women are men's subjects, she stands against her father's wishes to marry Paris without hesitation. Juliet remains true to her conscience and inner desires. She begs Friar Lawrence, "O, bid me leap, rather than marry Paris, / From off the battlements of any tower, / . . . And I will do it without fear or doubt" (183). She then acts on her words by drinking the sleeping drought, seeking comfort from neither her Nurse nor her mother. When she wakes in the tomb to find Friar Lawrence panicking and Romeo dead, she doesn't flee for safety with the Friar. As he departs in fear, she faces eternity and death alone. Her final deed is to violently stab herself without flinching. Throughout these trying scenes, Juliet debunks her society's notion that a woman is weak, inconstant, and incapable of bravery.

Although she commits the desperate act of suicide, Juliet can still be a model of certain strengths, helpful for young people to observe. Amidst a reckless feud, she displays morality, fortitude, and wit. Since nuances of characterization may be lost on readers unfamiliar with Shakespeare's language, teachers might assign a double-entry journal focusing on Juliet. In one column, students record quotations illuminating Juliet's character (what she says herself and what others say about her); in the other column, students express their personal responses to these lines, thus creating a dialogue to help them interact with the text. More broadly, discussion can focus on whether modern society still expects men and women to act according to the same gender roles enacted by the main characters in the play. For instance, are men still expected to withhold tears? Are women still expected to do as their fathers wish?

Juliet embodies a marvelous melding of innocence and foresight. Her innocence is clear as she is enraptured in the ecstasy of her first love; at the same time, she is perceptive enough to envision its brutal end. As her family engages in a fierce battle, charged by masculine antagonism, she remains resolute and heroic. Her strength must come from within, for her father seeks to dominate women and her mother accepts his right to do so. The question remains, then, why Juliet decides to commit suicide when her bravery should allow her to face her family or flee Verona; students should consider whether these, or other options, were viable in her time.

WORK CITED

Shakespeare, William. *Romeo and Juliet* [ca. 1599]. Ed. Barbara A. Mowat and Paul Werstine. New York: Washington Square–Pocket, 1992.

FOR FURTHER READING

Novy, Marianne L. "Violence, Love and Gender in *Romeo and Juliet*." *Love's Argument: Gender Relations in Shakespeare*. Ed. Marianne L. Novy. Chapel Hill: University of North Carolina Press, 1984, 99–109. Rpt. in Romeo and Juliet: *Critical Essays*. Ed. John F. Andrews. New York: Garland, 1993, 359–69.

Molly Bolts and Lifelines: Rita Mae Brown's *Rubyfruit Jungle* (1973)

Frances Ann Day

Rita Mae Brown's semi-autobiographical novel, *Rubyfruit Jungle*, was one of the first American books to portray a lesbian character in a positive way. Indeed, Molly Bolt, the novel's fiery, irreverent young protagonist, not only leads the way in avenging the wrongs done to lesbians in twentieth-century literature, but also, as her name implies, steadfastly holds on to her identity. Born lesbian, poor, and illegitimate, Molly rebels against the gender, class, and sexual identity restrictions placed upon her. Armed with remarkable gifts of resourcefulness, defiance, and grit, she storms through childhood with her self-esteem intact.

One of the first battles Molly fights is with her adoptive mother, Carrie, over what it means to be a girl. When Carrie embarks on a "crash program" to "make a lady out of [her]," Molly fights back with every fiber of her being. Refusing to cook, clean, sew, and "act right" (33), Molly spends her time climbing trees and taking old cars apart. One day, after Carrie beats her, Molly flees to the wheatfield behind the house. These acts of rebellion symbolize Molly's refusal to be imprisoned in the house and her rejection of the traditional role of women.

Similarly, when a friend tells her, "Girls can't have motorcycles," Molly responds, "I'll buy an army tank if I want to and run over anyone who tells me I can't have it" (63). Molly also defies tradition by wearing comfortable clothes. By riding motorcycles and choosing her own clothes, Molly makes a bold statement to the world: my body belongs to me; I will decide how I want to live my life.

In sixth grade, Molly falls in love with Leota, a classmate, and follows her own heart. Courageously, she embraces her sexual identity, takes enormous risks, and pursues her dreams. Students could analyze how Molly's various experiences strengthen her resolve, enabling her to overcome the obstacles she faces.

Rubyfruit Jungle is a powerful protest against lesbophobia and heterosexism. In this tough and sassy novel, Rita Mae Brown uses biting humor and sensitivity to engage her readers as she challenges social standards. Students can examine how humor is used in the book, selecting examples of the episodes, tone, and characterizations that make parts of it so funny.

Books of affirmation, such as *Rubyfruit Jungle*, are all the more important because of overwhelming heterosexism in schools. Although more than three million lesbian and gay teenagers live in the United States, their diverse voices are often excluded. Indeed, the statistics are chilling: because they live in a culture that is homophobic and heterosexist, young lesbian and gay people experience alarming levels of physical and verbal abuse, emotional isolation, parental rejection, depression, homelessness, dropout risk, and suicide. One way to provide hope for these at-risk youngsters is to share compassionate books that deal honestly with the very issues with which they are grappling. Discussing these books will also help heterosexual teens understand and support their lesbian and gay peers.

In areas where *Rubyfruit Jungle* might be considered controversial, teachers will want to become familiar with policies on the use of controversial materials. However, they should not avoid using this book just because a few parents or colleagues might object. An interesting teaching strategy involves researching books that may have been challenged in the district, state, and nation. Another fascinating strategy is to involve students in evaluating school district policies on discrimination. Does the policy include sexual orientation? If not, some students might explore reasons for its exclusion and ways the policy might be amended. During Banned Books Week (the last week in September), teachers may want to join other educators and librarians who use the week to discuss our First Amendment rights and the power of literature.

It is essential that schools provide safe, supportive learning environments for *all* students. For teachers concerned that some heterosexual students might resist, Vicky Greenbaum suggests introducing texts with potentially threatening topics later in the year, after trust has been established. Paula Alida Roy adds to this discussion by writing about the creation of a safe, inclusive classroom in which such topics can be considered openly and respectfully.

In *The Cat Came Back* by Hilary Mullins, the main character, Stevie, writes in her diary,

> "RUBYFRUIT REVELATION! This book is so great! It is the best book I have ever read! . . . Why didn't anyone tell me about this book before!!! Oh, but I know why, it's because Molly is so proud and nobody in the

world is going to stop her!!! . . . it's okay to feel this way after all. And I do feel better—thanks to Rita Mae." (98)

Like Stevie, we as readers applaud the tenacity and resiliency of Rita Mae Brown's brave protagonist. *Rubyfruit Jungle* celebrates individualism, dispels stereotypes, and invites a critical analysis of expectations based on gender, class, and sexual orientation. And perhaps this high-spirited book will provide a lifeline for isolated young lesbians, who, like Stevie, are desperately searching for positive images of themselves in literature.

WORKS CITED

Brown, Rita Mae. *Rubyfruit Jungle* [1973]. New York: Bantam, 1977.

Greenbaum, Vicky. "Literature Out of the Closet: Bringing Gay and Lesbian Texts and Subtexts Out in High School English." *English Journal* 83.5 (1994): 71–74.

Mullins, Hilary. *The Cat Came Back*. Tallahassee, FL: Naiad, 1993.

Roy, Paula Alida. "Language in the Classroom: Opening Conversations about Lesbian and Gay Issues in Senior High School." *Overcoming Heterosexism and Homophobia: Strategies that Work*. Ed. James T. Sears and Walter L. Williams. New York: Columbia UP, 1997, 209–17.

FOR FURTHER READING

Boutiller, Nancy. "Reading, Writing and Rita Mae Brown: Lesbian Literature in High School." *Tilting the Tower: Lesbians/Teaching/Queer Subjects*. Ed. Linda Garber. New York: Routledge, 1994, 135–41.

"A" as Hester's Autonomy in Nathaniel Hawthorne's *The Scarlet Letter* (1850)

Monika M. Elbert

Nathaniel Hawthorne's most famous novel, *The Scarlet Letter*, presents the modern reader with Hester Prynne, a Puritan woman living in the late seventeenth century, created from the perspective of a nineteenth-century New England writer. Although ostensibly about the Puritan way of life, the novel sheds even more light on changing gender roles in the nineteenth century. Women were traditionally supposed to take care of the home and hearth and not venture into men's world of business or public activity. Within the parameters of the "Cult of True Womanhood," middle-class women were relegated to the role of good housewife and mother in their separate domestic sphere. At first glance, Hester Prynne is certainly not the type of woman who would have been held up as a model of True Womanhood. Married to another, she has an illegitimate child, and then sets up a home of her own—without a husband by her side, as a single mother. Hawthorne has the good sense not to kill off his adulteress, a first in Anglo-American literature. Neither does he create Hester as some weak damsel in distress who needs a husband or father to guide and support her; rather, she is self-reliant, creative, and passionate.

Read within the cultural context of nineteenth-century feminism, Hester's character takes on an interesting, if enigmatic, dimension. Most likely influenced by such events as Seneca Falls Convention (1848) and the Married Women's Property Acts, Hawthorne creates a strong female protagonist, one whom he admires but also fears on some level. She shares the same New England Transcendentalist qualities, which Emerson extolled in his famous essay, "Self-Reliance" (1841), and which Margaret Fuller apparently rewrites for a female audience in her equally famous but longer work, *Woman in the Nineteenth Century* (1845). Although initially, the townspeople's fear of Hester seems to be of her blatant sexuality, by the end of the narrative Hester appears to have been tamed, at least superficially, so that she is rendered more and more passionless, marble-like, and statue-like. However, her potential threat to the community is more evident as she becomes increasingly introspective and intellectual. In "Another View of Hester," we hear that she

> assumed a freedom of speculation, then common enough on the other side of the Atlantic, but which our forefathers, had they known of it, would have held to be a deadlier crime than that stigmatized by the scarlet letter. (133)

Hawthorne has not, then, actually tamed or domesticated his Hester; instead, she grows from being excessively passionate to being serious and intellectual, no mere feat for a nineteenth-century woman.

In essence, Hawthorne celebrates (and Hester epitomizes) not just Woman Feeling, but Woman Thinking. Not merely a mother to her own child, Hester eventually becomes the angel of the household ministering to dying parishioners as well as nurturing lovesick girls. Herself having once been impassioned and lovesick, she excels as a counselor. This book celebrates feminine intelligence, creativity, compassion, while it downplays, to Hawthorne's (and Hester's) credit, the popular and sentimental image of woman as dependent, or even worse, as victim of her romantic fantasies.

Young readers, in particular, might be confused about Hester's source of power. Is she attractive because of her stunning beauty, her sexuality, her artistry, or her intelligence? If she does seem empowered (today we admire all those qualities), what qualities would the reader feel most compelling, most important for Hester not to sacrifice to public opinion? If society is superficial, judgmental, and oppressive, how can one live within its parameters and follow its dictates? Are actions based on principle or on honesty almost always construed as simply wayward? The message may be a bit frightening, as a total departure from the norm could lead to ostracism and alienation. It is more important to delve into one's own being to find one's hidden strengths and intelligence, a psychic space within (metaphorically, Hester's isolated cottage), as Hester does, than to create a new Eden (Boston as the "City upon a Hill"), based on time-worn traditions, as the judgmental Puritans do. Hester does not pander to patriarchal authority figures to please a hypocritical or shallow crowd. Readers who are used to conforming might respond with awe to Hester's courage and individualism. Others may be interested in comparing their own acts of rebelliousness—against their parents, teachers, and their community's expectations—to Hester's.

Most feminist critics analyze the process whereby Hester subverts the laws of patriarchy and lives according to a law of her own. She transforms the original meaning of the letter "A" (adultery) so that the judgmental community comes to see her stigmatized letter as a badge of honor: people assert that "it meant Able; so strong was Hester Prynne, with a woman's strength" (131). But Hester does not accept the community's new interpretation. After many years, when the town fathers ask her to remove the "letter" and forget the past, Hester refuses. As an artist creating embroidered beauty, Hester has infused the letter as well as her existence with her own meaning. The Puritan community, who initially tried to hush her, is now hushed. Various critics have interpreted her silence (her adamant refusal to name the father of her child; her vow of secrecy to Chillingworth not to identify his relation to her) as both empowering (she thwarts the Governor and other patriarchs from learning her secret) and disempowering (she feels threatened by Chillingworth's obvious and Dimmesdale's veiled attempts to hush her). Yet silence, in Hester's case, offers a type of passive resistance to male probing; thus, her injunction to Dimmesdale at the Governor's Mansion, "Speak thou for me" (98), ultimately forces him to confront his own demons rather than to project them onto her. One might finally ask whether Hester's voicelessness or Dimmesdale's voice has more presence.

Perhaps the most disheartening quality about *The Scarlet Letter* is the conclusive, cynical view of women in which the narrator calls for some ideal vision of Womanhood so as to redeem mankind from Hester's sin: "The angel and apostle of the coming revelation must be a woman, indeed, but lofty, pure, and beautiful, and wise, moreover, not through dusky grief, but the ethereal medium of joy" (201). With this apocalyptic vision in mind, readers might wonder if placing woman on a pedestal, demanding perfection and purity, oppresses all women who could be easily stigmatized with variations of the letter "A."

WORKS CITED

Emerson, Ralph Waldo. "Self-Reliance." *Selected Essays*. Ed. Lazar Ziff. New York: Penguin, 1987, 175–204.

Fuller, Margaret. *Woman in the Nineteenth Century*. Ed. Larry Reynolds. New York: Norton, 1998.

Hawthorne, Nathaniel. *The Scarlet Letter* [1850]. Ed. Ross C. Martin. Boston: Bedford Books, 1991.

FOR FURTHER READING

Elbert, Monika. "Hester's Maternity: Stigma or Weapon?" *ESQ: A Journal of the American Renaissance* 36.3 (1990): 175–207.

Person, Leland S., Jr. "Hester's Revenge: The Power of Silence in *The Scarlet Letter*." *Nineteenth-Century Literature* 43 (1989): 465–83.

Ragussis, Michael. "Silence, Family Discourse, and Fiction in *The Scarlet Letter*." *The Scarlet Letter*. Ed. Ross C. Murfin. Boston: Bedford, 1991, 316–29.

Female Freedom in Other Places and Inner Spaces: Suzanne Fisher Staples' *Shabanu: Daughter of the Wind* (1989)

Zarina Manawwar Hock

Shabanu, intended for young adults, portrays a girl's struggle to assert her independence in a patriarchal society. The first-person narrative, told through the main character, Shabanu (perhaps coincidentally, "Shah Bano," is also the name of a Muslim woman whose highly publicized divorce/alimony case in 1986 became a rallying point for feminist protest on the Indian Subcontinent), takes place in a culture that typical readers will find faraway and exotic—a wandering desert community in Cholistan, a province of Pakistan. Through Shabanu's story, Suzanne Fisher Staples holds up for scrutiny a society whose marriage customs will seem alienating and even barbaric to most Western readers. In doing so, she demonstrates how a spirited young girl comes to terms with oppressive practices of a male-dominated society.

Because she has no brothers, Shabanu enjoys many male privileges. Although she helps her father as a son would, she is also expected to cook for her father and be a dutiful daughter. In the patriarchal culture Staples depicts, girl children are a burden, their marriages depend on financial bargains, and parents must pay dowries to get them wed. Although the young narrator resists the restrictions and injustices she encounters, she knows that she must be unquestioningly obedient (28). When Shabanu comes of age, she loses the freedom she enjoys as a child: at eleven, she already knows that within a year she will be "owned" by the man her family chooses as her husband.

Gender inequities are underlined through the valorization of male children. "May she have many sons" (74) is a traditional blessing; women make pilgrimages to pray for sons. No one prays for a daughter. Shabanu's resistance to this inequity is best expressed in her own words: "I know Dadi [her father] thinks my bent for freedom is dangerous, and I'm learning to save my spirit for when it can be useful" (85). And indeed, Shabanu does learn to safeguard her daring spirit.

Inscribed in the characters of Shabanu and her sister Phulan is opposition between the *feminist* and the *feminine*. Phulan (whose name means "a flowering") is delicate and frequently helpless, joyfully embracing her family's marriage plans for her. Shabanu (meaning "the king's lady," hence "queen"), on the other hand, acts: she fights her father (61), rescues Phulan from a lascivious landowner (155), and takes charge in a crisis (158). Where Phulan slides starry-eyed into marriage—even though her murdered fiancé has been replaced by his brother—Shabanu runs away to avoid marriage. The attempt ends in disaster, and she is dragged—metaphorically and literally—kicking and screaming back into her father's home.

As the book's subtitle emphasizes, Shabanu is "daughter of the wind," untamed and free. Shabanu's identification with nature—especially visible in her passionate devotion to the camels—suggests that freedom is a natural condition for women. If closeness to nature symbolizes freedom, the *chadr* or Muslim head covering becomes symbolic of their cultural oppression. While Phulan welcomes this veiling—it is her rite of passage into womanhood (18)—for Shabanu, the *chadr* is nothing but a nuisance—at best an object to protect her from the sun (34) or to hold her money (49–50).

Another female character, Shabanu's favorite aunt Sharma, contests male domination and becomes, for Shabanu, an instrument of agency. Having left her abusive husband, Sharma lives independently and refuses to arrange her daughter's marriage (97). It is to this aunt that young Shabanu turns when she learns that she must marry the 55-year-old Rahim-sahib, a landowner with three other wives (192). Significantly, Aunt Sharma's seemingly liberated views contain an important caveat—a woman's dreams of freedom must remain hidden. Sharma's words of advice to Phulan—to "learn to please" her husband; to cultivate a mystique of the innermost self, one that will keep her attractive to him (217)—speak deeply to Shabanu, unhappily betrothed, who tries "to apply them like medicine to a wound" (218). Although such advice may surprise students when it comes from the novel's most subversive character, Sharma shows how independent women survive oppressive patriarchal societies.

Sharma's words, which Shabanu internalizes, empower Shabanu, enabling her to see her self-worth when she is "betrayed and sold" (239). As she journeys into adulthood, these words allow her access to her inner space—a space untouched by male tyranny. Typically, a *bildungsroman* "recounts the development . . . of an individual from childhood to maturity, to the point where the main character recognizes his or her place and role in the world" (Murfin and Ray 1998). As Laurie Grobman points out, the female *bildungsroman* "interrogates . . . patriarchal practices" but the protagonist's journey is a circular one, leading her to a private inner space (61–62). This is precisely what Shabanu finds in her final affirmation, when she echoes Sharma's words (240).

Teaching *Shabanu* offers opportunities to get beyond "just the story" to a critical reading of feminism in a non-Western context. The challenge is for students to look outside their own cultural frames and question assumptions— their own, those offered by the text, and those of the author. For example, students could examine ways that their *own* society, and not just the one Staples depicts, also commodifies women—by emphasizing the female body in advertising, in beauty contests, and in the media. To promote cross-cultural perspectives, teachers might ask: Why would a society arrange marriages for its people? Are readers from outside a culture justified in interrogating its traditions? What is cultural authenticity and should this matter in a work of fiction?

Additionally, students can be asked whether Staples conflates two traditions in her reading of marriage customs: the commodification of women and the arranged marriage. The first undeniably exploits women, who become victims of financial bargains and dowries. The second tradition can be understood only in a social context where individuals, *regardless of their gender*, often have little say as to whom they will marry. In this "other" paradigm of marriage, the community is valued above the individual; thus, the couple frequently welcomes the arrangement. Does Staples elide the cultural context and unintentionally privilege her "first world" view of marriage-by-choice, where Westerners are raised to honor their autonomy, above all else? By inviting students to question such cultural differences, teachers will extend discussion of this novel into how cultural mores and economic necessity shape gender roles in *any* society, including mainstream or minority communities within the United States.

WORKS CITED

Grobman, Laurie. *Teaching at the Crossroads: Cultures and Critical Perspectives in Literature by Women of Color.* San Francisco: Aunt Lute Press, 2001.

Murfin, Ross and Supriya Ray. *The Bedford Glossary of Critical Terms.* Boston: Bedford, 1998.

Staples, Suzanne Fisher. *Shabanu: Daughter of the Wind.* New York: Alfred A. Knopf, 1989.

FOR FURTHER READING

Rogers, Theresa and Anna O. Soter, eds. *Reading across Cultures: Teaching Literature in a Diverse Society*. New York: Teachers College Press/National Council of Teachers of English, 1997.

Gender in *Silas Marner* by George Eliot (1861)

Debra S. Davis

Silas Marner, set at the end of the eighteenth century, contains Victorian gender stereotypes. The male characters, active in the public sphere of politics and finance, wield what we would call "real" power today, while women are limited to influence in only the personal and domestic spheres. On the surface these gender roles would seem to privilege men; however, the motherless, morally corrupt Cass household clearly illustrates the value of feminine suasion. Left unchecked, male power leads to the immoral behavior of Dunstan and Godfrey. They drink and gamble, and Dunstan drowns after stealing Silas Marner's gold. Silas, exiled from his original community, is an outsider in the town of Raveloe. His eventual reintegration into society results from his relationships with Dolly Winthrop and his adopted daughter Eppie, as well as from his affirmation of the feminine traits he has suppressed. Read as a critique of masculine privilege, *Silas Marner* features strong women who counterbalance male social influence.

Eliot's novel, unlike many written by her male contemporaries, does not equate the feminine role with passive victimization (e.g., Dickens, *Little Dorrit*). Even Godfrey's first wife, Molly Farren, a barmaid and drug addict, dies in an attempt to confront the man who had hidden her away as his dirty little secret. Dolly Winthrop, a positive example of crucial feminine influence, demonstrates her goodness by her habit of rising at four-thirty in the morning to perform "duties" for others. She brings cakes to Silas after the theft and urges him to attend church. After the appearance of Eppie, Dolly never interferes with Silas' methods of raising the orphan; instead she offers advice and does the washing and mending for the pair. Despite her illiteracy, common among working-class Victorians, Dolly tries to help Silas make sense of his past and, along with Eppie, provides him with the motivation to recover from the theft by reestablishing a connection with humanity.

Eppie, the symbolic replacement for Silas' gold, exemplifies the power of female influence. Her presence transforms him from an isolated man who finds meaning only in work into a loving father; their appearances together in Raveloe turn Silas from a "queer and un-accountable creature, . . . looked at with wondering curiosity and repulsion" into "a person whose satisfaction and difficulties could be easily understood" (133). When Eppie's biological father Godfrey decides to claim her as his legitimate child, she rejects his offer, thereby asserting the power to decide her own destiny. Had she gone to live in the Red House as a member of the middle class, she would have gained material wealth but would have had to leave Silas and break off her engagement with Aaron Winthrop in order to marry a man befitting her new station in life, most likely one chosen for her by Godfrey.

Godfrey's vision of the women in his life evokes the classic virgin/whore stereotype. He idealizes Nancy—"she would be his wife and would make home lovely to him . . . and it would be easy, when she was always near, to shake off those foolish habits that were no pleasures, but only a feverish way of annulling vacancy" (92). He thinks of his sexual relationship with Molly as one of "those foolish habits" for which he denies responsibility. His telling Nancy that he "was led away into marrying Molly" (164) will undoubtedly anger young women and provide a good opportunity to engage students in a discussion of the age-old double standard for male and female sexual and courting behavior. It appears that Molly is punished for her transgression by freezing to death while her death rewards Godfrey in freeing him to marry the virtuous and virginal Nancy. However, Godfrey's marriage is not wholly fulfilling. The death of his and Nancy's child coupled with Eppie's rejection leaves him with no hope of producing an heir to the family name and fortune. Students can question whether Eliot intended tragic consequences for him owing to his callous treatment of Molly.

Gender can also be studied in the novel through a close examination of Silas who, as both mother and father to Eppie, represents the integration of feminine and masculine traits. As a weaver, Silas is linked to women from the start of the novel where Eliot places the linen weaver in a context alongside the "great ladies" with "their toy spinning wheels" (1). Moreover, his knowledge of medicinal herbs has come from his mother. By connecting Silas' two most useful skills with women, Eliot prepares the reader for his success in a maternal role. A close, directed reading on both the literal and symbolic level will alert students to Eliot's indication that Silas will adopt a feminine role: He hides his gold in a hole under the loom, representing his livelihood, but he discovers

Eppie in front of the hearth where he does his cooking. Students can discuss how Eliot subtly honors the feminine aspects of Silas' nature and whether they think so-called masculine and feminine qualities exist in everyone.

The challenges that George Eliot faced as a nineteenth-century woman writer might be another topic of class discussion. Her use of a masculine pseudonym underscores the difficulties that Victorian women encountered when entering the public sphere. As a critically and popularly acclaimed novelist in an age when women were not free to write for either livelihood or avocation, Eliot gave voice to female characters such as Dolly Winthrop and Dorothea Brooke (*Middlemarch*), who otherwise would have been silent. Ironically, she had to do it as a man.

WORK CITED

Eliot, George. *Silas Marner* [1861]. New York: Signet-Penguin, 1999.

FOR FURTHER READING

Alley, Henry. "*Silas Marner* and the Balance of Male and Female." *Victorians Institute Journal* 16 (1988): 65–73.
Ashton, Rosemary. *George Eliot: A Life*. New York/London: Penguin, 1997.
Conway, Richard. "*Silas Marner* and *Felix Holt*: From Fairy Tale to Feminism." *Studies in the Novel* 10.3 (1978): 295–304.

Empowerment through Writing in Mariama Bâ's *So Long a Letter* (1979)

Ellen S. Silber

The publication of *So Long a Letter* (*Une si longue lettre*) signaled the end of half a century's silence for French-speaking African women writers. Having been objects for male francophone authors, "spoken for rather than speaking" (Miller 259), women found in Mariama Bâ an authentic interpreter of their experiences in cultures that privilege men and leave women essentially without a voice.

The novel begins with the death of Modou Fall, which initiates a period, according to Moslem custom, when Modou's wives, Ramatoulaye and Binetou, must spend four months in seclusion. It is then that Ramatoulaye starts a long letter to her intimate childhood friend, Aissatou. She tells the story of her husband's decision to take a second wife, a much younger woman, a contemporary and friend of their daughter. Ramatoulaye also gives a past account (for the reader's information) of the marriage of Aissatou's husband Mawdo to a young co-wife chosen by his mother out of her disdain for Aissatou's family background. Additionally, Ramatoulaye writes of her youth, her French colonial education, the early period of her marriage, and her present life after Modou's death.

Bâ's critique of polygamy is a central theme of the novel. Men in modern Senegalese society are free to take more than one wife, whether for reasons of love, sexual desire, family connections, or status. Although Moslem law requires that co-wives be treated equally, such is often not the case. After his second marriage, Modou lives with Binetou, and no longer provides for Ramatoulaye and their twelve children. Under polygamy, Bâ shows, wives become rivals who vie for the economic and emotional resources of their shared husband. Women of different generations within a family become enemies, often in unspoken ways, as mothers arrange and destroy marriages with little regard for the children's feelings. Aissatou's mother-in-law grooms her young niece Nabou "[teaching] her that the first quality in a woman is docility" (29). Insisting that Mawdo (Aissatou's husband) take Nabou as his second wife, his mother fulfills her wish for a daughter-in-law of noble birth and assures her own continuing power over her son. Ramatoulaye's husband Modou falls in love with Binetou, a girl less than half his age. Her mother, who sees him as a wealthy match, forces her daughter into marriage for her own material gain. Such manipulations take place because women can gain economic security and a respected position in society only through marriage.

When Aissatou and Ramatoulaye are replaced by younger co-wives, Aissatou chooses to make a complete break with both her husband and her culture. She moves to the United States with her four sons. Ramatoulaye, however, chooses to remain. She too works hard at reconstructing her life, not by starting over in another place, but through writing her experiences and impressions to her friend, trying to figure out how to live as a modern woman while not completely deserting her native traditions. By writing, Ramatoulaye comes to understand and appreciate both her culture and her individual identity as a woman. She resists the subordination of women by allowing herself to value her own experience, developing, as she writes, a strong, confident, and honest voice in which she—and many other women like her—have not previously spoken.

By the end of her letter, Ramatoulaye has metaphorically and physically expanded her horizons; not only is she more aware of her inner possibilities, she is also able to drive the car given her by Aissatou, go to the movies alone, stand in a line with men to pay bills. More importantly, she has learned to express her feelings to men, who hold power. Earlier, when Aissatou's husband, Mawdo, and Tamsir, Mawdo's brother, had come to tell her of Modou's second marriage, she received them with a smile, stifling her feelings of betrayal. But when her period of mourning ends, and Tamsir proposes marriage for his own economic gain, Ramatoulaye responds passionately:

> You forget that I have a heart, a mind, that I am not an object to be passed from hand to hand. You don't know what marriage means to me: it is an act of faith and of love, the total surrender of oneself to the person one has chosen and has chosen you. (58)

Rejecting a patriarchal culture whose religious tradition as well as its economic and political systems allow women no voice, Ramatoulaye has, through her own efforts, acquired the power to speak up for her rights as an equal human being.

One realization of Ramatoulaye's is that relationships between women are far richer and more enduring than those between men and women. Her new-found security and long-standing feelings of unconditional love for her children enable her to raise them confidently without Modou. Taking pride in the loyalty of all her children, she encourages her daughters to live lives of greater freedom than she has been permitted.

An important model for Ramatoulaye has been the white headmistress of the French colonial school she and Aissatou attended. "She loved us without patronizing us," says Ramatoulaye (16). Inspiring her students to question their tradition, superstitions, and customs, and "appreciate a multitude of civilizations," she was able to envision for them "an 'uncommon' destiny" (15).

Finally, it is through her friendship with Aissatou that Ramatoulaye is able to find and express her profound sense of personal truth. In an intimate relationship free of hierarchy and subordination, founded on shared values, experience, and deep affection, Ramatoulaye comes to refashion her life. Her own liberation now expands to a vision of freedom for all women:

> I am not indifferent to the irreversible currents of women's liberation that are lashing the world. This commotion that is shaking up every aspect of our lives reveals and illustrates our abilities. My heart rejoices each time a woman emerges from the shadows. (88)

Students in the West might at first find this novel alien and confusing. Teachers can expect students to express how different Ramatoulaye's culture is from theirs. A good way to begin a conversation about *So Long a Letter* is by discussing polygamous marriages. Students can try to find out when and why polygamy began and any cultural needs it might still serve. Teachers might also want to bring up Western social practices that allow men considerable freedom in choosing female partners—for example, serial monogamy, that is, a man divorces his wife of many years to marry a younger woman (and he can do this again) or dates younger women "on the side." Another theme in Bâ's novel that will interest students is friendship. They may compare female friendships with those between males, examining particularly the differences they observe in qualities such as intimacy and trust.

WORKS CITED

Bâ, Mariama. *So Long a Letter* [1979]. Oxford: Heinemann International Literature and Textbooks, 1981.

Miller, Christopher L. *Theories of Africans*. Chicago: U of Chicago P, 1990.

FOR FURTHER READING

Mortimer, Mildred. "Enclosure/Disclosure in Mariama Bâ's *Une si longue lettre*." *The French Review* 64.1 (October 1990): 69–78.

Wearing "*Her* Favour in the Battle": The "Go-between" in D. H. Lawrence's *Sons and Lovers* (1913)

Maria Margaroni

D. H. Lawrence's *Sons and Lovers* is a *bildungsroman*, a novel that typically describes the formation of a male protagonist. In tracing his life from birth to adulthood/manhood, the *bildungsroman* aims at making sense of his disparate experiences as a progression toward a coherent individuality. As an example of this novelistic tradition, *Sons and Lovers* focuses on the development of its young male hero, Paul Morel, in a small working-class community of the British Midlands at the turn of the nineteenth century. Because Paul's journey toward manhood is portrayed as inextricable from his artistic awakening, "man" and "artist" seem to be synonymous in the novel. Indeed, not only is "man" defined as essentially an originator and controller of meaning, but the creative activity itself appears to be a male prerogative. There are hardly any opportunities for self-fulfilling, life-enhancing enterprise offered to women. Hence the desire to be men expressed by all three main female characters (Mrs. Morel, Clara, and Miriam): "If I were a man, nothing would stop me," Mrs. Morel tells a friend (16).

It is to Lawrence's credit that Mrs. Morel finds out that "being a man isn't everything." As *Sons and Lovers* demonstrates, both male and female natures are compromised in an industrialized, mechanized society. From a feminist perspective, where the novel is less successful is in its understanding of the *difference* between these two natures. Thus, whereas the realization of "manhood" is synonymous with the achievement of a creative and independent existence beyond the claims of love and family, the fulfillment of "womanhood" is conceivable only in the context of a relation to a man (be it a son or a lover). In this light, it is significant that there is no glimpse of a "progress" equivalent to Paul's in any of the young women's lives depicted in *Sons and Lovers*. Although apparently independent and determined to affirm her individuality, Clara is repeatedly portrayed as incomplete. It is no wonder that at the end of the novel she is reconciled to her husband and to that "ease of soul and physical comfort" which Paul considers fitting for feminine existence (314). Similarly, Miriam's continuing dependence on Paul (despite her pride in and commitment to her work as a teacher) seems to confirm his conviction that a woman's "real and vital part" is expressed only in her union with a man (505).

The problem with Lawrence's understanding of sexual difference is his inability to conceive it as other than natural. As a result, he often ends up reducing his men and women to the transient manifestations of a timeless male or female essence. The task then for a teacher in a gender-conscious classroom is to throw light on how, in the specific sociohistorical context, certain gender roles (e.g., those of wife and mother) are invested with power and promoted as "natural" while others (e.g., the roles of spinster, feminist, or the sexually liberated woman) are marginalized. It is in this light that students need to appreciate the apparently "normal" dependence of women on men and their failure to survive outside the institution of marriage. As an analysis of the characters of Mrs. Morel and Clara demonstrates, marriage offers women financial security and a socially respectable identity. It gives them the opportunity to become "mother[s] of men" which for Mrs. Morel is the next best thing to actually *being* a man (44).

It might be tempting to understand Mrs. Morel's attachment to her sons as an "abnormal" erotic fixation which cripples both sons emotionally as well as sexually. Such an understanding demands that we view Mrs. Morel as overly possessive and, hence, a "bad" mother. It is important, however, that we re-conceptualize the character's "possessiveness" as the symptom of a *political* rather than erotic desire; in other words, as the product of Mrs. Morel's frustration within a culture that denies her any direct access to power. What makes her seek consolation in her sons is precisely their ability to function as her own private army sent out "in the world" to "work out what *she* wanted" (127).

Thinking about Mrs. Morel's relationship to Paul in these terms will allow students to reconsider the significance of the first part of the novel, which (due to its focus on Mrs. Morel) has been perceived as having a merely "introductory" function. It will also help them view Paul's journey in a new light, for if Paul is set to attain a heroic individuality, this is pledged to his mother. His destiny, then, is to function as the mother's "go-between" (Finney 71), or, in Mrs. Morel's own words, the "knight who wore *her* favour in the battle" (101). This is emphasized in Paul's successive achievements after he "launches into life" (127–28, 226–27, 309–11). On these occasions both mother and son feel that "his work was hers" (227) because he was "derived from her," he was "of her" (128). Even after Mrs. Morel's death, Paul sees himself duty-bound to continue her struggle either through his painting or by begetting children (500).

It is this aspect of Paul that renders *Sons and Lovers* interesting from a feminist standpoint since it could be argued that the development traced in it is not that of heroic masculinity, but of a "third force" (Kermode 10) *between* masculinity and femininity. Indeed, in his vulnerable physique and his preference of solitary spiritual pursuits at home over communal physical activity in the coal mine or the fields, Paul constitutes "a new specimen of manhood" (178). Considering the semi-autobiographical nature of the novel, students may want to consider the extent to which the introduction of this "new specimen" in *Sons and Lovers* points to Lawrence's own dissatisfaction with the roles and choices open to him as a man at the turn of the nineteenth century. Finally, teachers may encourage students to explore the ways in which the character of Paul puts into question traditional models of masculinity as these are reflected in the novel and as they have survived in contemporary forms of gender representation (e.g., adolescent adventure stories, popular romantic fiction, post-1960s working-class literature).

WORKS CITED

Finney, Brian. *D. H. Lawrence:* Sons and Lovers. Harmondsworth, Middlesex: Penguin, 1990.

Kermode, Frank. *Lawrence*. London: Fontana, 1973.

Lawrence, D. H. *Sons and Lovers* [1913]. London: Penguin, 1948.

FOR FURTHER READING

Macleod, Sheila. *Lawrence's Men and Women*. London: Paladin, 1987.

Riding Tennessee Williams'
A Streetcar Named Desire (1947)

Elise Ann Earthman

A hard-drinking, abusive, down-to-earth man's man; a delicate flower of a woman, desperate to hide her sordid past behind her Southern belle charm; a loving housewife and sister torn between them: Tennessee Williams' second Broadway success, *A Streetcar Named Desire*, contains powerful material for an intensive study of gender roles as they were constructed in the mid-twentieth century.

In many ways, the play (followed by the 1951 Kazan film) depicts an epic struggle between ultramasculine and ultrafeminine forces. Stanley Kowalski, a "richly feathered male bird" (29), loves all that is male-identified: a good steak, bowling, poker, whiskey and Jax beer, crude jokes, and his "baby doll," Stella. Blanche DuBois, Stella's sister, arrives on the scene, trailing femininity like the scent of magnolia: she wears frilly cocktail dresses and white gloves, soaks for hours in a hot bath, lies about her age, refuses to be seen in strong light, and attempts to enchant every man she meets. Throughout the play, Stanley and Blanche struggle for the allegiance of Stella, a well-brought-up young woman who, though she loves her ethereal sister, is hopelessly devoted to her more earthy husband.

Williams masterfully creates characters of great complexity and ambiguity; we as readers/viewers find our allegiances growing more tangled as the play unfolds. The powerful Stanley—who strikes his pregnant wife and throws his dinner against the wall in a fit of rage—is, in his home (his *kingdom*), threatened by Blanche's presence. Over the course of her greatly extended stay in the tiny apartment, Stanley finds the simple joy of his household disrupted, as Blanche tries to win Stella's affections away from him and to convince Stella to leave Stanley. In a scene that must evoke our sympathy for Stanley, he overhears Blanche calling him "brute," "bestial," "ape-like" (71–72), and he reacts, in order to keep his marriage and home from being destroyed. Blanche —despite the fact that she lies about a shameful past, conceals her drinking, and nearly wins Mitch through deceptive "feminine wiles"—is a sensitive, wounded woman who has cared for dying family members one after the other, lost a young husband to suicide, and now, alone and completely without resources of any kind, has nowhere else to go. But the exaggerated femininity, which she feels has served her so well in the past, pushes Stanley into an exaggeratedly masculine position that ultimately results in her downfall.

Between them stands Stella, and what are we to make of her? A practical, down-to-earth young woman who rejects the "moonlight and magnolias" of her traditional upbringing; a modern woman who believes that "people have got to tolerate each other's habits" (65), she is so deeply attached to Stanley that she "nearly go[es] wild" when he is away for a week, and "cr[ies] on his lap like a baby" (25) when he returns. Midway through her first pregnancy when Blanche arrives, Stella tries valiantly to make a place for the sister whose past she shares, while keeping her husband happy.

Blanche's great strength lies in her ability to create illusion, and Stanley ultimately defeats her by tearing the illusions away one by one, forcing her to face the cold, hard facts of the identity he has pieced together through his investigations in Laurel, her hometown. Far from being the high-principled, refined schoolteacher that she would have people believe, Blanche was, in effect, ridden out of town on a rail, because she was intimate with strangers, with soldiers from the army camp, and with a 17-year-old student. Stanley's revelations to Stella and Mitch, the suitor Blanche hopes will arrest her downward spiral by marrying her, destroy their illusions about Blanche and any credibility she has, so that no one believes the "story" that Stanley has raped her. Stanley's sexual violation of Blanche while his wife is in the hospital giving birth graphically represents the complete defeat of everything Blanche is—the refined woman she would like to be, the "fallen" woman she tries to hide, the fragile, battered human being who tries to find a place of safety. Her only refuge, in the end, is madness, the final break from a world [that is] far too "real" for her to face.

Many have questioned whether *Streetcar* qualifies as a tragedy, the debate most often centering around Blanche as the tragic figure, and certainly her descent into madness has a "tragic grandeur" (Adler 49). Yet contemporary students may see another kind of tragedy in the choice Stella is forced to make between her husband and sister. Clearly, Stella feels she cannot afford to risk everything she has in order to take Blanche's side; though she is swayed enough by Blanche's influence to begin to see Stanley's flaws—to call him "pig" and to start giving him orders, in the end Stella abandons Blanche to take refuge in his strength and security. When Blanche accuses Stanley of rape, Stella tells

Eunice, "I couldn't believe her story and go on living with Stanley," to which the ever-practical Eunice replies, "Life has got to go on. No matter what happens, you've got to keep on going" (133). Faced by such an either-or choice, Stella opts for believing Stanley's lie, a home for herself and the baby, and a mental hospital for Blanche. Students might debate what possibilities were open to Stella, and thereby come to an understanding of the mid-century woman with little education and limited job skills.

Streetcar offers mature students many possibilities for critical thinking about gender relations. Who is the victim—Blanche or Stanley? What is Stella's responsibility for the events that occur? Mitch's? Any of the characters could be "put on trial" for their shortcomings—certainly Stanley, for his unforgivable act, but also Blanche for trying to break up Stanley's home, or Stella for abandoning her sister. Whatever direction the discussion takes, students will be enriched for having studied one of the twentieth century's greatest plays, which displays the tragic costs to both women and men of rigidly defined gender roles.

WORKS CITED

Adler, Thomas P. A Streetcar Named Desire: *The Moth and the Lantern*. New York: Twayne, 1990.
Williams, Tennessee. *A Streetcar Named Desire* [1947]. New York: Signet, 1974.

FOR FURTHER READING

Lant, Kathleen Margaret. "A Streetcar Named Mysogyny." *Violence in Drama*. Ed. James Redmond. Cambridge: Cambridge UP, 1991, 225–38.

Agent or Victim: Thomas Hardy's
Tess of the D'Urbervilles (1891)

Paula Alida Roy

Tess of the D'Urbervilles raises questions about biology as destiny and the crushing force of cultural attitudes, in particular, the double standard. Hardy may be seen as a nascent "feminist" in his obvious sympathy for Tess' victimization by men, yet his ambiguous portrayal of how freely Tess *chooses*, not once but twice, to live with Alec as his mistress complicates his heroine beyond poster girl for simple victimhood. Hardy's tone and the circumstances he depicts prompt consideration of issues still relevant today.

This episodic, melodramatic novel tells the old story of a young woman's hapless fall from innocence at the hands of the sinister but seductive Alec D'Urberville; her "respectable" marriage to the deceptively named Angel St. Clare; her second fall into despair and destitution as an abandoned wife; her return to Alec's keeping as mistress to rescue her family from poverty; and finally, her escape from bondage by her murder of Alec, followed by a brief idyll of reconciliation with Angel before she is apprehended while asleep, and taken to be executed. As Hardy, the famous fatalist, concludes, "the President of the Immortals . . . had ended his sport with Tess" (397). *His* sport, indeed!

Our first vision of Tess "club-walking" with her peers establishes her as desirable, with her "mobile peony mouth." She wears a red ribbon in her hair, "the only one of that white company who could boast of such a pronounced adornment" (14). Textual analysts trace this motif, connecting Tess to the color red, which here foreshadows her fateful sexual attractiveness and impinges on her innocence by suggesting dangerous sensuality. Red also prefigures blood, first of the horse Prince, whose demise, Tess' "fault," catapults her into Alec's orbit; finally, of Alex himself, dead at Tess' hand. At the outset, then, Hardy draws a causal link between Tess' biological charms and her destiny.

After Alec rapes Tess in the Chase, Hardy asks rhetorically, "Why is it that upon this beautiful feminine tissue, sensitive as gossamer, and practically blank as snow as yet, there should have been traced such a coarse pattern as it was doomed to receive?" (74). He offers as "answer" the country folks' conclusion, " 'It was to be' "; then concludes, at the end of the novel's first section, "An immeasurable chasm was to divide our heroine's personality thereafter from that previous self of hers" (74). Does Hardy suggest that Tess' essential nature has been altered completely by her unwanted violent transition from virgin to sexual experience? Does he further imply that woman, "personality" and "feminine tissue," is "blank" until changed for good or ill by contact with man? Alec's rape of Tess and her subsequent capitulation to him, which lead to pregnancy, will later be blamed by both Alec and Angel on Tess' red mouth, womanly figure, and passionate nature.

Students often misread the scene in which Alec violates Tess, the violence of which is obscured by Hardy's veiled language. A closer reading opens for some the question suggested by critics such as Linda M. Shires, who claims, "it remains unclear whether Alec rapes or seduces Tess" (152). The scene itself and such critical responses invite analysis of attitudes toward rape (what today would be termed "date rape"), then and now. Clearly, Alec holds a position of power over Tess, in terms of age, class, sophistication, and experience. She is "sleeping soundly" thanks to a "cordial" from a "druggist's bottle" that Alec "held . . . to her mouth unawares" to make her "feel warmer." Considering this language and Hardy's question, "But where was Tess's guardian angel?" (74), it seems difficult to argue for consensual sex. The fact that critics and students do so argue, reasoning that Tess would not willingly stay with Alec after being raped by him, calls for discussion of how often rape victims are blamed for the assault upon them, how often they blame themselves, and how the rape affects their lives.

In addition to being raped, Tess moves through a series of events in which her free will is compromised by gender and class. Among issues worthy of study for both historical context and contemporary relevance are: Tess' inability to provide, either in life or death, for her unfortunate child; the limits she faces in seeking employment; the obligation she feels to take care of her hapless mother and her siblings; and the dangerous combination of her beauty and her damaged reputation. Perhaps most interesting to student readers is the way Hardy explores (and deplores!) the double standard imposed on women in general by social mores and imposed on Tess by Angel on their wedding night. Enchanted by his own version of Tess as dairymaid cum blue blood, he, with impunity, dismisses her as she tries to tell him the truth of her life's experience. After he insists on confessing his dalliance, she, in a burst of relief, tells him her sad tale. But Angel cannot see the parallel that Tess draws between their pasts. As she begs him to forgive her "as you are forgiven," he echoes Hardy's diagnosis of Tess' altered personality after the rape: "Forgiveness does not apply to the case. You were one person; now you are another" (228).

When Angel leaves their unconsummated marriage for Brazil, Tess faces life as a disgraced woman and an abandoned wife. In the aftermath of both betrayals, however, we see Tess act with agency; after being *acted upon* by these two men who think they love her, she does *act*. In tracing the choices she makes—first leaving Alec without telling him she is pregnant and refusing his assistance; then making her own way in the world without availing herself of the resources of Angel's family—students may consider the degree to which Tess takes charge of her own life. As she capitulates to Alec again, it is not for herself but for her family, whose desperate need is beyond her means of rescue. To adapt Carol Gilligan's theory, Tess—unlike Alec who acts on impulses rationalized in a framework of class privilege and selfishness, and Angel who operates on a rigid code of honor without true empathy—makes choices informed by care for others and a quiet pride that insists she take responsibility for her actions: starting with the death of the horse Prince, and ending, terribly, with the bloody death it presaged, her murder of Alec.

That murder and the subsequent, brief reconciliation with her beloved Angel, who finally realizes the fidelity and essential purity of his ruined wife, stand as evidence that Tess is both victim of forces that enfold gender into the fabric of destiny and free agent. In patriarchal complicity with "the President of the Immortals," Alec and Angel *the men*, with all the attitudes and privileges conferred upon them by their sex, embody fate for Tess, *the woman*. Tess' last choice is a self-destructive one that links her to female characters from Antigone to Edna Pontellier, from Medea up to and including Thelma and Louise. Like these and other female "outlaws," Hardy's Tess leaves us with a troubling question: pushed to the margins by misogyny and sexism, is a strong woman's only choice her own destruction?

WORKS CITED

Gilligan, Carol. *In a Different Voice*. Cambridge, MA: Harvard UP, 1982.
Hardy, Thomas. *Tess of the D'Urbervilles* [1891]. New York: Penguin, 1998.

FOR FURTHER READING

Shires, Linda M. "The Radical Aesthetic of *Tess of the D'Urbervilles*." *The Cambridge Companion to Thomas Hardy*. Ed. Dale Kramer. Cambridge: Cambridge UP, 1999, 145–63.

An African-American Woman's Journey of Self-Discovery in Zora Neale Hurston's *Their Eyes Were Watching God* (1937)

Ken Silber

Zora Neale Hurston's *Their Eyes Were Watching God* is the story of Janie Crawford's search for personal fulfillment within a society that discourages women from acting freely. Her first two husbands impede her progress by confining and degrading her, but Janie finds true love with Tea Cake Woods, and the self-affirmation this love brings expands Janie's horizon. Offering her the freedom her previous husbands denied her, Tea Cake teaches Janie to drive and play checkers, invites her to speak her mind, and "tuh git round a whole heap" (169). Yet Tea Cake also makes sure everyone knows who's boss; "Janie is wherever *Ah* wants to be," he says (219). It is only after Tea Cake's death that, seizing the opportunity to experience all of life—both triumph and tragedy—Janie is able to realize herself truly, a groundbreaking achievement for a woman in the world of African-American literature in 1937.

Janie's journey begins in earnest at age sixteen when she comes upon a blooming pear tree and her imagination produces a vision of ecstasy: "She saw a dust-bearing bee sink into the sanctum of a bloom. . . . So this was a marriage!" (24). However, she has little time to pursue this vision before Nanny, her grandmother and an ex-slave, intrudes. Having endured terrible physical and mental abuse, Nanny values her granddaughter's future safety above all else, and she marries Janie off to ensure it: " 'Taint Logan Killicks Ah wants you to have, baby, it's protection" (30). But Janie refuses to remain trapped in a loveless marriage. Instead, she keeps a vigil at the front gate, gazing up the road, her mind and options open. When she escapes with Joe Starks, it is not for love, but because he speaks "for far horizon . . . for change and chance" (50).

Throughout twenty years of marriage, Starks strives to control and confine Janie, beating her down mentally and, at times, physically. But this treatment is no match for her robust will, about which Nanny had given her crucial instruction: " 'You can't beat nobody down so low till you can rob 'em of they will' " (31). On the surface, Janie plays the role of dutiful wife, marking time until Joe's death, while inside she has preserved intact the vision of the pear tree. When Tea Cake, the quintessential romantic hero, arrives in Eatonville, Janie hesitates at first, struggling with doubt and Nanny's cautionary influence, before acting decisively. "Ah done lived Grandma's way, now Ah means tuh live mine" (171) she confides to her closest friend, Pheoby Watson, before leaving for the muck.

With Tea Cake's help, Janie develops by great strides in many directions, from exchanging stories freely with her neighbors to learning how to handle a rifle (which proves crucial in saving her life). Unlike her previous husbands, Tea Cake loves Janie for who she is. The love Janie feels in return—which Hurston at one point describes as "self-crushing" (192)—compels her to defer to Tea Cake's judgment, supporting without regret his ill-fated decision to remain on the muck as a powerful hurricane approaches. The consequences—a flood that nearly kills them both, the rabid dog bite, and Tea Cake's illness—force Janie to draw upon inner strength she didn't know she had, and hasten her development into a fully realized woman.

Janie's deliberate decision to save her own life at the expense of Tea Cake's (she ensures that Tea Cake's pistol will click through three empty chambers before it fires) is a key manifestation of this growth. In a tradition where women were taught to value the lives of loved ones ahead of their own—or as Nanny put it, "tuh try and do for you befo' mah head is cold," (31)—Janie opts for self-preservation. At her trial for Tea Cake's murder, she learns that this choice has forfeited her standing in the Black community. The muck residents turn out in force to see her convicted; they cannot abide the woman who has killed Tea Cake. However, Janie is focused only on ensuring there be no misunderstanding of her relationship with Tea Cake. To Janie, were the jury to decide that she had wanted Tea Cake to die, it would be "worse than murder" (279).

The trial is an excellent scene to discuss with students because it offers an opportunity to explore these questions: Does Janie ultimately attain her own voice in this novel? At the story's end, is Janie an unfettered, autonomous woman, or is she still an object of men's possession? Scholars Mary Helen Washington, Missy Dehn Kubitschek, and Michael Awkward are among many to consider opposing points of view. Washington argues that Hurston's narrative voice obscures and silences Janie's voice during the courtroom scene, at a point when she has developed her own storytelling skills in the muck community (245). Kubitschek, however, sees Janie discover her voice in the Everglades locale, and realize it fully by relating her story to Pheoby (32).

Awkward recognizes the novel's duality of voice—considered a major flaw by many critics—as a sophisticated example of African-American collaborative storytelling (54). Students may find these arguments instructive in addressing the question: What does a woman of color need to achieve self-realization in a world dominated by men intent on restricting her?

Janie's greatest concern in telling her story is that her audience, be it on-lookers in the courtroom or her best friend, hear and understand her truth. Janie consistently uses speech to share truth and develop intimacy, in contrast to both Jody's grand discourse intended to subordinate (talking "tuh unlet-tered folks wid books in his jaws" [79]) and the Eatonville gossips and court-room spectators, who speak "with their tongues cocked and loaded" (275). Just as Janie took power over Jody simply by speaking her mind to him, her act of telling her story to Pheoby engenders the power of an entire novel. Nanny said it well: "Ah said Ah'd save de text for you" (32)—just what Janie did for Pheoby, and Hurston for her readers. Janie's return to Eatonville not only completes her emergence as a full-fledged participant in African-American storytelling culture, but results in a novel that defies a male-dominated literary tradition likely to overlook the significance of a conversation between women simply sharing their experiences. This community among women is Hurston's legacy to her readers and her literary descendants, and is a crucial model for the self-affirmation of female characters in novels such as *The Women of Brewster Place* by Gloria Naylor and Alice Walker's *The Color Purple*.

WORKS CITED

Awkward, Michael. *Inspiriting Influences: Tradition, Revision, and Afro-American Women's Novels*. New York: Columbia UP, 1989.

Hurston, Zora Neale. *Their Eyes Were Watching God*. Chicago: U of Illinois P, 1937.

Kubitschek, Missy Dehn. " 'Tuh de Horizon and Back': The Female Quest in *Their Eyes Were Watching God*." *Modern Critical Interpretations: Zora Neale Hur-ston's* Their Eyes Were Watching God. Ed. Harold Bloom. New York: Chelsea House Publishers, 1987, 19–33.

Washington, Mary Helen. *Invented Lives: Narratives of Black Women, 1860–1960*. New York: Anchor, 1987, 237–54.

FOR FURTHER READING

Johnson, Barbara. "Metaphor, Metonymy and Voice in *Their Eyes Were Watching God*." *Black Literature and Literary Theory*. Ed. Henry Louis Gates, Jr. New York: Methuen, 1984, 205–19.

Fragmenting Culture, Fragmenting Lives: Chinua Achebe's *Things Fall Apart* (1959)

Rebekah Hamilton

Chinua Achebe's *Things Fall Apart* begins with a reference to great wrestlers of the Igbo culture: Okonkwo (the novel's protagonist), Amalinze the Cat, and the unnamed, legendary founder of Umuofia, who wrestled "a spirit of the wild" day and night for one full week. This image of the wrestler becomes the dominant symbol of the novel, for characters must wrestle with the norms of Igbo culture, with the gods and goddesses of the tribe, and with their personal, conflicting desires.

One of the norms of Igbo culture is the sharp division between what is feminine and what is masculine. From simple farm crops to complex human actions and emotions, *Things Fall Apart* portrays a culture where real and symbolic gender distinctions abound. "[Okonkwo's] mother and sisters worked hard enough, but they grew women's crops, like coco-yams, beans and cassava. Yam, the king of crops, was a man's crop" (22–23). "Yam stood for manliness" (33). The difference signifies that it is harder and takes more time to cultivate and harvest yams than to raise other crops. There are female crimes, those committed inadvertently, and there are male crimes. Okonkwo's killing of Ezeudu's son as a result of an accidental gunshot is considered a female crime, punishable by seven years of exile in his motherland. Had he committed a male crime, Okonkwo's punishment would have been permanent exile or death by hanging.

Unoka, Okonkwo's father, was a talented musician who loved conversation but feared fighting. His son suffered as a child when a playmate told him his father was an *agbala*, the word for "woman" and "a man of no accomplishment." Okonkwo grew up ashamed of his father and came to hate characteristics associated in his culture with the feminine.

The society of the Igbo was dominated by men. Women of the clan lived strictly according to Igbo customs. One sign of status among Igbo men was to have multiple wives. Okonkwo's three wives each have their own living quarters, but the women are supportive of each other and of each other's children, who are raised as brothers and sisters. When Ekwefi is distraught that Agbala, the Oracle, has sent for Ezinma, for example, Nwoye's mother reassures her that her daughter will return soon. Ekwefi and Chielo are close and openly discuss Okonkwo's beatings. Okonkwo rules all his wives and children sternly and does not hesitate to beat them when they displease him, as when Ojuigo fails to prepare his meal on time or when Nwoye cries after Ikemefuna's death. The subjugation of women is most sharply drawn in Nneka, the woman whose four previous sets of twins have been abandoned in the Evil Forest according to custom, but who converts to Christianity in desperation to save her coming child. Okonkwo's daughter Ezinma, whom he always wishes had been a son, perhaps best represents the future possibilities for women of the tribe, yet even she acquiesces to the tribe's men. In their strongly patriarchal culture, the women take comfort primarily from each other and from the pleasures of their shared storytelling. The collaborative spirit of the women contrasts with the warrior's cult of violence and solitude.

Although Okonkwo is the novel's protagonist, his impulsiveness, his limited capacity for compassion, and his instinct to confront all problems with physical force isolate him from others. Because he fears emotions, he drives others away. His son Nwoye's attachment to Ikemefuna and his later conversion to Christianity are largely driven by his search for other, less punishing role models. Okonkwo's friend Obierika and his uncle Uchendu, while upholding traditional tribal ways, exhibit great wisdom and restraint. Ironically, Okonkwo's impulsiveness is most like Enoch's, the Christian convert whom he despises. Throughout most of the novel, Okonkwo reacts—often inappropriately—to events and people he cannot control. His final act of suicide shows the depth of his despair as his family and his culture make choices he cannot abide.

Critic Carol Boyce Davies writes that the journey of Ekwefi's daughter, Ezinma, with Chielo, the priestess, is important in many respects:

> Symbolically [it] takes her out of Okonkwo's/society's defined role for her as a young woman and suggests larger possibilities for her life. The Chielo/Ezinma episode is one of those situations over which Okonkwo has no control. . . . His machete, the symbol of male aggression, is of no use in this context. (247)

If Okonkwo's rise and fall stands for that of the clan at a significant juncture in its history, Achebe is suggesting that for survival, the qualities associated with femininity must be honored. Ekwefi's close relationship with her daughter is valued; Okonkwo's critical and violent relationship with his son is discredited. The price for rejecting the feminine, Achebe shows, is ultimately self-destruction (Davies 246).

Creative activities for students might include writing a brief sequel focusing on Ezinma's married life or a prequel highlighting Okonkwo's childhood relationships with his father and mother. The "generational saga" could dramatize changes in gender expectations and roles over time, even in highly traditional, patriarchal cultures. Students might also interview their relatives about changing gender roles in their own families. Reflective essays on the influences of religious beliefs and customs or of parental expectations on children would enable students to recognize similarities in generational conflicts from culture to culture. Investigating gender roles and ways in which expectations shift from one cultural group to another would help students become aware that all cultural practices cannot be judged by a single standard.

WORKS CITED

Achebe, Chinua. *Things Fall Apart* [1959]. New York: Anchor, 1994.

Davies, Carol Boyce. "Motherhood in the Works of Male and Female Igbo Writers: Achebe, Emecheta, Nwapa and Nzekwu." *Ngambika: Studies of Women in African Literature*. Ed. Carol Boyce Davies and Anne Adams Graves. Trenton, NJ: Africa World Press, 1986, 241–56.

FOR FURTHER READING

Iyasere, Solomon O., ed. *Understanding* Things Fall Apart: *Selected Essays and Criticism*. Troy, NY: Whitston, 1998.

"Just a Lady": Gender and Power in Harper Lee's *To Kill a Mockingbird* (1960)

Michele S. Ware

Harper Lee's Pulitzer Prize–winning novel, *To Kill a Mockingbird*, charts the development of a young Southern girl from a childhood of innocence and freedom to an awareness of cruelty, evil, and the limitations and constraints of her position in her culture. The first-person narrative of Jean Louise "Scout" Finch reveals her unusually perceptive account of three significant years of her childhood. The setting of the novel, a small town in Alabama during the mid-1930s, and the central conflict, the trial of a Black man falsely accused of raping a white woman, create an intersection of the issues of race, class, and gender as Lee explores the dynamics of racial prejudice, Depression-era poverty, and genteel Southern womanhood.

The novel begins in the summer before Scout enters the first grade. Scout is a tough little tomboy who spends her days playing with her older brother Jem and her evenings reading with her father, Atticus Finch. Fiercely independent, Scout resists any kind of limitations placed upon her. The author establishes Scout's carefree existence in order to dramatize all that threatens to destabilize her protected view of herself and her community. Atticus Finch will defend Tom Robinson in his trial for the alleged rape of Mayella Ewell, and the events precipitated by the trial will destroy Scout's illusions, forcing her to reconsider everything she holds to be true—about human nature, about individual power, and about justice.

Scout's primary identification with the masculine world of her brother Jem and her father stems in part from her mother's death when Scout was only two. She has no memory of her mother, so she looks to Jem and Atticus as her guides to appropriate behavior. According to Scout, power and authority are masculine attributes; to be a girl is to be marginalized and excluded. An important part of Scout's development is her growing comprehension that she will be forced to enter the world of women, a world that holds no attractions for her. In her description of a typical summer day in Maycomb, Scout includes a portrait of a Southern lady: "Ladies bathed before noon, after their three-o'clock naps, and by nightfall were like soft teacakes with frostings of sweat and sweet talcum" (5–6). Her assessment of what it means to be a woman underscores her dismissal of an apparently useless, decorative existence.

Various female characters influence Scout's social development and exemplify the range of gender roles available to her. Additionally, they represent cultural distinctions determined by race and class. Scout's responses to these women reflect her growing knowledge of where power resides in her community. Calpurnia, the Finch family's African-American cook and housekeeper, provides a strong and loving female presence and acts as a role model for her, but Scout's relationship with Calpurnia is marked at first by conflict and rebellion. Over the course of the novel, however, she and Calpurnia grow closer. Although Calpurnia has some of the qualities of the stereotypical "Mammy" figure, Lee's characterization extends beyond that limited portrayal. Calpurnia has a life and a mind of her own, and she is the necessary transitional figure who moves comfortably through both sides of this racially divided Southern town. Taking Scout and Jem to her church with her one Sunday, Calpurnia exposes them to another side of racism in Maycomb—the hatred of some members of the Black community. While Calpurnia protects Scout from insults and violence, she also trains her to see the reality of the world around her. Calpurnia teaches the Finch children about their shared common humanity with their African-American neighbors, and she acts as both a moral guide and an example of female authority for Scout. When Jem and Dill eventually exclude her from their play, Scout discovers female companionship with Miss Maudie Atkinson, their iconoclastic neighbor, a widow who defies convention by tending her garden "in an old straw hat and men's coveralls" (47). Miss Maudie successfully balances an independent spirit with traditional gender roles and therefore becomes a strong potential role model for Scout.

As she observes the trial of Tom Robinson, Scout begins to discern differences in class in her hierarchical Southern community. Mayella Ewell, who has unjustly accused Tom Robinson of rape, takes the stand and reveals her vicious racism, her ignorance, and the barren poverty of her existence.

Scout gradually begins to understand her own power and the power of women. During her father's confrontation with a group of vigilantes who come to lynch Tom Robinson, Scout single-handedly defuses the violence and shames the men by identifying them by name and asking about their families. Not all female power, however, is good. During the trial, it is clear to everyone that Mayella Ewell is lying, that she has accused Tom Robinson of rape to mask her own social crime of desire for a Black man. Yet the all-white jury finds him guilty despite evidence to the contrary. In this place and time, the word of a white woman counts more than that of a Black man. After the trial, Scout helps serve the women of the town at one of her Aunt Alexandra's "missionary circle" gatherings (261). There she witnesses the veiled but brutal and hypocritical pronouncements of racist white women intent on their so-called Christian duty.

Students respond with engagement to the conflicts presented in *To Kill a Mockingbird*. They may be offended by the use of racial epithets and the thinly veiled paternalism of the novel's white characters. In this racist Southern community, Atticus Finch is the moral center of the novel, and his attitudes and beliefs—about equality in the eyes of the law; about integrity, honesty, and fairness; and about the responsibility of those privileged by social status or race—become Scout's moral and ethical touchstone. The film version of the novel provides students with a memorable interpretation of the text and a visual frame of reference for the setting, but the movie's primary attention to the character of Atticus Finch detracts from the novel's narrative exploration of Scout's character development. Students may find it useful to compare the two characters as protagonists of the film and the novel.

Scout's narrative point of view is honest and often unintentionally humorous as she grapples for a complete understanding of her world. *To Kill a Mockingbird* can be read as a feminist *bildungsroman*, for Scout emerges from her childhood experiences with a clear sense of her place in her community and an awareness of her potential power as the woman she will one day be. Admittedly, her power is limited and her authority is circumscribed by the historical/cultural context of the novel; Lee's portrayal of Scout ends not in defeat but in a triumphant expansion of her knowledge, understanding, and sympathy.

WORK CITED

Lee, Harper. *To Kill a Mockingbird* [1960]. 40th Anniversary Edition. New York: HarperCollins, 1999.

FOR FURTHER READING

Johnson, Claudia D. *Understanding* To Kill a Mockingbird: *A Student Casebook to Issues, Sources and Historic Documents*. Westport, CT: Greenwood, 1994.

Women Righting Wrongs: Morality and Justice in Susan Glaspell's *Trifles* (1916)

Jerilyn Fisher

Produced just as turn-of-the-century Americans were conceding women's right to suffrage, *Trifles* dramatizes women acting decisively in response to men's condescension and sex role stereotyping both at home and in courts of law. Remarkable for its conciseness and craft, Glaspell's one-act play depicts the considerable, even fatal consequences that occur when men do not take women seriously. Inflamed by persistent insult to their sex, two ordinary, otherwise conventional housewives lie by omission to ensure a helpless neighbor's right to defend herself against her husband's brutality. Paradoxically, becoming "outlaws" by concealing criminal evidence seems the only way the principal female characters in *Trifles* can right the wrongs of men.

When John Wright's strangled body is found and his wife taken into custody, three men in official capacity come to examine the farmhouse to establish a motive and bring Minnie Wright to trial. While the suspect sits in jail, her neighbor (Mr. Hale), the Sheriff (Mr. Peters), and the County Attorney (Mr. Henderson) scrutinize points of entry into the Wrights' home. As their husbands search the premises, Mrs. Hale and Mrs. Peters search for the life story that Minnie Wright has left behind. In effect, as they wonder aloud about the kitchen mess, the two women seem engaged in dialogue with what they find. But the men, unlike their wives, approach the unfamiliar by "snooping around and criticizing" (1227). They aim, as Mrs. Hale observes, "to get her own house to turn against her" (1230). Yet, as if it were taking up her defense, Minnie's house remains unyielding to the probing of men; indeed, it acts the custodian of female secrets.

Blinded by their estimation that "kitchen things," like women themselves (1227), are undeserving of serious attention, the three investigators cannot see in the domestic details that surround them what their wives easily perceive:

Minnie Wright's victimization—exposed by erratic sewing, a roughly broken birdcage door, and a strangled canary. Emphasizing how sexism impairs the men's vision, Judith Fetterley considers "A Jury of Her Peers," Glaspell's narrative version of the play, "a story about reading" in which the men are unable to "read the text that is placed before them" (148). In contrast, the women read the past encoded in half-set bread and sloppy cupboards. Using as authority their own experiences, they invisibly write the life—and ultimately "right" the fate—of Minnie Wright, their defenseless sister-housewife.

Slowly stitching together the story of spouse abuse behind this murder, Mrs. Hale and Mrs. Peters realize the subversive power of their knowledge precisely *because* it remains devalued by the men. While the sheriff is blatantly trivializing women's interest in preserves and quiltmaking, and the County Attorney is repeatedly putting off until "later" (1225, 1228) recollections of John Wright's domineering nature (1231–32), the men sidestep clues that point to motivation for Minnie's desperate action. Tacitly, the women collude, dominating the men without their knowing of this great reversal. Enacting segments or all of this short play, students can also recognize the non-verbal inversion of power that occurs: At the very beginning, the women, hesitant to enter the kitchen, stay "close together near the door" (1225); by the end, the women have center stage.

Since they can do nothing to change the sexist attitude of these self-important men, Mrs. Hale and Mrs. Peters must seek justice, paradoxically, by going against the law. Their final deception—the act of hiding the dead canary—not only strikes back against John Wright for his cruelty, but also serves as retaliation against their own husbands' derisive sarcasm, unfairly directed at the domestic work women do to serve the very men who laugh at them.

Ironies in this play abound and thematically coalesce around all that the women know and do which the men can't fathom. Tracing evidence that the women find and the men ignore, students will enjoy probing verbal ironies which critique gender stereotyping ("Men's hands aren't as clean as they might be"; "what would we do without the ladies" [1227]); situational irony as expressed within the play's title; the ultimate irony (and creativity) in the way John Wright was murdered and in Mrs. Hale's decisive last line: "We call it— knot it, Mr. Henderson" (1234). Much can be made of Mrs. Hale's ironic final rejoinder. Knotting refers to the quilting skill that Minnie Wright put to use in killing her husband: her reaction, through "women's work," to his strangulation of her true desires, and, of course, his strangulating the extension of that once-lively self, the bird. Also, knotting symbolizes the seditious, binding connection among the three women. Finally, students can appreciate the clever irony in Mrs. Hale's seemingly honest, straightforward response to the County Attorney's repeated, facetious question ("Well, ladies, have you decided if she was going to quilt it or knot it" [1232]). Taking advantage of his low expectations for women's intelligence, Mrs. Hale's last line masks the two women's physical cover-up of evidence, thus ensuring Mrs. Wright's protection.

Further exploring the play's central theme of gender bias, students can discuss related issues that reach beyond the dramatic situation itself: What serious problems occur when women's voices, metaphorically and physically, are suppressed (voice as identity; voice as authority; voice as relational connection)? Should women, like Mrs. Wright, who murder psychologically or physically abusive husbands, be exonerated? With stage directions that emphasize the women's solidarity, what does Glaspell seem to say about effective tactics for disrupting sexism?

Paired with Sophocles' *Antigone* and/or Ibsen's *A Doll's House*, *Trifles* invites students to form opinions about whether women and men typically perceive what is right and wrong differently. Teachers interested in an interdisciplinary approach might introduce feminist psychological theory by both Gilligan and, jointly, Belenky, Clinchy, Goldberger, and Tarule. With *In a Different Voice*, students can consider controversial research about gender-related moral decision making (women often drawn to subjectivity—"an ethic of caring"—and men to objectivity—"principles of justice"); through *Women's Ways of Knowing*, students can examine gender-related, epistemological processes for discovering truth, knowledge, and one's own authority. After exposure to these studies, students will have some theoretical grounding to inform their impressions about gender, morality, and the law. Finally, they might ask, as Mrs. Hale does: What was the real crime here? "Who's going to punish that?" (1233).

WORKS CITED

Belenky, Mary et al. *Women's Ways of Knowing.* New York: Basic Books, 1986.

Fetterley, Judith. "Reading about Reading: 'A Jury of Her Peers,' 'The Murders in the Rue Morgue,' and 'The Yellow Wallpaper.' " *Gender and Reading.* Ed. Elizabeth A. Flynn and Patrocinio P. Schweickart. Baltimore, MD: Johns Hopkins UP, 1986, 147–54.

Gilligan, Carol. *In a Different Voice.* Cambridge, MA: Harvard UP, 1982.

Glaspell, Susan. *Trifles: Literature and Its Writers.* Ed. Ann Charters and Samuel Charters. New York: Bedford/St. Martin's, 2001, 1224–34.

———. "A Jury of Her Peers." Charters and Charters 207–22.

FOR FURTHER READING

Smith, Beverly A. "Women's Work—Trifles? The Skill and Insight of Playwright Susan Glaspell." *International Journal of Women's Studies* 5 (March–April 1982): 172–84.

"For Such as We Are Made of, Such We Be": The Construction of Gender in William Shakespeare's *Twelfth Night, or What You Will* (first performed 1602)

Terry Reilly

In *Twelfth Night*, conventions from romantic comedy—shipwreck, twinning, and cross-dressing—converge to explore complex gender relationships. *Twelfth Night* takes its name from the final day of the Christmas Revels, which in early modern England lasted from Christmas Day to January 6, the Feast of the Epiphany. During this topsy-turvy holiday period, normative structures of everyday life—such as social hierarchies and conventional gender expectations—were set aside. By focusing on the three female characters—Viola, Olivia, and Maria—and how each confronts love and marriage, students have an opportunity to discuss how ideas about gender norms are constructed, not only in this comedy but also in modern American life.

After a shipwreck strands Viola on the shore of Illyria, she asks a sea captain to help disguise her and send her to Duke Orsino, saying, "I'll serve this duke; / Thou shalt present me as an eunuch to him" (1.2.53–56). The Captain replies, "Be you his eunuch, and your mute I'll be" (1.2.62). Students and teachers familiar with Shakespeare's work will quickly recognize Viola's uniqueness: She does not attempt to dress as a page, squire, or a young man as other female characters in the comedies do. Instead, by insisting that Viola disguise herself as Cesario, "an eunuch," the playwright creates Cesario, a sexually ambiguous character who can be both either and/or neither gender.[1] Paradoxically, the more Viola tries to present herself as gender neutral, the more the other characters tend to characterize Cesario in terms of male and/or female sexuality. Noting Cesario's indeterminate sexuality can lead to productive classroom discussions about the social construction of gendered hierarchies and resulting biases. For example, in one of their early exchanges, when Viola (as Cesario) appears clad in the livery of a young male servant, Orsino notes Cesario's female features (1.4.31–34) and thus responds to Cesario as a female:

> Diana's lip
> Is not more smooth and rubious; thy small pipe
> Is as the maiden's organ, shrill and sound,
> And all is semblative of a woman's part. (1.4.31–34)

Conversely, immediately after their first meeting, during which Viola, once again as Cesario, tells Olivia, "I am a gentleman," Olivia says: "I'll be sworn thou art" (1.5.293). Here, Olivia regards Cesario as male, a fact Viola realizes shortly after this scene, as she says, incredulously, "I am the man!" (2.1.25).

One question central to representations of gender in the play is whether men or women love more, a topic that elicits lively class discussions. Orsino, speaking on behalf of men, asserts that he loves more passionately than any woman could:

> There is no woman's sides
> Can bide the beating of so strong a passion
> As love doth give my heart; no woman's heart
> So big, to hold so much; they lack retention.
> (2.4.93–96)

Viola, in the persona of Cesario, speaks "as a man," but counters with a woman's perspective:

> We men may say more, swear more, but indeed
> Our shows are more than will; for still we prove
> Much in our vows, but little in our love.
> (2.4.116–118)

The dialectic about which gender loves more centers around differences between outward, socially prescribed "shows" of love, and personal feelings of love, an argument that Olivia and Maria restate from different perspectives.

Olivia's character develops around her parentage, thus linking issues of gender and class. Although she is ostensibly mourning the deaths of her father and brother, Olivia's grief masks an aversion both to Orsino and to the institution of marriage: If she marries someone of her station or above, Olivia will lose everything—title, power, wealth. In addition, Olivia sees herself not as the subject of Orsino's love, but simply as the object of his desire for marriage, a fact she underscores when she inventories her beauty: "item, two lips, indifferent red; item, two grey eyes, with lids to them; item, one neck, one chin, and so forth" (1.5.247–249). Olivia thus regards marriage not as the mutual exchange of vows among loving equals, but rather as a social institution that privileges men while subjugating and disenfranchising women. Olivia's intention not to marry "above her degree" lends credibility to her steward Malvolio's perception that she intends to marry him.

Maria, Olivia's strong-willed, intelligent, and literate kitchen maid and the most interesting representative of the interplay of gender and power, contrives the devices that drive the plot, including the forged letter that leads Malvolio to believe Olivia loves him. Maria's efforts are not merely revenge against Malvolio's pomposity, since near the end of the play, Fabian tells us that "Maria writ / The letter at Sir Toby's great importance, / In recompense whereof he hath married her" (5.1.362–364). In a play based on the inversion of social hierarchies, it is fitting that a person at the foot of the social ladder controls the play. It is also the case that many other comedies of Shakespeare include powerful female characters who subjectively drive the action rather than be simply acted upon.

Like most female characters in Shakespeare's comedies, Olivia marries below her station, and this class distinction allows her to retain her autonomy which marriage to an equal or social superior would undermine. Maria and Viola, unlike many of Shakespeare's comic heroines, marry above their station. Maria weds the unappealing Sir Toby in a "rags to riches" scenario—her rise from kitchen maid to knight's wife is presented as a reward for her cleverness rather than a result of love. The relationship between Viola and Orsino is more complicated, however. As it evolves during the play from a homosocial friendship to heterosexual love and marriage, the question arises as to whether this is, in fact, a marriage of equals, or whether it will remain a type of master–servant relationship, as it has been for most of the play. The three marriages that conclude *Twelfth Night* provide varied perspectives for discussions about gender and marriage relationships both now and then.

NOTE

1. Although most editors of *Twelfth Night* tend to describe the character of Cesario as Viola dressed like a boy, the text indicates that any discussion about gender issues—undoubtedly crucial and central topics in the play—should consider Cesario as "an eunuch."

WORK CITED

Shakespeare, William. *Twelfth Night, or What You Will* [first performed 1602]. *The Riverside Shakespeare*. Ed. G. Blakemore Evans et al. 2nd ed. Boston: Houghton Mifflin, 1997, 437–76.

FOR FURTHER READING

Bloom, Harold, ed. *Modern Critical Interpretations of* Twelfth Night. New York: Chelsea House, 1987.
Gay, Penny. "*Twelfth Night*: Desire and its Discontents." *As She Likes It: Shakespeare's Unruly Women*. Ed. Penny Gay. London: Routledge, 1994, 17–47.

The Power of Mothers in Harriet Beecher Stowe's *Uncle Tom's Cabin* (1852)

Denise Kohn

Uncle Tom's Cabin, a didactic novel of epic proportions that interweaves the tales of white and Black American families, demonstrates Stowe's belief that slavery should be abolished. This best-selling novel looks at the political issue of slavery within the private sphere of the home, a tactic Stowe uses to emphasize the important role of women in American domestic, moral, and political life.

While most novels cast heroines as young, unmarried women within a marriage plot, Stowe's novel highlights the significance of women as mothers. The first mother presented is Eliza, a beautiful quadroon slave, introduced in a chapter entitled "The Mother," to counter the period's racist belief that slaves were incapable of loving their children in the same way as whites. When Eliza learns that her owner, Mr. Shelby, plans to take her son away from her and sell him down South, she plans their escape. Emily Shelby argues in vain with her husband that it is immoral to sell Harry and to separate mothers from their children. Powerless to stop the sale, Mrs. Shelby cleverly uses her control over meal times to defy both her husband and the law, thus enabling Eliza and Harry to escape. In one of the novel's most famous scenes, Eliza demonstrates heroic courage when she narrowly eludes her captors by jumping from one patch of ice to another to cross the Ohio River into the free state of Ohio.

In the North, Eliza befriends two women who illustrate the moral power mothers wield within their families and the bonds of motherhood between enslaved African-American and free Anglo-American women. The maternal Mrs. Bird uses both emotion and reason to persuade her husband, a senator, to defy the Fugitive Slave Law. The character of Mrs. Bird also highlights maternal love felt by both free and slave women, when she gives the clothes of her deceased child to Eliza for Harry. The runaways then travel to the home of Rachel Halliday, a Quaker who represents Stowe's ideal of American womanhood: a religious, educated, and loving older matriarch who enjoys a companionable marriage with her like-minded husband. Stowe writes of Rachel, "So much has been said and sung of beautiful young girls, why don't somebody wake up to the beauty of old women?" (149). She has taught her children a life of active Christian principle through her quiet, loving example, and they happily have followed her gentle commands. Her home's perfect order and cleanliness symbolizes the harmony of Rachel's life as mother and wife. Her references to Eliza as "my daughter" further illustrate similarities between all mothers, and thus the immorality of slavery.

The latter half of the novel shows that slavery in the Deep South degrades mothers, and consequently, homes and society. Marie St. Clare, an aristocratic mother in New Orleans, abdicates all responsibility and spends her days idle upon a couch, leaving her house in disorder. Stowe carefully depicts Cassy to show the sexual exploitation of female slaves in the Deep South and the desperation of enslaved mothers to protect their children. Cassy, a strong, sympathetic character, is moved to violence in response to cruel losses forced upon her—she once stabbed an owner who sold their son and daughter and later poisoned a baby she had by another master to save the child from slavery.

Any discussion of the novel needs to address Stowe's characterization of Uncle Tom, who is in many ways a feminized, maternal character. He takes care of Eva, helps weak and hungry slave women, and refuses to fight against Simon Legree. Indeed, the title *Uncle Tom's Cabin* emphasizes his role within the culture of domesticity. Although Stowe provides, through Cassy, a sympathetic portrayal of maternal love and protectiveness pushed to violence, Tom's self-sacrifice and non-violent protest is celebrated as the ultimate code of ethos and love within the novel. While students might find Tom subservient, Stowe wished her audience to see him as a martyr and a noble Christ figure. Before reading, students might be asked to explain what the epithet "an Uncle Tom" means to them and contrast that initial view, after reading, to their actual feelings about Stowe's character. Is he lowered in our esteem because he is more compliant and less aggressive than other men in (or outside) the novel?

Discussing Tom as Christ-like can also lead to a discussion of women's lives in the period. Mothers were often considered martyrs in their roles as self-sacrificing family caretakers and moral guides. Although Stowe's female characters might not seem feminist by today's standards, students can think of them as practicing a type of "domestic feminism" that allowed them to exert authority at home and thus change society. Although Stowe does not present women as inherently more moral than men—for instance, Marie St. Clare supports slavery and sells Tom against the wishes of her dead husband—often women must persuade, influence, or even actively oppose men to protect children. Many critics, notably Jane Tompkins and Elizabeth Ammons, have argued that Stowe's novel emphasizes values that were seen as typically feminine in the period and that the author gives women power by examining political issues through the eyes of mothers.

Stowe's positive portrayals of domesticity and motherhood can be compared with the homes and characters of Widow Douglas and Aunt Sally in Mark Twain's *Huckleberry Finn*. Other excellent texts for cross-study of these themes are Harriet Jacobs' autobiography, *Incidents in the Life of a Slave Girl*, which offers a first-person account of slave motherhood and sexual exploitation; and Toni Morrison's *Beloved*, which explores the same issues through Sethe, who, like Cassy, kills her baby to save the child from slavery.

WORKS CITED

Ammons, Liz and Susan Belasco, eds. *Approaches to Teaching* Uncle Tom's Cabin. New York: Modern Language Association, 2000.

Jacobs, Harriet A. *Incidents in the Life of a Slave Girl*. Ed. and Intro. by Jean Fagan Yellin. Cambridge, MA: Harvard UP, 1987.

Morrison, Toni. *Beloved*. New York: Alfred Knopf, 1987.

Stowe, Harriet Beecher. *Uncle Tom's Cabin* [1852]. New York: Penguin, 1981.

Tompkins, Jane. *Sensational Designs: The Cultural Work of American Fiction, 1790–1860*. New York: Oxford UP, 1985.

FOR FURTHER READING

Brown, Gillian. *Domestic Individualism*. Berkeley: U of California P, 1990.

A Chinese-American Woman Warrior Comes of Age: Maxine Hong Kingston's *The Woman Warrior: Memoirs of a Girlhood Among Ghosts* (1976)

Susan Currier

In *The Woman Warrior: Memoirs of a Girlhood Among Ghosts*, Maxine Hong Kingston redeems herself and all women of Chinese descent by fashioning a warrior-poet identity from legend, history, and autobiography. As a first-generation Chinese American growing up in mid-twentieth-century California, Kingston learns from family and friends that the Chinese call girls "maggots in the rice" (43), that they say, "feeding girls is feeding cowbirds" (46). A Chinese first-person feminine pronoun means "slave" (47), and her immigrant mother teaches Kingston that she will grow up to be "a wife and a slave" (20). But on other occasions, the same mother chants legends of women warriors in China, inspiring in her daughter dreams of honor and justice. Kingston's "memoir" is the story of her quest to translate legend into life in a medium accessible to Chinese and Americans alike.

To help students grasp the extraordinary contradictions that Kingston must reconcile, it's useful to consider connections among the five chapters of the work. In three of these, readers hear Kingston listening to her mother's cautionary tales about the destinies of women in her own generation. In the 1920s, famine forced Kingston's father, uncles, and other Chinese men to the United States ("Gold Mountain") and Hawaii to earn money to send home. War, the communist takeover, discriminatory immigration laws, and fading memories prevent their return. War, the same immigration laws, and restrictive social codes prevent their wives from joining them, at least for a long time.

In "No NameWoman," Kingston's father's sister gives birth to an illegitimate child, draws the wrath of the villagers upon her family's compound, and drowns herself and her daughter in the family well. Except that her story is once invoked as warning to her nieces, No Name Woman disappears from her family history. Whether she consented or was raped does not figure in the erasure of her being. In "At the Western Palace," Kingston's mother's sister, Moon Orchid, comes to the United States to confront the husband who never sends for her, only to find he has married an American. Moon Orchid can barely whisper, "What about me?" (153) before she goes mad.

From the stories of her aunts as well as conventional Chinese wisdom about girls, Kingston learns that Chinese women are negligible. Her own mother's story in "Shaman" is more inspiring, but also frightening. Following the departure of her husband, Brave Orchid's Chinese children die, so she uses the money he sends to attend a medical college founded for women by Europeans. Smart and courageous, Brave Orchid may remain a wife, but she will never again be a slave. As a doctor, Brave Orchid wins respect and status. However, as a doctor she also purchases a slave girl, attends the infanticides of girls, and witnesses the stoning of a madwoman without attempting to intervene. As narrator Kingston absorbs the strength of her mother, she also internalizes the suffering of the slave, baby girls, and madwoman.

The other two chapters of the work contrast legends of women warriors with the quotidian reality of Brave Orchid's children, particularly the author. For this generation, issues of race and class further complicate issues of gender. If the white ghosts assess her IQ at zero, they also tear down her father's laundry without adequate compensation for its loss. To restore her defeated father's strength, Kingston purchases a bodybuilding kit advertised in a comic. The A's she eventually earns in school seem no more efficacious.

Through her helplessness, however, Kingston recalls her mother's songs of women warriors, including Fa Mu Lan. In "White Tigers," she fantasizes her own training as a swordswoman. When she's ready, her teachers send her home, where she is welcomed as a son. Her parents carve their grievances in her back, and she departs on an epic battle against the tyranny that has devastated her family and her people. The chapter closes with the metaphorical nexus for the work: "The swordswoman and I are not so dissimilar. May my people understand the resemblance soon so that I can return to them. The idioms for revenge are 'report a crime' and 'report to five families.' The reporting is the vengeance—not the beheading, not the gutting, but the words" (53).

In "Song for a Barbarian Reed Pipe," Kingston retells her own favorite legend—of the warrior-poet Ts'ai Yen. When Ts'ai Yen tries to teach Chinese to the children she bears in captivity, they laugh, understanding no more of their mother's desolation than the barbarians around them. However, one evening, Ts'ai Yen sings a song so high and clear that it matches the music of the barbarians' flutes. Her children understand barbarian phrases in the song and sing with her. When she is ransomed and returned to China, she takes her songs with her and the Chinese adapt them to their own instruments. At least among the barbarians, Kingston has achieved swordswoman status. In 1976, when he reviewed *The Woman Warrior* for the *New York Times*, John Leonard pronounced it "dizzying, elemental, a poem turned into a sword." And he subordinated his discussion of the "big guns of autumn," the "howitzers" of Vonnegut, Updike, Cheever, and Mailer to it.

In the classroom, *The Woman Warrior* presents myriad opportunities to explore the experience of Chinese immigrants to the United States. It also invites discussion of the oppressive guilt that beleaguers American-born children who find they cannot afford to repay their parents' suffering and sacrifice in a currency of value to them. However, Kingston's triumph is as a "woman warrior" and discussion of this text should center on the dilemmas for Chinese-American women of discovering a self, creating an identity, and defining a sexuality in the interstices of two cultures that do not necessarily mean them well.

WORKS CITED

Kingston, Maxine Hong. *The Woman Warrior: Memoirs of a Girlhood Among Ghosts* [1976]. New York: Vintage International, 1989.
Leonard, John. "In Defiance of Two Worlds." *New York Times*, September 17, 1976, Sec. 3, 21.

FOR FURTHER READING

Kennedy, Colleen and Deborah Morse. "A Dialogue with(in) Tradition: Two Perspectives on *The Woman Warrior*." *Approaches to Teaching* The Woman Warrior. Ed. Shirley Geok-lin Lim. New York: Modern Language Association, 1991, 121–30.
Lidoff, Joan. "Autobiography in a Different Voice. *The Woman Warrior* and the Question of Genre." Geok-lin Lim 116–20.

The Will to Survive in Gloria Naylor's *The Women of Brewster Place* (1982)

Loretta G. Woodard

Gloria Naylor's award-winning "novel in seven stories" explores the lives of seven Black women of diverse backgrounds and ages who struggle to survive the deplorable conditions in which they live. Trapped in an endless cycle of racism and sexism, Naylor's women nevertheless attempt to rise above their unfortunate circumstances "like an ebony phoenix, each in her own time" (5), but find their real solace in their relationships with one another.

Naylor's title clearly indicates that the novel is about a special community of women. "The bastard child of several clandestine meetings" (1), Brewster Place is a dead-end street of decaying apartment buildings, where most of its "colored daughters" are forced to live "because they [have] no choice" (4). Black, female and poor, abused, betrayed, and abandoned by the men in their lives, Naylor's women are further alienated from the mainstream by a tall brick wall, an eyesore, erected by white city officials to keep them in their place.

The novel is made up of separate stories linked to one another, each of which tells about a different woman. Mattie Michael is the central character and emerges as the single, middle-aged matriarch who provides the other women with "light," "love," "comfort," strength, protection, and support, unselfishly and unconditionally. Pregnant in her youth by an unlikely suitor, Mattie has been brutally beaten by her heartbroken father and banished from home. Later she is deserted by her spoiled son, to whom she has devoted most of her life. Mothering instead her neighbors on Brewster Place, Mattie gently reprimands Cora Lee, the young, unwed mother with seven children whose only comfort comes from raising her babies: "You gonna have to stop this soon, Cora. You got a full load now" (123). As a true healer, she rescues the grief-stricken Lucielia from dying after her daughter's death: "Ceil moaned.

Mattie rocked . . . She rocked her into her childhood and let her see murdered
dreams. And she rocked her back into the womb, to the nadir of her hurt"
(103). As Kathleen M. Puhr writes, "Mattie extracts the splinter, rooted in
slavery and sexual oppression" (520), and helps Ceil to enter a new life. Students may see Mattie as heroic but ponder why she cannot change the women's
circumstances. They may conclude that women's power, expressed in acts of
love and nurturance, has no influence in the outside world where men are
dominant.

Mattie's relationship with Etta Mae stands out as an example of deep sis-
terly bonding. After Etta Mae fails to entice the hypocritical Reverend Woods
into marriage and thus shatters her hopes for a "respectable" life, she returns
home to Brewster Place, her spirit broken. "Etta laughed softly to herself as
she climbed the steps toward the light and the love and the comfort that
awaited her" (74). Mattie shows her understanding of the love women can
have for one another when she says to Etta Mae:

> Well, I've loved women too . . . I've loved you practically all my life. . . .
> I've loved some women deeper than I ever loved any man. . . . And there
> been some women who loved me more and did more for me than any
> man ever did. (14)

That kind of acceptance, however, does not extend to Lorraine and Theresa,
known as "the two," a pair of lesbian lovers who live on Brewster Place.
Sharing mainstream society's values in this case, most of the women cannot
abide the sexual love between them. When Etta Mae attempts to explain how
different Lorraine and Theresa's love is from the love the others share, Mattie
sums up their fears: "Maybe it's not so different . . . Maybe that's why some
women get so riled up about it, 'cause they know deep down it's not so different after all" (141). Critic Larry Andrews writes, in "Black Sisterhood in
Gloria Naylor's Novels":

> What Mattie comes to realize, through the insight of her own experience,
> is that the deep bond she has felt with women may have a wholeness and
> power (including the sensual) comparable to that of the lesbians and
> perhaps superior to any relationship that seems possible with a man in
> the distorted world of black relations. (4)

Focusing on Mattie's dominant role in the community will allow students
to discuss her effectiveness. Mattie's "collective" dream in "The Block Party"
suggests a new beginning, as it unites all of the women in a protest to destroy
the bloodstained wall, symbol for them of racist and class oppression. Al-

though this is not yet possible in reality, the women continue to dream, as they go about the ritual of their daily lives, and their dreams serve as a constant source of hope and inspiration.

The Women of Brewster Place is a scathing indictment of the discrimination and exploitation of women who have been deliberately and systematically excluded from society. More importantly, it is a celebration of their persistence in fighting against the terrible oppression that denies them more viable, productive lives. Bound together as mothers, daughters, sisters, friends, and lovers, Naylor's women find the will to survive by sharing love, intimacy, and friendship. Students might ultimately discuss how African-American women can, in addition, attain the education, political power, and wealth necessary to destroy the barriers of racism, sexism, and class discrimination that keep them at an "overall social status lower than that of any other group" (hooks 14).

Using Mattie as an example, teachers might want to help students analyze the historical causes of Black women's traditional portrayals as mothers, nurturers, and/or healers from slavery to the present time. Margaret Walker's *Jubilee* is an excellent start. Teachers might also assign *The Women of Brewster Place* in conjunction with other twentieth-century works by Black women writers such as Paule Marshall's *Brown Girl, Brownstones* and Alice Walker's *The Color Purple*, where Black women come together in nurturing communities.

WORKS CITED

Andrews, Larry R. "Black Sisterhood in Gloria Naylor's Novels." *CLA Journal* 33 (September 1, 1989): 1–25.

hooks, bell. "Black Women: Shaping Feminist Theory." *Feminist Theory: From Margin to Center.* Boston: South End Press, 1984, 1–15.

Marshall, Paule. *Brown Girl, Brownstones* [1959]. Old Westbury, NY: Feminist Press, 1981.

Naylor, Gloria. *The Women of Brewster Place: A Novel in Seven Stories* [1982]. New York: Penguin, 1983.

Puhr, Kathleen M. "Healers in Gloria Naylor's Fiction. *Twentieth Century Literature* 40.4 (Winter 1996): 518–28.

Walker, Margaret. *Jubilee.* New York: Bantam Books, 1967.

FOR FURTHER READING

Gates, Henry Louis, Jr., and K. A. Appiah, eds. *Gloria Naylor: Critical Perspectives Past and Present.* New York: Amistad, 1993.

Procrustean Bed: Gender Roles in Emily Brontë's *Wuthering Heights* (1847)

Barbara Z. Thaden

Emily Brontë's only novel, *Wuthering Heights*, is one of the most unusual and influential novels of the nineteenth century. Its heroine, Catherine Earnshaw, a headstrong and violent-tempered child, grows up isolated and scorned. She and her constant companion and foster-brother Heathcliff share an intense, unsocialized, almost symbiotic relationship as children, since they sleep in the same bed, are free to roam the moors together, and see no other children. However, Catherine's extended stay with the more genteel and wealthy Lintons begins her socialization as a woman. She must choose between poverty, shame, and boredom as the wife of the degraded Heathcliff, or wealth, comfort, and social status as the wife of Edgar Linton. She chooses Linton, only so that she can use his money to rescue Heathcliff, never understanding that the two men might not be amenable to this ménage a trois. Catherine's socialization into womanhood, her understanding of the passion and freedom she has given up, and her final refusal to choose between the two constitute the main events that can lead to feminist discussions of the text. Catherine finds that she cannot live within the societal bonds imposed on women, but there is no alternative available within the world of the living.

Both Catherine and Heathcliff despise the silly, pampered life they see through a window of the Linton residence, but Catherine is coddled and seduced into becoming a lady while recovering from being bitten by the Lintons' dog. This feminization of Catherine brings about a violent splitting of the self that causes emotional turmoil and physical illness. Heathcliff is similarly split off from his feminine self when his resolve to "be good" is crushed by Hindley's cruelty, and his need to be protected and nourished by Catherine is denied. He becomes a "fierce, pitiless, wolfish man" (80). Both long to return to their childhood bond, but the expectations of society force them apart.

When Catherine says that Heathcliff is "more myself than I am," she acknowledges that she is not the beautiful, partially socialized woman Linton thinks he is marrying; she is still the untamed, unsocialized, androgynous child psychically and psychologically fused with Heathcliff, her other half.

After her marriage, Catherine represses her disconsolation at Heathcliff's abandonment, but is forced to consciously acknowledge what she has lost when Heathcliff unexpectedly returns. The role of conventional wife and mother (Catherine is pregnant) is suddenly so stifling that Catherine's rage against its restrictive bonds results in freedom only through death. She is furious that Heathcliff and Edgar are violently jealous of each other, and that she cannot inhabit their two worlds simultaneously. While Catherine lies dying, she feels as if she has been violently wrenched from her childhood home "and been converted at a stroke into Mrs. Linton, the lady of Thrushcross Grange, and the wife of a stranger; an exile, and outcast, thenceforth, from what had been my world" (97). She longs to be a girl again, "half savage, and hardy, and free" (97), instead of imprisoned by stifling social conventions. But why does she never consider simply running away with Heathcliff, now that he is well-off? Students may speculate about a number of reasons, including perhaps that the nature of her passion for him has more to do with her own sexual and social identity than with romantic love or sexual desire.

Brontë contrasts Catherine's rebellious and headstrong nature with those of more conventional female characters. Isabella Linton is foolish and weak, the epitome of a young bourgeois female. Unlike Catherine, who has been shaped more by nature than culture, Isabella is a hothouse flower, the artificial creation of a corrupt and despicable society. In contrast, Nelly Dean, the housekeeper, is levelheaded and unromantic. She knows what is practical, and immediately senses that Catherine's plan to marry Edgar Linton and keep Heathcliff as her best friend is hopelessly idealistic or completely immoral. Nelly disapproves of wayward girls and passionate women who want more than marriage, because she is a supporter of the patriarchal order of things.

Catherine's daughter Cathy, born at the moment of her mother's death, is as isolated as Catherine and as sheltered as Isabella, but she is lucky enough to outlive her first, disastrous marriage (to Linton Heathcliff) and to move on to a worthier love. Students might discuss whether the author wants us to admire Catherine's rebelliousness or her daughter Cathy's more conventional feminine character.

Patriarchal oppression is a key thematic issue represented by the male heads of families: Mr. Earnshaw senior, Hindley Earnshaw, Heathcliff, and Edgar Linton, the possessors of money and property. It is also found in the religious and legal structure of society: Catherine is constantly rebelling against Joseph's religious tyranny, while Isabella Linton and Cathy Linton Heathcliff are enslaved by a legal system highly injurious to women. The laws of marriage contribute to women's imprisonment, since before 1882 in England, a married woman, all her goods, and all her children born in wedlock were the legal property of her husband. Isabella is fortunate that Heathcliff does not demand their son Linton before her death, since fathers were known to spirit away children to torture and punish their estranged wives. All of Cathy's personal property becomes Linton's when she marries him, but since Linton is too sickly to consummate the marriage, Heathcliff symbolically rapes her by brutally striking her on the face, making her mouth fill with blood. By tearing a locket from Cathy's neck and grinding her father's portrait into the floor, Heathcliff drives home the point that she owns neither the trinkets on her body, nor her body itself, nor her heritage as a Linton.

Students may find the relationships between men and women in this novel unusually passionate, violent, and desperate. Has Emily Brontë succeeded in laying bare the true relationships between the sexes, the emotions and motivations usually hidden under a veneer of civility? Also, are women today expected to give up more than men as they mature? Catherine Earnshaw, who finally refused to be owned by one man, is one of the most memorable female characters in all of English literature. How students react to her will form the touchstone through which they engage with the themes of the novel.

WORK CITED

Brontë, Emily. *Wuthering Heights* [1850]. Ed. William M. Sale, Jr., and Richard J. Dunn. New York: Norton, 1990.

FOR FURTHER READING

Allott, Miriam, ed. Wuthering Heights, *A Casebook*. London: Macmillan, 1992.
Gilbert, Sandra and Susan Gubar. *The Madwoman in the Attic: The Woman Writer and the Nineteenth-Century Literary Imagination*. New Haven, CT: Yale UP, 1979.
Stoneman, Patsy. Wuthering Heights: *New Casebooks*. New York: St. Martin's, 1993.

Negotiating Tight Spaces: Women in Michael Dorris' *A Yellow Raft in Blue Water* (1988)

Elizabeth J. Wright

With the interconnected lives of three generations of Native American women at its center, Michael Dorris' *A Yellow Raft in Blue Water* leads naturally to discussions concerning the complicated intersections of race, class, and gender. Set in western Washington and on an unnamed reservation in eastern Montana during the 1980s, the novel focuses on Rayona, a 15-year-old girl with a Native American mother and an African-American father; Rayona's mother, Christine, whose terminal illness convinces her to move with her daughter from Seattle back to Montana; and Rayona's grandmother, Ida, a traditional Native American woman who rarely leaves the reservation.

The book is divided into three sections: first, the story comes from Rayona's point of view, while Christine's and then Ida's stories dominate subsequent sections. This narrative technique enables Dorris to demonstrate, according to Gordon E. Slethaug, how "personal narratives are woven together," as well as how memories shift and change as a result of being framed by more than one perspective (21). In the telling, Dorris examines how these three women deal with the chronic unemployment, rampant alcoholism, and fragmented families that trouble Native Americans both on and off the reservation. In general, Native American literature abounds with strong women characters, who, like Rayona, Christine, and Ida, are unafraid to challenge social expectations. Yet as Dorris suggests in *A Yellow Raft in Blue Water*, resistance often renders women isolated from both the Native and non-Native worlds they encounter. To understand this dynamic more fully, students might research Native American culture, and specifically, dilemmas that Native American women themselves describe in writing about their own lives.

One effect of five hundred years' domination by European colonizers is that in Native American fiction, characters are frequently depicted as estranged, both from their tribe and the outside world. *A Yellow Raft in Blue Water* proves no different, as Rayona, Christine, and Ida are outsiders whose realities keep them separate from the communities in which they live. Rayona's isolation stems from being of mixed blood, a fact that makes her neither entirely Native American nor African American. Her sense of displacement becomes particularly evident when Rayona returns with her mother to Montana. There, Rayona finds herself instantly classified as "wrong color, outsider, skinny" (43). Like her daughter, Christine struggles to establish human connections. Since the death of her only brother, Lee, during the Vietnam War, Christine has lived with the knowledge that Ida blames her for urging Lee to enlist. As an adult woman returning to the reservation, Christine is viewed with a mixture of curiosity and scorn, a woman who left the reservation only to be forced to return. Ida's isolation stems from her reluctance to assimilate with the modern world. For example, she refuses to speak English, preferring instead to communicate in her Native tongue. Ida keeps silent in other ways, choosing to keep secret the knowledge that Christine is not her biological daughter but her half-sister.

Labeled as outsiders, the women in the novel often lack power, particularly in relationships with men. Male dominance over women becomes clear to Ida as a young girl when she, along with her invalid mother, cannot prevent her father from having an affair with his sister-in-law. When her parents decide to pass the child off as Ida's, Ida rationalizes the decision: "everyone must think us the perfect family" (300). Ida keeps the secret, fearing that, otherwise, she will lose Christine as a result. But her silence only furthers her isolation as she distances herself from her family and the tribe in an attempt to avoid disclosing any information that might be used against her. Christine, the child of the affair, is equally powerless when it comes to men. When her own husband, Elgin, begins having an affair, she cannot convince him to discontinue the relationship and return home. Among Rayona's experiences, readers witness the most disturbing absence of power when a priest rapes her during a church retreat. Dorris shows how women suffer to gain parity and empowerment in heterosexual relationships. He also emphasizes that their isolation stems from overcoming traumatic events often related to sex and sexuality, as illustrated by the conflicts that the three women in *A Yellow Raft in Blue Water* must confront.

Despite intermittent moments of weakness, Rayona, Christine, and Ida remain strong women, capable of withstanding others' withering judgments. Much of their personal power stems from their ability to subvert female gender role expectations. Among the Native Americans, Rayona refuses to be branded as a city kid unschooled in the ways of the reservation. She gains new recognition and acceptance after riding a bucking bronco during a local rodeo, proving that she can beat the reservation Indians at their own game. Christine subverts the rules concerning how a wife ought to behave. After her husband cheats on her, she responds by leaving him, thinking, "I hated the mess I made of myself" (241). Although she blames herself for their separation, she also blames Elgin and his unwillingness to remain devoted to his family. Because of this, Christine decides that she alone can provide their child with domestic stability by returning to the reservation. Courageously raising Christine as her own child, Ida mends the bonds broken after her father's affair. Later, Ida seduces a Native American man who is physically deformed and psychologically scarred from his recent war duty, an act that results in a biological child of her own. Such rebelliousness connects these three women to each other. Notwithstanding their differences, they are linked by their determination to endure.

Dorris' novel reaffirms the importance of repairing family ties when they threaten to unravel and sever. Although Ida, Christine, and Rayona each occasionally become enraged at each other, they stay connected, as Slethaug suggests, through their ability to overcome loss, including the loss of Rayona's virginity, the death of Lee, and the "imminent death of [Christine] through alcoholism" (20). David Cowart suggests that these women maintain connection through the complexities of family life, metaphorically captured by their "catching and letting go, in twisting and blending" (6). Indeed, Rayona, Christine, and Ida are entwined, like the hair braiding that Ida does so well. While they are flawed and have been hurt by men, they are strong women, unafraid to voice their opinions. In doing so, they teach us much about survival, a theme inherent in most Native American literature.

WORKS CITED

Dorris, Michael. *A Yellow Raft in Blue Water*. New York: Warner Books, 1988.

Cowart, David. " 'The Rhythm of Three Strands': Cultural Braiding in Dorris's *A Yellow Raft in Blue Water*." *SAIL: Studies in Native American Literature* 8.1 (Spring 1996): 1–12.

Slethaug, Gordon. " 'Multivocal Narration and Cultural Negotiation: Dorris's *A Yellow Raft in Blue Water* and *Cloud Chamber*." *SAIL: Studies in American Indian Literature* 11.1 (Spring 1999): 18–29.

FOR FURTHER READING

Owens, Louis. *Other Destinies: Understanding the American Indian Novel*. Norman: U of Oklahoma P, 1992.

Appendix: Thematic List of Books

As in any literary project, certain themes emerge from among the many readings published here. For example, several essays treat literary works, both "canonical" and new, in which young adolescent girls learn how or how not to grow into the women they are expected to be. In these works, a young girl's search for self results in her resisting and/or succumbing to convention. Sometimes the protagonist's choices are limited by her time, culture, or place; sometimes the protagonist's temperament doesn't allow her to transcend the limited gender roles that engulf her. Read as expressions of the difficulties girls have in growing up, these coming-of-age novels and plays sometimes feature females who act less than admirably, falling prey to peer pressure or their own character flaws. Interestingly, books about adolescent males, on the other hand, present boys' efforts at attaining "manhood," and often sexual prowess in the process. Yet, as with adolescent girls, peer pressure for boys to conform looms large in these books as well.

With this discussion in mind, we have identified below thirty such themes that we have noticed as we edited, followed by an alphabetical listing of corresponding fictional titles. Naturally, our thinking in compiling this list cannot be all-inclusive. We have carefully considered what titles to put into each category, but surely readers will see other possibilities for placing the literary texts and will come up with additional, equally discursive thematic descriptors.

1. Young Girls and Adolescents: *Annie John*, *The Bean Trees*, *Beauty*, *The Bluest Eye*, *The Crucible*, *The Diary of a Young Girl*, *How the García Girls Lost Their Accents*, *I Know Why the Caged Bird Sings*, *In Country*, *I Never Promised You a Rose Garden*, *Jane Eyre*, *Mag-*

gie: *A Girl of the Streets*, *The Member of the Wedding*, *The Mill on the Floss*, *Rubyfruit Jungle*, *Shabanu*, *To Kill a Mockingbird*, *A Yellow Raft in Blue Water*.

2. Young Boys and Adolescents: *The Adventures of Huckleberry Finn*, *All Quiet on the Western Front*, *The Bear*, *Bless Me, Ultima*, *The Catcher in the Rye*, *A Lesson Before Dying*, *Lord of the Flies*, *Night*, *A Portrait of the Artist as a Young Man*, *Sons and Lovers*.

3. Men's Power over Women: *Anna Karenina*, *The Bride Price*, *The Call of the Wild*, *Crime and Punishment*, *A Handmaid's Tale*, *The Good Earth*, *The Great Gatsby*, *Invisible Man*, *Madame Bovary*, *Maggie: A Girl of the Streets*, *1984*, *A Raisin in the Sun*, *The Scarlet Letter*, *So Long a Letter*, *A Streetcar Named Desire*, *Tess of the D'Urbervilles*, *Things Fall Apart*, *The Women of Brewster Place*.

4. Women's Limited Options within Marriage: *Anna Karenina*, *The Awakening*, *Bread Givers*, *The Bride Price*, *Ethan Frome*, *The Good Earth*, *Jane Eyre*, *Madame Bovary*, *Main Street*, *The Mill on the Floss*, *Pride and Prejudice*, *Trifles*.

5. Single Women: *Daisy Miller*, *A Doll's House*, *Florence*, *Jane Eyre*, *A Yellow Raft in Blue Water*.

6. Female Characters that Challenge Gender Stereotypes: *Antigone*, *The Awakening*, *The Book of the City of Ladies*, *Canterbury Tales*, *The Color Purple*, *Dessa Rose*, *A Doll's House*, *Florence*, *Herland*, *I Know Why the Caged Bird Sings*, *In Country*, *Jane Eyre*, *The Mill on the Floss*, *My Àntonia*, *Nectar in a Sieve*, *Rubyfruit Jungle*, *The Scarlet Letter*, *Shabanu*, *Their Eyes Were Watching God*, *To Kill a Mockingbird*, *Trifles*, *The Woman Warrior*.

7. Female Characters that Conform to Gender Stereotypes: *The Adventures of Huckleberry Finn*, *Bless Me, Ultima*, *Death of a Salesman*, *The Glass Menagerie*, *Herland*, *1984*, *Odyssey*, *Oedipus Rex*, *One Flew Over the Cuckoo's Nest*, *Pride and Prejudice*, *Pygmalion*, *Tess of the D'Urbervilles*.

8. Mothers and Daughters: *Annie John*, *Beloved*, *The Bluest Eye*, *Breath, Eyes, Memory*, *Daisy Miller*, *Florence*, *Herland*, *I Know Why the Caged Bird Sings*, *The Joy Luck Club*, *Maggie: A Girl of the Streets*, *The Picture Bride*, *The Scarlet Letter*, *The Woman Warrior*, *A Yellow Raft in Blue Water*.

9. Mothers' Responsibility to Their Children: *The Awakening*, *The Bean Trees*, *Beloved*, *Bless Me, Ultima*, *Breath, Eyes, Memory*, *Dessa Rose*, *A Doll's House*, *Florence*, *The Handmaid's Tale*, *Maggie: A*

Girl of the Streets, A Raisin in the Sun, Sons and Lovers, Uncle Tom's Cabin, A Yellow Raft in Blue Water.

10. Women and Work or Money: *The Bell Jar, Bread Givers, The Bride Price, The Color Purple, Crime and Punishment, Ethan Frome, Florence, The Glass Menagerie, Maggie: A Girl of the Streets, Memoirs of an Ex-Prom Queen, Pride and Prejudice, A Raisin in the Sun.*

11. Men's "Feminine" Sides: *All Quiet on the Western Front, The Color Purple, The Left Hand of Darkness, A Lesson Before Dying, Lord of the Flies, Moby-Dick, Night, Of Mice and Men, Silas Marner.*

12. Women's "Masculine" Sides: *Antigone, The Book of the City of Ladies, Gone with the Wind, Herland, The Left Hand of Darkness, Macbeth, The Member of the Wedding, My Àntonia, One Flew Over the Cuckoo's Nest, Rubyfruit Jungle, Twelfth Night, The Woman Warrior.*

13. Women as Sex Objects: *All Quiet on the Western Front, The Bell Jar, Brave New World, The Catcher in the Rye, Death of a Salesman, A Farewell to Arms, The Good Earth, The Great Gatsby, A Handmaid's Tale, Invisible Man, Maggie: A Girl of the Streets, Memoirs of an Ex-Prom Queen, 1984, Pygmalion, A Streetcar Named Desire, Tess of the D'Urbervilles.*

14. Women's Search for Freedom: *Anna Karenina, The Awakening, Beloved, Bread Givers, The Color Purple, Dessa Rose, A Doll's House, Florence, Gone with the Wind, A Handmaid's Tale, How the García Girls Lost Their Accents, Main Street, The Mill on the Floss, My Àntonia, A Raisin in the Sun, The Scarlet Letter, So Long a Letter, Their Eyes Were Watching God.*

15. Violence against Women: *Beloved, The Bluest Eye, The Book of the City of Ladies, The Bride Price, The Call of the Wild, Canterbury Tales, Crime and Punishment, The Crucible, Dessa Rose, A Handmaid's Tale, 1984, Odyssey, Of Mice and Men, One Flew Over the Cuckoo's Nest, Shabanu, Trifles, The Women of Brewster Place.*

16. Violence by Women: *Anna Karenina, Antigone, The Crucible, Daisy Miller, Dessa Rose, Hamlet, Jane Eyre, Macbeth, The Mill on the Floss, Oedipus Rex, Tess of the D'Urbervilles, Trifles, The Woman Warrior.*

17. Women and Suicide: *Anna Karenina, Antigone, The Awakening, The Bell Jar, Hamlet, Madame Bovary, Maggie: A Girl of the Streets, The Mill on the Floss, Oedipus Rex, Romeo and Juliet.*

18. Women and Madness: *The Bell Jar, The Bluest Eye, Hamlet, I Never*

Promised You a Rose Garden, Jane Eyre, Macbeth, A Streetcar Named Desire, Wuthering Heights.

19. Proto-feminists: *All's Well that Ends Well, Antigone, The Book of the City of Ladies, Canterbury Tales, The Color Purple, Dessa Rose, A Doll's House, My Àntonia, The Scarlet Letter, Their Eyes Were Watching God, The Woman Warrior.*

20. Woman as Femme Fatale: *Madame Bovary, Odyssey, Of Mice and Men, A Streetcar Named Desire.*

21. Marginalization of Women: *The Catcher in the Rye, Daisy Miller, Death of a Salesman, Hamlet, A Handmaid's Tale, Invisible Man, Lord Jim, Lord of the Flies, Maggie: A Girl of the Streets, Moby-Dick, 1984, A Portrait of the Artist as a Young Man, Things Fall Apart, The Women of Brewster Place.*

22. Men Failing to Understand Women: *Anna Karenina, Black Boy, Ethan Frome, Frankenstein, Madame Bovary, Main Street, Pygmalion, The Scarlet Letter, Trifles.*

23. Intersection of Race/Ethnicity and Gender: *Beloved, Black Boy, The Bluest Eye, Bread Givers, The Color Purple, Dessa Rose, The Diary of a Young Girl, Florence, How the García Girls Lost Their Accents, Invisible Man, A Lesson Before Dying, Picture Bride, A Raisin in the Sun, Their Eyes Were Watching God, Uncle Tom's Cabin, The Women of Brewster Place, A Yellow Raft in Blue Water.*

24. Gender and Cross-Cultural Themes: *Annie John, Bless Me, Ultima, Breath, Eyes, Memory, The Bride Price, The Good Earth, The Joy Luck Club, Nectar in a Sieve, Picture Bride, So Long a Letter, Things Fall Apart, The Woman Warrior.*

25. Nature versus Nurture, Biology, Technology, and Women's "Place": *Brave New World, Frankenstein, A Handmaid's Tale, The Left Hand of Darkness, The Mill on the Floss, 1984, Rubyfruit Jungle.*

26. Women Oppressing Women: *The Bluest Eye, Ethan Frome, The Glass Menagerie, How the García Girls Lost Their Accents, Maggie: A Girl of the Streets, The Prime of Miss Jean Brodie, A Streetcar Named Desire.*

27. Nature as Female Imagery: *Lord Jim, Moby-Dick.*

28. Social Construction of Gender: *A Handmaid's Tale, Herland, The Left Hand of Darkness, A Lesson Before Dying, Pygmalion, Rubyfruit Jungle, Twelfth Night, Wuthering Heights.*

29. Rewriting Herstory: *The Book of the City of Ladies, A Handmaid's Tale, Herland.*

30. Historical Perspective Helpful: *The Book of the City of Ladies, Florence, Great Expectations, The Great Gatsby, Maggie: A Girl of the Streets, Oedipus Rex, Of Mice and Men, Memoirs of an Ex-Prom Queen, Picture Bride, A Raisin in the Sun, The Scarlet Letter, To Kill a Mockingbird, Uncle Tom's Cabin, Wuthering Heights.*

Index of Literary Works by Author

Subject Index

Note: Page numbers in **bold** indicate main entries.

About the Editors and Contributors

JERILYN FISHER is Associate Professor of English at Hostos Community College, City University of New York, where she also teaches women's studies. She coordinated the National Women's Studies Association's Service Learning Project, co-editing *From the Campus to the Community: The Women's Studies Service Learning Handbook*. She has published articles on feminist pedagogy, fairy tales and feminist theory, and essays about the work of Kim Chernin and Buchi Emecheta. Previously, she and Ellen Silber edited *Analyzing the Different Voice: Feminist Psychological Theory and Literary Texts* (1998).

ELLEN S. SILBER is Professor of French at Marymount College of Fordham University, Tarrytown, New York, where she also teaches women's studies and is the director of the Marymount Institute for the Education of Women and Girls. She edited *Critical Issues in Foreign Language Instruction* (1991) and co-edited *Analyzing the Different Voice: Feminist Psychological Theory and Literary Texts* (1998) with Jerilyn Fisher. She was an associate editor for a special issue of the *Women's Studies Quarterly: Keeping Gender on the Chalkboard* (2001). Silber is especially interested in gender equity in education and currently has a Ford Foundation grant to work with a team on the creation of gender-equitable classroom materials for teacher educators.

PAUL BAIL has a doctorate in psychology from the University of Michigan and teaches multicultural awareness for the graduate counseling program at Fitchburg State College. He is the author of *John Saul: A Critical Companion* and *Anne Tyler: A Critical Companion*, and a contributor to *Great Women Mystery Writers*. A former peace activist with a lifelong interest in comparative religion, he has spent twenty years studying Hindu and Buddhist religious practices.

NASSIM W. BALESTRINI is Assistant Professor of English at Johannes Gutenberg Universitat in Mainz, Germany. From 1995 to 1997, she taught composition at the University of California, Davis. She has published several essays on Vladimir Nabokov; her research and teaching in Mainz has also focused on women playwrights and African-American poetry. Currently she is writing a book on libretto adaptations of fiction by Washington Irving, Nathaniel Hawthorne, and Henry James.

SHAKUNTALA BHARVANI received her Ph.D. from Bombay University in 1973. She studied at Exeter College, Oxford, on a British Council Fellowship in 1985, and again visited the United Kingdom as British Council Visitor in 1990. She teaches at the Government Law College, Bombay University, and has edited two anthologies for students: *The Best Word* and *The Best Order*, and authored a novel entitled *Lost Directions*. Her articles and reviews have appeared in a variety of academic journals and newspapers. Bharvani recently spent time in the United States, principally at the City University of New York Graduate Center, on a Fulbright Program.

KAREN BOVARD has taught high school theater, English, and history in Connecticut independent schools, where she has directed more than fifty productions. Formerly Artistic Director of Oddfellows Playhouse Youth Theater, the oldest and largest of New England's community-based youth theater programs, she is currently Director of the Creative Arts Progam at Watkinson School in Hartford. Recognized by Long Wharf Theater as one of the state's outstanding theater educators, she has published in *Stage of the Art*, *Teaching Tolerance*, and *Theater Journal*.

LESLEY BRODER currently teaches English at Mepham High School in Bellmore, New York. She has taught English Language Arts to students from grades six through twelve and English as a Second Language to college students. Her research interests include theories of gender and sexuality in Victorian and twentieth-century literature.

SHIRLEY P. BROWN, Program Administrator, Bryn Mawr/Haverford Colleges, has been responsible for implementing and evaluating a number of gender-focused pre-service and in-service projects. She has served as a researcher for Marymount College's project on gender in pre-service teacher education, as an evaluator for a project on geography and gender, and as a staff developer for programs addressing sexual harassment. She is presently on the National Writing Project's Task Force and is co-chair of the NWP's Teacher Inquiry Communities Network. She has published articles and book reviews in *Feminist Teacher* and *Women's Studies Quarterly*, among other scholarly journals.

EILEEN BURCHELL is Associate Professor of French and chair of Modern Languages at Marymount College, where she teaches a full range of language, civilization/culture, and literature courses. Her current research, publication, and professional presentations focus on Francophone women writers.

NORAH C. CHASE, Professor of English at Kingsborough Community College, City University of New York, is currently working on a biography of her grandmother, Elba Chase Nelson, who headed the Communist Party of New Hampshire for thirty years. She has taught all levels of English as well as Women's Studies courses and Labor Studies materials. She worked with high school teachers and students in the American Social History Project at the City University of New York.

MICHAEL G. CORNELIUS is a Ph.D. candidate in early British literature at the University of Rhode Island. His work has appeared in *Scotia*, *The Delta Epsilon Sigma Journal*, and *Fifteenth Century Studies*. He is the author of a novel, *Creating Man* (2000), and a forthcoming travelogue/memoir, *Errances, or Wanderings: One Boy's Journeys in Northern France* (2002).

KAREN CASTELLUCCI COX is a faculty member in the English Department at City College of San Francisco. Cox's research interests include women's literature, multicultural literature, and short-story theory. She has published in *College English* and recently had an essay published in an anthology on healing practices in the Caribbean tradition. A book-length study on Isabel Allende's novels is forthcoming from Greenwood Press.

SUSAN CURRIER is Professor of English and Associate Dean of the College of Liberal Arts at California Polytechnic State University in San Luis Obispo. She has published an essay on Virginia Woolf and James Joyce in the MLA volume, *Approaches to Teaching Woolf's* To the Lighthouse; an essay on Virginia Woolf and Margaret Drabble in *Analyzing the Different Voice: Feminist Psychological Theory and Literary Texts*; and essays on Maxine Hong Kingston, Pamela Hansford Johnson, Susan Cheever, Cynthia Ozick, and Fannie Hurst in the *Dictionary of Literary Biography*.

DEBRA S. DAVIS is a doctoral student in the Literatures of the Americas Program, English Department, Michigan State University, where she has begun writing her dissertation about the literature of the African-American Canadian Diaspora, a topic that reflects her interest in border studies.

FRANCES ANN DAY is the author of three award-winning guides: *Lesbian and Gay Voices* (Greenwood, 2000), *Latina and Latino Voices in Literature* (Greenwood, 2003), and *Multicultural Voices in Literature* (Heinemann, 1999). She has also written numerous articles, essays, book reviews, and newspaper columns. She conducts workshops nationwide, serves on the Advisory Board of the Center for Multicultural Literature for Children and Young Adults at the University of San Francisco, and teaches Chicano/a and Latino/a children's literature at Sonoma State University.

SUZANNE DEL GIZZO is a Ph.D. candidate in English and American literature at Tulane University. She is currently writing her dissertation, "Game: Recreation, Masculinity, and Identity in the Life and Work of Ernest Hemingway," and teaching at the University of Maryland.

MARY JEAN DeMARR is Professor Emerita of English and Women's Studies at Indiana State University. She has written books on adolescent females in American literature, Colleen McCullough, Barbara Kingsolver, and mystery and detective fiction. She is the long-time American editor of the *Annual Bibliography of English Language and Literature* (published by the Modern Humanities Research Association).

ELISE ANN EARTHMAN is Professor of English at San Francisco State University, where she teaches a variety of courses to those preparing to become either secondary or community college teachers. She has a long-standing interest in developing techniques for teaching canonical literature in contemporary classrooms, and has published articles on Shakespeare, classical mythology, and young adult literature.

MONIKA M. ELBERT, Professor of English at Montclair State University, is also Associate Editor of *The Nathaniel Hawthorne Review*. She has published widely on nineteenth-century American authors, and her edited collection *Separate Spheres No More: Gender Convergence in Nineteenth-Century American Literature 1830–1930* was published in 2000. Recently she received Montclair State's Distinguished Scholar Award.

KENNETH FLOREY is currently Graduate Coordinator of English Studies and former Department Chair at Southern Connecticut State University. He has published on such topics as African-American dialect in literature, *Beowulf*, Anglo-Saxon poetry, Mark Twain, genealogy, and the women's suffrage movement. He teaches courses and conducts research in African-American literature, mythology, and the history of the English language. He has been a board member of both the Connecticut Council of Teachers of English and the English Advisory Committee to the Connecticut Department of Higher Education.

MONTYE P. FUSE is Assistant Professor in the Department of English at Arizona State University. He has published numerous articles in the fields of African-American, Asian-American, and Chicano/a literature.

BEVERLY GUY-SHEFTALL is founding director of the Women's Research and Resource Center and Anna Julia Cooper Professor of Women's Studies at Spellman College. She teaches in the doctoral program at Emory University's Institute for Women's Studies. Her publications include: *Sturdy Black Bridges: Visions of Black Women in Literature* with Roseann P. Bell and Bettye Parker Smith; *Daughters of Sorrow: Attitudes Toward Black Women, 1880–1920*; *Words of Fire: An Anthology of African American Feminist Thought*; and most recently, *Traps: African American Men on Gender and Sexuality* with Rudolph Byrd. She has provided leadership for the establishment of the first women's studies major at a historically Black college.

REBEKAH HAMILTON is Associate Professor of English at the University of Texas-Pan American, where she teaches medieval and comparative literature. She is especially interested in literary depictions of religious conflicts and has published articles on Joan of Arc, *The Heimskringla*, and Schiller's *Maria Stuart*.

ZARINA MANAWWAR HOCK was born and raised in Lucknow, India, but received her graduate education in the United States, earning advanced degrees in English Literature, in the Teaching of English as a Second Language, and in Comparative Literature. Hock is Director of Book Publications and Senior Editor at the National Council of Teachers of English, with headquarters in Urbana, Illinois.

SARA R. HOROWITZ, Associate Director of the Centre for Jewish Studies at York University (Toronto), is author of *Voicing the Void: Muteness and Memory in Holocaust Fiction*, which received the Choice Award for Outstanding Academic Book. She has published extensively on Holocaust literature, women's studies, and contemporary Jewish writing. Currently completing a book called *Gender, Genocide, and Jewish Memory*, she co-edits the journal *KEREM: Creative Explorations in Judaism*. She also served as editor for fiction of *Jewish American Women Writers: A Bio-Bibliographical Critical Sourcebook* (Greenwood, 1994), winner of the Outstanding Judaica Reference Book Award from the Association of Jewish Libraries.

ERNECE B. KELLY has taught literature and composition at various colleges and universities including University of Maryland (College Park), Look College (Chicago), and Kingsborough Community College (City University of New York). Retired from teaching, she currently lectures on gender in Hollywood and independent film. She also writes film and theater reviews for a New York City–based newspaper, the *New York Beacon*.

DANA KINNISON is the Assistant Director of Composition at the University of Missouri, where she also teaches literature and writing courses. Her professional interests range from early-twentieth-century American women's farm novels to new contributions in writing program administration.

ELIZABETH KLETT is completing her doctoral degree in English at the University of Illinois at Urbana-Champaign. Her dissertation is entitled "Reproducing Shakespeare, Engendering Anxiety: Women's Cross-Gender Performance on the Contemporary British Stage." She holds a master's degree in Shakespeare Studies from the Shakespeare Institute in Stratford-upon-Avon, England. She has recently published in *Theater Journal* and *Retrovisions: Reinventing the Past in Film and Fiction*. She is also the Artistic Director of the New Revels Players.

DENISE KOHN, Associate Professor of English at Greensboro College in North Carolina, teaches courses in American literature, adolescent literature, and women's studies. Her research focuses on the work of early American women writers, including Susanna Rowson, Louisa May Alcott, Harriet Beecher Stowe, and Laura Curtis Bullard. She is an officer in the Stowe Society.

HEDDA ROSNER KOPF is adjunct Associate Professor of English and also teaches in the Women's Studies Program at Quinnipiac University in Hamden, Connecticut. She is book discussion scholar/facilitator in public libraries and lectures extensively on women writers and Holocaust literature. She is the author of *Understanding Anne Frank's* The Diary of a Young Girl: *A Student Casebook of Issues, Sources, and Historical Documents* (Greenwood, 1997).

MISSY DEHN KUBITSCHEK has authored two books, *Claiming the Heritage: African American Women Novelists and History* and *Toni Morrison: A Companion Volume* (Greenwood, 1998). She teaches at Indiana University Purdue University at Indianapolis, where she is Professor of English, Women's Studies, Afro-American Studies, and American Studies.

LAURIE F. LEACH, Associate Professor of English at Hawaii Pacific University, coordinated the Literature Program there from 1999 to 2002. Her research interests include nineteenth- and twentieth-century American literature, modernism, ethnic American literature, short fiction, and life writing. She is currently working on a biography of Langston Hughes for Greenwood.

NEAL A. LESTER, Professor of English and Affiliate Faculty of African American Studies at Arizona State University, teaches African-American literature. Author of *Ntozake Shange: A Critical Study of the Plays* (1994) and *Understanding Zora Neale Hurston's* Their Eyes Were Watching God: *A Student Casebook to Issues, Sources, and Historical Documents* (Greenwood, 1999), he has taught African-American drama; short-story, folklore, and children's literature; and has published on womanism and dance, African-American homoeroticism, Black female sexuality, African-American hair, and African-Americanist revisions of "the classics." Lester was recently named 2001 Distinguished Public Scholar by the Arizona Humanities Council.

KIM MARTIN LONG is Associate Professor of English at Shippensburg University in Pennsylvania. Long currently serves as the secretary of *MELUS* (Multi-Ethnic Literatures of the United States) and publishes on various American authors including Faulkner and Melville. She is also consulting editor for *American Periodicals* and the bibliographer for the Research Society for American Periodicals.

JANE MARCELLUS, a former reporter, taught English for eleven years, most recently as Professor of Journalism and English at Clark College in Vancouver, Washington. Her academic work has appeared in the *Journal on Excellence in College Teaching*, *Feminist Media Studies*, and *Victorian Periodicals Review*.

CRISTIE L. MARCH received her M.A. and Ph.D. from the University of North Carolina at Chapel Hill. Her research and published work has focused on gender theory and Anglo-Indian, Caribbean, and Scottish literatures. She is presently pursuing a joint J.D./M.B.A. at the University of Virginia and the Darden School of Business Administration.

MARIA MARGARONI is Assistant Professor of Foreign Languages and Literatures at the University of Cyprus. Her main publications are in the areas of twentieth-century British fiction and drama, literary theory, postmodern continental philosophy, psychoanalysis, and feminism. Her current research projects include a book on Julia Kristeva and an edited collection of essays on metaphoricity and postmodern politics.

CECILE MAZZUCCO-THAN has published articles on Cervantes, Henry James, Angel Ganivet, and Catharine Macaulay. Her research focuses on the relationship between culture, gender, and genre, and complements her teaching interest in multicultural literature. Several years ago, as she developed a course dealing with race and gender in contemporary American fiction, she developed a special interest in Amy Tan's work. She is the author of *A Form Foredoomed to Looseness: Henry James's Preoccupation with the Gender of Fiction* (2002).

LAURA McPHEE is a full-time instructor of English at Martin University in Indianapolis, teaching courses in language and literature of the African Diaspora. Her passion for postmodern gender studies continues to direct her teaching and research interests.

LUCY MELBOURNE, an English professor, lives in Raleigh, North Carolina, where she teaches interdisciplinary and feminist approaches to literature at Saint Augustine and Meredith Colleges. She has published a book, *Double Heart*, and articles on literary and pedagogical topics.

MAGALI CORNIER MICHAEL is an Associate Professor at Duquesne University, where she teaches a variety of undergraduate and graduate courses in twentieth-century fiction, gender studies, and feminist literary theory. She has published *Feminism and the Postmodern Impulse: Post-World War II Fiction*. Her most recent articles are "Rethinking History as Patchwork: The Case of Atwood's *Alias Grace* (*Modern Fiction Studies*, 2001), "Materiality and Abstraction in D. M. Thomas' *The White Hotel*" (*Critique: Studies in Contemporary Fiction*, 2001), and "Re-Imagining Agency: Toni Morrison's *Paradise*" (*African American Review*, 2002).

LUCY MORRISON, Assistant Professor of English at Penn State University, specializes in the British Romantic period and women writers. Her article about early nineteenth-century conduct books appeared in *Studies in Philology* in 2002. She is also working on an article considering Mary Shelley as biographer. She has published other essays in *Studies in Short Fiction*, *Keats-Shelley Review*, and *Southern Quarterly*. She is currently completing *The Encyclopedia of Mary Shelley*.

MICHELLE NAPIERSKI-PRANCL is an Assistant Professor at Russell Sage College for Women in Troy, New York, where she teaches courses in both sociology and women's studies, while continuing to conduct research in her specialty areas.

MARSHA ORGERON has written on various subjects, including the impact of film on American culture. Her recent articles can be found in the *Quarterly Review of Film & Video*, *College Literature*, *COIL*, *The Canadian Review of American Studies*, and *Enculturation*.

OSAYIMWENSE OSA is Professor of Education at Clark Atlanta University, Atlanta, Georgia, and founder and editor of the *Journal of African Children's and Youth Literature*. He has authored and edited a number of works in children's and young adult literatures.

DARLENE PAGÁN is an Assistant Professor of Ethnic Literature and Creative Writing at Pacific University in Forest Grove, Oregon. Raised in a bicultural family in Chicago, she has traveled extensively and lived in Illinois, Texas, and Oregon. Her poetry has appeared in *The MacGuffin*, *Evansville Review*, and *West Wind Review*. Her essays, "The Blue Shangri-la" and "In the House of Lovers," were awarded first place in the *Nebraska Review* creative nonfiction contest and the Literal Latté annual nonfiction contest, respectively.

ELEANOR PAM is Professor Emerita at the City University of New York and a pioneer in the Second Wave feminist movement; she joined NOW in 1967. She is a member of the Mayor's Commission to Combat Family Violence in New York City, former director of the John Jay College of Criminal Justice Domestic Violence Center, and has worked with the FBI. She has received many honors for her activities with women in prison and her involvement with issues of sexual harassment, domestic violence, gender discrimination, rape, and other acts of violence against women. She continues to speak out regularly about these issues in the media, lectures, and published articles.

LINDA C. PELZER is Professor of English at Wesley College in Dover, Delaware. As a specialist in American literature, she has published on Gail Godwin and Mary Higgins Clark. She is the author of *Student Companion to F. Scott Fitzgerald* (Greenwood, 2000). Her next book, *Revisiting Mary Higgins Clark*, will be published in 2003.

MELISSA McFARLAND PENNELL is Professor of English and Coordinator of American Studies at the University of Massachusetts, Lowell. A specialist in nineteenth- and early-twentieth-century American literature, she is author of *Student Companion to Nathaniel Hawthorne* (Greenwood, 1999) and coeditor of *American Literary Mentors*. Currently, she is writing *Student Companion to Edith Wharton* (Greenwood, forthcoming) and developing a book-length study on the work of Mary Wilkins Freeman.

YOLANDA PIERCE is Assistant Professor of English and African-American Studies at the University of Kentucky. She has written and lectured widely on early African-American literature, the Black Church tradition, and Black women's writings. Her other research interests include American slave narratives and African-American autobiography.

MARIANNE PITA is Assistant Professor of English at Bronx Community College of the City University of New York. She has written "Reading Dominican Girls: The Experiences of Four Participants in Herstory, A Literature Discussion Group" and is currently writing an article about Tamora Pierce's heroines.

TERRY REILLY is Associate Professor of English at the University of Alaska, Fairbanks. In addition to teaching Shakespeare, Renaissance Literature, and World Literature, she has contributed entries to several encyclopedias and reference works, and has published articles on various authors, including Shakespeare, Goethe, James Joyce, T. E. Lawrence, Doris Lessing, and Thomas Pynchon.

DEBORAH ROSS is Professor of English at Hawaii Pacific University, where she has taught literature, writing, and humanities courses since 1985. Her special research interest is female narrative and she is author of a book entitled *The Excellence of Falsehood: Romance, Realism and Women's Contribution to the Novel* (1991).

PAULA ALIDA ROY chaired the Department of English at Westfield High School for twenty years. She is currently a writer and consultant living in the Adirondacks of New York. She teaches courses at Mohawk Valley Community College and supervises/evaluates student teachers for Utica College. Her short stories have appeared as award winners in issues of *Middle Jersey Writers*. Her poetry has appeared in *Adirondac* and *Crone's Nest*. Articles about teaching and schools have appeared in *Overcoming Heterosexism and Homophobia* and journals such as *Women's Studies Quarterly*. She has served as director of the Old Forge library's summer writing workshop and leads writing workshops, co-funded by *Poets and Writers*.

ELLEN R. SACKELMAN has been teaching in the New Rochelle, New York public school system for the past nine years. Her previous teaching experience includes two years at the American School in Madrid and four years at J.H.S. 113 in the Bronx. Recently, she participated in an NEH seminar entitled American Women as Writers: Wharton and Cather.

SYDNEY SCHULTZE is Professor of Russian and member of the Women's Studies faculty at the University of Louisville. She is author of *The Structure of Anna Karenina* and *Culture and Customs of Russia* (Greenwood, 2000), editor of *Meyerhold the Director*, and author of numerous articles on Russian and Polish literature, detective fiction, and pedagogy. She has received three teaching awards and was named Distinguished Teaching Professor. She has traveled to Russia, China, Peru, Uzbekistan, and other countries with her husband, Thomas Buser, and children, Jack and Adrian.

ANN R. SHAPIRO, Professor of English at the State University of New York at Farmingdale, is the author of *Unlikely Heroines: Nineteenth Century American Woman Writers and the Woman Question*, and editor of *Jewish American Women Writers: A Bio-Bibliographical Critical Sourcebook* (Greenwood, 1994), which received the Association of Jewish Libraries Award for Outstanding Judaica Reference Book. The author of many articles on women writers, she is currently working on a biography of Edna Ferber.

KEN SILBER lives and works in the greater Boston area. Ken is currently studying voice, and also has a Masters of Fine Arts degree in Creative Writing from Emerson College. His first published story, "Requiem," received Special Mention in the 2002 Edition of *The Pushcart Prize: The Best of the Small Presses*.

JAMES R. SIMMONS, JR., an Assistant Professor of English at Louisiana Tech University, is the author of a number of published articles and reviews that have appeared in *Bronte Society Transactions*, *Victorian Studies*, *English Language Notes*, and *The Dickensian*. He also has a forthcoming book, *Factory Lives: Four Nineteenth-Century Working Class Autobiographies*.

CHARLOTTE TEMPLIN, Professor of English at the University of Indianapolis, is the author of *Feminism and the Politics of Literary Reputation* and the editor of *Conversations with Erica Jong*. She has published articles on twentieth-century women writers, as well as interviews with Susan Fromberg Schaeffer, Rosellen Brown, Carol Bly, and others. She is involved in a project analyzing cartoon images of Hillary Clinton. Her article on the Clinton cartoons appears in *Speaking of Hillary*, edited by Susan Flinn.

BARBARA Z. THADEN is Assistant Professor of English at St. Augustine's College in Raleigh, North Carolina. Her recent publications include *A Student Companion to Charlotte and Emily Bronte* and *The Maternal Voice in Victorian Fiction: Redefining the Patriarchal Family*. She is also the editor of *New Essays on the Maternal Voice in the Nineteenth Century* and has published articles on Elizabeth Gaskell, Jane Austen, Charles Johnson, Mikhail Bakhtin, and Jacques Derrida.

MICHELE S. WARE is Assistant Professor of English and American literature at North Carolina Central University. She is currently working on a manuscript about aesthetics and artists in Edith Wharton's short fiction. Her scholarly interests include the American short story and American women's political poetry.

MARY WARNER is Associate Professor of English and Director of English Education at Western Carolina University, Cullowhee, North Carolina. Mary has taught secondary and post-secondary English for over twenty-six years. Her publications include *Winning Ways of Coaching Writing: A Practical Guide for Teaching Writing, Grades 6–12* and numerous journal articles on Young Adult Literature, the poet Jessica Powers, and literature as site of the sacred.

BARBARA FREY WAXMAN is Professor of English at the University of North Carolina, Wilmington. She is the author of *From the Hearth to the Open Road: A Feminist Study of Aging in Contemporary Literature* (1990) and *To Live in the Center of the Moment: Literary Autobiographies of Aging* (1997). She also edited a collection of essays, *Multicultural Literatures Through Feminist/Poststructuralist Lenses*, in which her essay on Toni Morrison's *Beloved* appears. Her articles have been published in journals such as *MELUS, Women's Studies, College Literature, Frontiers, Reader, Mosaic,* and *The Gerontologist.*

LORETTA G. WOODARD, a former graduate assistant to writer James Baldwin, is Associate Professor of English at Marygrove College, where she teaches composition, speech communication, African-American literature, and freshman seminar. Woodard has published several essays and reviews on nineteenth-century, twentieth-century, and contemporary African-American writers. She has given lectures and conducted workshops on African-American writers and their works. Woodard recently received the 2001 presidential award for teaching at Marygrove. Currently, she is working on essays for a Harlem Renaissance project.

ELIZABETH J. WRIGHT, Assistant Professor of English at Pennsylvania State University, Hazleton campus, teaches courses in composition and American literature. Her current research involves a study of the shifting definitions of literacy in twentieth-century American women's writing.

JEANNE-MARIE ZECK, Assistant Professor at MacMurray College in Jacksonville, Illinois, teaches African-American literature, American literature, and women's studies. During her first year on campus, she founded an annual Take Back the Night rally. She also serves as faculty advisor for SOLACE, the Gay, Lesbian, and Bisexual student organization.